The World's Top Retirement Havens

Edited by Marian Cooper

Agora Books
824 E. Baltimore St.
Baltimore, MD 21202

The World's Top Retirement Havens

Publisher: William R. Bonner

Editor: Marian Cooper

Editorial Director: Vivian Lewis

Copy Editors: Kathleen Peddicord, Dianne McCann, Anne Bonner

Managing Editor: Jane Lears

Production: Denise Plowman, Becky Mangus

Interns: Anastasia Hudgins, Dave Robinson, Christoph Amberger, Deirdre Mullervy, Jennifer Delucca, Lynn Holden, Nancy McElwain

Contributing Writers: Richard Aiken, Patrick Alexander, D.G. MacDonald Allen, Freya Basson, Alice Bingner, Victor Block, Jane Butler, Marilyn and Will Cantrell, Richard Carpenter, Kay Carroll, Gloria Cole, Douglas Casey, Norman Darden, Leo Dahlmanns, Audrey Davis, Peter A. Dickinson, Jane Dolinger, Lee Dudka, Trish Durbin, Susan C. Ellis, Alice C. Fleming, Annamarie Gregory, Michael House, John Howells, Stuart M. Hunter, Richard le Grelle, Lora Holmberg, Anastasia Hudgins, Stuart Hunter, Louisa Jones, Vivian Lewis, Lois Lucas, Annette Lyons, Mark Magowan, Francine Modderno, Patrice Mullin, Gene Murphy, Kathy Murphy, Chad Neighbor, Jane Parker, Kathleen Peddicord, Elizabeth W. Philip, Harry Portman, Charles Powell, Margaret Range, Charles Romine, Marjorie Rose, Michael Sedge, Lee Setomer, Jim Shaw, Gary A. Scott, Jo Ann Skousen, Sheila Signer, Bruce Totaro, Becky Tozier, Warren Trabant, Gene L. Tyler, Patti Watts, Jack G. Wilson

Cover Design and Styling: French & French

Cover Photography: John Burwell

Parrot: Just for Pets

ISBN 0-945332-17-3

Table of Contents

Foreword

When we decided to write a book on retirement havens two years ago, we faced an enjoyable but difficult task. There are thousands of lovely, inexpensive, and interesting places in the world where you could retire. Yet each person's idea of paradise is a little different.

Many areas of the world are sunny, beautiful, inexpensive—and volatile. We counted out any countries with shaky political regimes or anit-American sentiments. Who needs that sort of trouble?

Other countries are peaceful, safe—and boring. We left them out too.

In the original edition of this book, we narrowed our havens down to Portugal (the Algarve in particular), Andorra, Austria, Britain, Ireland, the Caribbean, Costa Rica, France, Greece, Italy, Mexico, Spain, and —last but not least—behind the Iron Curtain. Why? Behind the Iron Curtain in Eastern Europe there are beautiful medieval towns, quaint villages, fine food, world-famous spas, and gorgeous beaches. And they are amazingly cheap. An American pension can provide a good life in Eastern Europe.

This year we decided the book needed to be updated and expanded. We added four more retirement havens: Canada (British Columbia and Nova Scotia, in particular), Ecuador, Israel, and Switzerland. We also added Bermuda to the chapter on the Caribbean. (Yes, we know, Bermuda is in the Atlantic. But it shares the charms and atmosphere of the Caribbean, which is not far away.)

How could we have overlooked Canada, our lovely neighbor to the north? Its coasts are spectacular and unspoiled. The language and customs are familiar. Medical care is good. The political climate is stable. Prices are slightly lower than in coastal areas in the United States. And it is a convenient distance from home.

Israel, that exotic little country where the world's three great religions evolved, is a paradise combining the fascination of ancient history with a Mediterranean climate. The Dead Sea is the world's greatest spa. And Israel's Mediterranean Coast is as lovely as Europe's, and less crowded.

Switzerland—what more could you ask for? A tax haven in the glorious Alps, with towns so clean you could eat from their streets.

The people are efficient and courteous, and often speak English. What's more, it is in the heart of Europe, just a hop, skip, and jump away from France, Germany, Austria, and Italy.

Bermuda, too, is a tax haven. Its beauties are opposite those of Switzerland—warm, sunny beaches, little unspoiled towns. But like Switzerland, it is prosperous and efficient. Don't let that laid-back atmosphere fool you.

Ecuador is a little-known retirement gem in South America. Bordering the Pacific, this mountainous country has a near-perfect climate. Temperatures along the coast are in the 70s and 80s all year. In the mountains, the climate is spring-like year-round, with average temperatures ranging from 45 degrees Fahrenheit to 78 degrees Fahrenheit. (The country's rain forests are hotter and wetter, but few people live in them.) Ecuador is also extremely cheap—the average retiree can afford to hire a maid, cook, and gardener here. And it is a peaceful, stable place.

Whether you seek sunshine, tranquility, a low cost of living, culture, or your roots, we wish you luck. In a few years, when we have finished paying our dues to the stress-ridden, work-day world, perhaps we'll join you! Let us know how it goes.

—Marian Cooper

Chapter 1

A Bird's-eye View

If you could retire anywhere in the world, where would you go? The sunny Caribbean? The French Riviera? How about the Canary Islands or the southern coast of Portugal? With a little capital—and a dose of ingenuity and courage—you can spend your retirement years in the place of your dreams. After working most of your life in a smoggy, hectic American city, wouldn't it be nice to retire in the sunshine of a sleepy beach town? Or maybe you're not looking for the sun. Perhaps you'd rather seek out your roots in the romantic lands of your forefathers: Ireland, Italy, Poland, Israel, Greece, or Yugoslavia. An American pension goes a long way in many areas of the world.

In places such as Ecuador and Mexico, for example, you can live like royalty on an American pension. While you might not be able to afford amenities such as a dishwasher or a trash compactor, you will easily be able to afford a maid, a cook, and a gardener. And while the roads may be rough and the public services primitive, food, clothing, and housing all go for a song.

However, in the North European countries, be prepared to live on a budget about 30% to 80% higher than in the United States. A couple needs a nest egg of $250,000 or more to enjoy a cushy lifestyle in Rome, London, or Paris. Although you need more to retire comfortably in these parts of the world, you are also able to guard your nest egg from the tax man with some savvy investing in Switzerland, the Isle of Man, or the Caribbean, for example.

To retire comfortably in most places described in this book, you should have enough in savings to yield a monthly income, after taxes, of $800 or more. (There is nothing magical about the $800 figure. It is simply enough to provide a reasonable standard of living anywhere in the world except parts of Canada and the more affluent countries of Europe.) If, for example, you can invest your savings to earn a yield of 8%, your nest egg should be $120,000 or more.

That's not as much as it sounds at first. Consider what your net worth would be if you sold everything you own and paid all your debts. If that wouldn't provide enough capital, consider investing in a high-yield vehicle. If you invest at a yield of 10%, for example, you need only $96,000; if you invest at 12%, you need $80,000; at 15%, you need $64,000. (Of course, the greater the yield, the greater the risk of the investment.)

Comparing retirement havens

If you're looking for a place to retire, begin by comparing the benefits and incentives offered in the countries you're considering. Create a chart similar to the one on pages 3 and 4, which compares the favorite retirement destinations of Americans. (When considering health benefits, note that U.S. Medicare does not reimburse medical costs overseas.)

A taxing situation

Many Americans retire abroad to avoid the pesky Internal Revenue Service (IRS). The Cayman Islands, the Isle of Man, Andorra, Switzerland, Austria, and the Bahamas are popular tax havens. Until recent years, this tactic worked fairly well. But beware. The IRS is undertaking a five-year plan to catch Americans overseas not filing U.S. tax returns. The task is so important to the IRS that it has created an International Division whose specific goal is to catch globe-hopping tax dodgers.

Congressional hearings and a study last year estimated that 61% of the two-million Americans who live outside the United States and do not work for the government are not filing returns. The estimate is based on simple statistics: two-million Americans in the United States file 840,000 tax returns, but only 275,000 tax returns are filed from abroad.

However, the figure of two-million overseas Americans is a guess. In addition, U.S. retirees, hippies, and underage children living abroad may not be earning enough income to have to file tax returns. It also is possible that some overseas Americans are filing returns in their home districts, which cannot be spotted.

Under the 1986 Tax Reform Act, Americans who get or renew passports must give the IRS mailing addresses and social security numbers—or face $500 fines. The IRS hopes that by 1998 this information will provide a list of all Americans living abroad, which will enable the IRS to provide guidelines (taxpayer profiles) to spot potential cheaters and to form a basis for compliance audits for Americans overseas.

The IRS also plans to obtain W-2 forms on earnings, 1099 forms on dividends and interest, and other data from foreign companies and banks. Provisions for foreign governments to collect this data on

Country	Required Income	Income Taxes	Inheritance Taxes	Health Care	Cost of Living	For More Information
Andorra	No specific requirements	None	None	Inexpensive insurance	Moderate	Syndicat d'Iniciativa de les Valls d'Andorra, Place Princep Benlloch 1, Andorra la Vella, Andorra
Bahamas	$25,000/year	None	None	Good in main cities; costs on par with U.S.	High	Embassy of Bahamas, 600 1601 Massachusetts Ave. N.W., Washington, DC 20008
Britain	$20,000/year	Worldwide income taxed	Worldwide property taxed for residents over 17 years	Inexpensive	High	Pre-Retirement Association, 19 Undine St., London, SW17 8PP
Costa Rica	$600/month	None	None	Inexpensive	Low	Embassy of Costa Rica, 2112 South St. N.W., Washington, DC 20008
France	Must submit written proof of income	Deductions for foreign taxes paid	Property in France taxed	Excellent, inexpensive	High	Embassy of France, 4101 Reservoir Road N.W., Washington, DC 20008
Greece	No specific requirements	Credit for foreign taxes paid	None for Americans	Good in major cities, mediocre elsewhere	Low	Embassy of Greece, 2221 Massachusetts Ave. N.W., Washington, DC 20008

3

Country	Required Income	Income Taxes	Inheritance Taxes	Health Care	Cost of Living	For More Information
Ireland	Must be able to support yourself	Social Security taxed	Yes; also, property and capital gains taxes	Good, inexpensive, free to members of EEC who earn less than about $110	Low	Embassy of Ireland, 2234 Massachusetts Ave. N.W., Washington, DC 20008
Italy	No specific requirements	Deductions for foreign taxes paid	Worldwide property taxed	Good, cheap	Moderate	Embassy of Italy, 1601 Fuller St. N.W., Washington, DC 20009
Mexico	$1,000/month	Credit for foreign taxes paid	None	Good, cheap	Very low	Embassy of Mexico, 2829 16th St. N.W., Washington, DC 20008
Portugal	No specific requirements	Social Security taxed	Property in Portugal taxed	Adequate, inexpensive	Low	Embassy of Portugal, 2125 Kalorama Road N.W., Washington, DC 20008
Spain	$4,000/year	Worldwide income taxed; credit for foreign taxes paid	Yes	Good doctor care, poor hospitals	Low	Embassy of Spain, 2700 15th St. N.W., Washington, DC 20008

4

behalf of the IRS have been written into 34 of the 35 bilateral tax treaties the United States has with other countries. However, the information is not now being provided.

The tax situation for American expatriates is more trying than that for foreign expatriates. Americans (and only Americans) are subject to a minimum U.S. tax of 21%, as well as taxes on earned income of more than $70,000. Only if the United States and the host country have a double-taxation agreement is the expatriate worker subject to taxes in only one claimant country (at the higher of the two rates).

To your health

Many American insurance companies, including Medicare and Medigap, do not cover travelers overseas. Before moving, contact your insurance company to make sure you're covered and to find out exactly what you're covered for.

Access America, *600 Third Ave., New York, NY 10163; (800)851-2800,* a subsidiary of Blue Cross/Blue Shield, covers medical expenses in foreign countries.

Europe Assistance, Worldwide Services Inc., *1333 F St. N.W., Suite 300, Washington, DC 20004; (800)821-2828,* is a travelers' assistance organization that offers a special Trip Protection program for worldwide travelers. The annual plan costs $450, and the family plan, which covers your spouse and up to six dependents, including students between the ages of 19 and 23, is $600 per year. The plan covers emergency medical payments up to $5,000; unlimited medical transportation; emergency cash advances; emergency travel arrangements; shipment of medication, including eye glasses; and repatriation of mortal remains.

When you have established residence in a country, you generally are eligible to apply for that country's medical insurance system. Often, medical insurance is less expensive overseas—another benefit of retiring abroad. Contact local health officials for more information.

The **International Association for Medical Assistance to Travelers** (IAMAT), *417 Center St., Lewiston, NY 14092; (716)754-4883,* is a nonprofit organization that collects and distributes worldwide medical information for the benefit of travelers. Membership is free.

When you join IAMAT, you receive a directory of English-speaking member doctors in more than 1,400 cities worldwide. These doctors are trained in Western medical practices and meet Western standards. They are on-call 24 hours a day. IAMAT also offers medical services at fixed prices worldwide. Member doctors charge $20 for office visits, $30 for local house calls, and $40 for night calls and visits on Sundays and holidays.

IAMAT membership entitles you to a Travelers' Clinical Record. Have your physician fill it out, then carry it with you when you travel. As an IAMAT member, you'll also receive a World Immunization Chart, a Malaria Risk Chart, a World Schistosomiasis Risk Chart, and a World Climate Chart. If you require other health and safety information, IAMAT often can help.

Most European countries do not require proof of immunizations other than those recommended for all U.S. citizens—polio, diphtheria, and tetanus. But there are exceptions. Cyprus recommends dengue fever shots for all visitors and hepatitis and typhoid fever shots for those planning to travel outside tourist areas. In Greece, you should have a typhoid fever shot if you plan to travel outside the tourist areas. Portugal requires yellow fever shots if you're arriving in or destined for the Azores or Madeira, but not if you're making only a plane connection. For more information on required immunizations worldwide, contact IAMAT.

A word to the wise

Before you decide to settle permanently in a foreign country, make sure you like it there. Visit several times and make sure you see it off-season as well as during the peak season. Consider renting there for a summer or trying a home-exchange program with residents of the area you're interested in. Many an idyllic town can turn sour when you find prices too high or goods too scarce. A thriving, bustling summer resort can be depressing during the winter. And a quaint seaside village can be invaded by loud-mouthed throngs when summer arrives.

When you have settled into a new home, get to know the local residents. The best way to do this is to learn their language. You won't get far in most places speaking only English. While the Austrians, for example, speak English well, you are more likely to make friends with them if you speak German. And in places such as Mexico and Yugoslavia, you are likely to be answered with blank stares if you try to get around speaking English rather than the native tongue.

Keep track of current events and the political situation in the country where you're considering retiring. You may want to reconsider your choice if rabid anti-American sentiment develops in your retirement haven.

You can hedge against financial disaster by keeping your money in subsidiaries of large international banks. Small local banks can be nationalized.

For more information

For more information on the countries discussed in this book, contact their respective embassies or consulates.

The **Consumer Information Center,** *Department 438-T, Pueblo, CO 81009,* publishes *Visa Requirements of Foreign Governments,* which lists visa requirements for U.S. citizens wishing to move to other countries and explains how to apply for the necessary papers. The cost is 50 cents.

The **U.S. Government Printing Office,** *Washington, DC 20402,* produces *Background Notes on the Countries of the World,* a series of pamphlets that provides information on the geographies, peoples, histories, political conditions, economies, and foreign policies of countries around the world.

Chapter 2

The Algarve
(and elsewhere in Portugal)

One-hundred miles of gorgeous sunny beaches stretch along the southern coast of Portugal, where the sun shines 3,000 hours a year. This region, known as the Algarve, is dotted with Moorish villages of whitewashed houses inhabited by Europe's friendliest people. Between these ancient towns are modern resorts catering to North Europeans, who line the beaches in bikinis and lounge in sidewalk cafés. Away from the crowds are secluded coves, their golden sand beaches shaded by high cliffs.

Flowers color and scent the Algarve. Geraniums decorate the windows and grow into great bushes on both sides of the roads. Orange groves cloak villages. Camellias, grapes, and figs grow everywhere. During the winter, white almond blossoms carpet the ground.

The climate is nearly perfect. During the summer, the average temperature is in the 70s. During the winter, days average 54 degrees Fahrenheit.

Although tourists have discovered the Algarve, the region's charming old ways persist. Women in shawls still wash clothes in the river. Donkeys carry baskets filled with fruit or pull carts loaded with pottery. Fishermen mend their nets on the beaches. Chickens and pigs forage in the gardens. And the lifestyle is easygoing.

Until recent years, Portugal (the Algarve in particular) was known as an incredible bargain for property hunters. But inflation has been high, and the word has gotten out. Hordes of British and West German retirees have moved to the Algarve, causing prices to rise. The days of finding a fisherman's cottage by the beach for next-to-nothing are over. In the past 10 years, the cost of property along the Algarve has doubled. This trend will surely continue.

However, property prices and the cost of living in Portugal are still lower than just about anywhere else in Europe. The Algarve is cheaper than the Costa del Sol or the Riviera and offers even more beautiful beaches.

Looking into the future

Thanks to careful zoning laws, the Algarve will not lose its charms as a result of development. It is a prime spot for real estate investment, and now is the time to buy. Because Portugal is a member of the European Economic Community (EEC), property prices are expected to increase dramatically. In 1992, citizens of other EEC countries will be able to live and work in this sunny land, and it will likely become the next Riviera. More British doctors and lawyers will practice here, a convenience for American retirees.

Other things are also changing. Until recently, citizens of the Algarve paid almost no annual property taxes (although home owners did have to pay income taxes on profits made by renting out their homes). Annual tax assessments are rising, and the government is zeroing in on rental income. However, taxes are still low compared with those in the United States.

A bridge is under construction across the Guadiana River that will connect the Algarve's main coastal highway (EN125) with Spain. It is scheduled for completion in time for Seville's World Fair in 1992 and the 500th anniversary of Columbus' discovery of the New World. The bridge will open up the Algarve even further, making property there a profitable investment. Land prices are already zooming in the Sotovento (eastern region). One real estate agent specializing in the area is Frances Belo, owner of **Sotovento,** *lda, Estrada Nacional 125, Cevadeiras (Alture), Algarve, Portugal; tel. (351-81)95165.*

The Faro Airport is being expanded to triple its capacity in a few years. In the spring of 1988, KLM began flying into Faro from Amsterdam (it flies once a week on Fridays). And now airlines are offering direct international flights to Faro.

The price of paradise

Portugal has the lowest cost of living of all the members of the EEC, according to the latest figures released by Eurostat. It is roughly half as expensive as Germany and France. And it is slightly less expensive than Spain and Greece. The nation's average per-capita income is $2,000. The same basket of goods would cost $5.60 in Portugal, $8.26 in the United States, $11.62 in Germany, and $14 in Denmark, according to the study.

While property is no longer a steal in Portugal, some developments are still relatively inexpensive, especially when compared with resort prices in the United States. Apartments of about 800 square feet begin at $40,000, and villas of about 1,300 square feet begin at

$90,000. (Prices depend on location as well as size.)

Rentals, food, and wine cost about half what they would at home. A two-bedroom apartment in the Algarve can be rented for about $400 a month. A liter of milk is about 15 cents.

Electricity for an apartment or small house—used for lighting, hot water, and refrigeration—costs about $30 a month. Because of the Algarve's moderate temperatures, central heating in homes is unusual. When necessary, rooms are heated with small electric, gas, or kerosene heaters.

All in all, once your property is paid for, you can expect the necessities of life to cost between $500 and $1,000 per couple per month.

Legalities

Portugal has a relaxed attitude toward immigration. Any self-supporting person of reasonable character can live here.

If you wish to take up habitual residence in Portugal, you must apply to the Portuguese consulate (consulates are located in Providence, Rhode Island; Newark, New Jersey; New Bedford, Massachusetts; and San Francisco and Los Angeles, California) before entering the country. Present a valid passport, the names of two people residing in Portugal who will vouch for you, a precise description of your financial means and what you propose to do in Portugal, and a clearance certificate showing you are not a criminal.

Within 90 days of arriving in Portugal, you must fully legalize your residence status by registering at the Serviços Estrangeiros (foreigners' department). For the first five years of your residence, you must renew your permit every year. Simply present your residence permission card to the **Serviços Estrangeiros,** *Rua Peéda Cruz 8, Portimão, Second Floor; tel. (351-82)25400,* or *Rua José Matos 14, Faro; tel. (351-89)27822,* to be stamped. You might be asked to show a current Portuguese bank statement.

If you are planning to stay less than 60 days, all you need is a U.S. passport. To stay longer, you must apply for an extension at the Foreigner's Registration Service seven days before the original 60-day period is to expire.

Buying a home

Typically, Algarve villas and apartments combine Moorish details with European practicality. Built of white stucco over cement block, they often include arches and terraces trimmed with hand-

11

painted tile, marble floors and bathrooms, laundry rooms, and fully equipped kitchens. Central heating usually is not provided (as mentioned above, it isn't necessary). New homes are equipped with dishwashers, but in older homes, the maids are the dishwashers.

No barriers are placed on foreign ownership of land in Portugal, which has a buoyant real estate market for both natives and foreigners. The Algarve is probably the best place in Portugal for land investment. Besides its scenic and climatic advantages, housing is easy to rent.

You can find a two-bedroom home near the ocean for as low as $80,000, depending on the location. However, houses are much more expensive in the popular resort towns. A two-bedroom, two-bath apartment in Faro goes for $135,000, and you may have to wait a year for it to be built. A few miles inland, however, a bungalow can cost less than half that.

Foreigners must purchase houses in cash, unless the developer offers mortgages. Banks do not lend money to non-Portuguese for real estate, so you usually must pay in foreign funds. To do so, you need a *boletim,* or importation license, from the Bank of Portugal. Your agent can take care of this. It takes about two months to get the license. (Although it *is* possible to buy property without an import license, you won't be able to take the money out of Portugal if you eventually sell the property.)

Before the transfer of the title of a piece of property can take place, a Property Transfer Tax (SISA) must be paid to the Inland Revenue Office (Seccão de Finanças). A 15% tax is levied up front on the purchase of most property (with the exception of villas and apartments costing less than 10-million escudos, which are not taxed). Land is not taxed. Neither are taxes levied on payments to builders. So you can save on taxes by building your own home.

Ignore suggestions that you declare a contract price lower than what you actually paid to save on the SISA. Portuguese tax authorities now keep computerized comparisons of property prices. If you under-declare the SISA, you can be forced to pay penalties, as well as the unpaid tax with interest. (For more information on property taxes in Portugal, see "The tax situation" below.)

Buying property in Portugal is less complicated than elsewhere in Europe. There are three phases: the signing of the promissory contract; the completion of the deal; and the registration of the deed.

The Algarve has a well-developed real estate market. Title searches are not necessary, as title records are available for inspection at the public records office. Before you are given permission to

12

import funds to purchase real estate, you must sign a *promessa* promising that you will make the purchase, and you must put down 10% of the purchase price. At settlement, a notary records the purchase and gives you a document called an *escritura*. You then register the property at the local land office, along with mortgage and lien details.

Before you sign anything, make sure you are dealing with a bonded, government-registered agent. Ask to see his registration. Scams abound, particularly in time-sharing deals.

A newspaper called the *Anglo-Portuguese News* is filled with real estate ads. For a copy, send $2.50 to **Nigel Batley,** *Director,* Anglo-Portuguese News, *Ave. de São Pedro 14-D, 2765 Monte Estoril, Portugal.*

As mentioned above, you can get around the Property Transfer Tax (SISA) by purchasing land costing less than one-million escudos, then hiring a builder to put a house on it. In a developed region, a two-bedroom house constructed by a respectable builder starts at about $32,000. Add another $10,000 for a pool.

Not all builders are reputable. *Algarve Magazine,* the local monthly, has written about an English couple that engaged a small builder on the recommendation of an intermediary, who was paid a finder's fee. The house was never built, despite a $500 down payment.

To avoid such rip-offs, be careful when dealing with a builder. To prevent any misunderstandings, you should speak good Portuguese or he should speak good English. Have a detailed contract drawn up by a lawyer, with staged payments linked to completion of building phases (and inspect the builder's progress before making any payments). Retain 10% of the price to guarantee final cleaning and last-minute details.

Recently advertised Algarve properties

• A one-bedroom apartment in Portimão with nice views and a large balcony is on the market for 4.8-million escudos. Call *(351-82)27655.*

• A renovated two-bedroom house in the center of Lagos is selling for 10-million escudos. Contact *Apartado 90, 8600 Lagos; tel. (351-Lagos)62286.*

• A fully furnished two-bedroom apartment on the top floor with a view of the sea is selling for £47,000. Call *(351-89)52548.*

• Two-bedroom apartments and three- and four-bedroom houses

in the Dunas Douradas development, adjacent to Vale do Lobo, are selling for £60,000 to £250,000. All have views of the sea. The development has an Olympic-size swimming pool, a restaurant, a bar, a mini-market, and tennis courts. The winding streets are shaded by orange trees. Contact **Dunas Douradas,** *Sitio do Garrão, Apartment 164, 8106 Almansil Codex, Algarve; tel. (351-89)96323.*

• One- and two-bedroom apartments and villas at the Quinta do Lago development are selling for £67,500 to £170,000. All homes have views of the development's golf courses, nearby lakes, or the sea. Management and renting services are available, and mortgages can be arranged. Contact the **Victory Village Club,** *Quinta do Lago, Algarve, Portugal; tel. (351-89)94629.*

• A fully furnished three-bedroom apartment in Portimão, with two balconies and two bathrooms, is on the market for £35,000. Contact **Sun and Sea,** *Edifício Luztur, Praia da Luz, Lagos; tel. (351-82)69168* or *(351-82)69604.*

• A furnished one-bedroom apartment in Praia da Luz with a view of the sea is on the market for £32,500. Contact **Sun and Sea,** *address above.*

• A two-bedroom apartment in Praia da Luz with a sea view, a large terrace, and furnishings, close to the beach, is selling for £42,500. Contact **Sun and Sea,** *address above.*

• A newly built bungalow near Faro with three bedrooms, two bathrooms, a covered terrace, and a garage is selling for 13-million escudos. Contact **Sun and Sea,** *address above.*

• A two-bedroom villa situated on 2.5 acres in Loulé is selling for 14-million escudos. The completely furnished villa has two bathrooms, a terrace, a large living room with a bar, a two-car garage, and magnificent views from its position on the side of a mountain. Contact **Sun and Sea,** *address above.*

• A three-bedroom villa with a heated pool, a wooded lot, and views of Portimão and Carvoeiro is selling for £180,000, including furniture and a nearly new Renault 9 GTL. Located in Caldas de Monchique, 10 miles north of Portimão, it has one-and-a-half bathrooms, a wood-burning stove, beamed ceilings, and a patio. A garden of plants and mature fruit trees surrounds the house. Contact **Vilas and Homes,** *Portimão Office, Edifício Vista Rio, Largo Heliodouro Salgado, 8500 Portimão; tel. (351-82)85271.*

• A four-bedroom, two-bathroom house near Loulé, Almancil, and Vilamoura is selling for £70,000. The large downstairs area can be converted into an apartment. The furniture is also available. Contact **Vilas and Homes,** *address above.*

• A new five-bedroom, two-bathroom villa with a large plot of land is selling for £52,000. The villa has a view of the city and the coastline. Contact **Vilas and Homes,** *address above.*

• One-bedroom apartments in Rocha Brava, a development just east of Carvoeiro with tennis courts, swimming pools, shops, and restaurants, are selling for £36,590. Some apartments have sea views and easy access to the beach. Contact **Vilas and Homes,** *address above.* For information on other Carvoeiro properties, contact *Paula Luyt,* **Algarve Marketing,** *tel. (351-82)52426.*

• A three-bedroom house in Lagos, with a mature orchard and a large garage, is selling for £45,000. Contact **Farley & Company Estate Agents,** *44-46 Old Brompton Road, South Kensington, London SW7 3DZ; tel. (44-1)589-1243.*

• A renovated farmhouse with a pool and a garage in Alcantarilha is selling for £95,000. Contact **Farley & Company Estate Agents,** *address above.*

• Homes in Balaia Village—a cluster of villas and apartments with swimming pools, tennis courts, and landscaped gardens, 10 minutes by car from Albufeira and Vilamoura—are selling for £38,500 to £70,000. Contact **Balaia Village,** *Sitio da Balaia, 8200 Albufeira, Algarve; tel. (351-89)50236,* or **Longcroft Properties Ltd.,** *Compton House, Main Road, Easter Compton, Bristol BS12 3QZ; tel. (351-89)50273 or (351-89)50277.*

• Apartments at the Carvoeiro Clube, located in a town east of Portimão, one of the oldest developments in the Algarve, are available for $90,000. Villas start at $350,000. Facilities at the development include a tennis center, a swimming pool, a riding center, restaurants, a laundry service, and a doctor. Developer **Euroactividade**, originally from West Germany, offers a full immigration service. The firm can help you obtain a second passport, identity card, residence permit, and work permit. Contact *Klaus Moeller Jr., tel. (351-82)57266.*

(Note: Lovely individual villas in the same beautiful location as the Carvoeiro Clube are being developed by well-known builder Robert Bachman at considerably less cost than those built by Euroactividade.)

Properties elsewhere in Portugal

Of course, there's more to Portugal than the Algarve. And homes are often less expensive away from the southern shore, where North Europeans are driving up the once very low prices. Outside the Algarve, a good place to settle is along the Atlantic coast, within driving distance of Lisbon. Popular towns include Sintra, Estoril, Setubal, and Sesimbra. One drawback to this region is its climate; the sun shines seldom, and rain falls often. Recently advertised properties in this area are listed below.

• A villa built in the 1940s, with two independent stories that could be connected, is selling for 13-million escudos. The first floor has four rooms, one bathroom, a kitchen, and a garage; the second floor has a living room, a dining room, a balcony, three bedrooms, one bathroom, and a kitchen. Contact **Sun and Sea,** *P.O. Box 49, P2735 Rio de Mouro; tel. (351-1)9261616 or (351-1)9264963.*

• A farmstead situated between Sintra and the ocean is available for 32-million escudos. It has a large living room with a fireplace, a modern kitchen, three bedrooms, two bathrooms, a terrace, solar heating, and a caretaker's house. Contact **Sun and Sea,** *address above.*

• A bungalow with 2.5 acres on Praia da Samarra, a beach near Sintra, is selling for 17-million escudos. Situated high on a rocky promontory, it has breathtaking views of the Atlantic, a fireplace, two bedrooms, one bathroom, a terraced veranda, a small orchard, and a garden. Contact **Sun and Sea,** *address above.*

• A two-family house in Malverira, between Lisbon and Mafra, with magnificent views of the surrounding countryside, six bedrooms, and a large garage is selling for 12-million escudos. Contact **Sun and Sea,** *address above.*

• A 19th-century house in Sintra with two bedrooms and a garden is available for 25.5-million escudos, including reconstruction fees. Call *(351-1)664297.*

• A three-bedroom villa in São João do Estoril with two bathrooms, a terrace, a garden, and sea views is available for 14-million escudos. Contact **George Knight,** *Ave. 5 de Outubro 115, 1000 Lisboa; tel. (351-1)76-88-87.*

• A semi-detached villa in São João do Estoril with four bedrooms, two bathrooms, a terrace, a garden, a modern kitchen, and sea views is selling for 16-million escudos. Contact **George Knight,** *address above.*

• A small cottage with four bedrooms and a garden, situated in a pine forest near Sintra, is available for 17-million escudos. Contact **George Knight,** *address above.*

• A period house in Sintra with four bedrooms, three bathrooms, a wine cellar, a split-level garden, and breathtaking views is selling for 17-million escudos. The house is more than 100 years old and needs renovating. Contact **George Knight,** *address above.*

• A two-bedroom villa in Sesimbra with views of the sea and the village and a split-level drawing room with a fireplace is selling for 21-million escudos. Contact **George Knight,** *address above.*

Renting out your property

Many non-Portuguese residents rent their properties several months a year to help pay the overhead and to give themselves a chance to explore Europe. The Algarve has a healthy rental market, especially in July and August. You can rent a house for the month of August alone and make a profit of $1,000 to $2,000 per year after expenses. One American man rents his villa out for $6,000 a month in the summer. You can do a lot of traveling on that money.

An agency can take care of rental details for you. (If you don't want to go through an agency, place an advertisement in the *International Herald Tribune* or *International Living, 824 E. Baltimore St., Baltimore, MD 21202.*) Your return is usually 50% or more of the actual rental price. This arrangement is especially good if you don't want to live in your house. People who try to rent their properties full-time generally find tenants for at least 20 weeks of the year, during European vacation months.

Inexpensive medical care

Medical care in the United States is much more expensive than equivalent care in Portugal. Public hospitals offer first-rate service for $30 a day in a private room. Private hospitals charge $40 per day. Medical helicopters are available to take patients to hospitals in Lisbon within 45 minutes if there is an emergency. An English-speaking, Portuguese doctor charges about $50 for a house call, $40 for an office visit. Cough syrup is $5.

According to some reports, Portugal has a severe shortage of hospital beds and doctors, especially in the Algarve. (Portugal has about five hospital beds per 1,000 people and 142 physicians per 100,000 people.) However, this may change when Portugal becomes a full member of the EEC, and foreign doctors can practice here easily.

The **British Hospital** in Lisbon, *tel. (351-1)602020* or *(351-1)603786,* has an English-speaking staff and provides good treatment. In the Algarve, hospitals are located in Portimão, *tel. (351-82)22132,* and Faro, *tel. (351-89)22011.*

The **Clinic at Plainiveste,** *Rua 25 Abril, Praia da Luz; tel. (351-82)69866,* is open every day and provides emergency care as well as house calls. Six languages are spoken.

The **Medico-Dental Clinic,** *Rua do Vale Formoso, Almansil; tel. (351-89)95453,* has an English dentist.

A new medical facility is being built in the central Algarve. It is being sponsored by an English firm and staffed with the firm's doctors. The facility includes apartments for the aged (most have been sold already, but it is possible that there will be resales in the future).

If you have an accident or suddenly become ill, go straight to the emergency room (*urgéncias*) of the local hospital. Take your passport, or *residencia* or *billete de identidade,* and a dictionary or Portuguese-speaking friend. You can also get emergency treatment at a Centro de Enfermagem (Nursing Station) or a Cruz Vermelha Portuguesa (Red Cross) post.

If you need an ambulance, call *115,* which is comparable to the American *911* emergency number.

Minor ailments can be dealt with at the local *farmacia,* where medications are often cheaper than in the United States. However, some *farmacias* are hesitant to sell items as innocent as vitamin C. (A product called Guronsan is the best thing sold in Portugal for a hangover or cold.)

All-inclusive British medical insurance is available in the Algarve for about $800 per year per couple, $400 per year per person. Portuguese plans are about $150 a year per person. Foreign residents contributing to the Portuguese national insurance scheme (Caixa) are covered. If you have American health insurance, make sure it will cover you in Portugal.

Portuguese spas

In various areas of Portugal, you can find elegant, old-fashioned spas catering not only to invalids, but also to people who want a rest from the stress of everyday life. Most are clustered in the countryside north of Lisbon. Despite their elegance, they are inexpensive. A first-class double room costs as little as $30 a night, and dinner costs $10 to $12 per person, including wine.

At **Luso,** a tiny town near Coimbra, the waters are slightly radioactive, which is thought beneficial for those suffering from arthritis and hypertension. The Grande Hotel das Termas, located next to the spa, is well-regarded. In the nearby forest of Buçaco is another good hotel. Built in the late 19th century, the Buçaco Palace Hotel accommodates guests for about $30.

Curia, six miles from Luso, is a much larger town. It is near the Roman ruins at Conimbriga and the beaches at Mira and Figueira da Foz. The Palace Hotel is the place to stay here.

Vidago is the largest of Portugal's spas (375 acres), and the Vidago Palace Hotel is pleasant. Pedras Salgadas, next to Vidago, is famous for its Grand Hotel.

For even a short treatment at one of Portugal's spas, you must first be examined by a spa physician. Generally, you must buy admission tickets for a week or two (which cost about $5 or $6).

For more information on spas, contact **Associação Nacional dos Industrais de Aguas Minero-Medicinais e de Mesa,** *Rua de São José, 93-1100 Lisbon.*

The tax situation

Residents of the Algarve must pay income taxes. You are considered a resident (and a taxpayer) if you live in Portugal more than 180 days a year. The tax rate is about 10% on the first $10,000 of taxable income and increases to 22% on $25,000 of taxable income.

The *imposto complementar* is an income tax levied on retirement pensions, regardless of source (even Social Security is subject to the *imposto complementar,* according to the Portuguese embassy). All income earned in Portugal is taxed. Income earned outside Portugal is not subject to Portuguese taxes other than the *imposto complementar,* but the entire amount of such income must be considered for determination of the amount of tax owed.

The *imposto complementar* is owed when the monthly income of a person who is single, widowed, divorced, or legally separated exceeds 80,000 escudos. For married couples, the minimum is 120,000 escudos. You must file before the end of July each year.

For each dependent child older than 11, you can take a deduction of 25,000 escudos; for each child younger than 11, the deduction is 15,000 escudos.

Local property taxes (*predial*) in the Algarve recently were raised dramatically. In some cases, residents paid 100 times more in 1988 than in 1987. Rates are calculated at 18% of the estimated annual rentable value of a piece of property. But the values of most older properties have not been reassessed in many years. And houses built in recent years have been considerably undervalued. Local finance offices are working now to bring assessments up-to-date.

An owner who last year got away with an official taxable value of less than 8,500 escudos may this year be faced with an assessment of more than 740,000 escudos net after a 30% deduction for repairs and maintenance. (These figures are for a luxury home.) A *predial* tax that has escalated during the past year from 1,500 escudos to 133,000 escudos is not unusual. (This information was excerpted from *Algarve News,* July 1, 1988.)

If you're considering living in Portugal, get reliable information on property taxes before you buy. Don't just talk to your real estate agent. Discuss taxes with local tax officials.

Getting your bearings

The Algarve stretches along the Mediterranean and is separated from the rest of Portugal by a spine of mountains. Cut off as they are from the rest of Europe, many Algarve towns resemble the villages of North Africa. Because the Algarve is a collection of villages strung out along the beaches, it is nice to have a car. However, excellent express buses connect Lisbon and the towns along the Algarve. Trains usually avoid the resorts and serve only the older towns inland.

Within the Algarve are distinct regions: the broad sandy beaches of the area east of Faro and the zone between Portimão and Lagos; the secluded cliffside coves typical of most of the western region; and the windswept ice-water beaches at the southwestern corner of Europe (Sagres and Cape St. Vincent). All beaches are public, but sometimes access is down steep cliffside steps or through rocky tunnels.

The coastline of the central Algarve, stretching about 30 miles west of Faro, is where most developments are located. Although certain sections have been spoiled by the unregulated and uncontrolled building of concrete ghettos, many of the projects here are well-designed, and many of the beaches remain uncrowded.

A similar length of coastline west of Portimão is much quieter, with a lower density of development. This is because traffic is held up crossing westward to Portimão by a single-lane bridge over the Arade River. However, the EEC's European Development Fund is financing a second span, and, as a result, new developments are planned for the near future. The older Luz Bay is a particular favorite among the British.

The third section of coastline to the east of Faro is the quietest and warmest. The reason for this is a series of islands running along the coast. The huge sandy beaches of these islands can be reached only by local ferryboat or rail services crossing the estuary. However, a marina is planned for the town of Tavira, and the construction of a bridge across the River Guadiana and a new highway crossing the length of the Algarve will make access much easier.

It's a good idea to choose a base camp in one of the coastal villages, then make easy day trips to the rest. **Faro,** the capital city of the Algarve, has ancient Moorish homes and defensive walls. Its magnificent lighthouse is world-famous. Faro has one rather macabre must-see: the **Chapel of Our Lady of Carmo,** built of thousands of human skulls and bones. The chapel is intended to remind worshipers of the fleeting nature of earthly life. The Spanish city of **Seville** is only a three-hour drive away, certainly worth the trip. On the way east you can visit **Olhão,** a former smuggling center, and **Tavira,** an ancient and beautiful fishing village that has a seven-arched Roman bridge.

About 10 miles northwest of Faro, in the hills, is the artisan town of **Loulé,** a great place to shop. A little farther west is the former Moorish capital of **Albufeira,** known as the St. Tropez of Portugal (Paul McCartney likes it here). Try Las Ruinas restaurant in Albufeira for a great view and good food.

Portimão, another 10 miles west, is the busiest fishing port in the Algarve and a good place for sport fishing. Try the restaurant known as the Catatua Sisters, where you can have steak and strawberry shortcake if you're homesick. But why not be brave and eat grilled fresh sardines on the pier in Portimão? Visit the **Dennis Inn,** *Rua 5 Octubre,* owned by two former lawyers from Toronto, Ann Lancaster and Pierre Larocque, who also run the elegant Catatua Sisters restaurant on the second floor. Portimão also has good shops and British-style pubs.

Lagos, a lovely harbor once a center for the African slave trade, has beautiful offshore rock grottoes. A string of beaches here is connected by natural rock tunnels. Lagos also offers museums and shops.

Westward from here is **Sagres,** the site of the navigational school founded by Prince Henry the Navigator (1394-1460), the leading promoter of exploration during the 15th century. Henry's fortress looks over the Atlantic. Here you can see a replica of the famous navigational device, the Compass Rose, laid out in multicolored stones. (The Compass Rose is the directional, 32-point star design often found in quilts. The traditional compass was based on this star.)

Sagres is also the site of one of the Algarve's two *pousadas* (government-run inns, often in historic buildings). The other is at São Bras de Alportel.

Cape St. Vincent, which adjoins Sagres, was believed to be land's end before the great explorations south and west began. Beyond this point, as one mapmaker put it, "there be dragons." As you look out from Cape St. Vincent, you see the view that inspired the explorations that brought an end to the medieval world and launched the modern era.

The Algarve's best beaches

The main attraction of the Algarve is its beaches, which are beautiful and varied. Some have strong surf, challenging enough for avid surfers. Others line calm waters, safe for children. Some beaches are long, wide, and sandy. Others are pebbly, with caves and cliffs. Fishermen pull their boats up onto some beaches. Topless North Europeans bedeck others. Here are our favorites, from west to east:

• **Beliche,** three miles north of Sagres, near Europe's southwestern tip, is a sandy beach at the base of a steep cliff. The surf is good, and the water is free of rocks. The wind can be stiff, however.

• **Martinhal,** one-and-a-half miles west of Sagres, is a wide beach with picturesque dunes. It is protected by a harbor and quite safe.

• **Salema,** a quaint fishing village between Budens and Figueira, has a lovely beach lined with fishing boats.

• **Boca do Rio** is the site of an underwater search for the remains of the French ship *l'Océan,* sunk in the Battle of Lagos in 1759. The surf is good and the beach wide.

• **Praia da Luz** is a wide beach with calm water filled with fishing boats. This is a good place for water sports.

• **Praia da Batata/Pinhoa,** west of Lagos, has small sandy coves, tunnels through the cliffs, and calm water.

• **Meia Praia,** east of Lagos, is one of the longest beaches in the Algarve. It is lined with dunes, washed by rollers, and popular among surfers. The currents are strong; be careful.

• **Praia do Vau,** west of Praia da Rocha, is a series of small coves. The view from the cliffs lining the beach is fantastic.

• You enter **Carvalho,** near the Alfanzina resort, through a tunnel. This was once a smugglers' beach.

• A fishing fleet pulls into **Armação de Pêra,** near Albufeira, and the fish market here is colorful. The beach is long, wide, and free of rocks. Surf fishermen like it here.

• **Praia da Galeé,** just up from Armação de Pera, has fantastic rock formations.

• **Praias de Albufeira, Barraquinho,** and **Fontainhas** are a series of coves, tunnels, and caves. Walk along the cliffs for a wide view of the sea.

• **Quinta do Lago,** near Almansil, is a long, beautiful stretch of beach with excellent surf. Pine trees line the sand. Nearby are saltwater lakes, good for windsurfing.

• **Manta Rota,** in the eastern Algarve, is a six-mile long sandy beach with rolling waves. The beach has six entrances, each with a restaurant.

Note: Flags on the beaches have specific meanings. Red means no swimming, dangerous currents; yellow means you are permitted to wade but not to swim; green means swimming is safe; and a check-ered flag means the guard is on his break.

Portugal away from the Algarve

All Portugal is *not* the Algarve. Above that tiny strip of beach lies another world. Northern Portugal is a bustling, thriving region full of authentic Portuguese culture, increasingly difficult to find in the Algarve.

The northern area of Portugal, around Porto and Aveiro, is agricultural. The people are earnest, hard-working, and friendly. The urban residents are more open than the country folk, but all are outgoing and eager to talk to foreigners. Many Portuguese speak a second language, often English.

Though cash poor, most of the Portuguese in this area own land. They tend their vineyards (this is port wine country) and raise cattle. Once the day's work is finished, they meet at the local *pastelaria* (café) for a few beers and friendly gossip.

Night life is strictly *Saturday Night Fever* revisited. In response to the dearth of social activities for expatriate adults, the foreign population (mostly British) has formed social clubs. Americans are welcome. A good club is located near Esphinho (which also has a great golf course).

Northern Portugal, which boasts a rich and far-reaching history, is incredibly scenic. Castles, 10th-century churches, and pre-Roman ruins perch on every hilltop. One particularly fascinating monument is the **Palace of the Dukes** in Guimarães, an authentic 10th-century castle-keep.

The **Costa do Sol,** running from the mouth of the Tagus to Cascais and Estoril, is a favorite among foreigners. Fortunately, the Portuguese population here is so great that it is capable of absorbing the foreign influx without sacrificing its charm and traditions.

The stretch from Estoril and Cascais to **Sintra** is beautiful, with mild weather. Spring is early, with a colorful array of flowers. Summer is long and dry, but never too hot, because of cool sea breezes. And the balmy evenings of autumn are followed by a short, mild winter.

Elsewhere in Portugal, poor roads and train service have deterred development, but this is changing rapidly. New highways and an improved rail system will cut journey times in half. In the next decade, a new airport will be constructed north of Lisbon, and the international airports of Oporto and Faro will be enlarged.

The mountainous region west of **Coimbra** and **Leiria,** with its fast-running streams, large lakes, beautiful scenery, and access to the beaches of the Costa da Prata, is a perfect place to retire. Two other good regions are **Nazaré/Obidos** and the Atlantic coastline south of **Setubal,** where, with the exception of the industrial center of Sines, you still can pick your own private section of beach.

Madeira—the garden island

Five-hundred miles south of Lisbon, off the coast of Morocco, is **Madeira,** a land of heady wines and orchids. The volcanic soil of this Atlantic garden is the fertile home to groves of citrus fruit, mangoes, and passion fruit, as well as jacarandas, birds of paradise, flamingo flowers, and hosts of orchids of breathtaking beauty. (About 200 species of orchids are found only on Madeira or mid-Atlantic islands, such as the Azores and the Canary Islands.)

Madeira's mild temperature ranges between 60 degrees Fahrenheit in winter and 72 degrees Fahrenheit in summer. During April and May, **Funchal,** the capital of Madeira, celebrates its garden festival. Any time of year, though, the city's botanical garden and its **Quinta da Boavista** (Orchid House) are worth visiting.

Against these natural beauties, the works of man fade. The churches range from the 15th-century **Capela de Santa Catarina** (in the Manueline style, a Portuguese version of Gothic characterized by nautical stone carvings) to the sé (cathedral), with its carved wood and gilt altars, to the **Church of Santa Clara.** Church paintings in Funchal and throughout the island show a strong Flemish influence.

Visit the palace of the **Conde de Carvalhal,** now the town hall. Note the early houses with black stone trim around their doors and windows—this is the volcanic rock of Madeira. The customs house in the harbor (Alfandega) is an often-overlooked site; especially noteworthy are the second-floor carved and painted ceiling and the 17th-century illuminated Bible, on which captains had to swear they had nothing to declare.

Most of the picturesque peasant flower sellers you see here come not from Funchal but from **Camacha,** in the mountains northeast of the city. This village is also the center of the island's wickerwork industry and fruit orchards. Madeira wickerwork furniture, baskets, place mats, handbags, and belts are lightweight and cheap. (Well-intentioned Victorians, mostly from England, brought these crafts to Madeira to save poor village girls from poverty and maiden's ruin. The Madeiran maidens learned well.) Cut orchids also can be bought and will travel and keep for months. (Note: U.S. residents may not bring home potted plants.)

Câmara de Lobos, on the coast on the other side of Funchal, is a quaint fishing village unspoiled by progress. Winston Churchill loved this place and painted many pictures of it. The village is a good place to try Madeira's version of bouillabaisse, which is called *caldeirada* (this may be the source of the English word *chowder*). To the west of Câmara de Lobos is Cabo Girão, the second-highest sea cliff in the world, a promontory with extraordinary views. Go at sunset. (The highest sea cliff in the world is the north coast of East Molokai Island, Hawaii.)

The island's vineyards are on the north coast, which is less developed. To reach this part of the island, take a taxi across the high mountains that form the island's backbone. From the peaks, where it rains, a system of irrigation canals takes the precious water down to the farmland around the coast. In places, the builders of the irrigation system (in the 16th century) tunneled through the mountains to help distribute the water to the dry south end of Madeira, including Funchal.

The island's smoky-flavored fortified wine is also known as Madeira. When early settlers reached the island, they burned off the thick forests. When vines were planted in this soil, so the story goes, the grapes acquired the characteristic smoky flavor.

Seixal is the center of the best Madeira wine growing. The driest Madeira wine, Sercial, makes an excellent aperitif. Verdelha, some-what sweeter, can be drunk with cheeses. Sweeter is Bual, and still sweeter is Malmsey.

Among the picturesque sites on the north coast are **Ponta Delgada,** with its Colonial-style homes, and **Santana,** which has cottages with curious pointed thatched roofs.

The sporting Madeira

Madeira offers all the sports you usually find on tropical islands, including horseback riding, golf on a nine-hole golf course snaking through the hills at Santa da Serra 15 miles above Funchal, and deep-sea fishing (for tuna and marlin from Câmara de Lobos, Machico on Zarco Bay at the eastern tip, or Porto Moniz, the northernmost point, where commercial charter boats are hired).

However, you also can practice a few special sports in Madeira. One is tobogganing, which you do in a wicker contraption with steel blades. Another is graded walking along the hills where the vineyards are. The paths follow the ancient irrigation channels (*levadas*) and are graded one to four (from easiest to most difficult).

For the hardest walks, you need more than hiking boots—you also need a good head for heights. On one side of the foot-wide paths is the irrigation stream, which may be running 18 gallons per minute, while on the other is a vertical precipice hundreds of feet high. The natives scurry up the paths, often carrying huge burdens on their heads.

Off the coast of Madeira is the second island of the range, **Porto Santo,** graced by golden sandy beaches fringed by palm trees and windmills.

Affordable accommodations

The best way to find a home on Madeira is to visit in person and ask around. The natives are the best sources of information and can find you the best deals.

Two local real estate agents you might contact are **Unicon,** *Rua de João Tavira, 9000 Funchal, Madeira,* and **Sociedade Interconti-nental da Madeira,** *P.O. Box 1, 9000 Funchal, Madeira.*

Hotels

While you are looking for a permanent home, stay in a hotel or pension—they are surprisingly inexpensive compared with those in the Caribbean or the Mediterranean.

The top-ranked **Casino Park Hotel,** *Aeroporto, Funchal, Madeira; tel. (351-91)33111,* near Funchal Airport, charges 12,500 escudos for a double room with a mountain view and 14,000 escudos for a double room with a sea view. (The price is for two people, including breakfast, taxes, service, and use of the pool, sauna, and tennis courts.)

Lower down the scale, apartment hotels such as the **Estrelicia** and the **Mimosa** (same ownership), *Caminho Velho da Ajuda, Funchal, Madeira; tel. (351-91)30131,* charge 6,000 escudos per day, double occupancy (discounts are offered).

Cheaper still are the **Pensão Astoria,** *Rua João Gago 10-3, Funchal, Madeira; tel. (351-91)23820* (2,500 escudos), and the **Pensão Palmeira,** *Porto Santo, Madeira; tel. (351-91)982112* (2,000 escudos).

If you would like to explore Madeira before committing to living there, try a six-night tour, starting at $723 per person, double occupancy, offered by **Abreu Tours,** *317 E. 34th St., Second Floor, New York, NY 10016; (212)661-0555.*

Bringing your belongings

Many apartments and villas for rent in Madeira come furnished, so you need to bring only your personal belongings. It is not practical to import televisions or other appliances from the United States, because of the differences in voltage and television conventions. (This is true throughout Europe).

Furniture and household effects may be imported if you have owned them for at least one year; if they were part of the furnishings of your previous residence; and if you do not already have a furnished home in Portugal.

A numbered list of the household goods you wish to import should be sent to the nearest Portuguese consulate. Include a Portuguese translation of the list and the following statement: "These household items have been in my possession and use for more than one year" (signature and date). All electric and electronic appliances must be declared, along with their serial numbers and manufacturers. Also enclose a check in the amount of $10.50.

The consulate will issue you a Certificate of Baggage (this certificate can be issued only after the resident visa is authorized), which should be presented together with your passport to the customs authorities for clearance of goods. Clearance through customs should take place within 90 days following the arrival of the goods in Portugal.

You can import an automobile to Portugal and keep it under foreign registry for one year. At the end of that time, you must register the automobile in Portugal or export it. You also must pay the customs duties at this time. Import duties are based on the length of time you have owned the car, not its actual age. Duties are high. If you have had a car for up to three years, it is assessed at 150% of its value. If you have had it for three to seven years, it is assessed at 40% to 50%. No import duty is assessed if you've had the car for more than seven years.

However, you don't need to import a car into Portugal, because new and used vehicles can be purchased or leased there at reasonable prices and favorable exchange rates. The U.S. consul in Lisbon suggests buying a used Portuguese car that already has been registered.

Car repairs are incredibly cheap in Portugal. North Europeans sometimes deliberately bring problem cars on vacation with them to the Algarve to have them repaired there.

If you are a prospective resident of Portugal, an American driver's license is acceptable for a period of three months following the date of your arrival. After that, you must get a local license.

Currency

The Portuguese currency is the escudo. In the summer of 1988, $1 bought about 149 escudos. There are 100 centavos to the escudo. One escudo is written 1$00 (1 escudo and 25 centavos is written 1$25).

Foreign currency brought into Portugal must be declared to the customs authorities at the time of importation.

Money intended for real estate purchase or other investment purposes must be imported through a bank with a *boletim*.

According to a rule set up by the Bank of Portugal, foreign banks may convert into foreign currency no more than 1,000 escudos per person. However, this law is being changed as foreign banks set up new branches in Portugal and the EEC moves to a common financial market by 1992.

You may not export more than 1,000 escudos when you leave Portugal, so do not change large amounts of money right before your departure. Also, you may take out foreign currency in an amount equal to no more than 25,000 escudos, unless you can prove that you brought more than that with you. In any single year you may not take out more than 150,000 escudos. Credit cards, personal checks, and traveler's checks are not subject to this limitation and are probably the best ways to buy things. The use of credit cards, especially Visa, is common.

Money is best changed at banks, which are open weekdays from 8:30 a.m. to noon and from 1 p.m. to 2 p.m. In addition, a currency-exchange service is usually open all day at major resorts, the border, airports, train stations, and hotels. Banks all give the same official rate, which is often much better than the rate offered by other exchange agents and certainly better than what you get from individual merchants. Hotel exchange rates are posted and usually worse than those given by banks.

Banking

Once you have a resident's card, you can open a non-tourist bank account. To import large sums of foreign money, you need a license from the Bank of Portugal, which your bank manager can help you obtain. It takes three or four weeks for a foreign check to clear.

To open a bank account, go to the window marked *"Expediente"* and fill out the appropriate forms. You will have to make a deposit. It's all right to write out the amount of the check in English—unless you are writing a check for something official, such as your taxes, in which case the written amount must be in Portuguese.

Portuguese banks:
- **Banco Borges & Irmão,** *Praça do Municipio 31, 100 Lisbon.*
- **Banco Nacional Ultramarino,** *Rua Augusta 24, 1100 Lisbon.*
- **Banco Espirito Santo & Comercial de Lisboa,** *Ave. da Liberdade 195, 1200 Lisbon.*
- **Banco Fonsecas & Burnay,** *Rua do Comercio 132, 1100 Lisbon.*
- **Banco Pinto y Sotto Mayor,** *Rua do Ouro 18/38, 1100 Lisbon.*
- **Banco Portugues do Atlántico,** *Rua do Ouro 110, 1100 Lisbon.*
- **Banco Totta y Açores,** *Rua do Ouro 88, 1100 Lisbon.*

American banks with branches in Portugal:
- **Bank of America.**
- **Chase Manhattan Bank.**
- **Chemical Bank of New York.**
- **First National City Bank of New York.**
- **Manufacturers Hanover.**
- **Morgan Guaranty Trust Company.**

A bit of history

Many of the major events of Portugal's history took place almost 500 years ago during Portugal's Age of Discovery. The history of the country up to the 16th century is one of looking outward to the water for trade and exploration.

The Algarve, isolated by its mountain range, was long considered a separate kingdom—the royalty of Portugal were "kings of Portugal and the Algarve." A rich site for marine products, the Algarve was used in ancient times by the Phoenicians as a trading base. Phoenicians were followed by Greeks and later by Romans. Present-day Portugal is located where the Roman provinces of Lusitania and part of Galicia once stood.

The Romans had a difficult time conquering Portugal, and Rome's rule was not really secure until the time of Augustus. Rome lost Portugal about the same time that Rome lost Rome, when the Visigoths took over in the fifth century A.D.

As in Spain, the Moors gained control in A.D. 711 and remained in power until the Reconquest was begun by Ferdinand I of Castile, who took the Moors' stronghold of Coimbra in 1064. By 1147, with the aid of foreign crusaders, Alfonso I conquered Lisbon. The Reconquest was complete by 1249, when the Moors were expelled from the Algarve.

The Iberian Peninsula during the Middle Ages was made up of many separate kingdoms. Portugal was separated by rivers, mountain ranges, and a distinctive language. As everywhere in Europe, the emergence from the Middle Ages was characterized by the struggles of nationhood and the crown versus the Church and landed gentry. But Portugal's struggles were further complicated by dynastic wars, particularly involving Castile.

After the rule of Ferdinand I, the Castilians were defeated by the Portuguese at Aljubarrota in 1385. This defeat established the Aviz dynasty, with João I as king. It was a son of João I, Prince Henry the Navigator, who gave Portugal its historical moment in the sun.

As already mentioned, Prince Henry founded a naval observatory and a school for the study of geography and navigation, based at Sagres, on the southwestern tip of the country. From here he planned the expeditions that made Portugal a major world power for approximately 200 years. From Lisbon, the explorer Vasco da Gama first sailed around Africa (1497-1499) and went on to establish a lucrative spice trade with India. Cabral, sailing across the Atlantic, is credited with the European discovery of Brazil in 1500. Almeida and Albuquerque went on to establish Portuguese dominance in Asia and to establish a Portuguese base in the Americas.

By this time, Portugal's traditional disputes with Spain had reached such a fevered pitch that the pope was called on to settle the rivalry between the two Roman Catholic countries. He drew a line bisecting the globe, giving the New World, except Brazil, to Spain and the Orient and Africa to Portugal.

The 16th century saw Portuguese colonies established in Africa, India, and the Far East. The Portuguese carried on lucrative trade with China, Japan, Macao, Goa, and many other sites along the African and Asian trade routes. Catholic missionaries were sent out to convert the heathen, while explorers and traders worked to enrich Portugal. The height of wealth and power was reached under Manuel I and João III. The highly decorated Manueline architectural style of the time displays this wealth, with its maritime symbols, gilded church altars, and ornate decor.

However, by the late 16th century, tiny Portugal had bitten off more than it could chew. The demands of colonization along with the expulsion of the Jews severely depopulated the country. Without adequate manpower, agriculture collapsed. In 1578, the young King Sebastian sustained major military defeats in Africa. In 1580, the house of Aviz died out, and Philip II of Spain, a nephew of João III, enforced his claim to the throne of Portugal.

While ruled by Spain, Portugal lost most of its colonial empire to the Dutch. In 1640, Portugal threw off the rule of Spain, then, in 1654, it allied itself with England. The English have retained strong trade and travel ties with Portugal to this day, and as a result, English is widely spoken throughout Portugal. A large Anglo-Portuguese colony exists still in the city of Oporto.

Throughout the 18th century, Portugal was ruled by absolute monarchs. At the end of the century, Portugal, with the help of the English, fought battles against the French and Spanish, who plotted to take over the country. While Portugal retained its independence, it lost its power throughout the world.

The royal family of Portugal sat out the Peninsular War against Napoleon in Brazil. The remainder of the 19th century was chaos: a long series of coups d'état and dictatorships that finished whatever remained of Portugal's former prosperity. In 1822, a democratic constitution was established.

In 1910, the last king, Manuel II, abdicated, and a republic was established. However, chaotic conditions (an average of one new government per year) continued until 1926, when General Carmona established himself as dictator. In 1928, Antonio de Oliveira Salazar took over.

Salazar maintained his grip until his death in 1968, although he was old, ill, and unpopular. Dr. Marcelo Caetano, a former minister and rector of Lisbon University, continued the dictatorship until April 25, 1974, when a popular and almost bloodless revolution overthrew the regime. This revolution is often referred to as the Revolution of Flowers, because many of the military put carnations into their gun barrels. After the revolution, Portugal gave up fighting wars in Africa to maintain its remaining colonies, and almost a million refugees from the colonies (primarily Mozambique, Angola, and Portuguese Guinea) poured into Portugal within the next year.

Politics

Political instability followed the revolution of 25 do Abril, as Portugal struggled to establish an elective democracy. The first provisional government resigned in September 1974. Banks, insurance companies, utilities, and large family-owned companies were nationalized in March 1975.

Four major parties emerged, with the Socialist Party, headed by Mario Soares, holding the majority. Communist Party agitation and an attempted coup took place in November 1975; however, the coup was defeated by army leaders led by General Eanes.

During the past 13 years, elections have shifted the government between the moderate right and the moderate left. Although the political situation has stabilized somewhat, the years of crisis, the preceding years of dictatorship, and Portuguese trade and debt payments have combined to produce a terrific financial burden.

Portugal continues to suffer its historic ills. While a surge in population followed the liberation of the colonies, many of Portugal's young people now emigrate to other European countries as temporary workers—because they see few industrial or professional jobs or entrepreneurial opportunities at home. This provides a cash inflow as the workers send money home, but it drains the country of its best manpower.

It is still possible to be imprisoned in Portugal for insulting the military or the government. Imprisonment without trial has occurred in isolated instances.

Demographics and statistics

Portugal covers 36,000 square miles, including the offshore island territories of Madeira and the Azores. Continental Portugal is a tiny country by North American standards, about 350 miles long, north to south, and about 235 miles wide, east to west. It is mostly mountainous, and is crisscrossed by the Tagus, Douro, and Minho rivers. The country has more than 500 miles of beaches. The only land border is with Spain.

Although once a major colonial power, Portugal's only remaining territory is Macao, 40 miles from Hong Kong.

Portugal's former possessions include Brazil (declared independent in 1822), Goa (which was conquered by India in 1961), Mozambique, Angola, Portuguese Guinea, the Cape Verde Islands, São Tome and Principe (granted independence after the Portuguese revolution of 1974), and Timor (annexed in 1975 by Indonesia).

For at least 30 years, the population of Portugal remained stable at about 8.7-million people. However, with the influx of former colonists in 1975, the population rose to about 9.7 million. An estimated 1.5-million Portuguese, particularly men between 25 and 40, emigrate to other West European countries as temporary workers. Their wages, sent home to their families for support and the purchase of real estate, provide an important cash infusion into the Portuguese economy. The average per-capita income is about $2,000 per year.

About 32% of the population is employed in agriculture; another 34% works in service industries, transportation, and government. Of the remaining work force, 40% is employed in the traditional industries of textiles, footwear, cork, and wood. About 2% is employed in steel, chemicals, oil-refining, paper, cement, tobacco, and beverage industries.

Agricultural yields are among the lowest in Western Europe, although the land is fertile. Antiquated methods (such as hand tools and oxen) are still used. The country has valuable mineral deposits, but the sites are small and scattered. Large-scale mining is difficult.

The language

Many in the Algarve speak English, but life is easier if you learn Portuguese. It is not difficult to read, especially if you know French, Spanish, or Latin. Try to find a volume of *Portugues Fundamental* and its companion grammar, produced by the Center of Linguistic Studies at the Lisbon Faculty of Arts. It reduces the language to 2,200 words, enough for a decent conversation. Or pick up the fact sheet called "Information on Study in Portugal," available from the Portuguese Tourist Bureau in New York.

The **Centro Audio-Visua de Linguas,** *Praça Luis de Camões 36, 1200 Lisbon; tel. (351-1)364988,* specializes in teaching foreigners to speak Portuguese in eight weeks.

Another school is **Centro Europeu de Linguas,** *Ave. Padre Manuel da Nobrega 3-A, 1000 Lisbon; tel. (351-1)808282 or (351-1)807425.*

An alternative is to hire a Portuguese tutor, which is a good way to meet locals. And watching Portuguese television and listening to the radio can help. But the best and fastest way to learn Portuguese is to live with a Portuguese family.

Transportation

TAP is the Portuguese national airline. Both TAP and Trans World Airlines fly from New York to Lisbon. International airports are also located in Oporto, Faro (the Algarve), Funchal, Madeira, and the Azores. You can fly from Lisbon to the Algarve, even though the trip takes only four hours by land. The round trip between Lisbon and the Algarve costs less than $40, or you can book it as part of your ticket from the United States. Express buses also make the journey.

You do not need a car in Lisbon, because public transportation is excellent. Buses and trains to the major tourist sites are cheap. A bus to the Algarve costs about $10. Service is good between Lisbon and most popular destinations, but it can be spotty between less-traveled routes.

While car rentals are cheap (as little as $10 a day plus mileage), gas prices are among the most expensive in Europe. The roads are not always the best; in fact, some of the old Roman roads are still in use. It is essential to get a good road map (such as the one put out by Michelin). Some Portuguese drive recklessly, so be careful. Beware of donkey carts, motorcycles, and ladies riding mules down the highways. Take a train or bus if you are worried.

On the plus side, most distances are short by American standards, and a car allows you flexibility when visiting the smaller villages.

Where to stay

While you're looking for a more permanent nest in the Algarve (or elsewhere in Portugal), stay in one of the country's lovely *pousadas*. These government-operated inns are often located in medieval castles or convents and serve excellent food. Dining rooms close at about 9:30 p.m. For information, contact the **Portuguese National Tourist Office,** *548 Fifth Ave., New York, NY 10035; (212) 354-4403.* For reservations, contact *Antonio Alonso,* **Marketing Ahead,** *515 Madison Ave., New York, NY 10022; (212) 686-9213.* Reservations are essential in May, June, September, and October. Following is a list of *pousadas*:

- **Pousada de São Teotonio,** *Valença.*
- **Pousada de São Bento,** *Canicada.*
- **Pousada de Santa Catarina,** *Miranda do Douro.*
- **Pousada de São Jeronimo,** *Caramulo.*
- **Pousada de Santo Antonio,** *Morisca do Vouga.*
- **Pousada de Santa Maria,** *Marvão.*

- **Pousada do Castelo,** *Obidos.*
- **Pousada de São Felipe,** *Setubal.*
- **Pousada de Palmela,** *Palmela.*
- **Pousada de São Bartolomeu,** *Braganca.*
- **Pousada de São Goncalo,** *Amarante.*
- **Pousada da Ria,** *Murtosa.*
- **Pousada de Santa Barbara,** *Povoa da Quartas.*
- **Pousada de São Lourenco,** *Serra da Estrela.*
- **Pousada de São Pedro,** *Castelo do Bode.*
- **Pousada de Santa Luzia,** *Elvas.*
- **Pousada da Rainha Santa Isabel,** Estremoz.
- **Pousada dos Loios,** *Evora.*
- **Pousada de São Tiago,** *Santiago do Cacem.*
- **Pousada do Infante,** *Sagres.*
- **Pousada de São Gens,** *Serpa.*
- **Pousada de São Bras,** *Bras de Alportel.*

In addition to *pousadas,* you'll find every type of accommodation, from budget to luxury, in the Algarve. In fact, more than 50% of Portugal's hotel beds are here. At Praia da Rocha beach, the **Hotel Alvor Praia** and the **Hotel Algarve** are famous. Rooms cost $22 to $65, depending on the season. If you're looking for something less expensive, go directly across the street from the Hotel Algarve. At the two-star Hotel Alcala, a clean double room with a bath costs about $20 in the summer, $13 in winter, including Continental breakfast.

Portimão has a Victorian-style hotel called the **Bela Vista,** as well as numerous inexpensive *pensão*-type hotels (about $20 to $30 per night). Try the **Hotel Eva** (Faro), the **Hotel Rocamar** (Albufeira), and the **Pensão Residencial Iberica** (Loulé). Reservations are not mandatory, except during the summer.

Listings of hotels and restaurants in all price ranges are available from the **Portuguese National Tourist Office,** *address above.*

Hurdles you'll face

You can wait as long as 10 years for a telephone in the Algarve. And local calls are expensive, so you'll have to learn to keep your conversations short.

You may not drive a foreign-registered car in Portugal if you are a permanent resident. Sell your car before leaving home and buy a Portuguese car when you arrive. You must get a Portuguese identity card before you can get a Portuguese driver's license; it's illegal to drive without one. Take your *residencia, bilhete de identidade,*

American driver's license, and three passport photographs to the U.S. consulate. There you get a translation of your American license and a certificate saying that you can read and write and do not have a criminal record. Then you must have a doctor examine you. Have all copies of his medical report notarized and deposit one copy at the local health center. Take all the other papers and photos to the Seccão de Viação, the transport department in the provincial capital, where you fill out more forms and finally obtain a provisional Portuguese license.

Any visitors to your residence in Portugal must be registered with the police. Go to the Servicio de Estrangeiros to buy a registration card, called a *boletim individual de alojomento*. Ask your visitors to complete the card as soon as they arrive; cards must be handed in to the police within 48 hours of their arrival.

In Portugal, bills (water, electricity, and telephone) are not mailed; they are delivered by hand. And the delivery man waits for the check. If no one is home, the bill is left in the mailbox, and you must pay it within a matter of days. If you don't pay the bill right away, your service is cut off.

Eating, Portuguese-style

As befits a seafaring nation with 500 miles of beaches, Portugal cuisine features great seafood. In fact, the word *tempura* is not Japanese but Portuguese. The Portuguese taught the Japanese how to deep-fry fish.

The Portuguese eat a lot, and you can expect large quantities of hearty fare. Food is robustly flavored with garlic and olive oil, and most parts of an animal are used in one dish or another.

The national dish is *bacalhau,* or salt codfish, which is reconstituted and served either with a tomato sauce or as a purée with garlic. It is an acquired taste—it can be salty. Wash it down with *vinho verde,* a young, slightly green white wine with a bit of bubble. Mussels and fresh fish are also popular, including fresh grilled sardines. The only expensive food is lobster, which is excellent.

Tripas à Moda do Porto is a historic specialty. Trying to supply a fleet setting out on a conquest of Morocco in 1415, the people of Oporto slaughtered all their cattle, keeping only the tripe to eat themselves. They made it into a stew, which today is combined with other meats, such as chicken and pork knuckles. It tastes better than it sounds. Another specialty is *broa,* a corn bread with a tart taste reminiscent of mushrooms. *Serra* is the local cheese specialty, made from mountain ewes' milk.

Other specialties include *leitão* (roast suckling pig); *caldo verde* (potato and cabbage soup); *porca à Alentejana* (fried pork in clam sauce); *cozido à Portuguesa* (mixed boiled meats); and *caldeirada* (the ubiquitous Mediterranean fish stew).

The Portuguese like their desserts sweet. *Pudim* is caramel custard with a sauce. *Pastelarias* sell marzipan candies that are molded and painted to look like fruits and vegetables.

In addition to *vinho verde,* you can enjoy a variety of local red wines (including Dão red), the Lancer's-type rosés (not overly popular with the Portuguese themselves, who like drier wines), and port, the pride of the Portuguese. While Americans think of port as a sweet dessert wine, it can be drunk before dinner as well. The aperitif port is called white port and is dry.

Most of the major wine shippers call Oporto home—Sandemans, Cockburn's, Gilbert's. You can sample port almost anywhere, but the best place is the port wine institute, the **Solar do Vinho do Porto,** *45 Rua S. Pedro de Alcantara, Lisbon.* It offers more than 100 different ports, beginning at about 30 cents a glass. Getting there is half the fun—take a funicular tram from the Palacio Foz.

Breakfast is a light meal consisting of savory pastries, such as ham baked in a roll, which you can enjoy at the local *pastelaria.* Lunch runs from noon until 2:30 p.m. and is the most social meal— the time for meeting friends. Even housewives, who eat breakfast and dinner at home, go out for lunch. The dinner hour begins about 7:30 p.m. While urban dwellers eat fashionably late, smaller towns put out the lights by 9:30 p.m.

In Portugal, every kind of coffee has a nickname. *Café con leche* is a favorite among American visitors. Another favorite is *galão,* which is espresso served in a tall glass with milk.

Milk is usually served hot and sweetened; coffee is black and sugared, French fries, which are fried in olive oil, and rice are universal accompaniments. Waiters are summoned by a "p-s-s-s-t," the loudness of which depends on the classiness of the restaurant.

Shopping for fun and profit

If you're wondering what to do with yourself in Portugal, shop! The bargains are remarkable. In Lisbon, for example, you can pick up a pair of Charles Jourdan shoes inexpensively at **Helio,** *Rua Garrett 41,* and **Helio Cinderela,** *Rua do Carmo 33.* Thick, hand-knit fishermen's sweaters are also cheap. Pottery is plentiful and colorful. The famous hand-painted tiles—*azulejos*—are everywhere: on

buildings, inset into walls, on table tops. One of the best shops is
Sant'Anna, *Rua do Alecrim 91, Lisbon,* where the tiles range from 50
cents to $5 each.

Oporto's old Municipal Library houses a craft center. Oporto is
also a good place for antiques. **Faro,** in the Algarve, is another.
Obidos, south of Oporto, is a famous handicraft center, known for its
ceramics. Also in the Algarve, the towns of **Lagos** and **Portimão** are
branches of Cristal Portugal, which sells Atlantis crystal at reasonable
prices. The Portuguese Vista Alegre porcelain, inspired by the
exploration into the Orient, is collected by David Rockefeller.

Festivals and holidays

Portugal is an overwhelmingly Roman Catholic country, and
most public holidays and festivals revolve around religious holidays.
Legal public holidays observed throughout the country are New
Year's Day; Good Friday; Anniversary of the Revolution (April 25);
Labor Day (May 1); Luis de Camões (Portugal's most renowned
writer) Day (June 10); Feast of Corpus Christi (June 21); Feast of the
Assumption (Aug. 15); Anniversary of the Proclamation of the
Republic (Oct. 5); All Saints Day (Nov. 1); Restoration of Independ-
ence (Dec. 1); Feast of the Immaculate Conception (Dec. 8); and
Christmas.

In addition to the legal holidays, many regional fairs and festivals
are held throughout the year; stop by the Portuguese Tourist Office
for a calendar. June is a particularly active festival season in Lisbon,
where each district has a giant block party in honor of its patron saint.

About a half-hour northeast of Lisbon is **Vila Franca de Xira,**
where the **Festival of the Red Waistcoats** takes place on July 6. It's a
big country fair featuring the herding of bulls through the city streets.
You can run before the bulls (don't worry; the bulls are stopped
before anyone is hurt).

One of the largest public events occurs twice a year, in May and
October, in the village of **Fátima,** about 220 miles from Lisbon. This
is the site where Catholics believe that Mary, the mother of Jesus,
appeared to three shepherd children in 1917. It is a major shrine,
basilica, and place of pilgrimage. Unless you have reservations well
ahead of time, it is impossible to secure a room during either of the
annual pilgrimages. Fátima is not exactly deserted at other times
either—religious tour groups consider it a de rigueur destination.

Portuguese bullfights

A Portuguese bullfight begins when the *cavaleiros* (horseback riders) charge the bull, planting several spears in the his back or neck. The *forçados* (matadors) then emerge and form a straight line, one behind the other, facing the bull. The object of the game is to wrestle the bull to the ground by grabbing his horns. Once accomplished, cows are led into the ring, then led away, followed by the bull in hot pursuit.

Fado: Portugal's sad music

While Spain has flamenco, an energetic dance of passion, Portugal has *fado*. Sad and heartfelt, fado is traditionally sung by women. Ask Portuguese friends to point you to a good fado club. And go late. Fado seldom gets going before midnight. Food is usually served.

Fun in the Algarve

Every summer, the Algarve hosts music festivals that feature concerts, recitals, and ballets performed by national and international artists. And in late summer, the **National Folk Festival** takes place, and dance groups from all over Portugal perform.

São Lourenço, near Almansil, has a cultural center offering concerts, art exhibits, and lectures.

The coast is the place for spectator sports: *futebol* (soccer), car racing, bike racing, show jumping, bullfights, and yacht races.

If you like gambling, *totobola* is the Portuguese football pool.

Fishing is popular. You can choose from saltwater, freshwater, underwater, and beach fishing. Freshwater fishermen enjoy the northern provinces of **Minho** and **Tras-os-Montes,** where there are rivers and streams, lakes, and reservoirs. The Minho and Lima rivers are great for salmon fishing.

Then, of course, you can spend time swimming, diving, sailing, golfing, playing tennis, squash, or cricket, riding, or hunting.

For more information

To have an in-depth look at the Algarve before you decide to move, consider a Retirement Exploration Tour. Jane Parker, a retired teacher, leads these tours, which include inspections of real estate; information seminars conducted by government officials, doctors, lawyers, business people, realtors, and cultural experts; and visits with Americans living in Portugal. Contact **Jane Parker,** *19414 Vineyard*

Lane, Saratoga, CA 95070; (408)257-5378, or **Marty Scutt,** *2900 Scenic Bend Drive, Modesto, CA 95355; (209)257-5378.*

You can also find out more about the Algarve by reading the following English-language publications: *Algarve Magazine, Rua 25 Abril, 8400 Lagos, Algarve, Portugal; tel. (351-82)52850; Algarve News,* a fortnightly published by *Algarve Magazine*; and *Anglo-Portuguese News, Ave. de Sao Pedro 14-D, 2765 Monte Estoril, Portugal.*

Other good sources of information are the **Portuguese National Tourist Office,** *548 Fifth Ave., New York, NY 10036,* and the **Embassy of Portugal,** *2125 Kalorama Road N.W., Washington, DC 20008.*

Information on doing business in Portugal can be obtained from the **Bank of Portugal,** *Rua do Comercio 148, 1100 Lisbon, Portugal.*

A good book on Portugal is *Living in Portugal, A Complete Guide,* by Susan Thackeray. You can order a copy from **Robert Hale Limited,** *Clerkenwell House, Clerkenwell Green, London EC1, England.* (This book is geared to the British, and some items are not applicable to Americans.)

"A Guide to Buying Property in Portugal," is a helpful pamphlet published by **Russell and Russell,** *9/13 Wood St., Bolton B11EE, England.* It is free and discusses how to seek legal advice, types of property ownership, the steps to take when purchasing property, purchase agreements, expenses, exchange controls, and timeshares.

Chapter 3

Andorra

High in the Pyrenees, hidden between Spain and France, is a retirement haven where no one pays taxes, poverty is nonexistent, the standard of living is high, the cost of living is low, the government has no army, and the scenery is lovely. What's more, this little principality offers social security and health benefits to anyone who lives there for more than one year! With political and economic stability, no strikes, virtually no unemployment, and the lowest crime rate in all Europe, Andorra is one of the most attractive retirement havens.

To top it all off, Andorra's clean dry air is especially good for the ailments of older people—bronchitis, rheumatism, and arthritis.

Andorra is three hours from Barcelona, Spain (and the closest international airport), but it is well-connected by mail, telephone, and telex. To get there, fly to the Barcelona Airport, then take the bus or a shared taxi to Andorra.

Andorra should become more accessible in the future. With the 1992 Olympics scheduled for Barcelona, plans are under way for a Trans-Pyreneean highway between Barcelona and Toulouse, France. This would make the drive to Andorra much faster. And the possibility of regular helicopter service from Toulouse and Barcelona to Seu d'Urgell, Andorra's airport, is under consideration.

The six deep valleys of Andorra are separated by high peaks, where skiing is popular in the winter. These mountains, snowcapped seven months of the year, shelter rustic houses with jutting roofs and wooden or wrought-iron balconies. The feudal principality covers 190 square miles and is home to 48,000 people. Only 12,300 of the residents are true Andorrans or hold Andorran passports; of the rest, 24,900 are Spanish, 3,300 are French, 1,800 are British, and 2,700 are of other nationalities.

About Andorra

Andorra is one of the oldest and smallest countries in Europe. A principality, it has two heads of state: the president of France and Spain's Bishop of Urgel. A 28-man General Council elected from the principality's seven parishes governs Andorra. The council is led by a sindic (president) and a six-man executive (cabinet).

The principality was granted independence by Charlemagne about A.D. 800 as reward for its services against the Moorish invaders of Spain. The present suzerainty dates from 1278, when the country came under the joint control of the French Comte de Foix and the Spanish Bishop of Urgel. After the French Revolution, the French head of state replaced the House of Foix.

Andorra's climate is varied, with four distinct seasons. Spring and summer bring wildflowers and cascading torrents overflowing from melting snow. Autumn, when the streams are full of trout, is rich with colorful foliage. Winter snows mean lots of skiing at the principality's seven resorts.

Andorra la Vella is the capital. This modern city is dominated by Charlemagne and Meritxell avenues, which are lined with shops, banks, theaters, cafés, and restaurants. The townspeople are well-dressed, and new cars fill the streets. The city exudes prosperity.

You'll find Dior, Cellini, Cacharel, and other favorite shops of the Rodeo Drive set. Pyrénées, the largest department store, is affiliated with the renowned Printemps of Paris. The second-floor food market rivals that at Harrods, and the liquor department sells the best brands at tax-free supermarket prices. Try a bottle of Chivas Regal for $6.

The valley of **Ordino** is a beautiful, pastoral region five miles from the capital. The residential section, called the Pleta, is made up of homes built in the typical Catalan style but equipped with all the modern conveniences.

The village of Ordino is quite old—some of its houses were built before America was discovered. But all the necessities are here: grocery stores, banks, pharmacies, a butcher who raises his own cattle, a general store stocking American and British newspapers, and French and Spanish post offices and schools.

A heavenly tax haven

Andorra is a tax haven. Andorrans pay no taxes on income, capital gains, inheritance, or profits. Neither are sales taxes or value-added taxes assessed. A flat import duty of 2% to 3% pays for government services. And local property taxes are nominal, paying for municipal services, such as road upkeep, trash collection, snow removal, and street lighting. The average annual bill varies from $34 for a studio apartment to $127 for a four-bedroom chalet.

You can change and use money without restriction in Andorra.

There is strict bank secrecy, including numbered accounts. Andorra has no national currency; the French franc and the Spanish peseta are used in business transactions.

The principality has seven banks (foreign banks may not open branches in Andorra): Credit Andorra, Banc Internacional, Banca Mora, Banc Agricol, Banca Cassany, Banca Reig, and La Caixa. Credit Andorra has an English-speaking staff. To open an account, you need your passport and a deposit of about $10.

Legalities

Apply to the local police for provisional residence cards good for 60 days.

A permanent residence permit (*residencia*) is easy to obtain if you are leasing or buying a house and giving up a former residence. You must prove that your income will support you without help from the principality. A minimum of one-million pesetas must be permanently available in your local bank in Andorra.

Officials prefer applicants of retirement age. You should be armed with good character references (the longer and more eloquent, the better), as well as penal certificates from your previous residences showing that you have no criminal record.

Applying for a permanent residence permit is a long procedure that must be conducted in Catalan. The procedure is normally conducted through the office of a *gestoria,* or administration bureau. There are many of these in Andorra, and most have English-speaking staff members. When all the paperwork is finished, which will mean living in Andorra for about six months, you may renew your resident's card annually. Once the officials get to know you, you can renew it every five years.

When you have been registered for six months, you may buy a car with Andorran matriculation plates, at almost duty-free prices. Or you may import a car that's less than three years old. You may buy only one car, but you can use a second car if it is registered in another person's name (spouse, child, or friend, for example).

You need an international green insurance card to drive in Andorra. French and Spanish insurance companies, as well as a helpful automobile association, operate in Andorra. From December through March, standard winter automobile equipment, such as snow tires, may be required on the Envalira Pass into Andorra from France, but not on the main roads from Spain. Top and standard grades of gasoline are available at two-thirds the cost in France and Spain.

Buying your piece of Andorra

Property values in Andorra have been increasing greatly. While that means slightly higher prices for buyers, it also means that Andorran property has proven to be a good investment. According to INVICO Ltd., a London-based real estate agency dealing in Andorra, property prices during the last 10 years have shown an average annual increase of 14%.

Old farms in the high pasture are virtually impossible to buy—the natives won't sell. But charming new *bordas*, large timber and stone houses with heavy slate roofs, are for sale. Prices range from $80,000 to more than $200,000. Apartments are available for $40,000 to $100,000.

Good places to look for property are the towns of La Massana, Arinsal, and Ordino in the northwest and Canillo and Soldeau in the northeast. These parish towns and the smaller hamlets surrounding them, along with the city of St. Julia de Loria, near the Spanish border, have the largest numbers of developments and houses for sale.

Andorran law restricts foreigners from owning more than one unit of housing or building land in Andorra. (Only 8% of the total land area of Andorra is available and suitable for development.) A plot of land, whether it has a house on it or not, may not be larger than 1,000 square meters (1,094 square yards). Average plots, however, are rarely larger than 500 to 700 square meters (545 to 763 square yards). A husband and wife count as a joint entity, but children over 18 can buy land separately.

Water, sewage mains, and electricity are available on almost all properties (all new housing developments have access to these services). While older properties may be off dirt roads or tracks, new developments are situated near main roads. If you choose an older property, you'll enjoy more seclusion, but you may have difficulty hooking up with the necessary services.

When purchasing property in Andorra, you are responsible for paying only the notary public's fee for drawing up the title deed. This is approximately 1% of the transaction price. Andorra has no land register; before any transfer documents can be drawn up, the vendor must prove his ownership to the notary public by producing his own purchase deeds. If any charges or mortgages are outstanding on the property, the only person to whom the deeds can be made available is the mortgager. Thus, property cannot be sold until the mortgage and all charges are cleared.

To register a property in your name, present a petition to the government formally requesting permission to have the property registered in your name. The registration takes about 24 hours.

If you buy property within the *comus* of Canillo or Escaldes, you must pay a once-time charge based on the constructed area of the property, about $12.33 per square meter.

Mortgages are available through Andorran banks; you can mortgage 60% of the value of the property with a 10-year term. **Cisa Andorran Properties** (Ian Purslow, director), *5 Princedale Road, Holland Park, London W11; tel. (44-1)221-6843,* or *12 Kings College Road, Ruislip, Middlesex, HA4 8BH; tel. (44-895)621617,* has offered mortgages of 60% of purchase price over 10 years at a rate of 10% to 15%.

If you decide to buy an apartment, remember that you will be required to contribute $340 to $680 annually for cleaning, repairs, insurance, lighting, caretakers, and maintenance of the building, gardens, and swimming pool.

Sample properties

Following are properties listed by **INVICO Ltd.,** *Roc Escolls III 4d, Av. Meritxell 20, Andorra La Vella, Andorra; tel. (33-628)20019,* in the early summer of 1988. It is likely that many have been sold, but their descriptions give you an idea of what's available and what you can expect to pay.

• Situated high above Andorra La Vella, this house has two double bedrooms, two baths, a large living/dining room, and a balcony. Built of quarried stone, with rough-hewn timbers, it offers distant views and is selling for $92,000.

• This converted mountain *borda* located in Anyos on 9,000 square feet has three bedrooms, 1 1/2 baths, a living room, a dining room/kitchen, a terrace, and a garden. It is selling for $115,000.

• This fully furnished flat in La Massana has a living/dining room, a small bedroom, a balcony, and a garage. It's listed for $40,000.

• This catalan-style village development in La Pleta, Ordino, has apartments with two to four bedrooms, charming antique-style interiors and exteriors, exposed beams, rough plaster, and fireplaces. Some have gardens, others have balconies. The apartments go for $120,000 to $220,000.

• This apartment-hotel in Soldeu offers fully furnished units. The complex has a restaurant, a pool, squash courts, and sauna facilities and is situated 1 1/2 miles from the ski slopes of Soldeu. You can rent out your property when you are not there. Each unit has a living/

dining room, a kitchen, a bath, and one double bedroom and costs from $115,000.

The following properties were advertised by **Cisa,** *Construccio Immobiliaria S.A., Edifici La Cabanota, La Massana, Andorra; tel. (33-628)35228* or *(33-628)35035.*

• La Cabanota, a two-bedroom, one-bathroom apartment with a garage and terrace, located in La Massana, offers views of the river and surrounding mountains. It's listed for $85,000.

• Hort del Sola, a two-bedroom, two-bathroom apartment has a garage, a terrace, and furnishings. Situated above La Massana and surrounded by communal land, where no further development is possible, the property offers panoramic views. It is selling for $100,000.

• Les Feixes, a two-bedroom, one-bathroom apartment with a garage and terrace, is situated on a peaceful hillside in Arinsal. It faces south and offers uninterrupted views. Arinsal skiing and La Massana are only five minutes away by car. The apartment complex has a swimming pool, a sauna, and exercise facilities. This apartment is listed for $100,000.

• Prats Sobirans, a two-bedroom, 1 1/2 bathroom apartment with a terrace and furnishings, is near the ski station in Arinsal. The apartment complex has a swimming pool and sauna. The apartment is going for $83,000.

Real estate agents

The many real estate agents dealing in Andorran properties include:

• **Construccions Catalanes S.A.,** *Verge del Pilar, Edifici Riberaygua, No 1-1-AiB, Andorra la Vella, Andorra.*

• **La National,** *Av. Carlemany 109, Escalades, Andorra; tel. (33-628)22-4-02* or *(33-628)22-5-29.*

• **Worldwide Properties Unlimited,** *Mr. Tom Pia, Av. Carlemany 71, Escalades-Engordany, Andorra; tel. (33-628)22-01-02.*

• **Anglo-Andorran Properties,** *Vivien Rostron, 2 Spurwood Cottages, Morris Lane, Halsall, Ormskirk, Lancashire, England; tel. (44-704)840561.*

• **Empresa de Desenvolupament Andorra, S.L.,** *Av. Princep Benlloch 71, Andorra la Vella, Andorra; tel. (33-628)20296.*

A wealthy yet affordable nation

While Andorra is one of the wealthiest countries in the world, it also has one of the lowest costs of living in Europe. Food, fuel, and electricity are cheap. Education is free.

Tourists flock to Andorra la Vella for good buys. Because Andorra has no sales tax, prices are low. And because of the active import/export business in Andorra, goods and delicacies from all over the world are available in most of the large supermarkets and department stores.

A liter of milk in Andorra costs about 38 pesetas; a whole chicken costs about 350 pesetas; and a liter of gas is about 64 pesetas. The cost of heating a three-bedroom apartment is about 861 pesetas per year.

Keeping healthy

Andorra has two well-equipped and modern state hospitals. Both are staffed by trained French and Spanish doctors and nurses, many of whom speak English. A private room is about $70 per day. Emergency ambulance service is free. The leading hospitals of Toulouse and Barcelona have facilities for major surgery.

Any member of the community can register for medical, dental, and hospital coverage. Current reimbursements for retired individuals are 75% of medical fees (which are low) and prescribed drugs. Hospital costs are reimbursed at 90%. Coverage extends to hospital and other medical expenses incurred outside Andorra.

When you become a resident, the cost of medical coverage is $45 a month. In addition, anyone under 65 and registered for medical coverage is eligible for the Pension Scheme. The minimum contribution for this is $35 a month. The pension becomes payable when you reach 65. The health plan fee is deducted automatically from your pension. After this deduction, you receive a minimum of $165 a month (depending on the amount of contribution) for the rest of your life!

If you are interested in less scientific health treatments, visit Andorra's sulfuric springs in **Escaldes.** The thermal springs, which are 50 to 183 degrees Fahrenheit, are good for the treatment of rheumatism and skin diseases. Andorra's dry climate in general is beneficial for people with respiratory or rheumatic problems. With no heavy industry and extensive traditional farming, the principality suffers little from pollution.

Andorran conversations

The official language of Andorra is Catalan, but French and

Spanish are widely spoken. Andorra also has many English-speaking residents, mostly British, so you should always be able to find someone to talk to. Many banks conduct business in English.

Entertainment

Little Andorra is surprisingly active, despite its isolation. Movie theaters show English-language and Continental films. And discotheques, nightclubs, bars, restaurants, and an indoor bullring add to the social life. The principality has one local radio station and good reception for radio and television programs from France and Spain. The BBC comes in clearly as well. During the summer, the six main villages hold festivals.

Skiing is a major attraction. The ski slopes are superb and the cheapest in Europe—ski passes are much less expensive than in the Alps. The country's resorts offer reliable conditions, smooth beginner slopes, and graded ski runs.

Other sports include trout fishing, swimming, riding, tennis, and walking. Hunters can stalk izard (a small, goat-like antelope), ptarmigan, partridge, and the occasional wild boar. With an average of 300 days of sunshine per year, you'll have plenty of time to enjoy the outdoors.

Andorra's superb health spas offer indoor swimming pools, tennis and squash courts, jacuzzis, and steam rooms. Memberships are less than $650 per year per couple (children under 16 are free). The **Centre Esportiu d'Anyos,** in La Massana, is good.

Where to stay while you settle in

Where should you stay while inspecting the property market in Andorra? You can choose from hotels of all classes, as well as camping sites in the ski areas, the small towns, or the capital.

In Andorra la Vella, try the **Eden Roc,** *tel. (33-628)21000.* Rooms are about 6445 pesetas per night for two, demi-pension. The hotel is within walking distance of the bus station.

Another good hotel in the capital is **Hotel Center,** *Carrer Dr. Nequi 8; tel. (33-628)24999,* which has double rooms, demi-pension, for 4,180 pesetas to 4765 pesetas. It is conveniently located.

In St. Julia de Loria, try the modern **St. Eloi,** *Centra d'Espanya; tel. (33-628)41100,* which has rooms for about 4050 pesetas.

If you'd like to get away from it all, try the **Hotel Babot,** *Centra d'Ordino a Canillo; tel. (33-628)35001,* in Ordino. Double rooms are 2,500 pesetas to 4,000 pesetas, demi-pension.

The village of Fontanada offers the **Refugi del Prat de l'Areny,** *tel. (33-628)41916,* a small restaurant/hotel. Double rooms are 3,100 pesetas.

Across the border in Seo de Urgell (known in Catalan as La Seu d'Urgell), Spain is a **Parador National,** *tel. (34-973)352000,* with an indoor swimming pool. This 60-room hotel is housed in a 14th-century building that has been restored and modernized.

Getting there

You can take a taxi or a bus from Barcelona to Andorra. The ride takes about 3 1/2 hours.

Shared Andorran taxis are much cheaper than Spanish taxis. They leave from four pick-up points in Barcelona: **Av. Meritxell 63,** *Andorra La Vella; tel. (33-628)28882;* **Bar Ruedo,** *Carrer Tarragona, Barcelona; tel. (34-3)2246530,* opposite the police headquarters and the exhibition center; **Hotel St. Agusti,** *Placa St. Agusti 3, Barcelona; tel. (34-3)3181658;* and **Hotel Lince,** *Carrer Tallers 11, Barcelona; tel. (34-3)3173712.*

Two buses a day connect Barcelona and Andorra. The buses depart *Plaça Universitat 4,* across from the university in the center of town, and the trip costs $10 to $12. The 2:45 p.m. bus gets you to Andorra before 7 p.m., in time to check into a hotel.

You can take a train to Andorra from Toulouse, France. To get to Andorra from Paris, take the train to l'Hospitalet. The bus that meets the train gets you to Andorra in an hour. (French train service to Andorra is suspended during the winter.)

If you're driving, take the Envalira Pass from France or the Seo de Urgell road from Spain.

If you're wondering about road and weather conditions or the availability of hotels, contact the **Sindicate d'Iniciativa de les Valls d'Andorra,** *Andorra la Vella, Andorra; tel. (33-628)20214.*

For more information

For more information, contact the **Andorra Tourist Bureau,** *1923 Irving Park, Chicago, IL 60613; (312)472-7660.*

For information on immigration, taxes, or conducting business in Andorra, contact the **Sindicate d'Iniciativa de les Valls d'Andorra,** *address above.* Ask for Mrs. Roser Jordana.

For information on banking, contact the **Bank Internacional,** *tel. (33-628)20607,* or any of the six other Andorran banks, which are listed above.

INVICO Ltd., *address above,* publishes a helpful booklet called *Andorra A-Z.*

INVICO also offers Inspection Flights of Andorra from London. They run once or twice a month and cost about $300, including air fare from London, bed, breakfast, and transportation to various Andorran properties. If you buy property in Andorra, the cost of the trip is refunded. Contact the United Kingdom office of **INVICO,** *Broomholm, Langholm, Dumfriessire, Scotland DG13 0LJ.*

Cisa, *addresses above,* also offers viewing weekends. The company flies you to Andorra from London, puts you up for three nights at the Anyos Park Centre, and takes you to see its properties for $323 per person. The trips go from Thursday to Sunday. Again, if you purchase property, the cost of the trip is refunded.

Gestandor, *Edifici El Triangle, Dr. Nequill 7, 30C, Andorra La Vella, Andorra,* an Andorran-based real estate agent, publishes a guide to properties in Andorra and Spain. The guide includes general instructions (in English) on how to buy Andorran and Spanish property, as well as facts about each locale. Also included are descriptions and prices of properties for sale.

Chapter 4

Austria

Some of the most beautiful mountain vistas in Europe and a rich cultural heritage combine to make Austria one of the most attractive countries for retirees. Nearly 2,500 Americans live in Austria and receive social security checks. They've caught on to a good thing.

Austria has good health services (1 physician for every 400 Austrians), and, as a result, its people have a long life expectancy. This is also one of the most politically stable countries in the world. It is neutral. Socialist and conservative governments alternate peacefully; the country suffers little from labor unrest; and strikes are few. The populace is highly educated in literature, music, and art. The crime rate is low. And although the cost of living is high, Austria has one of Europe's highest standards of living.

Imagine yourself enjoying morning coffee and pastry in one of Vienna's famous cafés, reading the paper, and watching the crowds go by. The simple pleasures are what make this country pleasant. But if you prefer more active pastimes, the Alps offer skiing, hiking, and mountain climbing. If you're looking for culture, meander through Vienna's museums, or spend the evening at the opera.

About Austria

Austria is in south central Europe, covering part of the eastern Alps and the Danube region. German is the official language, but many dialects are spoken. Most Austrians are Roman Catholic.

This landlocked country offers a variety of landscape, vegetation, and climate. Its 32,376 square miles are divided into nine provinces: Vorarlberg, Tyrol, Salzburg, Carinthia, Styria, Upper Austria, Lower Austria, Vienna, and Burgenland. Seven countries border Austria, making it a great base for travel: West Germany, Czechoslovakia, Hungary, Yugoslavia, Italy, Switzerland, and Liechtenstein.

Austria's landscape features mountainous terrain, with snow-fields, glaciers, and snow-capped peaks. Its highest peak is the **Grossglockner** (12,530 feet). The **Danube** (which is not blue) is Austria's most important river. Forests and woodlands cover 40% of the land area. Weather and geography differ greatly among the country's nine provinces.

The hills bordering the Alps have the most rainfall (often more than 80 inches annually), while less than 24 inches of rain fall in Austria's driest region, east of Lake Neusiedl. The average rainfall in Salzburg is 54 inches per year. In the Carpathians, Vienna, and northern Burgenland, the climate is drier but similar; annual rainfall in the Burgenland averages 23 inches. The highlands, the Alpine foothills, and the northern Alps share a moderate, humid, central European climate.

Annual temperature variation in Austria is not great, ranging on average (in Salzburg) from 35 degrees Fahrenheit in January to 65 degrees Fahrenheit in July.

Immigration procedures

If you decide to move to Austria permanently, you can apply for an immigration visa at the **Austrian Embassy,** *2343 Massachusetts Ave. N.W., Washington, DC 20008; (202)483-4474,* or an Austrian consulate in the United States (consulates are located in Atlanta, Boston, Buffalo, Chicago, Cleveland, Dallas, Denver, Detroit, Los Angeles, Miami, New Orleans, New York, Portland, San Francisco, and Seattle). Austrian officials will send your application to the Ministry of the Interior in Vienna, which will decide whether or not you may immigrate. To apply for an immigration visa, you need copies of your birth and marriage certificates, verification of good health from your doctor, a police clearance, and proof that you can support yourself and your dependents while living in Austria.

However, formally immigrating to Austria through these channels subjects you to Austrian taxation and exchange controls. And it does not remove the barriers against your buying real estate of certain grades or in certain regions. Consider the alternative.

A visa is not required if you plan to stay in Austria less than three months. Thus, you can remain in the country without formalizing your immigration by leaving for short vacations every three months.

Buying property

Restrictive laws keep most foreigners from buying property in Austria's Alpine region. As a result, virtually no property is sold to foreigners in the province of Tyrol.

Foreigners also must contend with restrictive laws when trying to purchase historic properties, such as castles. These are protected, and any purchase must be approved by the government's *Denkmalamt.* Sales are permitted only if no Austrians are interested in the property. However, it is not impossible for foreigners to purchase historic properties in Austria; some 70 Americans own castles or other historic residences there. When you purchase a historic property in Austria, you must inform authorities of any improvements you plan to make and guarantee that you will carry them out.

In Vienna, only older houses are available for purchase by foreigners. And foreign receipt of rental income is restricted.

On the positive side, up to 100% financing is available in Austria at an interest rate of less than 8%.

One way to get around restrictive laws is to have an Austrian nominee purchase property for you. In return, the Austrian gets a share in your property (for example, 0.5%).

Another way to get around the restrictions is to form a trustee ownership. In this way, you own the property by a secret (but legal) contract, but the previous owner *appears* to continue to own the property.

If you'd rather not deal with such complications, look for property in areas of Austria that are not restricted to foreigners. Some of the best buys are in Styria, near the Alps. The hill country called Burgenland is also a good bet. This area has been passed back and forth between Hungary and Austria many times. It is economically depressed and welcomes foreign buyers. Many restored and inexpensive houses and castles are for sale in the Eisenstadt area (where composer Joseph Haydn lived for 30 years).

For more information on purchasing property in Austria, contact *Helga Bonney,* **HVB International Ltd.,** *8800 Edgewood Drive, Capitol Heights, MD 20743; (301)261-8390.*

A leading Innsbruck realtor who can help you understand or overcome some of the obstacles to buying real estate in Austria is **Gunther Marent,** *A 6010 Innsbruck, Salurnerstr. 15/11, Austria; tel. (43-5222)20466 or (43-5222)31865.* Another is **J.A. Merrill,** *c/o Ball-Matic, Mollardgasse 20, 1060 Vienna.*

Renting—an attractive alternative

Renting is easier than buying in Austria, and prices are reasonable. Rents in Vienna, the most expensive area of Austria, average $130 a month. (Rents in New York City are six times more expensive; those in London are four times more expensive.)

For information on rentals, contact the following agencies:

• **Vienna's Housing Agency,** *Hodosy, Graben 31, Vienna; tel. (43-222)533-50-64.*

• **Pego Holiday Homes Rental for Austria,** *Peter Godula and Wilfried Saltzmann, A-6700 Bludenz, Sageweg 12, Austria; tel. (43-5552)301.* (This agency deals primarily with rentals in the Alps.)

• **Agency International Inc.,** *3033 Maple Drive N.E., Atlanta, GA 30305; (404)266-2200.*

• **At Home Abroad Inc.,** *Sutton Town House, 405 E. 56th St., 6-H, New York, NY 10022; (212)687-1255.*

• **Families Abroad,** *194 Riverside Drive, New York, NY 10025; (212)787-2434.*

• **Villas Abroad,** *123 E. 83rd St., New York, NY 10028; (212)759-1025.*

Where to stay while you look

Following is a list of some of Austria's most inviting hotels, perfect places to stay while you look for a more permanent residence.

In Vienna

North of Vienna is the **Schlosshotel Martinschloss,** *Martinstr. 34-36, Klosterneuburg bei Vienna; tel. (43-2243)7426,* where the Von Trapp Family Singers once lived. Made famous by the movie *The Sound of Music,* this baroque castle is decorated with antiques, including an arms collection that dates back to the castle's original owners. Many of the artifacts now on display were hidden in the depths of a 130-foot cistern during the German Occupation. Wild boar and deer can be hunted on the grounds. Rooms are 750 Austrian schillings to 1,800 Austrian schillings.

Kaiserin Elisabeth, *Weihburggasse 3, Vienna; tel. (43-222)51-52-60,* is a charming, centrally located hotel in a 14th-century building. Double rooms with bathrooms are 792 Austrian schillings to 1,100 Austrian schillings, including breakfast.

Less expensive Viennese hotels include **Pohl,** *Rathausstr. 20; tel. (43-222)424269;* **Schatz,** *Sonnenfelsgasse 9; tel. (43-222)521950;* and **König von Ungarn,** *Schulergasse 10; tel. (43-222)526320.*

In Innsbruck

Hotel Goldener Adler, *Herzog-Friedrich Str. 6, A-6020 Innsbruck; tel. (43-5222)26334,* is a 14th-century inn with good food and entertainment. Located in the heart of the old town, it has rooms decorated with antiques. Doubles are 400 Austrian schillings to 1,360 Austrian schillings, including breakfast.

Less expensive hotels include **Neue Post,** *Maximillianstr. 15; tel. (43-5222)26476;* and **Burg Reise,** *Hofgasse 12; tel. (43-5222)28445.*

In Salzburg

Hotel Elefant, *Sigmund Haffner-Gasse 4, 5020 Salzburg; tel. (43-662)843397,* is a medieval townhouse in the historic heart of Salzburg. The tall, narrow building is on a quiet pedestrian street five minutes from the opera house. The public rooms are decorated with inlaid furniture and old paintings, and the floors on the first floor are marble. The rooms on the upper floors are less elegant; some are small and plain. About half of the hotel's rooms have private baths. Double rooms are 840 Austrian schillings to 950 Austrian schillings.

Schloss Haunsperg, *tel. (43-6245)2662,* is a 14th-century castle hotel south of Salzburg. The spacious rooms are furnished with antiques. Schloss Haunsperg is near the autobahn that runs south from Salzburg past the airport; exit at Hallein and follow the signs to Oberalm and the castle. Double rooms are 590 Austrian schillings to 990 Austrian schillings.

For a bargain, try **Eden,** *Gaisbergstr. 38; tel. (43-662)74018;* **Blaue Gaus,** *Gretriedegasse 43; tel. (43-662)81317;* or **Roter Krebs,** *Mirabellplatz 8; tel. (43-662)81317.*

Bank secrecy

Austrian banks are safe and secret havens. But tight secrecy on foreign accounts is not the only reason to bank in Austria. In many ways, Austrian banks are more reliable than those in Switzerland for foreign account deposits. Compared with other European banks, Austrian banks pay handsome interest on checking and savings deposits. A range of accounts is available, so you're sure to find the one to fit your needs, and no withholding tax is assessed on earnings in these accounts. What's more, no limits are placed on the sums non-resident foreigners may deposit into Austrian accounts in any of the major currencies.

The only record that Austrian banks maintain of a secret savings account is the password or passbook number, which is also kept by the depositor. Banking secrecy laws may be breached only in connection with criminal proceedings before an Austrian criminal court.

Types of accounts

• **The personal bank account.** When opening a personal bank account or withdrawing funds from such an account, non-Austrians

55

are unimpeded by foreign-exchange controls. You must show your passport to prove you are not Austrian—but no one notes your name or number. You are free to dispose of your balance either by letter, in person, or by proxy at any branch office of the larger banks. This type of account is best for most American retirees in Austria.

• **The schilling current account.** You can open this type of account by letter or by visiting a bank's offices in person. (If the account is opened by mail, the bank may ask for authentication by your U.S. banker.) You can handle the account by mail (you sign a signature card that is kept by the bank), or, if you are a non-resident account holder, you can authorize an Austrian resident to manage the account for you.

Gold coins can be sold by this type of account, as can the proceeds of foreign bank note sales, without running into Austrian exchange restrictions.

A schilling current account is best for current business transactions or for those who wish to benefit from the strong Austrian schilling.

• **The foreign currency account.** This type of account is best for both current transactions and investment purposes. Unlimited amounts of foreign currency can be paid into or transferred from such an account, and proceeds from securities sales can be credited to the account. Interest is paid at the prevailing Euro-market rate on balances of more than $5,000.

• **The numbered account.** A (foreign) numbered account is kept in foreign currency or free schillings, not in your name but under an identification number. Such an account is used for long-term investment of large amounts. Your identity is known only by a few managers of the bank, who handle all your transactions. The bank is bound by law to observe the regulations of banking secrecy, and it can be sued or prosecuted if it fails to comply with this obligation.

• **The free schilling savings account.** This type of account earns interest. It can be opened in your name or anonymously.

Two Austrian banks
If you're planning to open a bank account in Austria, consider the following banks:

• **Creditanstalt-Bankverein,** *1010 Vienna, Schottengasse 6-8,* or **Bank Creditanstalt,** *Marko Musulin, 717 Fifth Ave., 11th Floor, New York, NY 10022.*

• **Oesterreichische Landerbank,** *1010 Vienna, Am Hof 2,* or

Austrian Landerbank, *Dr. Michael Franz, 11 Broadway, New York, NY 10004.*

Taxing questions

Austria has an agreement with the United States to prevent double taxation. Contact the Internal Revenue Service (IRS) for details.

Net worth is taxed at 1%, with deductions of 150,000 Austrian schillings per taxpayer and dependent. No wealth tax is assessed, although capital gains of more than 100,000 Austrian schillings are counted as income. Worldwide income is taxed from 10% to 50% progressively, with the following allowances: a 4,800 Austrian schilling personal allowance; a 3,200 Austrian schilling allowance for spouses; and allowances for alimony, charitable contributions, expenses, life insurance, medical bills, and social security.

If you have neither a residence nor a habitual domicile in Austria, you are not assessed Austrian tax on your bank balances. Nor is income tax assessed on interest earned on your savings.

In case of emergency

The emergency number for the police is *133;* the number for the fire department is *122;* and the number for an ambulance is *144.*

For a list of doctors and dentists, contact the **Amerika Haus,** *Friederich-Schmidt-Platz 2; tel. (43-222)31-55-11,* behind the *Rathaus* on Dr. Karl Lueger Ring in Vienna.

Austria has no shortage of hospitals. In Vienna, the following are respected: **Hospital of the Barmherzigen Bruder,** *Grosse Mohrengasse 9,* and **Universitatsklinik** in the **Vienna General Hospital,** *Alster Str. 4.*

Medicine in Austria is socialized, but it is not free. However, although you must pay, the charges are not nearly as great as in the United States.

Pharmacies, or *Apotheken,* are located throughout the country.

Special perks

Seniors are eligible for discounts on rail tickets in Austria. Inquire at railway stations for details.

Where to live

Austria has something for everyone. If you love music, dance, art, or fine food, you'll be drawn to Vienna or Salzburg. If you're a skier, mountain climber, or nature lover, head for the dramatic, snowy Alps. If you're a retiree looking for peace and tranquility, explore the less-known regions of southeast Austria, such as Styria or Carinthia.

Viennese charms

Vienna is a city of culture, intellect, and creature comforts. It is one of the most expensive places to live in Austria, but it offers so much: fine museums, great music, cozy coffee houses, and first-class restaurants. The Viennese waltz was created here, and the city's architecture is memorable. Viennese coffee houses and *Konditorien* (pastry shops) are inviting, serving tantalizing confections and great varieties of coffee.

Vienna's magnificent museums and art galleries contain priceless treasures from every period of Western civilization. The city's university, art colleges, and theater, opera, and concert programs contribute to its cultural life.

For centuries, Vienna was the capital of the multinational Hapsburg monarchy. During that time, the city acquired a special reputation for music. Famous Viennese include composers Johannes Brahms, Johann Strauss the Elder, Johann Strauss the Younger, Gustave Mahler, and Franz Schubert. Sigmund Freud and architect Otto Wagner also hail from this intellectual capital.

Vienna was built in concentric rings around a Roman and medieval core, originally protected by a wall. Baroque suburban areas surrounding the core were bordered by a second wall. In the 19th century, the walls were torn down and replaced by the **Ringstrasse** (nine boulevards that create a circle around the city).

Known as a music capital, Vienna offers traditional music houses, as well as avant-garde theater, mime, and film companies. The **Staatsoper** (state opera house) may be the best-known in the world. The opera and ballet performances staged here are among the best in Europe. Furthermore, ticket prices are reasonable; you can get a good seat for $10.

On any given night, you may have as many as seven classical music events to choose from. The two main concert halls, the **Konzaerthaus** and the **Musikverein,** have five different performing halls between them. You can get inexpensive tickets the day of a performance, if you don't mind standing in line.

Vienna has 28 theaters. To find out what's going on, pick up the current *Wien Programm,* a monthly schedule of music and theater events.

Two theaters offer plays in English: the **English Theater,** *Josefgasse 12,* and the **International Theater,** *Portzellangasse 8.* Two movie houses specialize in English-language films: the **Burg Kino,** *Opernring,* and the **Schotten Kino,** *Schottenring.*

For a more informal evening out, visit one of Vienna's greatest charms—its coffee houses, places for contemplation and conversation. Vienna's coffee houses offer magazines and newspapers if you'd like to sit alone and read, alcoves if you're looking for a place to have a private conversation, and marble-topped tables. Coffee is the main fare, of course, but sometimes the light white wine made in Grinzing, near Vienna, is also available. Two coffees and a pastry cost from $3 to $4, plus 50 cents for good service.

Try the **Café Schwarzenberg,** *Kaerntner Ring 17;* **Café Hawelka,** *Dorotheergasse 6;* or the open-air **Café Central,** *Herrengasse 14.* Each attracts a unique clientele. Order *Einspanner,* coffee in a tall glass with powdered sugar and whipped cream. Or perhaps you'd prefer *Mocca* (black coffee), *Brauner* (with cream), *Kaffee Brulot* (with brandy), *Turkischer* (boiled with sugar), or *Eiskaffee* (with ice cream and whipped cream).

While the world extolls the virtues of the Viennese coffee house, few people pay attention to the *Konditorei.* This noble institution deserves praise in its own right as a hallmark of Viennese civilization. Where else but in Vienna could you find such a seductive array of villainously tempting cakes dripping with icing and whipped cream or such a dazzling assortment of pastries? The fantasy displayed by the *Konditor* (pastry cook) is worthy of applause: a horse-shaped *Kipfer* (croissant) with shredded almonds or a *Schifferl* (small boat) oozing pink foam, with tiny strawberries for passengers.

Only **Demel's,** from its exalted position on the Kohlmarkt, dares to call itself *K.K. Hofzuckerbackerei* (imperial and royal sugar bakery). **Lehmann,** the leading *Konditorei* on the Graben, is only a *Zuckerbacker.* **Gerstner,** with its enviable position overlooking the Kaerntnerstrasse, is known as a *Café Konditorei.* It caters the Vienna Opera Ball. Like Demel's, Gerstner can claim royal recognition; Emperor Franz Josef prophetically remarked more than 100 years ago, "Gerstner will have a great future." Another landmark, famous for its dainty china as well as its delicious goodies, is **Heiner's,** with a *Café Konditorei* on both the Kaerntnerstrasse and the Wollzeile.

Another charming retreat is the **Backerei-Konditorei Karl Haag,** *Neuer Markt 9.* Well known to the Viennese for the excellence and variety of its baked goods, the small and inconspicuous Haag is not often frequented by visitors to the area—which is all the more reason you should go out of your way to have coffee and pastry here. For about $1.80, you can have a *Linzeraug* and a *Kleiner Schwarzer* (small black coffee).

Alpine retreats

Innsbruck, the capital of Tyrol, with 100,000 inhabitants, is one of the most beautiful cities in the world. It is also one of the biggest ski centers in Europe. The towering Alps can be seen from nearly every street corner. The **Nordkette,** a steep Alpine headwall, is the closest and most dramatic of the mountains that surround the city. Walk down Maria-Theresien-Strasse, the main street, for a splendid view of the mountains.

Just outside Innsbruck are miles of free cross-country ski tracks, as well as Olympic legacies, such as the Olympic bobsled run (which you can ride), a ski jump, and a large ice-skating and hockey arena.

The pointed, arched, and vaulted Gothic style prevalent in Europe from the 13th through the 15th centuries can be seen all over 800-year-old Innsbruck. Much of the city was built by order of Empress Maria Theresa and Emperor Maximillian I. Gothic arcades, forerunners of modern malls because they kept shoppers out of the weather, can be found off Herzog Friedrichstrasse.

Free ski buses take riders from the city to any one of the ski areas. For information, call *(43-5222)42457* or *(43-5222)25715.*

Salzburg is the city for music lovers. The famous **Salzburg Music Festival** (July 26 to Aug. 30) attracts musicians from all over the world. The emphasis is on Mozart, a native of this lovely city. For more information, contact **Austrian National Music Festivals,** *20th Floor, 500 Fifth Ave., New York, NY 10110; (212)944-6880.*

Dominated by a 12th-century fortress called the **Hohensalzburg,** this baroque city is surrounded by mountains. The **Salzach River** divides Salzburg into two worlds. On the left bank are narrow streets and 13th- to 15th-century buildings. The right bank is a modern city in the shadows of the Kapuzinerberg Mountain.

Alpine villages speckle the Austrian landscape. Snow-capped peaks loom above picturesque gingerbread villages with tidy little streets and flower-filled window boxes. Skiers flock to these areas in the winter. One popular resort is **Kirchdorf,** nestled in the heart of the Kitzbuheler Alps, near the slopes of Kitzbuhel, St. Johann, and Waidring. Together, Kirchdorf and **Erpfendorf** have six miles of ski runs and more than 36 miles of cross-country tracks.

Popular ski areas include the **Brand Valley/Bludenz,** with its pretty villages nestled beneath stunning mountains (for more information, contact the local **tourist office,** *tel.* *(43-5552)2170)*, and the **Montofon Valley,** with six major resorts and nearly 70 lifts covered by a single pass. The largest area is **Silvretta Nova,** accessible from St. Gallenkirch and Gaschurn (contact the local **tourist office,** *tel.* *(43-5557)6234* or *(43-5558)201)*.

The **Arlberg** is Austria's largest, best-known ski region. (The Arlberg ski technique originated here.) This region offers a combination of features not duplicated anywhere else: a high altitude that guarantees good snow; slopes for skiers of all levels of experience; interconnected villages that range from quaint to crowded to exclusive; serious ski instruction; and a cheery dose of *Gemutlichkeit,* or camaraderie.

The Arlberg region includes the large villages of **Lech** and **St. Anton** and the small, exclusive villages of **Zurs** and **Stuben.** For information on tiny, rustic Stuben on the west flank, call *(43-5582)761;* for information on elegant Zurs, call *(43-5583)2245.*

The Arlberg's most charming town is uncrowded **Kitzbuhel.** This friendly ski village has slopes for skiers of all levels and enough activity to keep even non-skiers happy. The slopes are well-groomed, and you can spend the evenings at the resort's casino. An ancient walled town, Kitzbuhel has crooked narrow streets and Tyrolean architecture, with gabled stone and stucco houses that date back to the Middle Ages. And the weather here is milder than in other ski areas.

Vorarlberg, the area between Lake Constance and the Arlberg, is Austria's westernmost province and the smallest. **Bregenz,** on Lake Constance, is the capital of the province, known for its summer festival. Good, inexpensive hotels in or near Bregenz include **Fahrenburg,** *Kirchstr. 21; tel. (43-5574)22406;* **Pfaerderhotel,** on a mountain peak; *tel. (43-5574)22184;* **Loewen,** at Hard, three miles from Bregenz, on the lake; *tel. (43-5544)5224;* and **Krone,** *Lustenau; tel. (43-5577)2246.*

The scenery around the lakes of the **Salzkammergut** is among the most beautiful in Austria. Visitors flock here during the summer to enjoy the water of the Atersee, the Traunsee, and the Wolfgangsee. Motorboats are banned to protect the stillness. This area's lake towns offer swimming, sailing, and fishing. The Alpine vistas are lovely, and the wildflowers are profuse. The Salzkammergut is also known for its health spas. Stay in Fuschl, at the **Hotel Waldhof,** *tel. (43-6226)264,* not in the more crowded town on the lake.

Southern comforts

Carinthia, the southernmost province of Austria, is surrounded by high mountains and filled with beautiful lakes. Especially popular is the Carinthian Riviera, the region around the Worther See near Klagenfurt, the Ossiacher See, and the Milstatter See.

Styria is Austria's greenest province. Forests cover half the area, and grassland and vineyards cover much of the rest. The provincial capital, **Graz,** was where officials retired in the days of the empire. A medieval city, its landmark is a clock tower on the Schlossberg.

Good but inexpensive hotels in Graz include **Zu den 5 Laerchen,** *Griesplatz 6; tel. (43-3122)86607;* **Goldener Ochs,** *Griesgasse 17; tel. (43-3122)81753;* and **Erzherzog Johann,** *Sakstr. 5; tel. (43-3122)97112.*

Chapter 5

Britain

Surprising numbers of Yanks dream of retiring to Britain, the land of their ancestors. They aren't drawn by visions of sunshine and warm weather. Nor are they tempted by low prices. Perhaps it is a yearning for the old ways, for civilization and afternoon tea, for history and culture. Or perhaps they are attracted by the desolate beauty of the moors, the poetry of the Lake Country, or the tranquility of the English countryside.

If these are the things you seek, 'tis sure you'll find them in the British Isles. This land is indeed rich in history; castles are as common (so to speak) as school yards. London offers fine theater, famous museums, lively night life, and restaurants by the thousand. The old ways are preserved in the countryside, where you can still enjoy tea with crumpets and heavy cream.

Retirement in Britain is pleasant. The people speak English. The customs are not as unfamiliar as in France or Spain. Health care is good and inexpensive. And you'll always find plenty to do. About 13,000 American retirees live in the British Isles. Their numbers are the best advertisement.

Of course, the weather is nothing to boast about. But it does make for conversation (it's the favorite British topic), because it is so variable. Any time you venture out for the day in Britain, you must be prepared for rain or a change in temperature. The greatest extremes of weather are in the mountains of Scotland, Wales, and northern England. The western areas of Great Britain are wet, but the temperatures are moderate. The eastern plains are windy and drier, with more extreme temperatures. The south is the sunniest area. Torquay, England's southernmost mainland, has palm trees.

Legalities

It can be difficult to obtain permission for permanent residence in Britain, unless you can prove that you are a person of independent means or that you have British relatives. (Your best bet is if you can prove both.) Because jobs are scarce in Britain, authorities are especially cautious about admitting anyone who might try to take one. And because medical care is socialized and more or less free, authorities are hesitant to admit anyone who might be a burden on the state medical system. (Anyone planning to stay in the United Kingdom more than six months must be examined by a medical inspector at the border. Admission to the country can be refused on medical grounds.)

To enter Britain as a person of independent means, you must have an entry clearance. To obtain this, you must show that you have £150,000 or an income of not less than £15,000 a year that is transferable to Britain. You must also prove that you can maintain and accommodate yourself and your dependents without working and without relying on public funds. In addition, you must demonstrate a close connection with Britain (close relatives or periods of previous residence, for example) or that your admission would be in the general interest of the country.

An application for residency takes several months to process. Initially, you are admitted for one year (you are prohibited from working in Britain during that time). You can apply for a year's extension at the end of the one-year period. You might be required to register with the police. This requirement is endorsed in your passport.

After you have lived in Britain for five years, you can apply to the Home Office for naturalization as a British subject. However, if you do so, you may risk losing your American citizenship. For more information, contact the British consulate nearest you or the **Embassy of Great Britain,** *3100 Massachusetts Ave. N.W., Washington, DC 20008; (202)462-1340.* Ask for the booklets *Residence in Britain (Notes for People from Overseas)* and *Immigration into Britain (Notes on the Regulations and Procedures).*

Where to retire in the British Isles?

Aha! The key question: Where to retire within those bonny British Isles? Many are attracted to London, because of its cultural opportunities. But London is expensive. Others prefer a more tranquil, less expensive retirement in the countryside. The British themselves tend to retire to seacoast towns, especially in the south and west of England, where the climate is milder.

The most popular places to retire to are Sussex, the Isle of Wight, Devon, Dorset, Cornwall, the Scilly Isles, Cumbria, Somerset, Norfolk, Kent, and Hampshire.

The south coast has the warmest temperatures and the least fog; South Devon and Cornwall are remote but warm. The most exclusive retirement areas are on the South Devon coast: Budleigh, Salterton,

Sidmouth, and Seaton. In Sussex, the places to retire are Eastbourne and Bexhill.

The east coast, from Lincolnshire to the Scottish border, also can be charming, although the winds are cold.

Wales is less expensive than England, and less developed. But it is rainier and cooler. And to retire here, you'll want to know a bit of Welsh. The most popular places to retire in Wales are Caernarvonshire, Merionethshire, Radnorshire, Cardiganshire, Denbighshire, Montgomeryshire, Caermarthenshire, Breconshire, Flintshire, and Anglesey.

If you are interested in Scotland, Edinburgh is a delightful city. As is Inverness (on Loch Ness); although the winters are cold and dark.

The more rural the area, the more difficult it is to fit in—unless you like riding, gardening, and fishing, the primary pastimes in the countryside.

Living in London like a Londoner

Americans who move to London and try to continue to live like Americans discover that life can be expensive. But life in this lovely city need not bust your budget; all you need to do is adopt the ways of the natives.

Londoners, for example, may opt to rent a bedsit rather than an apartment with a kitchen, a separate bedroom, and a private bathroom. A bedsit is the British equivalent of an efficiency. The bathroom is often down the hall, and the cooking facilities may be minimal. However, the better bedsits have private showers. Single bedsits start at about £40 a week; doubles are £50 to £80 per week. Or you can buy a bedsit starting at £50,000. One local estate agent that deals in bedsits is **Anscombe and Ringland,** *tel. (44-1)340-2600.*

Instead of renting a bedsit, you may prefer to share a flat or a house; the cost is comparable. This is a good way to get to know the British, and it gives you more space—perhaps even a back yard.

It's wise to take the cheapest accommodations you can live with. London is chock-full of attractions to keep you away from home.

The best resources for finding a bedsit or a flat are the *Evening Standard* and the *Hampstead and Highgate Express, Perrins Court, London NW3; tel. (4-1)435-9041.* To find an apartment to share, try either *Time Out* or *City Limits,* two London weekly magazines.

Even if you wouldn't dream of living without a car in the United States, try it in London. Public transportation is excellent and fairly cheap. The city has good subway (called the underground or the tube) and bus systems, as well as good train connections for travel around the country.

Travel on the underground is much cheaper if you buy a round-trip (return) ticket after 10 a.m. And train travel is cheaper if you purchase a day return ticket after 9:30 a.m. (Return tickets are much cheaper than two one-way tickets.) To save the most money, purchase weekly tickets for unlimited travel on the underground or trains. For more information, contact **Britrail,** *(212)599-5400.*

A bicycle is also a good way to see the city. London is fairly flat, and drivers are more careful of cyclists than in American cities.

You can cut your grocery bill in half by following British food-buying habits. Buy fresh fruit and vegetables at the markets scattered around the city, and shop for bread at the independent bakeries. Concentrate on fish rather than red meat.

And eating out, believe it or not, can be a money saver. Fish and chips and Indian and vegetarian food are especially affordable. The **Diwana Bhel Poori House,** *Drummond Street,* near Euston Station; *tel. (44-1)221-0721,* serves inexpensive Indian cuisine. The **Sea Shell,** *Lisson Grove,* near Marylebone Station, may be London's best fish and chips emporium. Pubs are good places for cheap and tasty lunches. Try shepherd's pie.

Even if you are on a budget, you can still afford high-quality entertainment. The British equivalent of Times Square's TKTS half-price ticket booth is in Leicester Square. Many theaters offer reduced prices for matinee or Monday night performances. During the summer you can listen to the best symphony orchestras in the world at the Royal Albert Hall for £2. The city's drama schools put on first-rate productions for as little as £1, and local film societies show movies for about the same price. Check local papers or libraries for listings.

If you're a sports fan, you can join a club offering everything from tennis to soccer for as little as £23. Avid soccer fans can save money at matches by doing what the British do—stand.

Property in London

London is the most expensive place to live in Britain. Even homes in the countryside outside London are pricey. One-bedroom apartments start at £65,000; houses go for £125,000 to £600,000.

Property in London is sold as leasehold or freehold. Freehold means you own the building and land outright; leasehold means you have the use of the land and building for the period of the lease, which can run from 999 years down.

Leasehold is an important concept in British property. It is rare to find anything freehold in London. Part of Belgravia and most of Mayfair are incorporated in the largest urban landholding in the world, an estate that belongs to the Duke of Westminster. The duke also owns part of Pimlico and a bit of the city of Westminster. Chelsea and the West End are almost exclusively owned by the Cadogan estate.

You can sell your leasehold property any time. The problem is that as the years dwindle, your leasehold becomes less valuable. However, as a leaseholder, you can apply to extend the term of your lease. And often you have the right to purchase the property freehold if you can afford it.

Choosing a piece of London

The desirability and prices of different sections of London vary. Belgravia and Mayfair are the most expensive and fashionable areas. Both are beyond the range of most Londoners and have become commercial centers and residences of foreigners and other "Mayfair mercenaries." Similarly chic are Hampstead and Highgate.

Lower-priced property with good potential for appreciation is available in Clapham, Kensington, Stockwell, Wandsworth, and Camberwell. More established but still available to bargain hunters are Battersea and Richmond. Shepherd's Bush and Acton have particularly good appreciation potential. Hackney is also considered up and coming—but it may take longer before the properties here appreciate. Parts of Hackney—Victoria Park and London Fields— have lovely period houses and high appreciation rates. However, other sections of Hackney are less attractive, with council flats. Houses go for £150,000 to £250,000.

Four up-and-coming areas are **Islington,** where three-bedroom houses are "good buys" at £300,000 to £500,000, **Fulham, Chiswick,** and **Little Venice.** Islington, a borough of London southwest of fashionable Hampstead, is popular because of its proximity to downtown London. Bankers, lawyers, and stockbrokers live here and walk to work in the city. The area saw a decline after the turn of the century, but the 1960s brought a brisk revival. Islington is filled with elegant Victorian parks and terraces. The smaller houses are good bargains. **Hotblack & Company,** *314 Upper St., London N1; tel. (44-1)226-0160 or (44-1)354-2664,* specializes in this area.

It's still possible to find bargains in picturesque Chiswick, although property values in the past year have risen 20%.

Prices in Fulham vary dramatically. A home selling in the Sands End area can go for half the price of a similar home in the smarter Hurlingham vicinity. But even in Hurlingham you can find bargains.

Little Venice is fast becoming London's mini-Belgravia. People such as John Mortimer live here, as do Jacob Rothschild and Boy George. The area is colorful, with a mixture of houses turned into flats and blocks of mansions. It is convenient to the West End. But the prices don't compare with the inflated costs of property elsewhere in London.

Until 1981, the vast estate encompassing Little Venice was owned by the Church of England. In 1981, the church put the estate on the market. Little Venice includes more than 2,000 residential units—this may be the largest single sale of high-class urban property in Europe since World War II. Prices range from £80,000 for a single flat to £1 million for a five-bedroom mansion. Many of the houses have period features.

Estate agents that deal in Little Venice and Fulham include **Vickers & Company,** *tel. (44-1)289-1692,* **Barnard Marcus,** *tel. (44-1)602-6111,* and **Foxton,** *tel. (44-1)221-3534.*

In addition, roof space in London is being converted into New York-style lofts that can be bought quite cheaply in areas such as Notting Hill Gate and Bayswater.

Sample London properties

Hotblack & Company, *314 Upper St., London N1; tel. (44-1)226-0160* or *(44-1)354-2664,* recently advertised the following properties:

• A one-bedroom apartment, *11 Saratoga Road, London E5,* on the second floor, is on the market for £58,000. It has a small reception room and a small kitchen and is being sold with a 94-year lease.

• A two-bedroom apartment, *3A Rectory Road, London N16,* on the third floor, is available for £69,950. It has a living room, a kitchen, and a bathroom. The lease is for 98 years.

• A three-bedroom apartment, *93 Sotheby Road, London N5,* on the top floor, is available for £92,500. It has a large living room, a kitchen, a bath, and a garden. Its lease is for 124 years.

• A modern, two-bedroom town house, *54 Springfield, London E5,* is on the market for £95,000. It is light and sunny, with a brass door, window seats, a patio, and a small front yard.

• An end-of-terrace home, *49 Mayola Road, London E5,* is available for £97,000. It has period features, central heat, three bedrooms, a bathroom, a living room, a kitchen/dining room, front and back yards, and a garage.

• A three-bedroom town house, *46 Avebury Court, Poole Street, London N1*, is available for £100,000. It is modern, with a bathroom, a spacious kitchen, a living room, and a back yard.

• A charming early Victorian cottage, *4 Hides St., London N7*, is going for £137,500. It has two bedrooms, a bathroom, a dining room, and a kitchen and has been renovated and restored, with new wiring and new plumbing.

You can always rent

Before you commit yourself to London, you may want to rent in the city for a while. The average rental for an unfurnished apartment is about £352 a month. Furnished flats in central London start at £300 a week for one bedroom; £450 for two bedrooms, one bath; and £500 pounds for two bedrooms, two baths.

A cottage in the English countryside

Although London is exciting, with its first-rate theater and lively night life, the English countryside is prettier—and much more peaceful. It's more conducive to a tranquil retirement (if that's what you seek). Property in the countryside within an hour's drive of London can be just as expensive as property within the city itself. For bargains, you must look farther from London.

Most pretty little country homes within driving distance of London cost between £100,000 and £150,000. Hamptons Bedford, in Bury St. Edmunds, recently advertised a three-bedroom, 17th-century cottage for £130,000. Farther north, the Nurseries at Runcton Holme, between King's Lynn and Downham Market, has an early 18th-century four-bedroom cottage with 4.5 acres on the market for £105,000.

However, not all property in Britain is expensive. For bargains, look in the remote rural locations, often isolated from cosmopolitan sophistication and big-city excitement. Low-priced houses are available in Norfolk, North Suffolk, Bedfordshire, East Kent, South Wales, Devon, Cornwall, and Sheffield. Prices in these locations begin at about £47,000.

The bucolic Cotswolds

Perhaps it is the famous Cotswold stone, honey colored and mellow, that gives this area just an hour-and-a-half northwest of

London its golden tranquility. The **Cotswolds** include Gloucestershire, Worcestershire, and Hertfordshire. The Cotswold economy originally was based on wool, and it is still predominantly agricultural. The region has rural farmland, country lanes, and old churches. A softly rolling ribbon of hills enfolds rustic villages of another, more romantic age. You can glimpse an occasional flock of sheep meandering across the scene. The 20th-century seems still in the future.

The towns and villages nestled in these hills possess a charming uniformity. Every structure is built of the local stone—an indigenous limestone—and topped with a steep slate roof. But the towns themselves vary in size and personality. The tinier villages are Old World, while the larger towns wear the trappings of modern society.

Unfortunately, the much-coveted Cotswolds have become expensive. Hamptons in Cheltenham recently advertised Shermershill Cottage in Bisley, Gloucestershire for £250,000. This 17th-century Cotswold stone house comprises two former weavers' cottages.

However, a few reasonably priced places remain in the Cotswolds, especially if you go farther west toward Stroud, Chapman, Prestbury, and Gotherington. A 17th-century stone cottage near Stroud was advertised recently for £89,500. Completely restored, this two-bedroom cottage includes a detached garage and gardens. Contact **Hampton & Sons,** *18 Imperial Square, Cheltenham, Gloucestershire GL50 1QZ; tel. (44-242)514849.*

If you're interested in renting in the Cotswolds, **Wayside Travel,** *10101 Kolin, Oaklawn, IL 60453; (312)423-2113,* rents completely furnished cottages with fireplaces for $170 to $370 a week. Wayside also has cottages dating from the 1500s and 1600s and converted wings of manor houses that rent for $190 to $470 a week.

The Lake Country

The **Lake Country,** so loved by the Romantic poets, is inspiring still. A land of whispering lakes lying in the shadows of England's highest mountains, it invites long ramblings through the countryside and deep reflective thoughts. If a poet lurks within you, this is where he or she will find contentment.

Here, you can live the life of a dreamy-eyed poet in a small cottage for £60,000 to £70,000. But buy now; prices are creeping up.

The Lake Country is in northwest England, primarily in Cumbria. Although it covers only 32 miles, it is uncrowded because of its distance from London. Mists shroud the mountain peaks and velvet valleys. Sheep graze in the meadows. Young and old hike for hours through the countryside, with the help of crooked sticks.

Don't move to the Lake Country if you are addicted to sunshine; sunny days are few and far between. But if you like the mystery of fog and soft drizzle, if you don't mind hiking about in rubber boots and a raincoat, this is the land for you. When the sun *does* shine, the Lake Country is a brilliant green.

This region is a land of great men and women. Across it runs **Hadrian's Wall,** built in the second century by the Romans to keep the wild Scotsmen at bay. William Wordsworth, one of the most loved English poets, was born at Cockermouth. Beatrix Potter, author of the Peter Rabbit books, lived near Hawkshead. John Ruskin, poet, artist, and social reformer, lived near Coniston Water and is buried at the village church in Coniston. Robert Southey, poet laureate, made his home in Keswick. So did novelist Sir Hugh Walpole.

Kendal is the southern gateway to the Lake Country. A small market town, it is near the lakeside resort of Windermere. But Kendal has its own attractions: the ruins of the castle where Catherine Parr (one of Henry VIII's wives) was born and a 13th-century church.

Windermere is on the eastern shore of Lake Windermere, England's largest lake. Nearby is Orrest Head, a good climb. From its summit you can see the highest peak in England, **Scafell Pike,** which rises 3,210 feet.

Not far from Windermere is **Bowness-on-Windermere,** also on the lake. This pretty town, filled with old buildings, is a hub for boaters and fishermen.

Wordsworth took refuge from the world at **Rydal,** a village on Rydal Water, one of the smallest lakes in the region. Wordsworth also lived in **Grasmere,** on Lake Grasmere, and is buried in the village graveyard.

The Southwest Peninsula

The **Southwest Peninsula**—Devon and Cornwall—is for people who enjoy tangy sea breezes, exploring fishing villages, walking harbor walls, swimming in the sea, and wallowing in England's maritime history. The southern coast faces the English Channel and has a mild climate. Gentle waves softly lap the secluded bays and ancient smugglers' coves. The northern coast of the peninsula faces the full force of the Atlantic. King Arthur, according to legend, lived at Tintagel, where a ruined Norman castle, circa 1145, still clings to the slate cliffs.

Inland are the granite moors. **Dartmoor, Exmoor,** and **Bodmin**

71

are designated National Trust areas. Protected from development, they remain as wild, free, and unspoiled now as they were at the beginning of time. Narrow country lanes twist through the region.

While houses in Cornwall usually sell for £90,000 to £100,000, some go for much less. A stone house in Delabole, Cornwall was advertised recently for £32,000. This three-bedroom house has a slate roof, exposed beams, a fireplace, and a garden. Contact **William Issacs,** *tel. (44-840)212788.*

Somerset and Dorset

Somerset and **Dorset,** serenely rural, are Thomas Hardy country. In Dorset, you'll find prehistoric chalklands, wildflowers, peaceful country lanes, and a wealth of Roman history. You can't miss the Cerne Abbas giant, a figure carved by prehistoric man into the chalk and visible for miles. It is renowned for its detail and lack of a fig leaf.

Houses are available in this region for £70,000 to £150,000. Recently, a terraced cottage in Shaftesbury, Dorset was on the market for £70,000. This restored two-bedroom cottage has beamed ceilings throughout, stonework, an inglenook fireplace, a garden, and superb views. Contact **Champman, Moore, & Mugford,** *9 High St., Shaftesbury, Dorset SP7 8JD; tel. (44-747)2400.*

The Southeast

The **Southeast** of England centers around London and is, therefore, more expensive than elsewhere in Britain. It includes the counties of Hampshire, Berkshire, Sussex, Surrey, and Kent. This area is particularly rich in National Trust properties, where stately homes bought by the trust have been preserved and opened to the public. East Kent probably has the best bargains, with homes going for about £52,000.

Hampshire is green and rolling, with fine views. Its **New Forest** offers quiet picnic spots, wild ponies wandering the roads, and quiet walks. Beaulieu (pronounced Bewley) is an unspoiled village within New Forest. It lies on the Beaulieu River and is enhanced by Lord Montague's stately home. Visit Montague's famous motor museum and the beautiful Cistercian Abbey ruins.

Kent is known as the Garden of England. Its rich soils nourish fruit orchards, crops, and cereals. Many of England's hedgerows date from the 16th century, and in Kent, they flourish, canopied with wild roses, honeysuckle, and blackberry brambles. The county is particularly famous for its hops and distinctive oast houses. Many of these taper-roofed, hops-drying kilns have been converted into homes.

The North Country

Traveling north, you will discover **East Anglia,** comprised of Essex (the East Saxons), Suffolk (the south folk), Norfolk (the north folk), and Cambridgeshire. The **Norfolk Broads,** 200 miles of navigable waterways, were thought to have been left by the glaciers that once covered the land. But recent excavations have revealed that they were in fact dug out—by hand—in the 11th century to provide peat as fuel for the nearby city of Norwich. The coastline here has miles of uncommercialized sandy beaches.

In East Anglia, property prices are high. A restored period cottage near Saffron Walden was advertised recently by **Hamptons Jennings,** *tel. (44-799)22628,* for £185,000. But it has lovely views across the hills, a fine beamed drawing room with inglenook, three bedrooms, and four bathrooms.

However, it is still possible, particularly in North Suffolk and Norfolk, to buy small cottages for £50,000 to £70,000.

Because of their proximity to London (a 40-minute drive), houses in Essex go for £70,000 to £120,000. Recently, a two-bedroom semi-detached brick house was on the market for £70,000. A three-bed-room single home with a large garden was advertised for £110,000. Contact **Strutt & Parker,** *Coval Hall, Chelmsford, Essex CM1 2QF; tel. (44-245)258201.*

Herriot Country

Yorkshire's wide-open spaces are now fondly called **Herriot Country.** The Scottish veterinarian and author of *All Creatures Great and Small* has retired, but it is rumored that once a week he returns to the pleasant market town of Thirsk to autograph copies of his book.

The dales of Herriot Country are dotted with picture-postcard villages full of history and odd traditions. The architecture in the town of **Bainbridge** dates back to its Roman beginnings in the first century A.D. This town has a strange custom. At 9 p.m. every Wednesday, from September through Shrove Tuesday, the Bainbridge Horn is blown to guide lost travelers to the hospitality of the village. Barry Thorpe's 15th-century **Rose and Crown Hotel** makes an ideal way station (bed and breakfast for £12).

The county of **Yorkshire** sprawls across the northeast of England, keeping its back to its old War of Roses rival, Lancashire. It faces Europe, which lies across the stormy North Sea.

Hull lies at the eastern end of the English motorway network. It's a bustling metropolis and has an excellent selection of moderately priced modern apartments and semi-detached homes.

The **Yorkshire Dales** once offered rural properties at low prices, but in recent years prices have risen, and it is now difficult to find a house here for less than £50,000. However, Henry Spencer & Sons recently listed a three-bedroom town house in Beverly for £35,000.

Tennants of Yorkshire recently listed a little two-bedroom semi-detached house in Gale for £50,000.

Dee & Atkinson listed a three-story, three-bedroom town house in the heart of Beverly for £68,000.

For more information on property in Yorkshire, contact:

• **Tennants of Yorkshire,** *27 Market Place, Leyburn; tel. (44-969)23451; 33 North End, Bedale; tel. (44-677)23911;* or *27A Market Place, Richmond; tel. (44-748)2149.*

• **Henry Spencer & Sons,** *42 Toll Gavel; tel. (44-482)881-888.*

• **Dee & Atkinson,** *14 N. Bar Within; tel. (44-482)869-389.*

• **Renton and Renton,** *3 King St.; tel. (44-748)5551.*

• **Peter Lucas,** *Stanilands, 45 Low Petergate, York YO1 2HT.*

Wales

North Wales is beautiful and inexpensive (**South Wales** is more industrial), with cottages for £30,000 to £40,000. A five-bedroom period house in Wales costs one-third the price of a comparable home in English Chester, just across the border. However, the high cost of property in southern England is pushing many people north, and prices are bound to increase. The stone villages in the Stamford-Melton and Mowbray-Oakham areas are popular.

If you are considering settling in Wales, learn a bit of Welsh (more than 40,000 inhabitants of the area speak this Celtic language; one-fourth of the inhabitants speak Welsh and English). It will make your life easier and charm your neighbors.

Scotland

The least expensive country properties in Britain are in the **Scottish Highlands,** where a cottage goes for £30,000. Also affordable are **Edinburgh** and **Glasgow,** where three-bedroom cottages sell for £41,000.

As the fortunes of the landed gentry in this area decline, their manors and estates enter the market at relatively low prices. For example, a Scottish castle with 79 acres near Glasgow and Edinburgh was advertised recently for £130,000.

Stately homes in the country

Historic properties (castles, parks, manors, halls, abbeys, chantry houses, and convents) go for as little as £97,000 at distress sales. However, most need extensive repairs, and you've got to be willing to do the work. For listings, write the **Department of the Environment,** *Historic Buildings Bureau, 25 Savile Row, London W1X 2BT.* **Period Property Register,** *Chobham Park House, Chobham, Surrey GU24 8HQ,* also has information on historic homes.

For listings of historic properties in Scotland, contact the Edinburgh office of **Strutt & Parker,** *tel. (44-31)226-2500.*

One word of warning: If you think thatched roofs are charming, remember that repairs can cost from £2,400 to £4,200. Re-doing a thatched roof can cost £12,000. If you are planning to restore or replace a thatched roof, contact the **Country Gentleman's Association,** *tel. (44-462)480-011,* for assistance.

Property listings

For more complete listings of properties available throughout the English countryside, contact:

• **Farar, Stead, & Glyn,** *656 Fulham Road, London SW6; tel. (44-1)731-4391.*

• **Hampton & Sons,** *6 Arlington St., London SW1; tel. (44-1)226-0160.*

• **Hamptons,** *96 New Kings Road, London SW1; tel. (44-1)493-8222.*

• **Hotblack Desiato & Company,** *314 Upper St., Islington, London N1; tel. (44-1)226-0160.*

• **Jackson-Stops & Staff,** *14 Curzon St., London W1; tel. (44-1)499-6291.*

• **Knight Frank & Rutley,** *20 Hanover Square, London W1R; tel. (44-1)629-8171.*

• **John D. Wood,** *23 Berkley Square, London W1; tel. (44-1)629-9050.*

• **Prudential,** *47 S. Audley St., London W1; tel. (44-1)493-6926.*

• **Prudential Property Services,** *Winchmore House 15, Setter Lane, London EC4A 1BR; tel. (44-1)528-9075.*

• **Roy Brooks,** *359 Kings Road, London SW3; tel. (44-1)352-0061.*

• **Strutt & Parker,** *13 Hill St., Berkeley Square, W1X 8DL; tel. (44-1)629-7282.*

Property listings can also be found in the following publications: *Country Life Magazine, Kings Reach Tower, Stamford Street, London SE1 9LS;* and *Savills, 20 Grosvenor Hill, London W1X OJQ; tel. (44-1)449-8644.*

Where to book a cottage

It may be a good idea to get a feel for the British countryside before buying property there. The way to do this is to rent a cottage. Stay during the winter season, to see if you can survive three months of damp, dark cold.

Character Cottages Ltd., *34 Fore St., Sidmouth, Devon, EX10 8AQ; tel. (44-3955)77001,* rents cottages, new homes, and converted barns. A two-bedroom modern terraced home in the Cotswolds rents for £185 a month in July and August. A three-bedroom cottage in Cornwall rents for £255 a month in July and August. An 18th-century converted barn near Cornwall rents for £255 a month in July and August, £180 a month in June or September.

You can also rent a cottage through **English Country Cottages,** *Claypit Lane, Faneknham, Norfolk NR21 8AS; tel. (44-328)4041* or *(44-328)4292,* or **Tayling's Holidays,** *14 High St., Godalming, Surrey GU7 1ED; tel. (44-4868)28522.*

You can rent a cottage in the Yorkshire Dales, the Lake District, York, Derbyshire, or Northumberland through **Country Holidays,** *High Street, Gargrave, Skipton, North Yorkshire; tel. (44-775678)776.*

Cottages can be rented in Pembrokeshire and Wales through **Rogeston,** *Portfield Gate, Haverford-West, Pembrokeshire, West Wales; tel. (44-43783)373.*

When writing for a brochure, enclose $2 to cover postage.

Buying British real estate

Buying property in England or Wales (Scotland is a different matter; it is discussed below) is a considerably different process than in the United States. To begin, you need a brief language lesson. A realtor in Britain is called an estate agent. The lawyer is a solicitor. If you are obtaining a mortgage in the United Kingdom, you deal with a building society (or bank).

By American standards, British estate agents are paid a tiny commission (2% to 3%). That's good news for your pocketbook, but it means the agents have little incentive to sell you anything.

In addition, estate agents are often uninformed about areas outside their locale. Take time to do your own research. Explore the area you are interested in. Find out as much as you can from long-time residents, the local papers, the town library, and historic records.

Once you have chosen a property, make an offer. You can make your offer directly to the seller, but this is usually handled by your estate agent. Offers commonly are subject to survey and contract, which means you may be able to back out—with penalty. A good-faith deposit boils down to lodging about £90 with the seller's estate agent.

The transactions following the initial deposit are usually handled by solicitors (both the buyer and the seller must engage solicitors). Your estate agent can recommend one. A solicitor's fees are about 1% of the purchase price. Stay on their heels, or settlement could take 10 months.

After you make a deposit, the seller's solicitor draws up a draft contract that describes the property in detail. Your solicitor reviews the draft and tries to dig up any additional information that might influence the future value of the property. He investigates to make sure that no plans exist to widen a road onto the property and that no outstanding payments are due. He finds out which council and water rates (taxes) are paid on the property, and whether there are any arrears.

All properties in England and Wales are in the process of being cataloged in a central Land Registry, where details concerning the title, covenants, and easements are being recorded. However, older properties are not registered. Their deeds can go back to the 1800s or earlier. These documents are often written in longhand, in Old English, and faded with age. But they must be read, in case any covenants are still applicable.

If a property has been registered, a single Land Certificate is all that you need to complete a purchase; if the property is mortgaged, a Charge Certificate is required. This not only makes conveyancing much easier, but it also makes the process less expensive for the buyer.

The draft contract is returned to the seller's solicitor after amendments or approval. When it is approved by both parties, a small down payment is required. Surveyors make the next important check on the property. The lender has the property surveyed, but you should have your own surveyor make a check as well (even though this is not required). Dry rot, flaws in plumbing, wiring, and roofing, and structural problems are all checked out. The cost of a typical survey is from £24 for a £12,000 house to £48 for a £60,000 house. As the buyer, you must pay for the survey. If the surveyors find a fault in the house, you can withdraw from the contract and collect your deposit and down payment.

To minimize the foreign-exchange risk, hedge your currency position in the currency forward market. For example, if you are buying a property for £250,000, and you think the pound might go up, buy a futures contract for £250,000.

Until your lender delivers the complete payment to the seller, watch out for gazumping. This is a peculiarly British way of taking the highest bidder at the last minute. If a buyer with a better offer comes in at any time before the complete payment has been made, you can be gazumped and lose your contract.

If you are not gazumped, the title of the property is transferred after the final payment has been made. Your solicitor then investigates the title and draws up the transfer document for the seller's solicitor to approve. When the document has been signed by both parties, you are the proud owner of a piece of British real estate.

In England and Wales, a mortgage is not transferable, as it is in the United States. Each vendor must pay off his mortgage when he sells a piece of property and take out a new mortgage on his new property. Properties are always sold unencumbered by any mortgages, legal charges, or liens.

The entire process, from the submission of the first draft contract to the securing of a mortgage and the receipt of your transfer document, can take several months.

Be prepared to pay a 2% stamp duty on properties costing more than £40,000. In addition, you may have to pay a land registry fee of about £210.

If you are a non-resident, it isn't easy to borrow money in England. You'll have better luck if you have a bank or building society account that has been established for a year or so.

It's easier in Scotland

Buying a house in Scotland is a breeze compared with the convoluted tangle of paperwork involved with property purchases in England and Wales. The same title search and investigations into local regulations ensue. However, all this is done after the exchange of contracts, which can be completed in a matter of hours or days after an offer has been made. And the vendor's solicitor does much of the paperwork, relieving your solicitor from all the burden.

You may not even need the services of an estate agent. Your solicitor can act in that capacity—most know the property markets in Scotland and can market the houses themselves. A Scottish solicitor can also arrange the survey and determine a reasonable bidding price. He can even make contacts for you with building societies.

Because bids can be made before the contract work is undertaken, either party may back out at any time, without penalty or wasted time. Once a bid has been accepted and contracts exchanged, of course, both parties are legally bound and cannot renege. But it's a great advantage to be able to find a house, make an offer, and wrap up the deal—or walk away from it—without waiting through the weeks, even months, of head-throbbing wrangling involved with buying property in England and Wales.

How to find a reliable realtor

Several organizations are responsible for upholding standards in Great Britain's real estate industry. They monitor complaints and generally keep an eye on things. Following is a list of these organizations, which you can contact for names of agents in any area of the country.

• The **Royal Institute of Chartered Surveyors** (RICS), *12 George St., London SW1P 3AD; tel. (44-1)222-7000,* founded in 1868 and incorporated by Royal Charter (the queen is a patron), monitors legislation-affected land and its development. The RICS has a library of more than 30,000 books on real estate procedures. It is affiliated with the International Real Estate Federation and has its own disciplinary board to deal with companies that fail to toe the line.

• The **Incorporated Society of Valuers and Auctioneers,** *3 Cadogan Gate, London SW1X 0AS; tel. (44-1)235-2282,* states that its "primary concern is to secure a standard of excellence in the public interest." The society also specializes in the valuation of industrial and commercial equipment.

• The stated objectives of the **National Association of Estate Agents,** *Arbor House, 21 Jury St., Warwick, Warwickshire; tel. (44-926)496800,* are "to promote unity and understanding among estate agents and to protect the public against fraud, misrepresentation, and malpractice." This company is limited by guarantee, and any estate agent that is a member should be reliable.

• The **Black Horse Agency,** *11/15 Monument St., London EC3R 8JU,* owned by Lloyds Bank PLC, has 410 offices in 44 countries.

This agency can send you a list of its offices, plus a magazine entitled *Maison* that lists properties throughout Great Britain, along with prices.

• **Home Location,** *2 Cabot Drive, Swindon SN5 6HG,* is a personal-service agency. For $75 and full details of what you're looking for (including price range), Home Location will send you particulars of properties offered by reputable estate agents. This avoids the time and paperwork of writing to one of the above-mentioned organizations and then to the recommended agents. Home Location can even make appointments for you to inspect properties.

After you have bought your property, Home Location can arrange a caretaking staff if you don't intend to live in the house full-time.

Buying at auction

In Britain, buying property at an auction can bring great bargains. It also saves time. The deal is sealed with the final bid, bypassing the delay of ticklish, drawn-out negotiations.

More and more country houses are being sold at auction, as the great demand brings lively bidding. The heaviest competition usually surrounds houses in the £93,000 to £240,000 range. Properties in need of renovation also have been selling well at auctions. Developers, recognizing the potential gains on fixer-uppers located in the right areas, are adding to the competition (competition is fiercest in the winter months, when developers are looking for projects to keep their work forces busy).

To take advantage of the auction marketplace, do some planning before the sale. (Auction particulars are usually publicized two to three weeks before the date of the sale.)

Arrange for the financing of a 10% deposit on the property you want to buy. The final bang of the auctioneer's hammer creates an instant contract requiring this initial deposit. Banks in Britain are now better prepared to meet such deadlines.

Organize surveys, valuations, and legal searches before the sale.

Set a realistic ceiling price and drop out of the bidding when the property goes over that amount. Sometimes houses are withdrawn from a sale if the bidding does not reach a set price. If this happens, you may have the opportunity after the auction to negotiate privately.

If you can't attend the auction in person, appoint a representative to bid for you, preferably a solicitor or a member of the auction house's staff.

For more information and sale announcements, contact **Barnard**

Marcus & Company Auctioneers, *66 Shepherd's Bush Road, London W6; tel. (44-1)602-6111.* This is Britain's busiest auction house.

Medical services

Good medical care is inexpensive—and in some cases free—in Britain. Emergency medical treatment is free for U.S. citizens, but subsequent care is not. Residents are not charged for treatment in case of emergency or for the diagnosis and treatment of certain communicable diseases.

Short-term visitors and newcomers (those who have lived in Britain for less than a year) must pay the full costs of any hospital treatment. Even if you must pay, you will find that the costs are generally lower than in the United States.

To find out if you are eligible for coverage under the National Health Service, write to the **Department of Health and Social Security,** *Health Services Division, 3B Hannibal House, London SE1 6TE.*

However, under the National Health Service, it can take up to two years to get a non-emergency operation. For this reason, we recommend private hospital insurance, which costs about £120 to £300 a year per person.

Your U.S. health insurance may cover you overseas. If it does, you may want to continue with your U.S. company for the first year or two that you live in Britain (until you are firmly established as a resident).

If you decide to go with a private British company, consider one of the following, which are the three largest private health insurance companies in the country:

• With **British United Provident Association** (BUPA), *Provident House, Essex St., London WC2R 3AX; tel. (44-1)353-5212,* family insurance ranges from £972 to £1,513 per year. This isn't the best insurance for retirees, however; it covers you only up to age 74.

• With **Private Patients Plan** (PPP), *Eynsham House, Crescent Road, Tunbridge Wells, Kent TN1 2PL; tel. (44-1)388-2468,* family insurance ranges from £478 to £964 per year. This is the best insurance for retirees; PPP has a special retirement health plan that costs only £17.90 per month. It works in conjunction with the National Health Service.

• With **Western Provident Association** (WPA), *Culver House, Culver Street, Bristol BS1 6AB; tel. (44-1)409-0414,* family insurance ranges from £365 to £516 per year.

81

Great Britain has 1 physician for every 680 people. (The United States has 1 physician for every 500 people).

British life insurance

British life insurance (called assurance) rates are less expensive than those in the United States. British companies offer some of the lowest rates in the world.

English companies, among the oldest and most experienced in the world, are free from government investment restrictions. Thus, they are able to make greater returns to pass on to their customers. In addition, British insurers tend to pay lower commissions to their sales staffs, which further reduces costs. A premium that costs £218 in the United States, for example, is £120 in Great Britain.

The cost of living

The British may spend more on some essentials, but they spend much less on entertainment than Americans. A good orchestra seat at a West End theater in London costs only £7 pounds (a comparable seat costs £15 to £30 in New York).

To retire comfortably in Great Britain, a couple needs an income of about $15,000 a year; an individual needs about $11,500 a year.

While groceries and restaurants are reasonably priced in Britain, bus and subway fares can be high.

The tax man cometh

Britain has a double-taxation agreement with the United States to avoid taxing U.S. expatriates twice for the same income.

The basic income tax rate in Great Britain is 25% on taxable income up to £19,300; beyond that amount, the flat rate is 40%.

Tax write-offs include interest payments on mortgages on primary residences up to £30,000 and investments in some companies whose shares are not listed on the stock exchange.

Great Britain has no wealth tax. Capital gains of more than £5,000 per person are taxed 25% (however, capital gains from the sale of your residence are exempt from this tax).

A 15% value-added tax is assessed on goods and services sold in Britain, which raises prices.

For information on taxes, contact the *Secretary,* **Board of Inland Revenue,** *Somerset House, London WC2R 1LB.*

Banking

London has more foreign banks per square mile than any city in the world. It's an account-holder's cafeteria; whatever banking services you're looking for, you should be able to find them here. More importantly, British banks have a well-deserved reputation for soundness and experience. They weathered the worldwide banking crisis of the 1930s without any major bank shutdowns. Today, unlike American banks, they have little farm debt.

British banks also offer privacy. This tradition is rooted in English common law and widely respected. Under British law, a banker has a contract of privacy with his client. An English banker will not give information about your account to anyone without your permission or a court order. Recently, for instance, a large New York bank was subpoenaed in the United States for its London branch bank records. An English judge placed an injunction on the English branch, prohibiting it from releasing the data.

England has none of the automatic reporting transactions that regulate the U.S. banking system. English banks don't keep used checks or microfilm checks. Once your checks are returned, only you know what the checks were issued for and in what amounts.

It is easy to gain worldwide spending power with your English bank account. Most London bankers will give you a credit card that enables you to spend money all over the world and have it paid from your London bank account.

You will find that in Britain, the best bank isn't necessarily on the corner. Check around to see which banks offer the most comprehensive services. The **National Girobank,** *tel. (44-1)301-5757,* which operates through the mail and at post offices, offers free checking with no service charge, no charge for checks, and no minimum balance. The penalty for a bounced check is only 85 pence. At National Girobank, you can also buy foreign currency at a better rate than that offered by the major banks. And you can obtain checks that can be cashed abroad.

Savings are best kept in a building society, the equivalent of an American savings and loan.

The four major English banks are National Westminster, Barclays, Lloyds, and Midland. A checking account at Lloyds offers numerous advantages. Lloyds has a special program with American Express that provides an overseas gold card. If you qualify for this program, you receive a checkbook, a special cash card (which enables you to write and cash checks for up to £50 in almost any shop in

England and to receive cash advances of up to £300 a day from any branch of Lloyds), overdraft protection of £7,500 (this allows you to borrow on an unsecured basis at a favorable 2.5% above the London prime rate), and the ability to receive pounds from a cash machine without paying any exchange fees. With an overseas gold card, you don't have to carry cash when you travel in the British Isles.

Lloyds also offers loans, savings accounts, special savings plans that pay higher rates of interest, savings with life insurance, savings with mutual funds, investment management services, advice on taxes and wills, checking accounts (called current accounts), bill-paying services, and multi-currency or foreign-currency accounts. For more information, call **Lloyds** in New York, *(212)514-9100.*

English banking is inexpensive. Banking at Lloyds is free provided your account balance does not fall below £100 at any time during the quarter. Even if your balance does drop below £100, you're not necessarily charged. The bank gives you an allowance of 2.5% against costs on your credit balances. If, for example, your account balance one month was £6,000, your allowance for that month would be £12. This amount would be offset against any charges.

If you establish a good rapport with your English banker, he will usually negotiate checks for you. If, for example, you deposit a check from the United States, he will give you immediate credit, even though it will take up to four weeks before the check clears.

A paradise for green thumbs

Britain is a land of gardeners. The climate, with its plentiful rain, mild winters, and warm summers, provides a congenial environment for trees and plants, particularly in the south. The country's climate has inspired the British to create a rich national heritage of beautiful parks, arboreta, herb farms, plant nurseries, and cottage gardens.

Gardening is a good way to meet the British, especially the country folk (as is horseback riding). If you, too, have a green thumb, consider cultivating your hobby and a few new friends through one of the following English garden societies:

• As a member of the **Hardy Plant Society,** *214 Ruxely Lane, West Ewell, Surrey,* you'll have a chance to learn about plants through garden visits, meetings, and free bulletins.

• The **Royal Horticultural Society,** *80 Vincent Square, London SW1 2PE; tel. (44-1)834-4333,* runs the famous Chelsea Flower Show and the largest and finest garden in England. Members receive free admission to both, a monthly newsletter, advice on gardening, and admission to England's finest garden library.

• The **Garden History Society,** *Membership Secretary, 66 Granville Park, London SE13 7DX; tel. (44-1)852-1818,* is for people interested in the conservation and restoration of historic gardens. Members attend lectures, visit gardens of historic import, and receive a semiannual journal.

Volunteering

If you're interested in volunteering, you'll find great opportunities in Britain:

• The **Council for British Archeology,** *112 Kensington Road, London SE 11 GRE; tel. (44-1)582-0494,* has information on archeological projects in England that accept volunteers.

• The **National Conservation Corps,** *10-14 Duke St., Reading, Berkshire RG1 4RU,* is made up of volunteers working to conserve Britain's wildlife and countryside.

The following voluntary service organizations work with the poor and handicapped in Great Britain. Write for details.

• **Mencap Holidays Office,** *119 Drake St., Rochdale, Lancashire OL16 1PZ.*

• **The Simon Community,** *St. Joseph's House, 129 Malden Road, London NW5 4HS.*

• **Community Service Volunteers,** *237 Pentonville Road, London N19NJ.*

Scholarly pursuits

For information on higher education in Great Britain, including a directory of where you can study specific subjects, consult *Higher Education in the United Kingdom: A Handbook for Students from Overseas and Their Advisors.* It is published by the British Council and the Association of Commonwealth Universities and is available from **Longman Inc.,** *95 Church St., White Plains, NY 10601-1505; (914)993-5000,* or from **Longman Group,** *Longman House, Burnt Mill, Harlows, Essex, UK CM202SE.*

Organizations for retirees

The **Pre-Retirement Association of Great Britain and Northern Ireland** (PRA), *19 Undine St., Tooting, London SW 17 8PP; tel. (44-1)767-3225,* encourages local authorities and employers to organize pre-retirement programs and conducts seminars for workers. PRA sells a comprehensive *Approach to Retirement* kit that contains up-to-date material on finances, health, housing, leisure, and legal matters. **Saga Club,** *P.O. Box 65, Folkestone, Kent,* organizes holiday tours, produces *Saga News,* and provides a matchmaker service that can help you find a mate or companion.

For information on retirement communities in Great Britain, contact the **Retirement Home Association,** *47 Albermarle St., London W1X 3FE.*

Drawbacks

The British consider Americans brash, materialistic, and uncultured. They are more reserved than we are and slower to develop friendships.

Services are slower and less efficient in Britain. Take your own bag to the grocery store; you'll have to pack it yourself. Twenty-four-hour service is unheard of, and you'll find that repairs take forever.

The weather is usually cool and damp, which can be difficult for people with arthritis or rheumatism. The average daily temperature in Edinburgh is 43 degrees Fahrenheit in January and 64 degrees Fahrenheit in July. In London, temperatures vary from 45 degrees Fahrenheit to 70 degrees Fahrenheit. The average rainfall is about 40 inches. London gets about 23 inches each year, and the Lake District and Highlands get more than 60 inches.

For more information

The following agencies may be able to help you get settled in Great Britain:

• **British Embassy,** *(202)462-1340.*

• **British Information Services,** *(800)223-5339* or *(212)752-5747.*

• **Commercial Reference, British Embassy,** *(202)898-4346.*

• **Cornwall Tourist Board,** *tel. (44-872)74282.*

• **London Tourist Board,** *tel. (44-1)730-3488.*

• **Scottish Highlands & Islands,** *tel. (44-349)63434.*

• **Townsend Thoresen Cross Channel Ferry,** *tel. (44-1)583-9330.*

• **U.S. Embassy in London,** *tel. (44-1)499-9000* (24-hour number).

• **Wales Tourist Board,** *2 Maddox St., London W1; tel. (44-1)409-0969.*

Chapter 6

Canada

$\mathbf{W}$hile the majority of Americans looking for retirement havens head south to warmer climes, not everyone enjoys tropical heat. If you think you'd feel more at home among polar bears than beach bunnies, head north to Canada. This country has a cool climate, but it is not the iceberg that most imagine. Northern Canada is frosty, but the coastal regions are temperate.

The Pacific coast near Vancouver enjoys Canada's warmest winters; temperatures seldom drop below freezing (they range from 32 degrees Fahrenheit to 43 degrees Fahrenheit). Summers are mild (temperatures range from 54 degrees Fahrenheit to 74 degrees Fahrenheit), with an average of eight to nine hours of sunlight per day.

In Nova Scotia, the weather in January is similar to that in the northeastern United States, with temperatures ranging from 15 degrees Fahrenheit to 32 degrees Fahrenheit. Like Vancouver, this Atlantic island province has marvelously cool summers, with temperatures ranging from 54 degrees Fahrenheit to 74 degrees Fahrenheit.

Canada has more to offer than scenery and mild weather, however. It suffers less from violent crime than the United States. According to the *Book of City Rankings, 1986,* Toronto has an average of 2.1 homicides per 100,000 residents, compared with 35 per 100,000 residents in Washington, D.C. Halifax has even better statistics: 1.3 homicides per 100,000, compared with 58.5 per 100,000 in St. Louis, Missouri.

Because of the exchange rate, the cost of living is slightly lower in Canada than in the United States. And Canadian savings accounts often earn higher interest than U.S. savings accounts. In Canada, senior citizens are offered discounts on travel, services, and entertainment. Canada's government-run health care is inexpensive; patients are charged on a sliding scale.

If you love the outdoors, you'll think Canada a paradise. It offers excellent skiing, fishing, canoeing, sailing, hiking, mountain climbing, hunting, bird-watching, and swimming.

Last, but not least, most Canadians speak English, eliminating any language problem (except in Quebec province). And Canadian customs and traditions are similar to those in the United States, with a few charming differences. The government is a parliamentary democracy, allowing the same freedoms and civil liberties we enjoy at home.

This chapter concentrates on two attractive coastal areas: the region around Vancouver in the west and Nova Scotia in the east. Both are beautiful and unspoiled, with scenic ocean views and relaxed ways. Prices are reasonable, much lower than those in Ontario (which should be avoided; Toronto can be more expensive than New York City). And both regions are popular among retirees, who are attracted by the scenery, climate, and tranquility. The Southern Coast of Nova Scotia, especially, attracts quite a few American retirees, including many writers.

A look at the Vancouver area

If you stand in the heart of **Vancouver,** you'll see snow-capped mountains in all directions. To the east are the **Coast Mountains,** rising 4,000 feet and flanked by superb ski slopes. To the west are the mountains of **Vancouver Island,** across the Straits of Georgia. They cradle mirror-like lakes, where canoers paddle silently. To the south, in Washington, U.S.A., is **Mt. Rainier's** glowing peak.

Skiers, especially, enjoy Vancouver. Snow seldom blocks the roads along the coast, but it is heavy in the mountains, and skiing conditions are excellent throughout the winter.

The city of Vancouver, on the mainland, is not to be confused with Vancouver Island, a 280-mile strip of land across the Straits of Georgia from the city. The two are connected by ferries, but worlds apart. While Vancouver City is cosmopolitan and sophisticated, with fine restaurants, hotels, and museums, Vancouver Island is peaceful and relatively unspoiled. Most of the half-million people on Vancouver Island live on the east coast. The west coast is rugged, cut by fjords and piled high with mountains. It has only a handful of fishing villages.

The main city on Vancouver Island (and the capital of British Columbia) is **Victoria,** which retains a British air and the constant scent of flowers. This lovely city has twice the national average of retired people (they make up about 16% of the population)—and for good reason. Victoria enjoys Canada's nicest weather. Spring comes early, and winter temperatures seldom fall below freezing. And less rain falls on this city than elsewhere along the west coast.

Vancouver and Vancouver Island combine the best of two worlds: the mountains and the sea. While floating in the warm, calm waters off the east coast of Vancouver Island, you can look across the Straits of Georgia at the snow-covered peaks of the Coast Mountains. If you go out into the sea in a boat, you'll likely find yourself trailed by curious sea lions. The Pacific coast of Vancouver Island has a rugged beauty found nowhere else in North America. You can wander alone for hours along sandy beaches between surf and virgin rain forest.

Outdoor activities are a big draw in this region. Golfers say they never miss a day. Sailors race the wind in every season. And scuba divers claim that the waters around Vancouver Island are the clearest and most prolific in the Northern Hemisphere.

The **Gulf Islands,** between southern Vancouver Island and the mainland, are also beautiful and peaceful. British Columbia ferries sail regularly from Swartz Bay to all the Gulf Islands. Saltspring is the largest and most populated. Mayne is rustic and historic.

Senior citizens in British Columbia receive free public transportation; a 25% discount on car insurance; a free newspaper called *The Elder Statesman*; and discounts at many restaurants, theaters, and shops.

For more information, contact the **Federated Legislative Council of Elderly Citizens Association of British Columbia,** *#410, 1755 W. Broadway, Vancouver, BC V6J 4S5.*

A look at Nova Scotia

If you love the ocean, **Nova Scotia** is the place to retire. During the summer, fog rolls in off the water, shrouding the towns. It is caused by the temperature difference between the warm waters of the Gulf Stream and the cold Labrador current, which carries icebergs south even in summer. At night you can hear the surf pounding and the fog horns blowing. Nova Scotia's coast is lined with nooks and crannies, carved by the sea, each a secret treasure for you to discover. The **Bay of Fundy,** which washes the west coast of the province (and separates the 375-mile peninsula from New Brunswick), has the highest tides in the world. And the **Northumberland Strait** has the warmest salt water north of the Carolinas.

When you step off the boat in Nova Scotia, you have the uncanny feeling that you're in Scotland, not Canada. *Nova Scotia* means *New Scotland,* and much of the province was settled by Scots. It is as picturesque and unassuming as any little town on the north coast of

Scotland, with miles and miles of dramatic coastline lined with quaint fishing villages, bobbing boats, and centuries-old lighthouses. Woods, apple orchards, and pastures end suddenly at the edges of cliffs, which drop suddenly into the sea.

The two main regions of the province, Nova Scotia proper and Cape Breton Island, drew boatloads of Scotsmen during the wave of immigration from the Highlands in the 1700s. The Cape Breton immigrants left before they felt the full impact of King James VI's law of 1616, which prohibited the use of Gaelic and the wearing of kilts. Today, even in such remote regions of Scotland as the Isle of Skye, the use of this ill-fated language is rare.

However, on western Cape Breton Island, most adult residents have Gaelic-speaking parents, and you are apt to overhear some conversations in Scottish Gaelic among the older residents. They'll switch to English to be polite in the company of strangers.

Fiddlers in this province retain a Scottish style abandoned by most Scottish musicians long ago. "This, not Scotland, is the real McCoy," says Celtic record distributor Dan Collins of Shanachie Records. You'll find informal music sessions throughout the island— participants and dancers welcome—at all hours. A stretch along the coast from the causeway at Port Hastings to Margaree Forks is known as the **Ceilidh Trail**; here, traditional music and dance survive and flourish.

Of course, the Indians inhabited the island first. Later, the French settled here. But it was the Scots who left their traditions and accent.

For information on services for seniors in Nova Scotia, contact the **Nova Scotia Senior Services Secretariat,** *Dennis Building, P.O. Box 2065, Halifax, NS B3J 2T7.*

Immigration procedures

You can apply to immigrate to Canada at a Canadian embassy, high commission, or consulate outside Canada. If you are visiting Canada and decide you want to live there, you cannot stay in Canada while applying for residency; you must apply while living abroad.

The selection system separates applicants into three groups: "family," which means you have a relative living in Canada who has legally promised to help you financially; "refugee"; and "independent," which means you are applying on your own, with or without the financial help of relatives in Canada.

Most American retirees apply as independents. To immigrate as a retiree, you must be at least 55 years old and prove that you have enough money to support yourself (bank records, proof of pension, investments, property titles, or tax records may be used). The amount required varies, depending on your age and the area where you wish to live, but you should have at least US$10,000 per person per year, before taxes. Retirees must also pass a medical examination. Because Canada has a form of socialized medicine, the government doesn't want to take on anyone who may prove an undue burden on federal funds.

Your application is most likely to be approved if you can prove some ties with Canada, through relatives or friends. Owning a summer home may help.

While applications are processed as quickly as possible, thousands are received each year. First priority is given to family members and refugees. Independents must wait longer.

Officials may ask for birth or baptismal certificates, separation or divorce papers, educational transcripts, technical or professional certificates, and letters of reference. If your application is approved, you will need these papers when you get to Canada.

If your application for residency is approved, you can bring with you, without paying tariffs or taxes, most household and personal goods you used before arriving in Canada. But you must keep all these goods for at least 12 months after arriving in Canada; if you don't, you'll have to pay normal duties and taxes. Cars and trucks you owned and used before arriving in Canada can be brought into the country if they meet Canadian safety regulations. However, they can be used only for family transportation.

Applicants for permanent residence must pay a processing fee of C$125 (this is not refunded if your application is denied).

If your application is denied, or if you would rather avoid all the red tape, you can stay in Canada up to three months at a time without a visa. To extend your stay, go to an immigration office at least a week before your three months is up. Or just cross the border for a day or two and then return.

For specific legal information, consult the 1976 Immigration Act and Regulations. Or contact the **Embassy of Canada,** *1746 Massachusetts Ave. N.W., Washington, DC 20036; (202)785-1400.*

Buying Canadian property

As an American, you can buy property in Canada even if you are not a full-time resident. The amount of land you can purchase is limited in some provinces, but you can buy a one-acre lot anywhere.

Generally speaking, the procedure for buying a house in Canada is the same as in the United States. You make the purchase through a realtor, who must be licensed in the province where you wish to buy. It is wise to have a lawyer review the contract before you sign. And you must perform a title search. A down payment of at least 25% of the purchase price is required, unless you have mortgage loan insurance (in which case you must put 10% down). Most retirees prefer to pay cash, because mortgage interest is not deductible in Canada.

The details of real estate transactions are governed by provincial real estate associations. For complete information, contact a real estate agent or the real estate association in the province where you wish to live.

For general information on Canadian real estate, call the **Canadian Real Estate Association** in Ottawa, *(613)234-3373.*

For information on property in British Columbia, contact the provincial real estate association, *Suite 309, 1155 W. Pender, Vancouver, BC V6E 2P9; (604)683-7702.*

For information on property in Nova Scotia, contact the provincial real estate association, *5687 West St., Halifax, NS B3K 1H6; (902)423-9145.*

Homes in and around Vancouver

Prices for homes in Vancouver range from C$27,000 in East Haney to C$300,000 in Coquitlam. East Vancouver is an inexpensive area of the city, with condominiums and town houses starting at C$40,000.

A novel way to live in Vancouver is in a houseboat. You can buy a houseboat in the development called Sea Village for about C$125,000 or in the development known as Annacis for C$90,000.

The **Sunshine Coast,** extending from Langdale to Lund near Vancouver, is popular among retirees. A varied, scenic stretch, it has peninsulas, lakes, islands, and fjords. One of the nicest places along the coast is the town of **Gibsons,** where housing is inexpensive. Waterfront house lots cost C$20,000 to C$30,000. For more information, call the **Gibsons Chamber of Commerce,** *(604)886-2325.*

The hub of the Sunshine Coast is the town of **Sechelt,** on a strip of land between Sechelt Inlet and the Strait of Georgia. A coastal rain forest is nearby, as is the spectacular Gray Creek Falls. Housing prices are comparable to those in Gibsons. For more information, call the **Sechelt Chamber of Commerce,** *(604)885-3100.*

Richmond, on two islands between the north and south arms of the Fraser River, is 30 minutes from Vancouver and 30 minutes from the U.S. border. Although the town is flat, it has views of the mountains. Single-family houses start at C$70,000. Condominiums are C$55,000 to C$130,000. The town's best residential areas begin with the word *maple*: Maple Grove, Maple Land, Maple Wood. Another good neighborhood is Park Lane West. For more information, call the **Richmond Chamber of Commerce,** *(604)278-2822.*

Prices in **Coquitlam,** which is within commuting distance of Vancouver, are higher. Three- and four-bedroom town houses in River Heights Estates go for C$120,000 to C$189,000. For more information, call **Anson Realty,** *(604)876-9222,* or the **Coquitlam Chamber of Commerce,** *(604)464-2333.*

White Rock is a prime seaside community 27 miles from Vancouver. Bordering the warm, shallow waters of Semiahmoo Bay, it is in the southwest corner of the lower mainland. Retirees flock here for the town's beauty and perfect weather. Houses are relatively expensive, from C$100,000 to C$200,000. Seapark Development has luxury condominiums for C$78,000 to C$152,000. For more information, call the **White Rock Chamber of Commerce,** *(604)536-6844.*

Vancouver Island tends to be less expensive than the mainland. The median price for single family homes in **Victoria** is C$83,000, a good deal less than in White Rock. In addition, Victoria is a pretty, lively city that you may find a more stimulating place to retire.

Nanaimo, on Vancouver Island, has the lowest housing prices in Canada; housing in general is less than C$100,000. A three-bedroom house here rents for C$450 to C$550 a month. Fine homes in choice locations go for as little as C$50,000. A new three-bedroom home on the waterfront can be had for C$56,000.

While Nanaimo isn't a pretty town, it is on the spectacular Strait of Georgia and has gorgeous beaches. It also has more shopping space per capita than any other town in North America. And it has an airport, which makes it convenient. For more information, contact the **Greater Nanaimo Chamber of Commerce,** *100 Cameron Road, Nanaimo, BC V9R 2X1.*

Campbell River, also on Vancouver Island, has homes for C$65,000 to C$75,000. The town is not far from Strathcoma Provincial Park, known for its spectacular waterfalls.

If you'd like to build your own home in Vancouver, contact **United Properties Ltd.,** *201-1195 W. Broadway, Vancouver, BC V6H 3X5; (604)736-3864.*

Buying a house in Nova Scotia

A three-bedroom bungalow in **Halifax,** the lively capital of Nova Scotia, costs about C$100,000. A comparable house in the countryside is about C$60,000. And housing on **Cape Breton** is even less expensive.

The most popular place in Nova Scotia among American retirees is the **South Shore,** around Bridgewater, Yarmouth, and Digby. Here, along Mahone Bay and in Chester, lovely homes overlook the water.

Two other popular retirement havens are along the **Northumberland Strait** on the main island and along the shores of **Bras d'Or Lake** in Cape Breton. A one-acre lot on the Northumberland Strait costs C$12,000 to C$15,000. That same acre a few miles inland is only C$3,000. Construction costs also vary considerably. They run C$55 per square foot in the countryside; in the Halifax metropolitan area, they are C$70 per square foot; and along the waterfront, expect to pay C$60 per square foot.

Following is a list of recently advertised properties on the South Shore:

• A two-story traditional house, with 17 acres of land overlooking the LaHave River, is on the market for C$119,000.

• A three-bedroom pine summer cottage overlooking Lake Annis is available for C$28,000.

• A four-bedroom home with a view of Riverport Cove is going for C$69,000.

• A three-bedroom home with 500 feet of frontage on Hennigar Lake and a deck over the lake is available for C$63,900.

• A three-bedroom home in Dublin Shore with views of the ocean, Douglas Fir woodwork, and hardwood floors is on the market for C$69,900.

• A three-bedroom cottage on Ponhook Lake with a fireplace and a deck is available for C$55,000.

• An A-frame cottage on the shores of Molega Lake is available for C$44,900.

For more information on properties available in Nova Scotia, contact **HomeLife/Pat King Real Estate,** *84 Dufferin St., Bridgewater, NS; (902)543-4688,* or Ron Hollett, owner of **Remax**, *Halifax, NS; (902)465-3788.*

For general information on real estate on the South Shore, contact Anne Moyle at the **South Shore Real Estate Board,** *(902)543-4688.*

To find a lawyer in Nova Scotia, contact the **Nova Scotia Barristers' Society,** *1475 Hollis St., Halifax B3J 3M4; (902)422-1491.*

A question of health

The provincial governments in Canada are responsible for administering health services. Each province has an insurance policy that ensures that all residents receive necessary hospital care, including physicians' care, nursing care, meals, laboratory procedures, and many drugs. Out-patient services and mental-health services are included only in some provinces. The costs of ambulance services and extended care must be met partially by the user.

If you are over 65, hospital coverage is virtually free, as are most medical procedures. And the price of dental care is reduced.

Although doctors' services are paid for by government insurance plans, most doctors charge extra fees. And dental fees are higher than in the United States—C$1,000 to install a fixed bridge, for example.

The federal government contributes substantially to the costs of maintaining provincial hospitals and medical-care facilities. Contributions are based on costs incurred by the provinces on a per-capita basis. The provinces use tax revenues to contribute to the costs of hospital services; in Alberta, British Columbia, and Ontario, contributions come from taxes and authorized charges to patients.

Tourists, transients, and visitors are not covered by hospital insurance policies. For a new resident, the usual waiting period before insurance begins to cover medical services is three months after residency has been established. Age, economic status, and previous medical conditions are not considered when coverage is determined.

One U.S. insurance company that will cover you in Canada is Blue Cross. You can also get insurance through Canadian branches of Blue Cross. For more information, contact **Ontario Blue Cross,** *150 Ferrand Drive, Don Mills, ON M3C 1H6,* or **Blue Cross of Atlantic Canada,** *P.O. Box 220, Moncton, NB E1C 8L3.*

Health care in Nova Scotia is rated among the best in Canada, aided by the presence of Dalhousie University Medical School in Halifax, which attracts top researchers and specialists. The province has 51 hospitals, with 5,667 beds and 1,588 doctors (this is 1 doctor for every 539 residents). Access to the provincial health-care system is universal under the Medical Services Insurance (MSI) program; no individual premiums are paid. For more information, contact **MSI,** *P.O. Box 500, Halifax, NS B3J 2S1.*

When you arrive as a resident in Nova Scotia, contact the MSI office at **Maritime Medical Care Inc.,** *Spring Garden Road, Halifax, NS; (902)465-9700* or *(902)429-8800.* This private insurer administers the provincial plan under the direction of the Nova Scotia Health

Services and Insurance Commission. You will be covered under the MSI plan the first day of the third month following your arrival in Nova Scotia.

For more information, contact the **Nova Scotia Department of Health,** *Community Health Services, Halifax, NS; (902)424-4434.*

British Columbia has 135 hospitals, 18,422 beds, and 5,265 doctors (this is 1 doctor for every 510 residents).

Taxing questions

The federal government charges a minimum tax of 34% on income of more than C$53,376. Provinces add their own taxes to this, the amount of which varies greatly. In British Columbia, combined federal and provincial taxes are 50.46%. Sales tax is 6%. Nova Scotia residents pay a total tax of 51.85% and a sales tax of 8%.

Everyone is entitled to a basic deduction of C$2,890. If you receive a pension or American Social Security, you can add C$1,000 to the deduction. And people born before 1915, or who are blind or disabled, can add an additional C$1,810 to the deduction.

For more information, contact **Revenue Canada,** *875 Heron Road, Ottawa, ON K1A 0L8; (613)598-6275.*

Don't forget the fun

Canada is for those who love the outdoors. It offers every kind of outdoor sport, from skiing and sailing to canoeing and white-water rafting.

Skiing in British Columbia

British Columbia has some of North America's best skiing. The province's sparkling, powder-covered slopes are varied and include the Rockies, the Bugaboos, the Purcells, the Selkirks, Chilcotin, Cariboo, and the Monashees. The longest fall line in North America runs through British Columbia, which boasts the highest serviced vertical drop.

Mount Washington is Vancouver Island's biggest ski area and has lift service from 3,600 to 5,168 feet. This area enjoys one of the highest average snowfalls of any ski region. A 2-hour drive from the Nanaimo ferry terminal, and a 4-hour drive from the Victoria ferry terminal, Mount Washington offers more than 20 downhill runs serviced by 2 triple and 2 double chairs.

For information on ski packages, contact **Mount Washington,** *2040 Cliffe Ave., Courtenay, BC V9N 2L3; (604)338-1386.*

Whistler Mountain offers the highest serviced vertical drop in North America. It has more than 60 runs, trails for skiers of every level of experience, and a season that runs into May. It also has racing camps under the direction of World Cup Downhill racer Dave Murray. Nearby are the longest fall-line runs in North America, with uninterrupted skiing for up to three miles at Backcomb.

It's easy to get to Whistler from Vancouver. You can go by car (follow Highway 99), which takes about two hours, or by bus or train.

Gibson Pass, in the Cascade Mountains three hours from Vancouver, offers excellent cross-country skiing. The area also has two powder runs and two chairlifts for downhill skiers.

Fishing for compliments

If you want to catch the biggest fish of your life, go fishing in Canada. The oceans, lakes, and rivers are chock-full. Some say Canada has the best fishing in the world.

Generally, the farther north you go, the better the fishing. Salmon fishing is good in British Columbia. Rockfish, cod, flatfish, perch, and dogfish are abundant along the Pacific coast. These white-meat fish are relatively easy to catch. Rocky areas, pilings, reefs, and kelp beds are likely spots.

The big hunt

Canada has a profusion of wildlife. You can see brown bears and grizzlies in British Columbia and the Laurentians of Quebec. You can spot buffalo in Alberta. Elk and moose wander Saskatchewan. The Northwest Territories and the Yukon have polar bears, musk oxen, caribou, seals, walruses, and penguins.

Most of these animals are protected. Hunting laws are detailed and outline specific seasons and registrations. For more information, contact the Ministry of Natural Resources in the area where you wish to hunt.

A sailor's delight

Nova Scotia is a Shangri-la for boaters. Its harbors and rolling hills make perfect refuges for Atlantic sailors. If you're looking for a place to park your yacht, consider one of the following clubs:
- **Armdale Yacht Club,** *Halifax.*
- **Bedford Basin Yacht Club,** *Halifax.*
- **Bras d'Or Yacht Club,** *Baddeck.*
- **Canadian Forces Sailing Association,** *Shearwater.*

- **Cornwallis Sailing Club,** *Annapolis—French Basin.*
- **Dartmouth Yacht Club,** *Bedford Basin.*
- **Lennox Passage Yacht Club,** *D'Escousse.*
- **Lunenburg Yacht Club,** *Herman's Island, Lunenburg County.*
- **Royal Cape Breton Yacht Club,** *Sydney.*
- **Royal Western Nova Scotia Yacht Club,** *Montague Row, Digby.*

Weekly boat charters are available through **Baddeck Marine and Sports.** Contact Charles Weaver, *P.O. Box 667, Baddeck, NS B0E 1B0; (902)295-3318.*

For more information

For more details on how to retire to Canada, contact the **Embassy of Canada,** *1746 Massachusetts Ave. N.W., Washington, DC 20036; (202)785-1400.* The **Embassy Library,** *1771 N St. N.W., Washington, DC; (202)785-1400,* has a wealth of information and is open to the public on weekday afternoons.

For tourist information on British Columbia, call *(202)223-2856.* For tourist information on Nova Scotia, call *(800)341-6096.*

Chapter 7

The Caribbean

J ust a few hours from New York or Miami are some of the most beautiful places in the Western Hemisphere—the islands of the Caribbean. These idyllic islands offer white sand beaches, an average temperature of 78 degrees Fahrenheit year-round, affordable domestic help, low taxes, bank secrecy, and tranquility.

Stretching from Florida to Venezuela, there are thousands of these little beauties, and each is different. Some are mountainous, some are flat. Some are independent countries, some are dependencies of the United States, Britain, France, or Holland. You can swim, sail, scuba dive, hike, snorkel, and sunbathe on nearly all of the islands. On some, you can also gamble, dine in fine restaurants, and dance the nights away. Others offer an escape from modern civilization.

Choosing an island can be confusing. To guide you, we will share some of our insights. If you would like to retire to a Robinson Crusoe-style desert isle, consider one of the islands in the Turks and Caicos chain. If you would like to retire without a lot of paperwork and red tape, the U.S. Virgin Islands are the best bet. If beautiful views are important, head for Dominica. Francophones like Martinique and Guadeloupe. Those looking for a Latin culture are drawn to Puerto Rico and the Dominican Republic. Our own favorites are St. Kitts and Nevis, two former British colonies with breathtaking scenery and natives who speak a lilting English.

Below are descriptions of some of the many worlds the Caribbean offers. We will begin with English-speaking islands, following them roughly from north to south. Next, we will describe a handful of Spanish-speaking islands, again working from north to south. We will also discuss a mixed bag of islands with French and Dutch backgrounds. Finally, we will consider Bermuda. Although not technically a Caribbean island, because it is in the Atlantic, Bermuda shares many of the attractions of its southern neighbors.

The Bahamas: 700 choices

The Bahamas are made up of 700 islands and several thousand coral and sand cays spread across 750 miles of blue sea. Most are flat, with white sand beaches. Duty-free shopping, nightclubs, and casinos are the attractions, along with fishing, sailing, and snorkeling.

Now independent, the Bahamas were ruled by Britain until 1973. They are sunny, easily accessible, and good places to invest—a great combination for retirement. Only about 20 are inhabited. The chain begins only 50 miles off the coast of Florida, with the island of Bimini, and stretches toward Haiti. The principal island is New Providence, where more than half the Bahamians live. Nassau, the biggest tourist center, is the seat of government. The other major island is Grand Bahama, where Freeport is located. The less developed islands are called Out or Family islands.

Although they are scattered and subtropical, the Bahamas have a high standard of health. Major tropical diseases are nonexistent. In Freeport are Rand Memorial Hospital and a private clinic. Nassau has the Rassin and White hospitals, the Princess Margaret Hospital with about 500 beds, and a geriatrics hospital with 140 beds. Curative services are available in Nassau and New Providence. All the islands are served by private medical centers and clinics. A Flying Doctor Service flies to remote islands, and serious cases can be flown to Florida. A visit to the doctor costs about $25.

The Bahamian dollar is on a par with the U.S. dollar, but the cost of living here is slightly higher than in the United States (it drops about 10% to 35% during the summer). Eating can be expensive if you want foods not native to the islands; however, the fresh fruits, vegetables, and fish from the islands are inexpensive and delicious.

Buying a home

Real estate bargains can be found throughout the Bahamas. (You must engage a Bahamian attorney for any real estate transaction.)

A 1,500-square-foot fully furnished condominium in Freeport goes for about $85,000 (maintenance fees are about $150 a month). A furnished home in Freeport costs $100,000.

In Nassau, you can rent a small one-bedroom house for about $700 a month or $3,000 a quarter. The sale price would be about $100,000.

A 10,000-square-foot lot in a West End township on Grand Bahama was advertised recently for $6,000. Contact **Joe Bartoszek,** *7455 Camio Ave., Cocoa, FL 32927; (407)631-2572.*

Two adjacent lots on Great Exuma, each 85 by 125 feet, were advertised recently for $9,950. Taxes are $30 a year. Contact **James F. Robertson Jr.,** *2218 Holly Oaks River Road, Jacksonville, FL 32225-3087; (904)641-9700.*

An 80-by-125-foot homesite 10 miles north of Georgetown on Great Exuma was advertised recently for $3,000. Contact **John Soafer,** *c/o Shirley Saxton, 11514 Rochester Ave., West Los Angeles, CA 90025; (818)986-4260.*

Less expensive real estate is available on Abaco, Eleuthera, Andros, and the Cat Islands. Most property must be paid for in cash; little financing is available.

An attractive two-bedroom cottage on three lots just five minutes from Coco Bay, Abaco was advertised recently for $92,000. Contact **Virginia Realty,** *P.O. Box 6986, Charlottesville, VA 22906; (804)973-1111.*

For more information on property purchase, contact the following developers and real estate agents in the Bahamas:

• **Churchill & Jones Realty,** *Box F2480, Freeport; tel. (809)373-2576.*

• **Michael Lightbourn,** *Box N1110, Nassau.*

• **C.W. Maguire,** *P.O. Box 1, South Caicos, BWI; tel. (809)322-4148.*

• *Bill Hertz,* **Treasure Cay,** *Abaco.*

Other organizations that can help include the *Secretary,* **Bahamas Real Estate Association,** *P.O. Box N-4051, Nassau, Bahamas; tel. (809)325-4942,* and **Caribbean Management Ltd.,** *tel. (809)322-8618.*

Renting in the Bahamas

It's a good idea to rent a home in the Bahamas before buying. One way to find a rental is through **Bahamas Home Rentals,** *230 Lawrence Ave., Pittsburgh, PA 15238; (412)828-1048.* (This organization charges a $39 service charge.) Rentals start at $450 per week, depending on the size of the home, the size of the party, and the length of your stay.

On a short-term basis, you can live at **The Two Turtles Inn on the Pond,** *(800)327-0787,* near George Town on Great Exuma. These apartments have their own kitchens. One bedrooms start at $76 per night; two bedrooms are $116.

Becoming a resident

You can apply to become a permanent resident of the Bahamas at any time. The cost is $5,000. But it's best to live in the Bahamas a few years before starting the application process. To be granted permanent residence, you must demonstrate financial security and a desire to live on the islands permanently. Contact *Mr. Pratt,* **Bahamas Immigration Board,** *(212)371-7203.*

Annual residence certificates are easier to obtain than permanent certificates. Foreigners may live in the Bahamas for up to eight months each year—at the discretion of the Immigration Board.

For more information, contact the **Honorable Consul General of the Commonwealth of the Bahamas,** *25 S.E. Second Ave., Suite 104, Miami, FL 33131,* or the **Bahama Tourist Office,** *30 Rockefeller Plaza, Room 52, New York, NY 10020; (212)758-2777, 255 Alhambra Circle, Coral Gables, FL 33134; (305)442-4860,* or *875 N. Michigan Ave., Suite 1816, Chicago, IL 60611; (312)787-8203.*

A tax haven

In addition to their beautiful weather and inexpensive real estate, the Bahamas are also a tax haven. Nassau is one of the largest offshore banking centers, with more than 300 banks. It provides a convenient center for booking Eurodollar deposits and loans.

In the Bahamas you pay no taxes on income, capital gains, dividends, interest, estate, inheritance, gifts, royalties, sales, or withholding. The only direct tax is a small real estate tax. Bahamian banks maintain strict secrecy laws. And Bahamian banks offer certificates of deposit with higher yields than are usually available in the United States.

The most reliable international banks in the Bahamas are:

• **Bank of New Providence Trust Company,** *Claughton House, Shirley Street, Box N4723, Nassau.*

• **Bank of Nova Scotia,** *P.O. Box N7518, Nassau.*

The Bahamas are also ideal places for business investments, if you'd like to retire only partially. In the Out Islands, small guesthouses are in short supply, and the tourist trade is growing.

A portrait of the Bahama Islands

• **Andros.** This huge island borders the Great Bahama Bank, the third largest coral reef on earth.

• **The Biminis.** These islands, the closest to the United States, are big-game fishing paradises. This is where Hemingway wrote *The Old Man and the Sea* and Ponce de Leon sought the Fountain of Youth. Life centers around Alice Town, which comes alive during spring fishing tournaments.

• **Cat Island.** The highest island in the Bahamas, with hills rising

200 feet above the sea, Cat has sandy beaches and two excellent harbors.

• **Eleuthera.** The oldest settled island, Eleuthera has 100 miles of pink sand beaches, limestone cliffs, and two championship golf courses.

• **The Exuma Cays.** These isles are ideal for sailing. George Town is the site of a regatta each April. The lifestyle here is old-fashioned (and expensive).

• **Grand Bahama.** This popular island is 70 miles off the coast of Florida and is divided roughly into two sections: West End and Freeport/Lucaya. West End has a port and a resort area. Freeport/Lucaya has luxurious resorts, a casino, golf courses, nightclubs, restaurants, schools, medical facilities, and two international airports.

• **Grand Guana.** A hideaway off Great Abaco, Grand Guana has no telephones, no electricity, no traffic, and little crime. About 30 houses pepper this island, which has a fabulous beach and great snorkeling. Several modest homes are available for rent.

• **New Providence Island.** Nassau, the capital of the Bahamas, is here. It draws millions of tourists, with its throbbing nightclubs, casinos, fine restaurants, colonial forts, and shops.

• **Northern Bahamas.** The Abacos, settled by Loyalists after the American Revolution, are a popular retirement destination. They stretch for 150 miles, and the climate is delightful. Hopetown dates from 1785. The island has no realtors; you must find your own property. But land is plentiful and inexpensive.

• **San Salvador.** Columbus landed here in 1492. The last unspoiled, untouristed island of the Bahamas, San Salvador's lovely beaches can be reached by bicycle. Guest houses offer full board.

• **Southern Bahamas.** Long Island and Inagua, off the coasts of Haiti and Cuba, are relatively undeveloped. Long Island has an old-time charm. Inagua is home to 50,000 flamingos.

For more information, contact the **Bahamas Tourist Office,** *address above.*

One family's Bahama experience

Jo Ann Skousen and her family moved to the Bahamas, where they found their own paradise. Her story is excerpted from International Living *(October 1986).*

I was hanging clothes on the line under a deep blue sky, a gentle breeze whipping the cool, damp cloth against my skin. Through the open gate, I could see my children on our dock, dangling makeshift fishing lines into the blue-green ocean. I was surrounded by a garden of roses, hibiscus, hollyhocks, poinsettias, gardenias, and banana, lime, cherry, peach, kumquat, orange, and mango trees. It was truly a little paradise. "I love living here," I heard myself saying aloud.

Our decision to move to the Bahamas had been sudden. We went first to Nassau to check it out. Three short weeks later our family of 6 was heading for a new island home with only 6 suitcases and 10 boxes of belongings.

Why the Bahamas? We had considered moving to several other countries, particularly Costa Rica, England, and Switzerland. Countries with income taxes were ruled out. We travel frequently to the United States for speaking engagements, so we wanted a country with easy travel connections. Even more important, we wanted to move to a place where we'd feel warm, welcome, and happy. The Bahamas, an English-speaking country just 35 miles from Miami by plane, seemed the perfect choice.

Like most countries, the Bahamas is particular about who can stay permanently. Employers must convince the government that no Bahamian is qualified for a particular job before a work permit is issued. And you are not guaranteed that your work permit will be renewed. However, certain professions, such as teachers and nurses, are always in demand. (For information on teaching or nursing in the Bahamas, contact the **Embassy of the Bahamas,** *600 New Hampshire Ave. N.W., Washington, DC 20037; (202)944-3390.* Special applications are available.)

Because my husband and I are writers, we didn't need work permits. No one else could do our writing, and it wasn't being sold to Bahamians anyway.

We entered the Bahamas as tourists and were able to remain there legally for up to six months. This worked fine for us, because we travel frequently on business.

Temporary residence can be arranged through an attorney (many Bahamian attorneys specialize in residence applications) and is advisable if you plan to maintain your home in the United States as well as your new residence. Temporary residence acts as proof that you are indeed living abroad and not just vacationing frequently.

We found a lovely old estate on the beach just two miles east of Paradise Island. The main house had high ceilings and huge windows that let in the sea breezes. We never missed air conditioning. Also on the grounds was a two-bedroom guesthouse. A Haitian gardener named Willie kept the grounds in beautiful condition for $30 a week, and I had a full-time maid for $70 a week.

Rents in Nassau are expensive by U.S. standards. A simple three-bedroom house in a middle-class neighborhood away from the beach can cost as much as $2,000 a month.

Utilities also are expensive. Water is especially costly, because it is brought to Nassau from Andros by barge. However, we had a well, so we didn't have to pay for water. Services are antiquated by U.S. standards. Electric power goes out frequently, and the phone lines are always getting crossed. Telephone service is costly—$1 a minute to the United States and as much as $4 a minute to other countries.

The roads are narrow, winding, and full of potholes, making driving treacherous. Those who survive auto accidents often are victims of paramedics—we call them paramaniacs, because of their irresponsible, shoddy service.

Because no income tax is collected, the Bahamian government collects revenue from an import duty that reaches as high as 42%. Food is not exempt from this high tax, so groceries cost much more than in the United States. A gallon of milk, for example, costs more than $4.

The local supermarket sells leftovers from the chain's American parent company. Around Christmas the store is filled with boxes decorated for Halloween; Christmas promotions arrive in the spring. It seems that the U.S. parent store clears its shelves of unsold products and ships them down to Nassau. However, you can usually buy any food items that you would find in the United States.

Other items, such as clothing, household goods, and toys, cost at least twice as much as in the United States. A toaster costs about $100. The best solution is to fly to Miami to do your shopping. If you maintain your tourist status, as we did, you should be able to return to the Bahamas without having your bags inspected, thus avoiding import duties.

The one exception to the high prices in the Bahamas is cars. Because environmental and safety standards are lenient, automobiles are about the same price as in the United States. We bought a brand new Nissan Sunny (Sentra) for less than $9,000.

Medical treatment is readily available. Bahamian doctors are adequate for routine illnesses and checkups, but when our daughter was attacked by a Doberman pinscher, I was relieved that Miami Children's Hospital was less than an hour away. An air ambulance is on call 24 hours a day. The cost is $2,000. An insurance policy available to Americans living abroad covers the air ambulance, as well as medical care in the foreign country. For information, contact *Robert Edgar,* **Edgar Ward Ltd.,** *15 Minories, London EC3N 1NJ, England; tel. (44-1)480-7108.*

105

I never felt unsafe living in Nassau, even on the numerous occasions when my husband was away, leaving me alone with the children. Houses generally have bars on the windows for safety. While the robbery rate is high, most incidents involve disgruntled domestic help who have access to their employers' belongings. Bearing this in mind, care should be taken when screening potential household help.

Living in the Bahamas has its ups and downs. It can be expensive, and life is old-fashioned in many ways. If you're easily frustrated by slow service, inefficiency, and a standard of living below that in the United States, the Bahamas might not be the place for you.

When we first arrived, we were overcome by the natural beauty and the opportunities for outdoor recreation—sailing, swimming, snorkeling. However, social activities on the island are severely limited. If you don't like bars, casinos, or cabarets, you won't like the night life.

Nassau has few movie theaters. The one television station doesn't begin broadcasting until the afternoon. However, many people have satellite dishes to receive other stations. We didn't even bother to keep a television, and our children didn't miss it. They loved to read and played with one another outdoors.

The Nassau Operatic Society, a musical theater group that has been around for more than 25 years, provided us with one artistic oasis. The society performs two musicals a year, and we participated in three of them during our stay on the island. Those rehearsals and performances were some of the happiest times our family has known. I recommend the experience to anyone moving to Nassau who can carry a tune.

Since returning to the United States, I've had pangs of homesickness for the blue sky, the voluptuous ocean, and the brilliant fruits and flowers. If you've never had the experience of walking through pine trees to the top of a hill and suddenly seeing a vast expanse of clear turquoise water and white sand, I say, "What are you waiting for?"

The Turks and Caicos Islands

If you want to retire to a near-desert isle—to the Caribbean the way it used to be—consider the Turks and Caicos Islands. Until recently, these British Crown colonies really were undiscovered. They have become better known, but they are nowhere near as developed as their closest neighbors, the Bahamas, 30 miles to the northwest. In fact, some of the 30 islands in this archipelago are still undeveloped.

Only one, Grand Turk, has sidewalks. None of the islands have movie theaters, traffic lights, or fast-food chains. And crime (except for reports of drug trafficking) is rare. Most islanders leave their homes unlocked and their keys in their cars.

The islands are divided into two groups: the Turks and the Caicos. Eight are inhabited: Grand Turk, Salt Cay, Providenciales (Provo), Pine Cay, Parrot Cay, and Middle, South, and North Caicos. Grand Turk, the seat of government for the islands, is home to about 700 expatriates. Provo, the most developed island, is even more popular; about 1,500 expats live here. South Caicos has a good natural harbor and is popular with fishermen. North Caicos is the greenest island, with rugged cliffs and farms. Middle Caicos is the largest, with cliffs, caves, bluffs, and palm trees. About 25 expats live here.

Red tape
U.S. citizens need proof of identification (a birth certificate, voter's registration card, or passport) and an onward or return ticket to visit. To become a resident, you must present a character reference, a police report, a bank statement, and $250. After five years, you can apply for naturalization. The process is quicker and easier than in most Caribbean islands. For more information, contact the **Chief of Immigration,** *tel. (809)946-2972.*

Although they are British, the Turks and Caicos use American currency and the same system of weights and measures as the United States.

These islands have been a well-known tax haven since 1979. Residents pay no income taxes. However, departure, hotel, and property transfer taxes, as well as import duties, are imposed. Bank secrecy laws protect investors, except in cases of drug-related investigations.

Buying property
Buying property on the Turks and Caicos Islands is much easier than on other Caribbean islands. You do not need special licenses or a residence permit to make the purchase, and closing is reached quickly. However, because much of the land on the islands is owned by the British Crown, it is available only to Turks islanders. You will have to conduct a concentrated search to find land available for sale to foreigners. Houses and condos are scarce. Houses on Provo are often sold before they are built.

When buying property, you can borrow up to 50% of the selling price (for a five-year term) from local banks.

Prices for homes range from about $100,000 to $1.5 million. Apartments and condominiums start at about $70,000. Waterfront land is scarce. If you plan to build, expect to pay $75 to $100 per square foot. It takes four to nine months to build a home, depending on the size.

For more information on buying property on the Turks and Caicos, contact the following real estate agents:

• **Butterfield Gold,** *Airport Road, Provo; tel. (809)946-4214.*

• **Caicos Realty,** *Lighthouse Road, Grand Turk; tel. (809)946-2224.*

• **Out Island Realty,** *Third Turtle Inn, Provo; tel. (809)946-4384.*

• **Russell De Coudres,** *Turtle Cove, Provo; tel. (809)946-4253.*

Recently, a two-story villa on a hill in Turtle Cove on Providenciales Island was advertised for $185,000. It has two bedrooms, 2 1/2 baths, a view of the Turtle Cove Marina and the north shore of the island, a screened porch, and solar hot water. It can be rented for $10,800 per year. For information, contact **Russell DeCoudres,** *P.O. Box 52-6002, Miami, FL 33152; tel. (809)946-4253.*

A three-bedroom house on the waterfront on Grand Turk, with three bathrooms, was advertised recently by Caicos Realty for $600,000. Caicos also advertised a three-bedroom waterfront home with two acres for $750,000.

The best places to look for rentals are Provo or Grand Turk. Two- to three-bedroom villas rent for $500 to $2,000 per week. For more information, contact **Bahamas Home Rentals,** *(412)828-1048.*

The cost of living

Food and utilities are expensive on Turks and Caicos. Expect to pay 30% to 50% more for food here than in the United States. Fresh milk is $8 per gallon; chicken is $1.40 per pound ($1 per pound in quantity). Maids charge $20 to $27 per day, gardeners $2.50 to $3 per hour. The service charge for telephones is $17 per month. New and used cars are expensive, because they are shipped from the United States. Gas costs $1.82 to $2.35 per gallon. Lunch in an average restaurant is $5.

For more information

For more information, contact the **Turks and Caicos Tourist Board,** *121 S.E. First St., Suite 510, Miami, FL 33131; (305)577-0133, (800)441-4419,* or *(809)946-2321 on Grand Turk.*

The Cayman Islands: shipwrecks and scuba diving

The Caribbean's best scuba diving is off the three Cayman Islands (Grand Cayman, Cayman Brac, and Little Cayman). Part of the British West Indies, they lie 180 miles west of Jamaica. Magnificent white beaches, colonial villages, pleasant weather (temperatures range from 75 degrees Fahrenheit to 85 degrees Fahrenheit year-round), and tax breaks make the Cayman Islands popular among retirees.

Although the Caymans were hit hard by Hurricane Gilbert in 1988, they had recovered by the time this book was printed. Cayman Kai is one hotel that was damaged by the storm, but it has been renovated.

The Cayman Islands are a British Crown Colony with a British-appointed governor who works with an executive council of three appointed and four elected members. A legislative assembly of 12 elected members elects the 4 executive council members.

People of the Cayman Islands speak English. As in Britain, drivers keep to the left. If you have a U.S. driver's license, you are entitled to a Cayman Island driver's license, which costs $45 for three years.

Bank secrecy

The Cayman Islands are a major international offshore financial center, offering Euro-currency and financial services. No exchange controls exist. Under the 1976 Confidential Relationship Law, it is a criminal offense for any person in the Cayman Islands to divulge information provided in the course of business under conditions of express or implied confidentiality. The punishment is a fine, which is doubled if the violator is a professional—and quadrupled if he acted in response to a bribe.

One bank on the island boasts a gold MasterCard processed by Caymanians in the Caymans. It gives you access to your money in the United States and in 140 other countries without leaving any traces—the identity of the cardholder is known only to the administration of the bank, which is subject to the Caymanian secrecy law. For more information on this service, contact **Finsbury Bank and Trust,** *Transnational House, West Bay Road, P.O. Box 1592, Grand Cayman, BWI; tel. (809)947-4011.*

Banking regulation is by the Cayman Islands inspector of banks, who is overseen by the governor general (appointed by the queen of England) and the popularly elected legislature. Only class A banks, which have a high capital requirement, may take deposits. Class B

109

Caymanian banks may operate only offshore from the Caymans. Moreover, new class B banks must be located in and use the administrative support of class A banks; this is to ensure some control over their activities. However, class B banks are essentially unregulated by the Caymans. (Note that older B banks may escape this regulation.) All the banks listed below are either class A banks or new class B banks:

• **BankAmerica Trust & Banking Corporation (Cayman) Ltd.,** *P.O. Box 1092, Grand Cayman, BWI; tel. (809)949-7888.*

• **Cayman National Bank & Trust Company,** *P.O. Box 1097, Grand Cayman, BWI; tel. (809)949-4655.*

• **Cayman Securities Ltd.,** *P.O. Box 275, Grand Cayman, BWI; tel. (809)949-7722.*

• **Eurobank Corporation,** *P.O. Box 1792, Anderson Square, George Town, Grand Cayman, BWI; tel. (809)940-8721.*

• **Guiness Mahon Cayman Trust Ltd.,** *P.O. Box 887, Grand Cayman, BWI; tel. (809)949-4653.*

• **Midland Bank Trust Corporation (Cayman) Ltd.,** *P.O. Box 2192, Transnational House, West Bay Road, George Town, Grand Cayman, BWI; tel. (809)947-4063.*

• **MIM Britannia International Investments Ltd.,** *P.O. Box 609, Washington Bank Building, Grand Cayman, BWI; tel. (809)949-8144.*

• **Swiss Bank & Trust Corporation Ltd.,** *Swiss Bank Building, P.O. Box 852, Grand Cayman, BWI; tel. (809)949-7344.*

The above information was excerpted from *Banking Secrets of Financial Survivors,* a report published in 1988 by **Agora Inc.,** *824 E. Baltimore St., Baltimore, MD 21202.*

Money matters

The Cayman Islands dollar is pegged to the U.S. dollar at the rate of CI$1=US$1.20. Traveler's checks are accepted in most hotels, restaurants, and shops. American Express, Visa, and Access are accepted in most hotels and duty-free shops, but not at all restaurants.

The cost of living is generally higher than in the United States, because most commodities are imported. (However, this is partially offset by the absence of income and property taxes.) Monthly rents in prime areas are usually much higher than for comparable properties in the United States. Gas, electricity, and water fees are also more expensive.

Finding a home

Apartment rentals are easy to find on the Cayman Islands, especially on Grand Cayman, but they are expensive. Rental of a two-bedroom furnished apartment or house is likely to be at least CI$700 a month—and it can be more than CI$3,000 for a select property.

You may have difficulty finding a long-term lease, because owners get higher rents on daily or weekly rentals during the November to April tourist season. The most expensive apartments are along South Sound and Seven Mile Beach. Next are apartments in George Town. The least expensive rentals are in East End, North Side, and Breakers.

Building lots are easy to find. Prices vary according to location and size. Land registration ensures that the title is authentic, and no restrictions are placed on foreign ownership of land. Lots can be found for as little as CI$5,000 in Lower Valley, Savannah, or Prospect, or as much as CI$100,000 in George Town on the South Sound. Waterfront lots vary from CI$3,000 to CI$7,000 per foot of beachfront property on Seven Mile Beach to CI$750 per foot for canal frontage and $650 per foot for ocean frontage at Cayman Kai's Sand Point (jutting out into North Sound). Prices are lower in West Bay, Northwest Point, Savannah/Pedro, Lower Valley, North Side, and East End, ranging from CI$400 for rocky coastline to CI$750 for sandy beach.

Recently, seven half-acre oceanfront lots on a sandy cove were advertised for US$75,000. For information, contact **Edward Rhodes,** *Box 1097, Carolina Beach, NC 28428; (919)458-8941.*

Property prices in the Cayman Islands have risen recently. Your best bet is a studio apartment. You will need a bit of guidance when selecting your agent. One place to begin is the **Cayman Islands Tourist Office,** *tel. (800)441-4419.*

Two-bedroom condominiums on Grand Cayman with ocean views, air conditioning, two baths, and a pool were advertised recently for US$125,000 to US$135,000, with flexible financing. Contact **Herbert L. Snyder,** *47 Highwood Drive, Manchester, CT 06040; (203)645-5020.*

Temporary digs

While you are looking for a more permanent home, consider staying in one of the following housekeeping accommodations:

• The **Coconut Harbour Hotel,** *West Bay Road; tel. (800)552-6281.* Rates for two are US$135 to US$165 a night, including a kitchen. The complex has a restaurant and a bar, and a good reef for diving is just offshore from the hotel. A grocery store is within walking distance.

• The **Coral Caymanian,** *West Bay Road; tel. (809)949-4054.* Rates for two are US$135 a night, including a kitchen. The Coral Caymanian is on the beach, within walking distance of two grocery stores.

• The **Cayman Kai,** *North Side Beach, Grand Cayman; tel. (809)947-9556.* One-bedroom apartments are US$120; two bedrooms are US$185, including a kitchen. A local grocery store delivers free to the Cayman Kai. The hotel has a restaurant and a bar and offers scuba diving.

Health care

Health care is provided by the government's Health Services Department, which operates 2 hospitals: a 52-bed facility in George Town, Grand Cayman, where there is an 8-bed extended-care unit; and the 12-bed Faith Hospital in Cayman Brac. The government also runs four district clinics in Grand Cayman. And private practitioners, including a remarkably wide range of specialists operating from group clinics, are easy to find.

There are no endemic tropical diseases, and the islands are non-malarial. Costs for medical treatment in government hospitals and clinics compare favorably with rates at private hospitals in the United States.

The art of eating

Crayfish and conch are plentiful and tasty, as are the island's fruits. A typical Caymanian dinner might include lobster, crab, conch or turtle stew, red snapper with breadfruit chips and fried plantains, and almond pie with homemade coconut ice cream.

If you eat local products, food is not expensive. However, if you eat imported goods, your grocery bills will be high.

Having fun

The favorite island sport is treasure hunting. Local treasure hunters have unearthed rusty cannons, swords, ducats, and pieces of eight. You also can explore pirate caves and bicycle across the islands (there are 22 miles of sandy roads to cover).

Night life on the Caymans centers around Pedro's Castle on Grand Cayman, an old fortress that has been turned into a restaurant and disco. Islanders dance to *mento* music (Cayman calypso).

The lay of the land

Grand Cayman's capital, **George Town,** is a free port, where German cameras, Swiss watches, and luxury items can be bought for less than U.S. prices. Many of the Caymans' 23,400 residents live in George Town, which is filled with historic buildings, good restaurants, and hotels. West Beach (or Seven Mile Beach), also on Grand Cayman, is grossly over-developed.

Cayman Brac, which is slightly less expensive than Grand Cayman, offers 12 miles of lush, tropical vegetation and beautiful beaches. You may be able to board with a Cayman family.

The word *brac,* Gaelic for *bluff,* defines this island's most striking feature—a rugged limestone cliff running most of its length and rising to a height of 140 feet. Covered with exotic foliage, including aloe, rare orchids, papaya, and mangoes, the bluff provides a refuge for rare species of bird, including the elusive green, blue, and red Caymanian parrot. The Brac is honeycombed with caves, many of which remain undiscovered. Legend has it that fabulous pirate treasures are buried in these cliffs.

Most of the Brac's 1,700 inhabitants live along the north shore. One main street runs the length of the island, meandering through rural communities with names such as Stake Bay, Watering Place, Cotton Tree, Spot Bay, and Halfway Ground. Cayman Brac has the best scuba diving in the Caribbean (if not the world); it is a near-perfect marine wilderness.

Little Cayman, only two miles from Cayman Brac, is for those looking for an escape. It has miles of deserted white-sand beaches, crystal-clear water, tarpon fishing, and lots of privacy. The island's resorts include The Southern Cross Club and Pirates Point, as well as Sam McCoy's Fishing Lodge.

Red tape

It's easy to arrange a visit to the Cayman Islands. A birth certificate, voter's registration card, or passport and a return ticket allow you to stay up to six months.

For permanent residence, apply to the **Chief Immigration Officer,** *Department of Immigration, P.O. Box 1098, George Town, Grand Cayman, BWI; tel. (809)949-8344.* You must prove that you can support yourself and your dependents financially without seeking employment in the islands. In addition, you must be able to invest at least CI$150,000 in a Caymanian home or enterprise. You will also need a passport, a police clearance certificate from your last place of residence, a certificate of health, three written references from nonrelatives who have known you for some years, and one full-face and one profile photograph.

Once your application for permanent residence has been approved, you must deposit CI$1,500 with the Cayman Islands government. An entry certificate will then be issued. Present this to the immigration officer when you land. He will enter an endorsement in your passport, giving you permission to remain in the islands for an initial period of six months. This authority is renewable at six-month intervals at the discretion of the chief immigration officer. However, at any time after the initial six months, you can apply to the Department of Immigration to have the residence permit made permanent. The department will take into consideration whether you have bought a home in the islands.

The local government doesn't want you taking jobs away from Caymanians, so strict limitations are placed on foreigners working here. However, after two years of residence in the Caymans you may, in some cases, seek employment. For more information, request *Acquisition of Permanent Residential Status in the Cayman Islands* from **Government Information Services,** *Third Floor, Tower Building, George Town, Grand Cayman, BWI; tel. (809)949-7999.*

Where to stay while you settle in

You'll probably want to stay in a hotel while you're looking for a more permanent residence in the Caymans. One of the least expensive is the **Ambassadors Inn Diving Resort,** *P.O. Box 1789, Grand Cayman; tel. (809)949-7577,* which charges US$75 for a double room in high season. It is 200 yards from the beach and one mile from town. **Brac Reef Beach Resort,** *P.O. Box 235, Cayman Brac; tel. (809)948-7323* or *(800)327-3835,* charges US$79 to US$99 for a double room in high season. It is on the beach and five miles from town. For more information, contact **Hotel Information,** *(800)327-8777.*

In some cases, you can rent an apartment for less than the cost of a hotel. **Driftwood Village,** *P.O. Box 35, Northside, Grand Cayman; tel. (809)947-9415,* has two-bedroom cottages on the beach, 25 miles from town, for CI$85. The Driftwood was closed for renovations following the 1988 hurricane, but it should be open again soon.

For more information

The Cayman Islands have one daily newspaper, the *Caymanian Compass;* one weekly, *Tourist Weekly;* and two bimonthly publications, *Newstar* and *Horizons.*

114

The **Cayman Islands Tourist Office,** *P.O. Box 67, Grand Cayman, BWI; tel. (809)949-7999,* or *420 Lexington Ave., Suite 2312, New York, NY 10170; (212)682-5582,* also can provide information on life on the Caymans.

Getting there

The Cayman Islands' national carrier is Cayman Airways, which offers nonstop jet service from Miami, Houston, Atlanta, and Tampa. The Caymans are also served by Northwest, Eastern, and Air Jamaica.

The U.S. Virgin Islands

The U.S. Virgin Islands, together with Puerto Rico, may be the easiest places to retire to in the Caribbean. They are English-speaking, and the red tape involved with getting a residence permit is minimal. For more information, read *The Settler's Handbook for the U.S. Virgin Islands, Douglas S. Burns Productions, P.O. Box 894, Christiansted, St. Croix, USVI 00820.*

Paperwork

To obtain a residence permit in the U.S. Virgin Islands, you must first establish residence, then present a birth certificate, a voter's registration card, or a passport.

If you live in the U.S. Virgin Islands as a non-resident, you must pay taxes on income earned there, then claim a credit when filing your U.S. federal taxes. Capital gains are treated as on U.S. federal income tax forms. Real estate taxes are 1.25% of 60% of assessed value. Excise taxes are charged on many imports.

A portrait of the Virgin Islands

St. Thomas and St. Croix have near-perfect climates year-round. They also have more hotels, restaurants, shopping centers, and fast-food stands than any other island in the Caribbean. St. Thomas is a duty-free shopping center and the West Indies' busiest cruise port of call.

Of the two islands, we prefer St. Croix, which is slightly less developed. Reports of crime and resentment of well-heeled outsiders shadow better-known St. Thomas.

Condos in Teague Bay sell for as much as $250,000. Southgate and Goldenrock are less expensive; you can find condos here for $100,000. Contact **R. Bidelspacher Real Estate,** *3 N. Grapetree Bay, Christiansted, St. Croix, USVI 00820; tel. (809)773-0071* or *(809)773-5040.*

A one-bedroom condo at Ft. Augusta near Gallows Bay was advertised recently for $149,000. For information, contact *Patrice Kelly,* **Erikson Schindler Hamilton,** *Caravelle Arcade, Christiansted, St. Croix, USVI 00820; tel. (809)773-3300.* One-acre lots near the water, a marina, and a golf course were advertised recently for $40,000 by **Christine Christle,** *54 King St., Christiansted, St. Croix, USVI 00820; tel. (809)778-8595.*

Housekeeping accommodations are common in St. Croix. Most are west and east of Christiansted. Mill Harbor has air-conditioned condos for $180 per night for two. It offers tennis courts, a pool, and a restaurant. A supermarket is a mile away. For reservations, call the **St. Croix Hotel Association,** *(800)524-2026.*

Chenay Bay Beach Resort, *tel. (809)773-2918,* has housekeeping units for $115 to $125 per day. The complex has a small restaurant. The nearest grocery store is two miles away.

On St. Thomas, houses are generally $250,000 to $500,000. Lovely homes can be found in East End, Nazareth Estate, Estate Peterborg, and Skyline Drive. One-bedroom condos in the Red Hook development were advertised recently for $117,000 to $151,000. Residents can use the pool, health club, hot tub, paddle ball court, restaurant, and lounge. The development is near marinas, shops, and restaurants. For more information, contact **Arguin McLaughlin Realtors,** *100 Blackbeard's Hill, St. Thomas, USVI 00802; tel. (809)774-6780.*

St. John: paradis *au naturel*

The least-spoiled U.S. Virgin Island is **St. John,** where Laurance Rockefeller deeded large chunks of property to the National Park Service in 1965. Today, 12,600 acres of magnificent trees, tropical plants, and beach are preserved by the park. This acts as insulation against over-development, which has practically destroyed neighboring St. Thomas. However, St. John is not immune to development; it is more discovered than it was six years ago. While this brings more people and more crime, it also brings more amenities and more entertainment.

St. John is a great place to retire to. Because it is a U.S. island, you don't have to contend with foreign documents. Most islanders speak English (some speak an English Creole). The currency is the dollar. Medical facilities are American. Temperatures average 77 degrees Fahrenheit to 82 degrees Fahrenheit, with low humidity. And the island is beautiful, with soft, white sandy beaches.

Property is more expensive on St. John than elsewhere in the U.S.

Virgin Islands. Food prices are high (a quart of milk is $1.40; ground beef is $3.50 per pound). And, unlike elsewhere in the Caribbean, domestic help is not cheap. Maids charge about $25 for six hours of cleaning. Gardeners and laborers earn about $7 per hour.

Making friends

The best ways to meet the people of St. John is to join church and community groups, to frequent the local bars and restaurants, and to volunteer to help the park service or the historical society. Or you can join Business and Professional Women, the Audubon Society, the Lions, the Lionesses, or the St. John Yacht Club.

Medical care

St. John has a combined hospital and community center, as well as a clinic. If you need emergency care and it isn't available on the island, you will be taken by ambulance to the ambulance boat, which will take you to St. Thomas. If help is not available there, you will be taken by air ambulance to Puerto Rico. Some retirees recommend seeing your U.S. physician and your U.S. dentist once a year.

Buying property

Buying property on St. John is relatively uncomplicated. Because the island belongs to the United States, you do not have to contend with foreign real estate laws or currency conversions.

But island living has its problems. St. John has no fresh water; rain water must be collected and stored. Most houses have specially designed roofs that collect water and pipe it into basement cisterns. If you don't have such a cistern, or if you run out of water, you can buy it from a water truck. The imported water costs about three cents a gallon.

Because St. John is shaped like a Hershey Kiss, rising straight out of the ocean, it is difficult to find land flat enough to build on. And the hillier a plot, the more expensive it is to build on.

Most building materials must be shipped to the island from St. Thomas, adding considerably to the cost of building a house (it costs about $150 per square foot to build a conventional wooden home). Keep in mind, though, that central heating isn't necessary, and most home owners choose not to install air conditioning, relying instead on the cool trade winds. It takes about a year to complete a home.

Although St. John is relatively small, the terrain and property values differ considerably from one side of the island to the other. House prices range from $250,000 for two or three bedrooms to $2.1 million for a grand design. Most are $400,000 to $450,000. Condominiums range from $75,000 for a studio to $350,000 to $400,000. New townhouses at the Pond Bay Club are $400,000 to $625,000.

Condominium fees start at $250 per month.

In the **Cruz Bay** area, development is reaching the saturation point, and real estate prices are sky high. Large homes with bay views cost about $300,000. In general, homes are $225,000 to $400,000. However, Cruz Bay Realty recently advertised a three-bedroom wood-frame house on three-quarters of an acre for $195,000. (The house does not have a water view.)

Around the corner from Great Cruz Bay, **Chocolate Hole** has been slower to develop. Some well-placed plots are still available at reasonable prices; half-acre lots start at $85,000, and houses start at $275,000. However, houses on the water are $500,000 to $600,000. St. John Investments recently listed a two-bedroom condo in Chocolate Bay with a bay view and hardwood floors for $130,000.

However, the real bargains are on St. John's **East End**—but they probably won't last long. Here the vegetation is drier and the terrain rockier, thanks to parching trade winds from the east. The beaches and rocky shorelines are just as beautiful as on the posher Cruz Bay side of the island, but they are barely populated. Goats trot across the single road; houses and small farms dot the hillsides. The occasional shop is a casual, family-run business.

Coral Bay has become one of the most desirable areas on the island. As a result, it is a good place for real estate investment. Plans are under consideration to build a marina in Coral Bay, which would make it more accessible but less isolated and private.

It is more common to buy property in Coral Bay than a house. Property costs $10,000 to $15,000 less than in Cruz Bay. **St. John Investments,** *address below,* recently advertised five acres in Coral Bay for $200,000. While the land is not right on the beach, it is just a short walk away.

Real estate agents on St. John include:

• **Coral Bay Real Estate,** *1-DC, Bethany; tel. (809)776-6133.*

• **Cruz Bay Realty Inc.,** *1E-96, Cruz Bay; tel. (809)776-7001.*

• **Gallows Point Real Estate Sales,** *Cruz Bay; tel. (809)776-7655.*

• **Islandia Real Estate,** *Box 56, Cruz Bay; tel. (809)776-6666.* Rene Servant specializes in the east end of the island.

• **Peter Griffith Holiday Homes,** *Mongoose Junction, Bay Street; tel. (809)776-6776.*

• **St. John Investments,** *20 2AC, Cruz Bay; tel. (809)776-6656.*

• **Theovald Moorehead,** *5-F Cruz Bay; tel. (809)776-6464.*

For more information on property for sale, consult *Tradewinds* or the *Virgin Islands Daily News,* published on St. Thomas. Residents also can tell you what is available.

Renting

You may find it more affordable to rent on St. John than to buy. Villas can be rented for $1,000 to $2,200 per week; condos for $175 to $275 per night. One-bedroom apartments go for $450 per month, not including utilities. Two local rental agents are **Lisa Durgan,** *tel. (809)776-6462,* and **John Kellam,** *tel. (809)776-6322.*

Getting there and getting around

Flights to St. Thomas depart daily from New York (a four-hour trip) and Miami (a three-hour trip). From St. Thomas, you can take a sea plane or a ferry to St. John. The flight takes only 10 minutes and costs US$20 one way.

Once in the U.S. Virgin Islands, the best way to get around is by car. A U.S. driver's license is good temporarily. However, if you plan to become a permanent resident, you must obtain a Virgin Islands license.

Four-wheel drive vehicles are best for the islands' winding, steep terrain. Expect to spend about $4,000 for a three-year-old vehicle, or $305 a week for a rental car. Gas costs about $1.60 a gallon. Remember to keep to the left—and look out for potholes. The speed limit is 20 miles per hour.

St. Kitts and Nevis

The tiny green islands of St. Christopher (St. Kitts) and Nevis together make up a lush, volcanic Caribbean island nation. On the map, they are located between St. Martin and Montserrat on the eastern side of the Leeward Islands chain. Formerly a British colony, St. Kitts and Nevis became an independent nation Sept. 19, 1983.

While these islands are rather poor, they are rich in the Caribbean luxuries that attract retirees: gorgeous sandy beaches, balmy trade winds, perfect temperatures (70 degrees Fahrenheit to 85 degrees Fahrenheit, with little rainfall), tropical fruits, a relaxed atmosphere, fresh fish, picturesque villages, mountain and sea views, and miles and miles of ocean separating them from modern civilization. The natives have a word for the easygoing island pace: *liming*. It means doing nothing in particular and enjoying it.

St. Kitts is a favorite vacation spot of Prince Charles. It boasts English-style inns, old sugar plantation houses, and a 19th-century port. And, because it changed hands several times between the English and the French, it has a pinch of French ambience.

Nationals on the islands pay no personal income tax; however, aliens are taxed on 20% of their income (this is not applicable to U.S. citizens). No sales tax is imposed.

Domestic help is widely available. Domestic servants working 30 hours or more are paid 56 cents an hour, minimum, or $20.37 a week, minimum. Part-time workers are paid a minimum wage of 61 cents an hour, or $16.67 per week. Domestic help is paid double on Sundays and holidays and time-and-a-half for overtime.

The cost of living on St. Kitts and Nevis is reasonable. Local seamstresses can make you a dress or suit very cheaply. Liquor, especially rum, is also cheap. Property taxes are lower than in the United States.

The local currency is the Eastern Caribbean Dollar, which is pegged to the U.S. dollar and has an exchange rate of US$1=EC$2.70.

St. Kitts and Nevis have four hospitals (three on St. Kitts, one on Nevis), with a total of more than 200 beds.

To enter the country temporarily, you need only proof of citizenship (a passport, birth certificate, or voter's registration card) and a return ticket. For information on arranging longer stays and residence permits, contact the **Embassy of St. Kitts and Nevis,** *2501 M St. N.W., Suite 540, Washington, DC 20037; (202)833-3550.*

Before driving a car in St. Kitts and Nevis, you must obtain a local driver's license from the Police Traffic Department. This is easy if you have a U.S. or international driver's license. The cost is EC$30. Traffic is on the left.

Local banks include Barclays International, Royal Bank of Canada, Bank of Nova Scotia, St. Kitts-Nevis National Bank, Development Bank of St. Kitts-Nevis, Eastern Caribbean Central Bank, Nevis Co-operative Bank, and the Bank of Nevis Ltd.

St. Kitts

Called Liamuiga (Lee-a-moo-ee-ga) by the original Carib Indian inhabitants (decimated by English and French settlers), St. Kitts is a fertile volcanic island with miles of green sugar cane fields. It is peppered with restored plantation houses that have been converted into inns. The island is shaded by fig trees and scented by frangipani. Worshippers of the sun swim, tan, windsurf, snorkel, and sail in its waters.

The islanders live in tiny pastel-colored homes with high-pitched roofs and cooling shutters. Above their villages looms Mt. Misery (formerly Mt. Liamuiga) at 3,792 feet. Vervet monkeys, tree frogs, butterflies, and crickets play in the woods.

St. Kitts has both a rain forest, where you could be lost for days,

120

and a lively city, Basseterre (population 15,000). Here, crowds mill around The Circus, which surrounds an ornate cast-iron clock tower. Reggae blasts from the windows. Cafés and bars are crowded with people. The smells of spicy island cooking (goat, plantains, red bean soup, chowders) waft from the windows. The alleys are filled with chickens and goats. Along Bay Road and the beach is a lively fish market.

Many of St. Kitts' beaches are of black volcanic sand. The best golden-sand beaches are along the peninsula known as Frigate Bay and around Salt Pond.

Property is expensive. Recently, a plot of land just under one acre was advertised for US$99,000. The property is on a hillside with panoramic views and is near a golf course, casino, and beach. For information, contact **Dr. Britt,** *P.O. Box 443, St. Kitts; tel. (809)465-8359.*

St. Kitts has both an international airport accommodating wide-bodied jets and a deep-water seaport that accommodates large cruise ships and cargo vessels.

Nevis
Until the Napoleonic Wars, Nevis was hailed as the Queen of the Caribees, a social resort for West Indian planters. Fashionable aristocrats and belles crowded the streets of **Charlestown,** the capital. Alexander Hamilton was born here, and Admiral Nelson was married here.

Life on Nevis is now simpler and more peaceful. The plantation owners are gone, and the pace is slow and friendly. About 12,000 residents live on the island. Ruined sugar mills and mansions stand as memorials to the old ways.

However, Nevis is not rundown. It is majestic—a cloud-capped volcano ringed by white, sandy beaches. **Pinney's Beach,** north of Charlestown, is one of the finest in the Caribbean. A coral reef encircles the six-by-eight square mile island. Snorkeling, fishing, and relic-hunting are popular pastimes.

The island is easy to get to from St. Kitts, just two miles away. The Carib Queen ferry leaves Basseterre Harbor for Nevis several times daily, except Thursday or Sunday, jammed with passengers, both human and animal. The trip costs US$8 per person round trip. And the small Newcastle Airport provides connections with neighboring islands.

Charlestown (population 1,300) is a palm-shaded rainbow of pastel-colored cottages with tin roofs and shady gardens. Expatriates

121

gather here at Don Williams' Longstone bar for a dose of island gossip. Nearby, at the Nevis Handicraft Cooperative Society, you can buy local wines made from exotic fruits, including pawpaw, sorrel, and genep.

An 18-mile road rings the island, passing the once-fashionable Bath Hotel, whose subterranean sulphur baths are said to be therapeutic, and, occasionally, the ruins of a great house from one of the island's long-gone cotton plantations.

Many expats choose to live in the American Colony, as it is known. This group of newly built air-conditioned villas is in the hills near the rain forest, where temperatures are cool. The development is attractive, but it is removed from the charm and atmosphere of Charlestown and other island settlements.

The north and west coasts of the island have beautiful white beaches fringed by palm and mango trees. Dream here, mesmerized by hummingbirds and the scent of wild orchids.

You can rent a house in Charlestown for a year, but if you plan to stay, your best bet is to build a home. Foreigners are allowed to buy 5- or 10-acre tracts, and land is usually available. Government land is affordable, but you must promise to improve it with a house or agriculture within two years. Costs for building are about the same as in Florida.

To give you an idea of property prices, a three-bedroom, two-bathroom house in Nevis was advertised recently for US$130,000. The house is situated on two acres just a few minutes from three beaches. For information, contact **John C. Miller,** *Landfall, Jones Estate, Nevis; tel. (809)469-5348.*

Getting there
BWIA (British West Indies Airways) has direct flights to St. Kitts and Nevis from New York on Thursday and from Miami on Friday.

Pan Am has direct flights from New York on Saturday, Sunday, and Wednesday.

Prinair has daily scheduled services from Puerto Rico, St. Thomas, St. Croix, and St. Martin.

LIAT (Leeward Islands Transport), Winair, and Prinair offer daily connections to international carriers (American Airlines, Eastern Airlines, British Airways) serving North America and Europe.

LIAT has daily scheduled services to Antigua, St. Martin, St. Thomas, St. Croix, Montserrat, Dominica, Guadeloupe, Martinique, St. Lucia, St. Vincent, Barbados, and Grenada. It has weekend service to Puerto Rico.

American Eagle has charter service on Sunday between Chicago and St. Kitts.

Evergreen has charter service between New York and St. Kitts on Sunday.

A bit of history

The first known inhabitants of St. Kitts landed about 3,000 B.C. and lived a simple life, relying on shellfish for sustenance. They were followed by the Saladoid Indians, who arrived in the first century, made colorful pottery, and depended on agriculture to survive. No trace of their culture has been found after A.D. 650; no one knows why they disappeared. When Columbus discovered St. Kitts during his second voyage in 1493, it was populated by yet another tribe, the fierce Carib Indians.

Although it was owned by Spain, Britain first colonized the island in 1623. France colonized it in 1624, and intermittent wars broke out between the French and English for years, as the island was passed from country to country. Finally in 1783, the island was ceded to Britain under the Treaty of Versailles.

Nevis, too, was discovered by Columbus in 1493. But this island was forgotten until 1628, when it was colonized by the British. The prosperity of these settlers aroused the envy of the Spanish, who captured the island in 1629. Although Nevis suffered periodically from Spanish and French attacks, the island remained both British and prosperous.

In 1816, St. Kitts, Nevis, Anguilla, and the British Virgin Islands formed a single British colony. From 1958 to 1961, this island group was part of the West Indies Federation. In 1966, St. Kitts, Nevis, and Anguilla joined in a State of Association with Great Britain. St. Kitts and Nevis gained independence from Britain on Sept. 19, 1983. (Anguilla remains a British dependency with a separate administration and elected representatives.)

Today, St. Kitts and Nevis is a democratic federal state with a parliamentary system. The governor general is appointed by the queen of England. He, in turn, appoints a prime minister, who is a member of the House of Assembly.

For more information

The following organizations can help you plan your retirement to St. Kitts and Nevis:

• **Embassy of St. Kitts and Nevis,** *2501 M St. N.W., Suite 540, Washington, DC 20037; (202)833-3550.*

• **St. Kitts and Nevis Chamber of Industry and Commerce,** *P.O. Box 332, Basseterre, St. Kitts, W.I.; tel. (809)465-2980.*
• **St. Kitts and Nevis Tourist Board,** *Box 132, Basseterre, St. Kitts, W.I.; tel. (809)465-4040.*

Anguilla: the most beautiful beaches

Anguilla, a British island, has the best beaches in the Caribbean, a perfect climate, and a low cost of living. While it remains one of the Caribbean's least discovered islands, it is also one of the easiest to get to. Anguilla is the perfect retirement spot if you're looking for peace and tranquility. Swimming, snorkeling, scuba diving, fishing, and enjoying steel band music are the only forms of entertainment.

Anguilla is 32 square miles of flawless beaches, reefs, and cays. The ocean bottom is evenly sloped to a distant string of rocks that attracts sea creatures and snorkelers (underwater, look for coral gardens, elkhorn reefs, star and flower coral, squirrel fish, sergeant fish, and damselfish). The island has few trees, but vegetables and cotton are grown in the rich bottom lands.

Shoal Bay is one of Anguilla's most beautiful beaches, a two-mile stretch of white sand. To get here, follow the road west out of Island Harbour on the north coast until you reach the turnoff for the bay. While in Shoal Bay, visit the Fountain, a large cave once used by pirates.

The romantic should head to **Captain's Bay,** on the northeastern edge of Anguilla. There you are unlikely to meet anyone or anything but white sand and clear water—it is the perfect place to escape civilization.

During the first week in August, the Anguilla Sailboat Races spawn offshore parties and general merriment.

The place to shop is the capital city, called **The Valley.** Note the traffic light—it is the only one on the island. Near The Valley you are likely to see a match of this British island's main sport: cricket.

Real estate is becoming more expensive as Anguilla becomes more discovered. However, you may still be able to find good buys inland. One-bedroom condos sell for US$25,000 to US$80,000; two-bedroom condos go for US$70,000; and two-bedroom houses are US$60,000.

If you eat the island's food—fresh meat, milk, butter, eggs, and vegetables—you can live cheaply. And cooks and maids charge little. But if you choose to live on imported products, your costs will be much higher.

The island has a small hospital, four banks, a supermarket, and a movie house. It has a resident population of 6,000.

To live on Anguilla permanently, or to purchase property on the island, you must get permission from the commissioner (it is usually granted). To stay up to six months, you only need identification papers and a return ticket. To take up residence, you may be asked to make a deposit of $1,000.

A good place to stay while you are looking for a permanent home on Anguilla is Easy Corner Villas, which overlooks Road Bay at Sandy Ground. A one-bedroom villa is US$125; a villa with three bedrooms is US$400. Villas have their own kitchens, allowing you to cook at home, which saves a good deal on restaurant bills. The villas are represented by **I.T.R.,** *(212)840-2039.*

You can fly Winair or take a boat to Anguilla from Marigot Bay, St. Martin. Boats leave every 40 minutes, take 25 minutes, and cost US$8 one way. Or you can fly to Anguilla from San Juan, Puerto Rico via American Eagle.

For general information on retiring to Anguilla, contact the **Anguilla Department of Tourism,** *Caribbean Tourism Association, 20 E. 46th St., New York, NY 10017; (212)682-0435.*

For legal information, contact **Joan Medhurst,** *(516)673-0150,* or the **Attorney General of Anguilla,** *tel. (809)497-2457.*

For information on real estate and business opportunities, contact the **Office of Community Development,** *tel. (809)491-2317.*

Antigua

Antigua has 365 white coral sand beaches and lots of rich yachters. Its English Harbour is the Williamsburg of the Caribbean.

Accommodations on Antigua range from luxury villas to simple housekeeping units to picturesque old English inns. One of the cheapest accommodations in the Caribbean is on Antigua, the Main Road Guest House, which is a 10-minute walk from St. John's. A basic but clean double room is only US$7 a night. The guesthouse is run by an elderly woman with a lovely singsong Antiguan lilt.

If you really search, you can find real estate bargains on Antigua. A furnished one-bedroom villa in Halcyon Heights was advertised recently for US$75,000. It has two balconies and an ocean view and is a 10-minute walk from the beach. Contact **Tony Frank,** *85 Skymark Drive, #2105, Willowdale, Ontario M2H 3P2 Canada; tel. (416)499-1225.*

A three-bedroom, two-bath house on Long Bay Road on the east coast of the island was advertised recently for US$85,000. A traditional West Indian cedarwood house with two bedrooms and two bathrooms was advertised for US$180,000. For information on these properties, contact **K.R. Scales,** *P.O. Box 123, Hodges Bay, Antigua, W.I.; tel. (809)462-4920.*

A fully furnished townhouse with a pool, tennis courts, an art gallery, and a restaurant was advertised for US$150,000 to US$175,000. Contact **Egen W.M. Warner,** *P.O. Box 976, Ottos Main Road, St. John's, Antigua, W.I.; tel. (809)462-2415.*

Beachfront condos with three bedrooms have been listed recently for US$275,000. Contact **Egen Warner,** *address above.*

For more information, contact the **Antigua and Barbuda Department of Tourism,** *610 Fifth Ave., Suite 311, New York, NY 10020; (212)541-4117.*

Stunning St. Lucia

The British and the French fought long and hard over St. Lucia, an island of stunning natural beauty. Volcanic mountains loom above palm-lined beaches. The most famous of the 3,000-foot peaks are the Pitons, dropping a half-mile into the transparent ocean below.

St. Lucia is 27 miles long and 14 miles wide. It lies halfway between St. Vincent and Martinique. Part English, part French, many islanders still speak a Creole patois (although English is the official language) and cook a rich Creole cuisine.

The island's natural beauty and modern conveniences make it a popular retirement spot. This former British colony has superb beaches, a mild climate (temperatures range from 70 degrees Fahrenheit to 90 degrees Fahrenheit), lots of lobster, an exciting night life, good fishing, and many creature comforts. However, the cost of living here is slightly higher than on other Caribbean islands.

The currency in St. Lucia is the Eastern Caribbean dollar (EC$). But U.S. dollars are acceptable tender. Most credit cards and traveler's checks also are accepted.

No vaccinations are required to visit St. Lucia. The water is safe to drink. Doctors and dentists are available.

The lay of the land

To get a feeling for St. Lucia, drive through the cool, lush highlands where deep valleys bisect the island's interior. Explore the banana plantations, the rain forests, and the island's drive-in volcano, whose hot sulphur springs are believed to cure respiratory problems. Don't miss Diamond Waterfall, which crashes through the forest into

126

a brilliant green pool. The water shoots over rocks brightly colored from mineral deposits.

The capital of St. Lucia, **Castries,** is a harbor town surrounded by hills. It has a bustling market selling fresh fruit, vegetables, straw goods, and pottery.

The village of **Gros Islet** throws a street party every Friday night. Town residents line the street with their merchandise, and then dance the night away.

Marigot Bay is truly idyllic. Here the film *Dr. Doolittle* was made. Banana plantations overlook the bay.

The typically West Indian town of **Soufrière** is guarded by the twin peaks of the Pitons. It is near Sulphur Springs and Diamond Waterfall.

St. Lucia's hot night spots include the Spanish Dance Club, the After Deck, Splash (in St. Lucia's Hotel), Club St. Lucia, Monroe's (in Grand River), and The Lime. During the day, you can mountain climb, windsurf, fish, snorkel, skin dive, water ski, sail, golf, play tennis, ride horses, and swim.

Island accommodations range from guesthouses to apartments to deluxe hotels. The island's hotels are concentrated in the north near Castries, in Soufrière, and in Vieux Fort. Try the **Halcyon Beach Club,** *P.O. Box 388, Castries; tel. (809)452-5331* or *(800)223-9815,* which has chalet-style rooms on a sandy bay; **Marigot Bay Resort,** *P.O. Box 101, Castries; tel. (809)453-4357,* where double rooms are US$90 to US$125 per night, or **The Islander,** *P.O. Box 907, Castries; tel. (809)452-8757* or *(800)223-9815,* an inexpensive self-catering complex.

Buying real estate
In the undeveloped mountainous areas of the island, houses sell for US$50,000 to US$70,000. In the words of Gene Cowell, editor of *Island Properties Report,* they are "nothing fancy, just nice. They have kitchens, power, water, and bedrooms."

To buy real estate on the island, you need an Alien Land Holding License. A local attorney can apply for this license for you. To qualify, you must pay 7.5% of the purchase price to the government of St. Lucia. Renting a self-contained unit or an entire house is relatively easy and inexpensive.

Neither is it difficult to arrange to buy land. A half-dozen real estate developments have been started for people interested in retiring to St. Lucia. Lots, usually near golf courses or yacht clubs, are offered at Florida prices. Among them are Cap Estates, Yacht Haven at

Marigot Bay, Santa Lucia Club and Grand Anse Beach Development, the Carib Riviera Club Estates, and Coubaril Park Estates.

A one-bedroom villa on 10 acres in Cap Estates was listed recently for US$195,000. A half-acre of land in Cap Estates was on the market for US$22,000.

Rodney Bay is the most expensive area, with land going for US$3 to US$4 per square foot.

Recently, a three-bedroom villa in Coubaril, Castries was advertised for US$65,000. It has two bathrooms and is situated on 22,000 square feet of sloping land overlooking the Hotel La Tock golf course and the Caribbean Sea. For information, contact the **Property Shop,** *P.O. Box 130, Castries; tel. (809)452-8288.*

Getting down to business

About 500 Canadians and Americans have built homes and retired to St. Lucia. And some have started small businesses in electronics, textiles, or computers. Liberal tax concessions make starting a business an attractive proposition. Taxes on land are low, and St. Lucia has a double-taxation agreement with the United States so that American incomes are not taxed again on the island. Up to US$2,000 worth of used furniture can be imported to the island duty free.

Red tape

You can visit St. Lucia for six months if you have a return ticket, a photo identification, and proof of citizenship. To extend your stay, apply to the chief immigration officer. To stay on the island permanently, you need a passport, a financial statement attesting that you have enough money to support yourself, a written statement explaining why you want resident status, and a police report. And you must have lived in St. Lucia continuously for seven years.

Getting there

St. Lucia has two airports: Hewanorra (in the south) for international flights and Vigie (in the north) for inter-island flights. There is a departure tax of EC$10 for other Caribbean destinations and EC$20 for international destinations.

For more information

For more information, contact the **St. Lucia Tourist Board,** *Box 221, Castries, St. Lucia, W.I.,* or *Suite 315, E. 42nd St., New York, NY 10017; (212)867-7295.*

St. Vincent and the Grenadines

St. Vincent and the Grenadines make up a largely undeveloped independent island nation in the eastern Caribbean. This 17-square-mile archipelago 100 miles west of Barbados consists of 32 main islands. St. Vincent is the largest, 18 miles long by 11 miles wide. To the southwest are the smaller Grenadines, a diver's paradise. Unlike St. Vincent, which is volcanic, the Grenadines are coral islands, with white coral beaches. The total population of St. Vincent and the Grenadines is 110,000.

Because of its black sand beaches, St. Vincent has not been discovered by tourists and remains uncrowded and unspoiled. This exotic tropical island has good accommodations, low prices, and a peaceful charm. It is largely mountainous with forests and a mild climate.

Kingstown, the capital, is a red-roofed village set on a bay. Boats filled with fruit and produce glide into town. The view from Ft. Charlotte is superb. Kingstown has two movie theaters and a public library.

St. Vincent's lush climate is perfect for growing fruit and vegetables. The island's hotels, guesthouses, and restaurants charge some of the lowest rates in the Caribbean. And all hotels have membership arrangements with local social clubs, where you can play tennis and meet the island's residents.

Inland, you can explore Soufrière mountain, little villages, and arrowroot plantations. The best beaches are Indian Bay and Tyrrell Bay, where you can rent cottages and apartments.

Most of the people on St. Vincent and the Grenadines are descendants of black African slaves brought to the islands during the colonial period. English is spoken.

While St. Vincent was discovered by Columbus, it wasn't settled by the English until the 1700s. Failing to subdue the native Carib Indians, colonists had them deported in 1797. The island was granted self-government in 1969 and full independence in 1979.

Cooks, maids, and gardeners are easy to find and charge reasonable rates (per-capita income here is low, although educational levels are high). Electricity, telephone service, sanitation, doctors, dentists, a hospital, and pure water are available. Hurricanes are rare. And the island's residents are friendly.

Establishing your home

If you want to build your retirement home, you'll find that lots are readily available. Good spots to build include Cane Garden, where lots overlook Kingstown, the Villa, Edinboro, Tyrrell Bay, and Ratho Mill.

Recently, a single-story beachhouse on an 11,843-square-foot hillside lot was advertised for US$63,000. It has three bedrooms, a maid's room, 1 1/2 baths, and is a one-minute walk from the beach. Contact **Judith Nelson,** *802 South Drive, Fargo, ND 58103; (701)235-6809.*

Paperwork
When you arrive on St. Vincent, immigration will grant you from one to three months to stay, at its caprice. After that, you must apply for renewed permission to remain on the island each month. The charge is about EC$20 (about $7.50). The bad part is standing in line first at immigration, then at the treasury to pay, then at immigration again to show the receipt and to recover your passport. Figure on wasting a hot, frustrating half-day each month in the process.

You can stay on the island up to a year as a visitor. After that, you must apply for a residence permit from the Foreign Ministry. Prepare for many frustrating months of waiting, followed by the payment of several hundred dollars. The amount seems to be calculated on the Foreign Ministry's guess as to your ability to pay.

The Grenadines
Near St. Vincent are the small Grenadine islands, which number about 100 and are connected twice a week by a ferry called the *M.V. Snapper.* Most accommodations on the Grendadines are small and inexpensive, except for resorts on Palm Island and Petite St. Vincent—as well as an exclusive hideaway on Princess Margaret's Mustique.

For more information
The following organizations can help you plan your retirement to St. Vincent and the Grenadines:

• **Caribbean Tourist Association,** *20 E. 46th St., New York, NY 10017; (212)682-0435.*

• **St. Vincent Tourist Board,** *Box 834, Kingstown, St. Vincent, W.I.; (212)687-4981 in New York.*

Healthy living in Barbados
Lying well out in the Atlantic Ocean, to the east of the lower end

of the Antilles chain, this 166-square-mile island has one of the healthiest climates in the West Indies. A former British possession, Barbados retains some of its colonial heritage, including a Westminster model of government, an Anglo-Saxon legal system, and a passion for cricket.

Barbados, settled by the English in 1627, has the world's second oldest House of Assembly. While the island is relatively flat, the interior is hilly and covered with sugar cane. Temperatures vary little, ranging from 72 degrees Fahrenheit to 86 degrees Fahrenheit. Constant gentle trade winds cool the island. Rainfall is slight.

Barbados has good health facilities: Queen Elizabeth, an acute general hospital; two maternity hospitals; a leprosarium; five district hospitals; three private hospitals; and a psychiatric hospital.

The Barbados dollar is pegged to the U.S. dollar.

About 200 British, Canadian, and American retirees live on Barbados. Americans who retire to Barbados say they live twice as well on half the money. Most live in St. James Parish near Holetown.

The cost of living *is* relatively low, but only if you eat and drink local products, such as flying fish, dolphin, saltfish cakes, crab, *christaphene* (a mixture of cucumber and avocado), papaya, mangoes, and limes. Fresh local fruit is sold on the roadsides for next to nothing. (Wash it carefully.) The local Mt. Gay Rum is about $4 a bottle, and Banks Beer is 60 cents. Both are superior to many American products. You can have a dress made by a local seamstress for $10. Maids cost about $60 a week.

Finding a home

For a listing of houses for rent, contact the **Barbados Board of Tourism,** *800 Second Ave., New York, NY 10017; (212)986-6516.* Handicapped people might be interested in the special facilities at Sandy Beach. Contact **Knightsbridge Marketing Services,** *1661 Worcester Road, Framingham, MA 01701.*

The Soroptimist International of Barbados has sponsored a Senior Citizens Village at Eden Lodge, St. Michael. The village has 25 units, a day center, and a sick bay. For information, contact the **Soroptimist International of Barbados,** *c/o Super Mare Hotel, Worthing, Christ Church, Barbados, W.I.*

For more detailed information on real estate, write **J.C. Corbin & Company,** *P.O. Box 708 C, Bridgetown, Barbados, W.I.,* or **Lucas Realty,** *P.O. Box 839 E, Bridgetown, Barbados, W.I.*

Taxes
Foreign nationals working in Barbados are subject to income taxes ranging from 10% to 70%. A non-resident withholding tax is assessed on dividends, interest, rents, premiums, royalties, management fees, commissions, and annuities. However, Barbados has a tax treaty with the United States that avoids double taxation.

A temporary home
An inexpensive place to stay while you get your bearings in Barbados is the **Angler Guest House,** *Derricks, St. James, Barbados, W.I.; tel. (809)432-0187.* It is 5 minutes from the beach and 15 minutes from Bridgetown. Single rooms are only US$12 per night, including kitchen facilities and a television. A charming couple who spent many years in London runs the guesthouse. Noise is the only drawback—the house is right on the main south coast highway. In addition, the local roosters have no sense of time and crow at all hours of the night, setting the neighborhood dogs barking.

Getting your papers
A passport and visa are not required for stays up to six months. Tourists must have a return ticket and proof of citizenship. For information on residence permits, contact the **Embassy of Barbados,** *2144 Wyoming Ave. N.W., Washington, DC 20008; (202)939-9200.*

The **American Consulate** in Bridgetown, *tel. (809)436-4950,* also might be able to help.

Dominica: beauty and longevity
The most beautiful Caribbean island is Dominica, situated between Guadeloupe and Martinique. Here, mountains rise 5,000 feet above sea level, waterfalls tumble, sulphur springs steam, steep cliffs swoop to the sea, ancient forests endure, and calm lakes repose. More than 135 species of bird live here, including two species of rare parrots found only on this island.

Life is peaceful on Dominica (too peaceful, some say). Perhaps this explains the famed longevity of the island's residents. This is the place for escapists, people looking to retire to a place with heavenly scenery, peace and quiet, and no crowds.

Dominica's mountains are cool, and the climate is good for nervous complaints (daytime temperatures are between 70 degrees Fahrenheit and 80 degrees Fahrenheit).

Unfortunately, Dominica is very poor. However, because of this, the cost of living is about half that on the more fashionable islands. Maids and gardeners work for little. Fruits, vegetables, and fish are cheap.

The island is crossed by hundreds of walking trails and 300 rivers. But if you're not interested in hiking or boating, Dominica also offers a tennis club and a drama society. Calabashie has the best beach on the island. And you can visit boiling cauldrons in the Valley of Desolation.

Self-governing since 1967, Dominica is a British island. Although the official language is English, a French patois can be heard in the countryside.

Roseau, Dominica's quiet little capital, is the place to go for dentists, doctors, and a drugstore. **Portsmouth** is the island's best harbor. Inland, you can visit the Caribbean's only Carib Indian reservation. Safari trips can be arranged through the island's tropical rain forest.

U.S. citizens need proof of citizenship to visit Dominica.

Cooking is by kerosene, wood, or charcoal. The island has no poisonous snakes, but malaria is a problem.

A house to call home

If you decide to escape to Dominica, look into building a house rather than buying one. Housing is scarce, but building costs are lower than on more developed islands. Real estate agents and other expatriates or islanders can help you find property. Before you begin your search, hire a competent island attorney. Land prices quoted to Dominicans may be lower than those quoted to foreigners.

Most expatriates prefer to live close to the city. Some fear the Dreads, members of a guerrilla movement, who live in the countryside. Dreads were thought to have killed whites in the 1970s, but no such crimes have occurred for several years.

You need an alien landholding license to buy property. To get one, you must have a residence permit. Foreigners are generally limited to purchasing one acre of land. Submit house plans with your license application.

Most lots are 10,000 to 12,000 square feet and cost about $1.48 per square foot. Dominica has good builders and materials. A house can be built in six months for a reasonable price.

If you decide to buy an existing house, it is possible to find a good deal. Recently, land with a lovely view and a ramshackle house was advertised for US$25,000.

For more information on building a home on Dominica, contact the *Permanent Secretary,* **Ministry of Agriculture,** *Government Headquarters, Roseau, Commonwealth of Dominica, W.I.; tel. (809)445-2401.*

A temporary home
A good place to stay while you explore the island is the **Anchorage Hotel,** *P.O. Box 34, Roseau, Dominica, W.I.; tel. (809)445-2638.* A moderately priced inn, it is near the docks at Castle Comfort. Rooms have sea views. Boating, fishing, snorkeling, and water skiing are available nearby.

For more information
For help planning your retirement to Dominica, contact the **Caribbean Tourist Association,** *20 E. 46th St., New York, NY 10017; (212)682-0435.*

Grenada: the prettiest towns
The most picturesque harbor towns in the islands are in Grenada, which also has a healthy climate and gorgeous beaches. Its guesthouse rates are among the cheapest in the West Indies.

Grenada has mountain lakes, tall ferns, fertile valleys, dramatic waterfalls, sugar cane fields, and spice plantations. Fishing villages dot the shores, and there is no obvious poverty. Most of the natives speak English, although a French patois is spoken in the country. The temperature is 80 degrees Fahrenheit year-round, with little humidity.

Grenada boasts one of the Caribbean's most beautiful beaches, **Grand Anse,** a two-mile stretch of white sand. Offshore you can enjoy deep-sea fishing and snorkeling or scuba diving among 40 species of coral.

St. George's, the island's capital, is the hilliest city in the Caribbean. It is set around a harbor filled with sloops and schooners. Houses are painted in bright colors and reached by terraced, cobblestoned streets that climb steep hills. Dominating the town are Ft. George, Ft. Frederick, and Ft. William Henry, which at one time were all connected by tunnels. St. George's is filled with the smell of spices, and the sunset across the harbor is breathtaking.

Grenada's primary landmark is **Carib's Leap,** near the town of Sauteurs. Here, the last of the native Carib Indians leapt over a steep cliff 100 feet into the sea rather than face defeat at the hands of French colonists.

The island's natural beauties are many. **Levera National Park** preserves the seabirds of the islands off the coast of Grenada, including Sugar Loaf, Green, and Sandy. The park includes a large mangrove swamp filled with aquatic birds. Coconut palm, cactus, and woody scrub growth occupy the uplands. Here you can see iguana and land crabs. The white sand beaches in the park are important hatching grounds for turtles, while the marine areas are famous for their coral reefs and sea grass beds.

Grand Etang National Park overlooks Grand Etang, or Great Lake, a large volcanic crater. The forest around the lake is lush, washed by more than 160 inches of rainfall each year. It is filled with plant life that has adapted to the moisture-laden, windswept environment. The thick, leathery leaves have drip tips, and the trees are smaller than usual.

Sailing is heavenly in the waters surrounding this 133-square-mile island of 100,000 residents. Life is peaceful (despite the U.S. military intervention in 1983).

A capsule history

Grenada was discovered by Columbus on Aug. 14, 1498. He named the island Concepción. In the next century, both English and French colonists attempted to settle the island but were driven away by the Carib Indians. Eventually, the French, using harsh measures, vanquished the hostile natives. For years, the English and French fought over the island, which was passed between the two powers several times. The British finally won.

Grenada joined the Federation of the West Indies as an independent member on Jan. 3, 1958 and remained a member until the federation dissolved in 1962. At that time, a governor was appointed by the British Crown for the self-governing state, which became associated with Great Britain.

On Feb. 7, 1974, Grenada became an independent nation within the British Commonwealth. According to Grenada's constitution, the governor general is named by the British Crown, and the head of government is the prime minister.

The Grenada invasion

On March 13, 1979, the government of Sir Eric Gairy was overthrown in a coup d'état led by the New Jewel Movement. Maurice Bishop was named prime minister, and a Peoples Revolutionary Government was formed. On Oct. 19, 1983, elements of the Peoples Revolutionary Army staged another coup, and Maurice Bishop and several other cabinet members were killed.

The governor general, Sir Paul Scoon, called on the Organization

135

of Eastern Caribbean States, Jamaica, Barbados, and the United States to help him restore law and order. On Oct. 25, 1983, a combined force landed in Grenada, and the military junta was put down. General elections were held in December 1984, and Herbert A. Blaize of the New National Party was elected prime minister.

Moving in

Visit Grenada in the summer before you retire there permanently. Good cottage rentals can be found on Morne Rouge overlooking Grand Anse Beach.

Once you decide to settle permanently, building a home is your best bet. Reasonably priced lots are located near the beach. The best places to settle are Belmont, St. Paul's, Grand Anse, and Fontenoy, all of which are close to town and the beach and have public utilities.

Recently, two lots, each approximately 11,000 square feet, one with an ocean view, were advertised for US$20,000 and US$25,000. Contact **Axel R. Ottens,** *6049 Ambertree Lane, Lake Worth, FL 33463; (407)969-0131.*

Finding a house is more difficult than finding a plot of land, but bargains are available. **Carriacou,** north of Grenada, is one inexpensive place to live. But this pretty little island is difficult to get to. Not long ago, a two-bedroom house overlooking the beach here sold for US$60,000 through **T.G. & S.M. McKinstry,** *Prospect, Carriacou, Grenada; tel. 443-7380* (you must go through the international operator to call Grenada from the United States).

Money matters

The cost of living on Grenada is not high. Meat, fish, vegetables, fruit, sugar, jams, spices, and jellies are produced on the island, and fresh seafood is plentiful.

As the tourist economy expands, so do opportunities for small businesses. Several American retirees have opened businesses that have allowed them to stay permanently on the island. One example is the Nutmeg, a popular St. George's waterfront bistro. Most pioneer business ventures are entitled to liberal tax concessions.

Paperwork

To remain on the island for up to six months, you need only a round-trip ticket and enough money to support yourself. For a residence permit, contact the **Embassy of Grenada,** *1701 New Hampshire Ave. N.W., Washington, DC 20009; (202)265-2561.*

For more information, contact the **Grenada Tourist Board,** *P.O. Box 293, St. George's, Grenada, B.W.I.,* and request the retirement brochure.

The Dominican Republic

The Dominican Republic is an independent Spanish-speaking country. Although it shares the island of Hispaniola with Haiti, it does not share Haiti's poverty and strife. This could be a tremendous retirement spot, but most Americans are scared away by the Spanish language and foreign culture. Real estate is remarkably inexpensive, and the scenery and beaches are spectacular.

This lovely island is the home of the first European settlement in the New World. Columbus thought it was the world's most beautiful island. It is the most mountainous island in the Caribbean, with the highest peaks rising to more than 10,000 feet.

The Dominican Republic has extravagant hotels in the Spanish vein—at less than top luxury prices. Fashion designer Oscar de la Renta's flair for style can be seen in the interior designs of several of the island's luxury hotels. Conquistador forts, monasteries, narrow streets, the oldest cathedral in America, and a palace built for Columbus' son are waiting to be explored.

Popular amusements include cockfights (if you can stand them) and polo, which was introduced by the nephew of the Maharajah of Jodhpur. Night life centers around Caribbean music shows and big casinos. Local shops sell beautiful semi-precious jewels, and huge handicraft markets dot the island. Outside the city, the magnificent beaches are developing rapidly in response to the influx of tourists.

Some say the greatest resort in the Caribbean is **Casa de Campo** at La Romana. Frank Lloyd Wright designed the main building, and the interior was designed by de la Renta.

Altos de Chavon, the Dominican Republic's international artists' village, attracts artists, sculptors, musicians, and dancers from around the world.

The Dominican Republic's climate is more seasonal than elsewhere in the Caribbean. The mountains are cooler and wetter than the rest of the country. And the north coast is almost twice as wet as the south coast, where Santo Domingo is located. Average daily temperatures in Santo Domingo range from 66 degrees Fahrenheit to 84 degrees Fahrenheit in January and from 73 degrees Fahrenheit to 88 degrees Fahrenheit in August.

137

Buying real estate

Local real estate bargains exist—if you don't insist on luxury developments by the ocean. The Puerto Plata area, for example, has good buys. A condo in this new development sells for about US$30,000. Oceanfront land goes for $500 an acre. Efficiencies in Sosua go for US$20,000. Contact **Orange Coast Real Estate,** *214 Brevard St., Titusville, FL 32780; (305)268-0520,* or **General Realty, S.A.,** *Sosua, Puerto Plata; tel. (809)571-2604.*

Recently, two-bedroom condos in Sosua with views of the ocean were advertised for US$110,000. Contact **Bommarito Realty,** *Sosua, Puerto Plata; tel. (809)571-2604* or *(809)571-2389.*

A 1,350-square-foot lot in the Hills of Marbella, Sosua was advertised recently for US$25,000. For an additional US$50,000 you can have a two-bedroom, two-bath townhouse with ocean views, a pool, and parking facilities built on the lot. For more information, contact **Anthony Vogelaar,** *Calle Pedro Glisante #1, Sosua; tel. (809)571-2121.*

Four two-bedroom condos in Sosua, each with a bath, balcony, pool, rental program, and view of Sosua Bay, were on the market for US$47,500. Contact **Carole Ann Berkowitz,** *9 Crescent St., Natick, MA 01760; (617)653-8228.*

A two-level Spanish-style house on a 1,000-square-meter lot with an ocean view and a jacuzzi was advertised for US$75,000. Contact **Vincent Nardone,** *922 56th St., Brooklyn, NY 11219; (718)851-2699.*

A fully furnished four-bedroom, three-bath home on a hill overlooking Sosua Beach was advertised for $140,000. It has two balconies and is within walking distance of the beach. Contact **Mr. and Mrs. Mendez,** *Sosua, Puerto Plata; tel. (809)571-2563.*

A spacious oceanfront four-bedroom home with a swimming pool, in Punta Goleta, was advertised for $185,000. Contact **Bommarito Realty,** *Sosua, Puerto Plata; tel. (809)571-2604.*

For more information

For help retiring to the Dominican Republic, contact the **Embassy of the Dominican Republic,** *1715 22nd St. N.W., Washington, DC 20008; (202)332-6280,* or the **U.S. Embassy,** *corner of Calle Cesar Nicolas Penson and Calle Leopolda Navarro, Santo Domingo; tel. (809)682-2171.*

Puerto Rico: an Atlantic Hawaii

Puerto Rico is often compared to Hawaii, a fellow U.S. island.

But Puerto Rico is much more accessible than Hawaii; it's only 3 1/2 hours from New York. This mountainous island, lying between the Atlantic to the north and the Caribbean to the south, is fringed with white beaches. Sugar, coffee, and banana plantations climb the green hills. And the average temperature year-round is 77 degrees Fahrenheit.

Puerto Rico covers a total area of 3,435 square miles. It is crisscrossed by more than 3,000 miles of highways leading to old Spanish towns and picturesque villages, tropical rain forests, and gorgeous beaches.

This densely populated Caribbean island (the population density is 680 people per square mile) has the highest literacy rate in Latin America. Unemployment is 20%, and slums are a problem. In 1987, 3,335,970 Puerto Ricans emigrated to the mainland to find better job opportunities and a higher standard of living. On the other hand, 3,326,036 people immigrated to the island, some of them American retirees seeking sunshine and Caribbean beauty.

Puerto Ricans are American citizens—the island is part of the United States Federal Union. They enjoy most benefits of the Union but pay lower taxes. Puerto Rican residents pay no taxes on income earned in Puerto Rico. They can vote in national primary elections but not national presidential elections.

Puerto Rico (or Borinquen, the original Arawak Indian name) was discovered by Columbus on Nov. 19, 1493. Ponce de Léon conquered it for Spain in 1509 and established the first settlement at Caparra, across the bay from San Juan. Sugar cane was introduced in 1515, and slaves were imported three years later. Gold mining, which attracted the Spaniards to the island in the first place, petered out in 1570. And the Spanish fought off a series of British and Dutch attacks. In 1873 slavery was abolished.

Under the Treaty of Paris, Puerto Rico was ceded to the United States after the Spanish-American War in 1898. Today, the commonwealth of Puerto Rico is a self-governing part of the United States with a primarily Hispanic culture. The island's citizens have virtually the same control over their internal affairs as do citizens of the 50 states. Puerto Rico is represented in Congress by a resident commissioner, who has a voice but no vote, except in committees.

Living in Puerto Rico is almost like living in the United States. The towns are Spanish and cockfighting is legal, but the legal tender, post offices, and medical facilities are American. Although Spanish is the native language, most Puertorriqueños speak some English.

The climate is perfect—it is summer year-round. Temperatures average between 70 degrees Fahrenheit and 80 degrees Fahrenheit in January and between 75 degrees Fahrenheit and 86 degrees Fahrenheit during the summer. (If you prefer cooler temperatures, the mountains are 10 degrees cooler.) The northeast coast gets the most rain. The sun shines 335 days a year.

Health and medical standards are comparable to those in the United States. The island has hundreds of excellent doctors and specialists, well-equipped hospitals, and familiar drugstores.

The water is drinkable, and the milk is pasteurized.

. The drawbacks? Some beaches near San Juan are reportedly polluted. And purse snatchings and muggings are common in parts of San Juan. Life is expensive if you live in the upper-class areas.

A home of your own

However, outside the high-rent areas, two can live comfortably on $700 a month. You can rent a pleasant, two-bedroom apartment in the suburbs of San Juan for about $275 a month.

And if you avoid the luxury developments by the ocean, you can buy a home for a reasonable price. Keep in mind that the asking prices for properties are often much higher than the prices actually paid. Last year, a rural lot sold for $5,000 through **Richard Hoeger, G.P.O.,** *P.O. Box 4908, San Juan, PR 00936; tel. (809)753-7676.*

Many American retirees choose to buy modern homes in one of the new housing developments. The IBEC Housing Corporation has built thousands of moderately priced homes in the hills above San Juan—you can purchase attractive two- and three-bedroom masonry homes on one-acre lots at Florida prices. Older homes are even less expensive, and mortgages convert to liberal savings on U.S. income taxes. You can build a home in the country for half the price of construction in San Juan.

Away from San Juan

Many retirement towns, beach resorts, and villages are situated outside San Juan. **Arecibo,** for example, on the north coast, is an ancient city with beautiful beaches. **Mayaguez,** Puerto Rico's university town, has a fine beach. **San German** is a historic colonial village. **La Parguera** is a fishing village and resort. **Guanica** is an old Spanish town and beach resort. **Ponce,** Puerto Rico's second largest city, has ancient streets, wrought-iron balconies, Spanish architecture, good beaches, and a red-and-white striped fire house.

Barranquitas is a pleasant summer resort with cool temperatures. **Guyama** is a rural town at the foot of the gorgeous

Cayey Mountains, slightly inland from the island's south coast. **Las Croabas** is a picturesque fishing village.

The island of **Vieques,** nine miles off the eastern tip of Puerto Rico, is a marvelous retirement spot. The U.S. Army owns part of the island, but the rest is in civilian hands. It is a paradise of beaches, snorkeling, fishing, tropical fruits, stucco homes, and relaxation. This little-known 21-mile-long island lies due east of Puerto Rico. Wild horses and cattle roam the roads, hills, and empty beaches. Small boats cruise Phosphorescent Bay. Mahogany and rubber trees reach through the small rain forest's ceiling. White sand beaches slip into clear, calm waters, some near colorful coral reefs. Home to 8,000 Spanish-speaking natives and, on the west coast, 100 U.S. sailors and Marines, Vieques is informal, low-key, and inexpensive.

For accommodations in villas owned by mainland U.S. citizens, contact *Nancy and Ray Sherwin,* **Island Homes Rentals,** *P.O. Box 1483, Vieques, PR 00765; tel. (809)741-8136.*

Inexpensive accommodations are available at Bananas and Trade Winds (about $40 a night), both of which are restaurants with guestrooms.

Property listings

For listings of homes, condos, and apartments, consult the following publications: *El Mundo, El Nueva Día,* and *El Vocero* (the local Spanish daily newspapers); the *San Juan Star* (the local English daily newspaper); and *Caribbean Business* (the business English weekly newspaper).

The cost of living

Imported foods are 5% to 10% more expensive in Puerto Rico, because of shipping costs. But locally produced seafood, poultry, fruits, and vegetables are not expensive. And you can purchase a bottle of Bacardi rum for very little (the world's largest rum plant, the Bacardi Distillery, is located here).

Driving

If you want to import your car to Puerto Rico, do so within 90 days of your arrival on the island. If you wait longer than that, you'll have to pay excise taxes based on the car's wholesale selling price, make, model, year, and accessories. For more information, call the office of the **Arbitrios Generales,** *tel. (809)724-3040,* preferably early in the morning. New cars sell here for about 30% more than in New York.

141

Entertainment

You should never lack for recreation in Puerto Rico. San Juan has varied cultural entertainment, beginning with the Drama Festival from January through March and continuing with the Theater Festival from March through May, the great Casals Festival in June, and the symphony season, which begins in November. The island offers concerts, exhibitions, plays, opera, and ballet. Baseball is popular, as are basketball, boxing, soccer, tennis, fishing, and golf. Horse racing, .riding, gambling, fishing, snorkeling, and hunting provide variety.

San Juan has an English-language radio station, several Spanish-language television stations, and cinemas showing American and foreign films.

Business opportunities

Opportunities exist in Puerto Rico for retirees to open small businesses. Guesthouses and small resorts are needed outside San Juan. Villages need small supermarkets. And there is a market for locally produced fruits and vegetables.

For more information

For more on retiring to Puerto Rico, read *Off the Beaten Path* by Norman D. Ford, **Harian Publications,** *1 Vernon Ave., Floral Park, NY 11001.* Or contact the **Chamber of Commerce,** *100 Tetuán, P.O. Box 3789, San Juan, PR 00904,* or the **Puerto Rico Tourism Office,** *1290 Avenue of the Americas, New York, NY 10019.*

For more information on the tax situation in Puerto Rico, send for *What You Should Know About Taxes in Puerto Rico,* which is available free from the **Treasurer of the Commonwealth of Puerto Rico,** *Box 4515, San Juan, PR 00903.*

One couple's Puerto Rican retirement

Gene Murphy describes retirement in Puerto Rico. This article first appeared in the September 1987 issue of International Living.

My wife and I were introduced to the town of Rincon, Puerto Rico through an adventurous former classmate, Charlotte Sirutus, and her husband, Yustin. They had been vacationing in the cabins on the shore here for 25 years. When Yustin, a former golden gloves heavyweight contender and a physical education teacher, became arthritic, they decided to move to Rincon so he could swim year-round in the calm 80-degree water.

We bought a house after spending three winters in a delightful two-bedroom, two-bath cottage. Our house is separated from the sea and the sunsets by a tropical garden. The lure of the southwestern Puerto Rican climate, the attractive investment opportunity, the enjoyment that our children and grandchildren get from their visits, all these things sold us on retirement in Puerto Rico.

Now at our own Pelican Beach cottage, we have a Bermuda grass lawn to the beach, a fence of hibiscus, overhead fans in all the newly painted rooms, and polished terrazzo floors. We expect a telephone to be installed this year. We found a store about a half-hour away by car that sells the Sunday *New York Times* for $5.75. We stretch it out until Thursday. And we are busy taping movies on our video-cassette recorder to share with our neighbors, a scene reminiscent of television's early days, when guests were invited over to see Uncle Miltie.

We wake up to the sounds of barking dogs and crowing roosters, then take a dip in the calm Caribbean before breakfast. For breakfast, we have freshly squeezed orange juice, sliced pineapple, or papaya, all from a street vendor or our garden. We leave the house for a few hours to make room for the housekeeper and gardener; usually we stroll to town to buy the *San Juan Star* and a loaf of cheese bread from the bakery and to check for mail.

On more adventurous days, we help the fishermen on the beach pull in their nets. If it's a good catch, we buy a red snapper for dinner. Later, we take another swim before strolling along the beach and boning up on recent real estate opportunities for the evening's cocktail chat.

We get the latest neighborhood news from a native, along with advice on how to prepare rice and beans to accompany the snapper. From the porch, we watch the sunset, the whales, and the atmospheric phenomenon known as the green flash.

In downtown Rincon is a plaza with a supermarket, a bakery, a tropical bar, and restaurants where the vendors speak English and trade is conducted exclusively in U.S. currency. The plaza is surrounded by Catholic and Protestant churches, a post office, the town hall, a bank, a health clinic, a drug store, a travel agency, a surf shop, and a variety store, as well as Carlos' Tropical Bar and Danny's Restaurant.

Each weekend morning during high season, markets are set up along the beach in front of the resort hotels where you can shop for hammocks, custom-made or precut shirts and skirts, gift items woven from palms, and jewelry made of sea glass and shells.

Happily, all the hustle that goes with casinos, high-rise hotels, gourmet food, and fancy boutiques is a three-hour drive away in San Juan. That safe distance also separates the west coast from half the island's population and 90% of its tourists.

Drawbacks brought on by this isolation are few. We have trouble finding stateside newspapers and usually have to settle for the *San Juan Star*. American television networks are inaccessible without a satellite dish. And telephone connections, when made, are choppy.

Until 25 years ago, the beaches of Rincon were covered with palm trees and backed by fields of sugar cane. Most of the palms still .stand. But the cane has given way to poor squatters who were permitted to buy their 10,000-square-foot lots for $1 each. They planted mango, banana, citrus, papaya, breadfruit, and other fast-growing tropical trees, along with colorful hibiscus and ornamental foliage.

And during the past few years, Rincon has been undergoing other changes as well. Two modest resort hotels have emerged, attracting more and more American retirees. Those who can't get reservations rough it in tiny cabins.

When the U.S. government ceded Ramey Air Force Base to the Puerto Rican government, the largest air strip in the Caribbean was made public. This eventually brought about the demise of a pictur-esque golf course that had charged modest fees and sported fewer players than a private course on the U.S. mainland.

Recently, about a dozen regular visitors to the island bought beachfront shanties and upgraded them to attractive stucco cottages with modern conveniences. These $80,000 homes now dot the coast. The two resort hotels are thriving.

This somewhat sleepy but well-managed town is growing as a result of the influx of outside spenders. And this year Rincon was blessed with a *parador* (a traditional and modestly priced govern-ment-run hotel)—which should contribute even more to the town's development.

Where to stay in Rincon

Rincon offers limited rental accommodations, especially during January and February (the peak season). Rates range from $600 to $2,500 per month.

Cottages can be rented through:

• **Selma Waldman,** *5 Seven Bridge Road, Chappaqua, NY 10514; (914)238-3567.*

• **Patrick Moscatello,** *262 Laurence Ave., Oakhurst, NJ 07755; (201)531-8484* or *(201)870-9293.*

144

• **Elizabeth Hartage,** *P.O. Box 14, Rincon, PR 00743; tel. (809)823-3905.*

• **Marie Vohs,** *P.O. Box 2216, Montauk, NY 11954; (516)668-9088.*

Condominiums can be rented through:

• **Charlotte Sirutis,** *P.O. Box 1001, Rincon, PR 00743; tel. (809)823-1025.*

• **Dr. Fred Bake,** *312 Upper College Terrace, Frederick, MD 21701.*

• **Willy Ramos,** *Marbella 6, 133 D St., Agua Dilla, PR 00603.*

Charlotte Sirutis recently listed a 2 1/2-room apartment for rent on the beach in Rincon for $700 a month.

The French West Indies

The French West Indies, which include Martinique, Guadeloupe, St. Martin, Iles des Saintes, Marie-Galante, La Désirade, and St. Barthélemy, offer the Caribbean's best food, most fashionable cities, and sexiest nude beaches. These islands are lush, covered in flowers, and considered by many to have the most beautiful women in the Caribbean. The French Empress Josephine is history's most famous Martinique beauty.

Martinique

Martinique's **Ft.-de-France** is the Paris of the Western Hemisphere, with wrought-iron grillwork and narrow streets. Gauguin's Caribbean home was here. Ft.-de-France has a lively musical night life, one of the Caribbean's best Mardi Gras, and St. Pierre, the Pompeii of the Caribbean. French luxury goods are available at bargain prices. And the island has a full range of accommodations, from luxury (including French colonial manor houses) to spare, rock-bottom French digs.

Oddly enough, Martinique has good real estate buys. Property goes for as little as FF360,000. This island may be the perfect retirement haven for Francophones, but if you don't speak French, you might not feel at home here.

For more information on Martinique, contact the **Martinique Office of Tourism,** *tel. (596)637-960.*

Guadeloupe

Guadeloupe, lying 100 miles north of Martinique, 45 miles south of Antigua, is known as the Emerald Island. It is a quieter, more rustic, less expensive version of Martinique, and we prefer it to Martinique as a retirement haven. With Mediterranean-style fishing villages and a steaming volcano, it has some of the most spectacular scenery in the Caribbean. Guadeloupe's pre-Columbian inhabitants called the island Karukera (land of beautiful waters), because of its waterfalls, cascades, and hot springs.

Like Martinique, Guadeloupe is a French territory (*région*), and Guadeloupeans are French citizens. But unlike Martinique, it is not content with the status quo. A small group of Guadeloupeans is striving for independence, and about three years ago it made its wishes known by setting off car bombs throughout the island. But things have been calm since then. The island's economy is almost completely dependent on France, which subsidizes local businesses, provides jobs, and builds roads and schools.

Guadeloupeans speak French and Creole, and the island is known for both its French and Creole restaurants. Island festivals celebrate Creole music and dance. The official currency is the French franc, but you can open bank accounts in the U.S. dollar as well.

If you're looking to get away from your fellow Americans, Guadeloupe may be the place for you. Fewer than 100 Americans live here. And if you decide to retire to Guadeloupe, learn to speak French. The islanders are not particularly friendly to those who don't.

The island is rainy. The most intense rainfall in modern times was recorded in Barst in 1970, when one-and-a-half inches of rain fell in one minute. The rainiest months are September, October, and November; the least rain falls from December through April.

While it can be humid, Guadeloupe is cooled by trade winds (les Alizés). Temperatures range from 72 degrees Fahrenheit to 86 degrees Fahrenheit on the coast and from 66 degrees Fahrenheit to 81 degrees Fahrenheit inland. The temperature of the water is 70 degrees Fahrenheit to 80 degrees Fahrenheit.

Guadeloupe proper is actually two islands: **Basse-Terre** and **Grande-Terre,** connected by a bridge over the Rivère Salée (Salt River). Basse-Terre has a 74,000-acre nature park with waterfalls, rain forests, lakes, and rivers. It also has a dormant volcano, black sand beaches, and mountains. Grande-Terre has white-sand beaches, plains, plantations, hotels, and a big city.

The city of **Basse-Terre,** capital of the island of the same name, is situated at the foot of La Soufrière (4,870 feet), the island's volcano. The city is a banana and sugar cane port with French colonial buildings. Nearby are fumaroles, cauldrons, and sulphur fields.

Buying property

If you decide to buy property on Guadeloupe, you will find that the process is time-consuming but not complicated. The most expensive properties are on Grande-Terre (because it rains less here than on Basse-Terre). The lowest prices are in the countryside. It is difficult to buy property on small satellite islands, where land tends to stay within families and available properties are not advertised. The process is further complicated because these islands have no real estate agents.

By Guadeloupean law, notaries handle all real estate transactions. Expect to pay at least 10% of the purchase price in notary fees and stamp taxes. You don't need a residence permit to buy a house, apartment, or land.

When you eventually sell your home, you will have to pay capital gains of about 33.33% of the profit, deflated for the cost-of-living increase during the years of your ownership.

Apartments cost from FF360,000 to FF900,000, depending on the location, size, and quality. You will also have to pay maintenance fees. Houses range in price from FF249,000 to FF4.8 million. The average is about FF900,000.

Two-story houses are considered one-story houses in Guadeloupe (the ground floor doesn't count). A three-bedroom house is called a three-room home—you can assume that it also has a kitchen, living room, and bathroom.

Expect to pay FF2,760 to FF4,980 per square meter to build (.093 square meters equals one square foot). Land ranges from FF138 to FF150 per square meter in the country and from FF138 to FF300 per square meter near the water.

To get a building permit, you must submit building plans from a contractor or an architect. Expect it to take at least eight months for your house to be constructed. Most homes are built of concrete with wood trim.

You might be able to arrange a mortgage. You can count on a 20% down payment, an interest rate of 10.5%, and a 15-year term.

For a list of real estate agents, contact the **Office du Tourisme,** *5 Square de la Banque, 97110 Pointe-à-Pitre, Guadeloupe, F.W.I.; tel. (590)82-09-30;* the **Chambre de Commerce et d'Industrie de Pointe-à-Pitre,** *Assainissement BP 64, 97152 Pointe-à-Pitre Cedex, Guadeloupe, F.W.I.; tel. (590)82-51-15;* or the **Préfecture de la Guadeloupe,** *Palais d'Orléans, 97109 Basse-Terre, Guadeloupe, F.W.I.; tel. (590)81-15-60.*

Cost of living

Food prices are high in Guadeloupe, but the variety of products available is surprising. A box of cold American cereal goes for FF24; a chicken is FF13.50 per pound; and steaks are FF36 per pound. A tube of American toothpaste is FF15.30. Sterilized milk, imported from France, keeps for three months at room temperature; it's fine for cooking but not great for drinking.

You can hire a full-time maid for about FF1,800 per month. (You'll have to pay for health insurance as well.)

A normal electricity bill is FF1,020 for three months—higher if you have air conditioning. Outages occur when workers strike.

Expect to pay FF66 every two months for telephone service, plus a charge for each call you make.

Rentals are FF900 to FF6,000 per week, depending on location. The highest prices are in St. François and other resort areas; the lowest prices are in the country and on satellite islands. Cheaper rentals don't include hot water.

Legalities

To stay in Guadeloupe for up to three months, you must have a valid passport and a return ticket. You will be issued a free, temporary visa upon arrival. To stay for longer than three months but less than six months, you must obtain a long-stay visa. After that, you must apply for a residence permit. Visas are available only from French consulates in American cities.

Approval for a visa or residence permit takes six to eight weeks. The cost is FF90. Island officials reviewing your application will want to know the condition of your health (if you are applying for a residence permit you must pass a physical examination), your occupation, the reason for your stay, and how you will support yourself while on the island. In addition, you must supply personal references in the United States and on Guadeloupe, if possible.

Driving a car

You can drive in Guadeloupe for up to 20 days on a U.S. driver's license. If you stay longer, you'll need an international driver's permit, which you must get in the United States. If you become a resident of the island, you must get a French driver's license, which means you must attend a local driving school and take the driver's test. For information, contact the **Préfecture de la Guadeloupe,** *Palais d'Orléans, 97109 Basse-Terre, Guadeloupe, F.W.I.; tel. (590)81-15-60.*

Rather than importing your American car, we recommend that

you buy a new or used French car in Guadeloupe. Spare parts are difficult to find for American cars.

Gasoline is about FF17 a gallon.

Entertaining yourself

Guadeloupe offers the standard Caribbean activities: swimming, snorkeling, scuba diving, sailing, and water skiing. (Jacques Cousteau calls a diving site off Pigeon Island—one of Guadeloupe's satellites—one of the world's 10 best.)

The island also boasts an 18-hole Robert Trent Jones golf course and several marinas. If you want something more exotic, go to a cockfight or a nude beach. Local Caribbean music groups give frequent concerts.

Taxes

You must pay both French and U.S. taxes on income of more than FF420,000 earned on the island. If you earn less than that, you pay taxes to France only. Property taxes vary according to the statutes set by each town or village. They are usually about 1.5% of a property's value. Estate tax, called succession tax, is computed on the value of the share of an estate that each heir receives, not on the value of the entire estate.

Getting there

You can fly to Guadeloupe from New York or Miami. Flights leave daily from New York, stopping in San Juan, and take five hours, not including stopover time. Flights from Miami depart Saturday and Sunday, sometimes stopping in Haiti. Flying time is four hours. Le Raizet International Airport is about two miles from Pointe-á-Pitre.

Iles des Saintes

The Iles des Saintes, reached by boat or small plane from Guadeloupe, are eight dots in the Caribbean, way off the beaten path. They are the diving grounds of Jacques Cousteau. **Terre-de-Haut,** the only one of these islands with tourist accommodations, has lovely beaches and a tiny, primitive Victorian town populated by fishermen who are descendants of Breton corsairs. Some of these Breton fishermen offer rooms in their homes. Four nondescript hotels on Terre-de-Haut offer the cheapest accommodations in the Caribbean.

St. Barthélemy

St. Barthélemy, the American millionaire's island, has a Swedish atmosphere (it belonged to Sweden for a century before the French won it back in 1878). Owners of the island's spectacular mansions include Rockefellers and Rothschilds. Inhabitants are descendants of

Breton and Norman fishermen, who dress in the provincial costumes of the old country.

Away from the millionaires, life on St. Barts can be homey and moderately priced. Housekeeping accommodations are available, good places for families to vacation.

For more information

For more information on retiring to the West Indies, contact the **French West Indies Tourist Board,** *610 Fifth Ave., New York, NY 10020; (212)757-1125,* or the **French Government Tourist Office,** *9401 Wilshire Blvd., Beverly Hills, CA 90212; (213)272-2661.*

St. Martin/Sint Maarten: *paradis continental*

St. Martin/Sint Maarten is half-French and half-Dutch. The French side—St. Martin—is famous for its restaurants and Bohemian ambience. Artists choose Marigot, St. Martin's waterfront square, to set up their easels. Small fishing boats pull into port with their catches. Vendors sell their wares under brightly colored umbrellas. And travelers meet at La Vie en Rose to chat over fresh, exquisitely prepared seafood.

For information on residence permits, taxes, or buying property on the French side of the island, contact the **French West Indies Tourist Board,** *address above.*

Sint Maarten, the Dutch side, is known for its well-run hotels and shopping bargains. Cruise ships dock in the harbor in Philipsburg to allow passengers to take advantage of duty-free prices on jewelry, linen, crystal, and cameras.

Both sides offer sailing, jet skiing, windsurfing, scuba diving, snorkeling, deep-sea diving, golf, and tennis. You can rent motor bikes, cars, or convertible jeeps to explore the island.

Monolingual Americans prefer the Dutch side of the island, because English is the primary language of communication there (although Dutch is the official language).

Constant trade winds keep the daytime temperatures at an annual average of 80 degrees Fahrenheit. The only months with the threat of bad weather are August, September, and October, when rain and tropical storms are common.

Buying property

No restrictions are placed on foreigners who want to own property in Sint Maarten, and many of the non-native home buyers and business operators on the island are Americans. To start a business in Sint Maarten, you must establish an NV (Namenlose Vereenschaap—literally, a "company with no name") through a local notary. By naming yourself managing director of the NV, you gain a residence permit, the right to operate the company, and the right to purchase property. Establishing an NV costs about $1,200.

Property transactions are also handled through a notary, who represents neither the buyer nor the seller but acts as a friend of the court. Notaries are appointed by the queen of the Netherlands.

There are three ways to take possession of property on Sint Maarten. The first is fee simple ownership, which involves paying for the property, receiving a deed, and owning the property forever. The second way is called government leasehold. If you go this route, you get a 60-year lease from the government, which is automatically renewed after the first 60 years. After 120 years the government can refuse to renew the lease, but it must pay you, the owner of the lease, for improvements to the property. The third way to take possession of property is called private leasehold. In this way, you lease property from a private party, and the terms of the contract are determined entirely by you and the other party.

When making a real estate purchase, you must pay a transfer tax to the government of 2.75% of the purchase price, as well as $60 for a Foreign Exchange License. You must also pay the notary's fee, which depends upon the amount of work performed when preparing the deed. Although title insurance is available, it's unnecessary because the notary's signature, authorized by the queen, is never questioned. Sint Maarten imposes neither real estate nor personal property taxes.

Real estate, especially developed property, is expensive in Sint Maarten. Because materials must be shipped from the United States or Latin America, construction costs are high. Cement foundations cost about $100 per cubic yard. Other construction costs can run $75 to $110 per square foot.

But you can find good deals. A half-acre of land high on Paradise Peak was advertised recently for $65,000. From the lot, which has an access road, electric lines, and telephone service, you can see half the island and miles out to sea.

Denfield Knight, a local real estate appraiser, estimates that Sint Maarten real estate has appreciated an average of 10% per year over the last 10 years. Undeveloped land may be the best investment. There's no doubt that those who purchased property 10 years ago have done well on their investments. However, it's unlikely that people who buy Sint Maarten real estate now can expect the same return. Local businessmen estimate that the economy is overheated as the result of heavy tourist traffic.

Because available capital on the island is limited, borrowing money is difficult. The Central Bank of the Netherlands Antilles, comparable to our Federal Deposit Insurance Corporation, requires a long-term deposit (contra account) to back a long-term loan. Generally, financing doesn't exceed 65% over four years and is available only to residents. In May 1985, interest rates averaged 13% for residential loans and ranged from 11% to 17% for personal loans. The Central Bank can influence terms of the loan.

Real estate agents
Real estate agents dealing with property in St. Martin/Sint Maarten include:

• **Ambria International Realty, NV,** *Ned Durham and Sharon Lee Sagat, 180 Front St., Philipsburg, Sint Maarten.*

• **Real Estate & Developement Company, NV,** *Irene Morris, P.O. Box 205, Phillipsburg, Sint Maarten.*

• **Soskin-Deher Real Estate,** *Michel Deher, P.O. Box 262, Great Bay Marina, Sint Maarten.*

• **Tendal Holdings, NV,** *Walt Kassel, 11 Front St., Philipsburg, Sint Maarten.*

For more information on buying property, contact the **Chamber of Commerce,** *Mr. Louis Peters, P.O. Box 372, Philipsburg, Sint Maarten,* or consult the *Sint Maarten Business Journal* (available from the Chamber of Commerce). Another good source of information is *The Clarion,* available through **Allan S. Richardson,** *P.O. Box 206, Philipsburg, Sint Maarten.*

Banking
Interest earned on an account in Sint Maarten isn't reported to the Internal Revenue Service (IRS). However, most of the local banks have U.S. branches, which means the parent bank is vulnerable to IRS pressure. Although deposits are not insured, the Central Bank requires that all banks maintain liquidity equal to 20% of resident deposits and 100% of non-resident deposits. That has kept the banking industry extremely solvent.

A tale of two entrepreneurs
From a lawn chair overlooking the blue Caribbean, life on Sint Maarten looks pretty good. That's what Earle and Betty Vaughan

thought when they decided to move to the island from Fryeburg, Maine. And they haven't regretted their decision since. They are now proprietors of the Horny Toad Guesthouse on the Dutch side of this 37-square-mile island in the Netherlands Antilles.

The Vaughans first visited the island in 1978 and fell in love with the gentle climate, beautiful beaches, and friendly people. They vacationed on the island again in 1979. When they returned to their home in Fryeburg, they were half-committed to a permanent move.

In October 1980, Betty took a year's leave of absence from her job as a school nurse, and Earle decided to retire. They rented out their house and headed for Sint Maarten to explore opportunities on the island.

The couple was soon helping to manage the guesthouse where they were staying, and when illness in the family prompted the owners to move back to the United States, Earle and Betty stepped in as full-time managers. They established an NV through the local notary and received residence permits (while retaining U.S. citizenship). Within a short time the Vaughns acquired the Horny Toad from its absentee owners.

If you'd like to talk to the Vaughans about their island retirement, you can contact them at *Box 397, Philipsburg, Sint Maarten, Netherlands Antilles.*

For more information

For general information, contact the **Sint Maarten Tourist Office,** *c/o Mallory Factor Inc., Gail Knopfler, 1500 Broadway, Room 2305, New York, NY 10036; (212)840-6655.*

Saba: St. Martin's charming neighbor

Saba, a five-square-mile volcanic island respectfully called the Unspoiled Queen, can be glimpsed as a hazy mountain silhouette from the west side of St. Martin, 28 miles away. Movie buffs might recognize it as the beautiful but dangerous Cannibal Island in the original version of *King Kong.*

You can get to Saba from St. Martin Airport via a Windward Islands Airway 30-seat twin-engine airplane. The flight takes 15 minutes. You can also get there from St. Martin by boat.

From the air, Saba is a wall of jagged black and gray rock shooting up 3,000 feet from the white caps of the surf. Its summit is lost in the clouds.

Outside the single-story, cinder-block airport building waits a constant line of parked vehicles. The drivers smile and wave enthusiastically, waiting to serve as tour guides. They will spend a day showing you around the island for less than $5.

Saba's only highway (called the Driveway by locals) is nine miles long. It was carved by hand along the sides of the mountains and down through the valley. When Sabans asked their central government to build a road, engineers studying the project came to the conclusion that it was impossible. One Saban, J.L. Hassell, disagreed. After finishing an engineering correspondence course, he built the road himself, by hand. The road snakes through picturesque villages with names such as Hell's Gate, Windwardside, and the Bottom.

Throughout Saba, small white houses with red tile roofs, each with its own family graveyard, peek through the thick tropical vegetation produced by the rich volcanic soil. Because most of the houses are built on slopes, each has a magnificent view. Cultivated crops cut into the sides of the island's steep hills like steps.

The island is immaculate. Streets and public buildings are completely free of garbage and debris. To accomplish this, each village assigns its residents clean-up duty on a rotating schedule.

Saba also has a reputation as a world-famous diving spot. More than 25 diving areas, each with visibility beyond 100 feet, are located around the island. In 1988, the Saba Marine Park opened, complete with a self-guiding marine trail. Diving instructions and certification are offered at Saba Deep, a diving shop owned and operated by two Americans at the Last Chance harbor.

Hiking is the other major activity on the island. Rugged footpaths wind through Saba, shrouded by elephant ears, ferns, palms, and banana and mango trees. At the end of Mountain Road is Mt. Scenery, a 3,000-foot-high extinct volcano. You can reach its summit by climbing the 1,064 concrete steps embedded in its surface.

Saba is a quiet, intimate, enchanting place. The people are genuinely friendly and want to know the island's visitors. If you stay overnight, the local radio station will announce your visit, and you'll be greeted by name the next morning.

The **Bottom**, the island's capital, is at the center of a valley surrounded by steep walls. Here is the grand Administrator's Mansion, as well as small wooden houses with tiny cemeteries for back yards.

Windwardside is the island's second-highest town, at 1,500 feet. The town's small inn is a good place to stay the night or to stop for a meal.

Hells Gate, a village jutting out from the face of the mountain, sits 600 feet over the sea. It has five bucolic houses, some thatched, some roofed in red.

At an altitude of 1,600 feet is **Upper Hells Gate,** the highest town on the island. Only 700 inhabitants live in the village's rustic cottages.

Saba only has one beach, located by the wharf in the Bottom. While it is by no means the most spectacular beach in the Caribbean, it is never crowded. And you can watch the local fishermen bringing in their catches.

Buying a house

Many Americans own houses on Saba. Real estate values on the island vary considerably, but comfortable homes can be found for as little as $80,000. Recently, a furnished house in Booby Hill with 400 square meters of land was advertised for $85,000. For more information, contact Eric Johnson in Windwardside.

Many houses for sale throughout the island are advertised on a bulletin board in the airport. Most people, though, find property by word of mouth. One American who found his house that way spends about six months a year there and rents the property the rest of the time. He bought the house, which was in need of repairs, for $45,000. After all the work he's done on it, he could easily sell it for twice that.

If you would rather go through a real estate agent, contact **Island Realty Alliance,** *P.O. Box 468, Philipsburg, Sint Maarten; tel. (599-5)44397.* It lists properties on Saba.

Foreign residents on Saba cannot take jobs that would otherwise go to Saban nationals. However, foreign residents can own and operate their own businesses on the island.

Before you decide to settle permanently on Saba, visit for a while. A good place to stay while you're exploring the island is **Cranston's Antique Inn,** *the Bottom; tel. (599-4)-3203.* Built in 1850, this old frame structure was once a government guesthouse that regularly hosted Queen Juliana. Each of the six rooms has a four-poster bed. Breakfast is complimentary, and prices are reasonable.

The Saban currency is the Netherlands Antilles guilder, or florin. U.S. currency is accepted everywhere on Saba, but credit cards are not. While the nationality and the official language are Dutch, English is the first language of nearly all Sabans. (For 200 years the Dutch and English fought over the island, which changed hands 20 times in the 17th and 18th centuries. The Dutch won, but the islanders chose English as their language.) Of the 1,000 Sabans, 60% are white. Don't be surprised to see red-haired, freckled islanders.

To visit Saba, you will need proof of citizenship (a birth certificate, voter's registration card, or passport).

A good source of information on Saba is a book called *Islands to the Windward* by Brian Dythe, available for $9.95 from Palm Tree Books.

For general information, contact the **Saba Tourist Board,** *275 Seventh Ave., New York, NY 10001-6788; (212)989-0000.*

Bermuda: the Atlantic isle

Mark Twain once said of Bermuda, "You go to Heaven if you want—I'll just stay right here." Sunny, warm Bermuda has soft pink-white sand, coral reefs, historic towns, good restaurants and hotels, and an average temperature of 72 degrees Fahrenheit. And you'll never lack for recreation. The island has facilities for golfing, tennis, horseback riding, and scuba diving. And Bermuda is an international yachting center.

While Bermuda is not actually part of the Caribbean, it offers the same island seclusion and beauty as its southern counterparts. This tiny island in the Atlantic is 600 miles from Cape Hatteras, North Carolina and 911 miles northeast of the Bahamas. It is made up of 150 separate islands, with a total land area of 21 square miles. (Greater New York City is 15 times larger.) Bermuda is 22 miles long and less than 2 miles wide.

Bermuda is Britain's oldest colony. Totally self-governing, it retains ceremonial ties with the queen, who appoints the governor. The governor, in turn, appoints the island's premier.

Bermuda has a distinctly British air. Bermudans take tea at 4 every afternoon. Their lawyers wear wigs. Island policemen are known as bobbies. And cricket is the national craze. Businessmen wear Bermuda shorts. Drivers keep to the left. And the Bermuda Regiment marches in crimson and gold uniforms.

Bermuda has just two seasons, spring and summer. Spring temperatures, from mid-November through mid-April, range from the high 60s to the low 70s Fahrenheit. Summer temperatures are in the 70s and 80s Fahrenheit. The highest temperature recorded during the past 40 years was 91.8 degrees Fahrenheit. Nighttime temperatures are about 10 degrees cooler, so be sure to bring sweaters or jackets when you visit.

The island has both 18-hole and 9-hole golf courses, nearly 100 tennis courts, and a riding school.

The *Royal Gazette* is Bermuda's daily newspaper. Two weeklies, the *Bermuda Sun* and the *Mid-Ocean News,* are published on Friday.

Flying time from Boston, New York, Philadelphia, or Washington, D.C. is less than two hours. From Chicago, the flight is less than five hours.

Moving in

For a short visit to the island (of up to about three weeks), all you need is a return ticket. Unless you have authorization to land from the Bermuda Immigration Authorities, don't arrive without a return ticket—you will not be admitted.

If you are interested in taking up residence in Bermuda, you will not be permitted to land unless you have prior authorization from the Department of Immigration. To apply for authorization, contact the *Chief Immigration Officer,* **Department of Immigration,** *Ministry of Home Affairs, P.O. Box HM 1364, Hamilton 5, HM FX, Bermuda.* (The office is located on the first floor of the **Government Administration Building,** *Parliament Street, Hamilton.*)

Don't expect to move to Bermuda and find a job. When a job vacancy occurs, the employer first must advertise in the local newspapers. Only after he has proven that no Bermudian is either qualified or available can he apply to the Minister of Home Affairs for permission to hire a non-Bermudian.

Renting a home

Cottages, houses, and apartments are available for rental on a seasonal or long-term basis to temporary visitors. (Seasonal rental is considered to be from one week to three months—sometimes up to six months. Long-term rental is more than six months.) These private homes, which are not specifically designated as tourist accommodations, are handled through real estate agents in Bermuda. Most are located in residential areas throughout the island and are not available on a regular basis. (Note: Apartment complexes officially designated as condominiums cannot be rented to visitors.)

An average house can be rented on a long-term basis for about $1,800 a month. If you want a house with a pool, maid service, and other luxuries, expect to pay between $4,000 and $10,000 a month.

Two-bedroom seasonal rentals are approximately $1,500 to $3,500 a month. However, some seasonal rentals are as much as $15,000 a month, depending on location and amenities. Electricity, gardening, and telephone services (excluding long-distance calls) are often included in seasonal rentals, but not in long-term rentals.

Often owners request that their permanent domestic help be hired along with their house, sometimes at an extra charge. Permission to import your own maids or cooks must be obtained by writing in advance to the *Chief Immigration Officer,* **Ministry of Home Affairs,** *address above.* A fee of $160 must accompany the application.

For more information on real estate in Bermuda, contact the **Secretary of the Bermuda Chamber of Commerce Real Estate Division,** *Visitors Service Bureau, P.O. Box HM 655, Hamilton HM CX, Bermuda; tel. (809)295-4201.* The following banks and real estate agents also may be able to help:

• **Allan Cooper Real Estate Ltd.,** *Commerce Building, Reid Street, Hamilton; tel. (809)292-7533.*

• **Bank of Bermuda Ltd.,** *6 Front St., Hamilton; tel. (809)295-4000.*

• **Bermuda Realty Company Ltd.,** *Queen Street, Hamilton; tel. (809)295-0294.*

• **Bermuda Universal Realty Ltd.,** *Reid Street, Hamilton; tel. (809)295-1546.*

• **Collier Real Estate,** *Sherwood Building, Pitts Bay Road, Pembroke; tel. (809)295-5487.*

• **Decouto & Dunstan,** *P.O. Box HM 933, Hamilton HM DX; tel. (809)292-0616.*

• **Donald Adderley Real Estate,** *Parliament Street, Hamilton; tel. (809)295-1631.*

• **Dorchester Realty Ltd.,** *Insco House, Church Street, Hamilton; tel. (809)295-5252.*

• **G.E. Kendall Real Estate,** *P.O. Box PG 276, Paget PGBX.*

• **Geoffrey Bird and Company,** *P.O. Box HM 1312, Hamilton, HM SX; tel. (809)295-1567.*

• **Gerald D. Paley Realtor,** *Eurotile Building, Woodland Road, Pembroke; tel. (809)292-6208.*

• **Hope B. Bowker Real Estate,** *Vallis Building and Bermudian Road, Hamilton; tel. (809)295-0444.*

• **John Trimingham Realty,** *P.O. Box HS 10, Harrington Sound; tel. (809)293-2414.*

• **Lancelot Swan Real Estate,** *P.O. Box HM 318, Hamilton HM BX.*

• **Leonard O. Gibbons Real Estate,** *P.O. Box 875, Hamilton HM DX; tel. (809)292-4905.*

Buying a home

Non-Bermudians are not allowed to buy undeveloped land; houses with annual rental values of less than $37,000 (a house with an annual rental value of $37,000 costs about $1 million to buy); or multi-unit dwellings, apartments, or condominiums not included in the developments listed below, unless they have annual rental values of more than $13,200 (a condo with an annual rental value of $13,200 costs $300,000 or more to buy) and the buyer has a residential certificate or is related to a Bermudian.

Non-Bermudians *can* buy apartments or condominiums that are included in the developments listed below and that have annual rental values of more than $13,200. However, these apartments or condos cannot be rented out or used for tourist purposes.

Non-Bermudians can buy apartments or condominiums in the following developments: Mizzentop, Warwick; Deepdene, Smith's Parish; Mt. Wyndham; Pomander Gate Town Houses, Paget Paris; Inwood, Paget Parish; Villa Developments, Warwick Parish; Southdown Farm, Southampton Parish; Landmark, Southampton Parish; Grove Apartments, Smiths Parish; Panorama Apartments, Paget Parish; Cloverdale Apartments, Devonshire Parish; Grosvenor Apartments, Pembroke Parish; Queen's Cove, Pembroke Parish; Roxdene Apartments, Pembroke Parish; and St. James Court, St. James Village.

If you are interested in buying property in Bermuda, submit the necessary forms through a local lawyer. You must supply a banker's reference as well as two personal references from Bermudians or non-Bermudians (subject to the approval of the minister) who have known you for at least three years. You'll have to pay a fee of 15% of the purchase price of the property.

Domestic help

You can find domestic help through real estate agents for short-term rentals or through the **Government Employment Office,** *tel. (809)5-5151.* The average wage is $7 to $8 an hour for general maid service. Cooks are more expensive.

Every employer in Bermuda must pay a weekly contribution to social and medical insurance plans for employees who work more than four hours a week. For more information, contact the supervisor of the **Social Insurance Department,** *tel. (809)295-5151, extension 1136.*

Health care

Bermuda has a modern, well-equipped general hospital, King Edward VII Memorial, in Paget Parish. It is staffed by physicians from Bermuda, Great Britain, Canada, and the United States. The island has more than 60 doctors and 30 dentists, as well as 4 optometrists in Hamilton.

Foreign prescriptions are not honored in Bermuda. So it is advisable to see a Bermudian doctor immediately to establish a local contact.

Strangest sight

Bermuda's **Gombey Dancers,** grotesquely masked and costumed dancers, perform ritualistic dances on Boxing Day (Dec. 26) and Easter Monday. They are a strange sight that you shouldn't miss seeing. Listen for their haunting, rhythmical drum beat—and follow it.

Pets

You can bring animals into Bermuda if you have the proper papers. The island has no quarantine facilities, so animals arriving without proper documentation are returned to their points of origin. All animals need general health certificates issued by a licensed veterinarian within 10 days prior to arrival in Bermuda. Dogs and cats also need proof that they have not spent any time within the last six months in an official quarantined rabies area, as well as proof that they have been vaccinated since reaching the age of three months with an anti-rabies vaccine. Applications for bringing pets into Bermuda are available from the Bermuda Tourist Offices in New York and Chicago. For information, contact the **Department of Agriculture,** *P.O. Box 834, Hamilton 5.*

Banking

Several banks in Bermuda offer external U.S. accounts that allow you to deposit U.S. dollars and to write checks for most Bermuda charges without paying conversion fees. Check around—each bank has its own policy.

Brain fuel

The main branch of Bermuda's library is on Queen Street in Hamilton. Smaller branches are in St. George's and Somerset. You can get a library card free by presenting identification.

Adult education courses are available through Bermuda College and Warwick Academy. Watch for announcements in local newspapers. Pottery making is taught at the **Department of Commerce and Technology,** *tel. (809-292)5205.*

You can also take courses at Bermuda College and the U.S. Naval Air Station, which has branches of the University of Maryland, Los Angeles Community College, and Webster College. Call *(809-293)5111* for more information.

From September through June, Bermuda College operates two inexpensive cooking school restaurants, one in Warwick and the other in St. George's. Call *(809-292)6107* for more information.

Drawbacks

Portuguese men-of-war, which give a painful sting, are found in Bermuda's waters. Take some meat tenderizer or ammonia with you when you go to the beach. In emergencies, urine will help soothe the sting. For severe cases, go to the hospital for observation.

Rip tide is another hazard of the ocean. Note signs on public beaches and follow directions.

Mildew is a less dangerous, but more pervasive, part of life in Bermuda. It never seems to go away. Air out your house whenever possible, and consider buying a closet heater or a dehumidifier. A good tip for furniture (even antiques) is to dilute one-half cup of bleach in one gallon of water and wipe the area with the solution. Then wipe dry immediately. This should kill spores for a while. Local stores sell chemicals that soak up moisture.

Because Bermuda has few sources of fresh water, it depends on rainfall caught on roofs and stored in underground tanks. (House roofs are painted every two years with a lime substance that helps purify the water as it falls into the tanks.) Because of the short supply, Bermudians are very conscientious about conserving water.

Recommended reading

The following helpful books are available in Bermuda bookstores:
- *As A Matter of Fact,* published by the Altrusa Club.
- *Bermuda's Story* by Terry Tucker.
- *Dining Out in Bermuda, Lunch and Dinner Menus.*
- *Every Cyclist's Guide to Bermuda.*
- Fodor's *Bermuda.*
- *Guide to Bermuda's Public Parks and Beaches.*
- *Bermuda Islands Guide—Maps and Information.*

How to get to your Caribbean island

The following international airlines connect the United States with islands in the Caribbean:

• **Anguilla:** Air Anguilla, Carib Air, Crown Air, Winair, and LIAT.

• **Antigua:** Air Canada, American, BWIA, LIAT, and Pan Am.

• **Aruba:** American, and ALM.

• **Bahamas:** Air Canada, Bahamasair, Delta, Pan Am, TWA, United, Chalk's International, Trans Air, and other small carriers from Florida.

• **Barbados:** Air Canada, American, BWIA, Pan Am, and LIAT.

• **British Virgin Islands:** Air BVI, Crown Air, and LIAT.

• **Cayman Islands:** Cayman Airways and Northwest Airlines.

• **Dominica:** Air Caribe, Air Guadeloupe, Air Martinique, and LIAT.

• **Grenada:** BWIA and LIAT (connections via Barbados and Trinidad).

• **Guadeloupe:** Air Canada, Air France, Air Guadeloupe, American, and LIAT.

• **Puerto Rico:** American, Delta, Arrow, TWA, Air BVI, ALM, Arrow Air, BWIA, Coral Air, and Crown Air.

• **St. Kitts/Nevis:** BWIA, LIAT, and Pan Am.

• **St. Lucia:** Air Martinique, BWIA, LIAT, and Pan Am.

• **Sint Maarten/St. Martin:** American, Pan Am, Winair, Air Guadeloupe, ALM, BWIA, LIAT, and St. Lucia Airways.

• **St. Vincent:** Air Martinique and LIAT.

• **Trinidad and Tobago:** ALM, American, BWIA, LIAT, and Pan Am.

• **Turks and Caicos:** Atlantic Gulf, Bahamasair, Pan Am, and Turks and Caicos National Airlines.

• **U.S. Virgin Islands:** American, Pan Am, Midway, Air BVI, Aero Virgin Islands, Crown Air, LIAT, and Virgin Island Air.

For more information

Our favorite source of information on the Caribbean is a monthly newsletter called *Island Properties Report,* published by Gene Cowell, *P.O. Box 58, Woodstock, VT 05091; (802)457-3734.* An introductory subscription, which includes eight issues, four Quarterly Regional Reports, and membership in the Island Properties Report Travel Savings Plan, is $39 a year.

Other good sources of information include *Blueprint for Paradise* by Ross Norgrove, available from **Palm Tree Books,** *5500 Little Falls Road, Arlington, VA 22207,* and *How to Retire to the Caribbean* by Sydney Hunt, available from *Island Properties Report, address above.*

Chapter 8

Costa Rica

S̲ome 15,000 Americans live in Costa Rica; 6,000 of them are
retired. These numbers speak for themselves. Americans find this
Latin American country an attractive place to live. Costa Rica has
long, empty beaches and cool mountains, lush jungles filled with wild
orchids, a lively capital, an educated populace, and a stable government.

The pensionado program

And that's not all—Costa Rica also has a liberal pensionado
program that allows Americans to retire there on little money and to
import cars and household goods free of taxes or import duties. If you
have a secure income from a pension or retirement fund of at least
46,740 colons a month, you can become a resident of Costa Rica. And
you will be taxed only on income generated within the country.

The purpose of the pensionado program is to attract foreign
capital—and it's succeeding to the tune of $4.5 million per month.
Pensionados are granted all rights of citizenship, except the right to
vote. They are not permitted to earn a salary from a Costa Rican
employer or company, but they can own and manage businesses in
Costa Rica.

Under the laws of the pensionado program, you can import a
freezer, refrigerator, stove, microwave oven, washer, and dryer duty-
free (as long as they are intended for your own use only). However,
the government permits you to avoid only up to 543,300 colons in
import duties. After that, you must pay the taxes.

You can also import duty-free (or purchase duty-free through a
Costa Rican auto dealer) one automobile worth no more than 1.3-
million colons. You must pay a 10% sales tax and a 5% customs fee
on the total value of the car. If you decide to import your own car,
consider its age. It can be difficult to get spare parts for American cars
in Costa Rica, and not all roads are paved.

On the other hand, buying a car in Costa Rica is an expensive
proposition—a Honda Civic, for example, goes for nearly three times
as much as in the United States. However, the Costa Rican legislature

is considering cutting taxes and duties to 50% on certain economy cars, which would bring the cost within reach of the general population.

If you import a car, you may not sell it for five years. And you may lend it only to dependents and other non-Costa Ricans.

As a pensionado, you must reside in Costa Rica at least four months per year. And each year you must prove that your income is stable and permanent.

For details on how to apply to become a pensionado, contact the **Costa Rican Embassy,** *2112 S St. N.W., Washington, DC 20008; (202)234-2945,* or a Costa Rican consulate in the United States. A Costa Rican attorney will complete and file all appropriate application documents for 46,740 colons to 779,000 colons. It takes about 2 1/2 months to be approved as a pensionado.

A tax break

Costa Rica taxes only income generated inside the country. The rate is from 5% for incomes of 5,000 colons (after 15,000 colons and items such as life insurance and some bank deposits have been deducted) to 50% for incomes greater than 350,000 colons. No capital gains taxes are imposed.

A lower cost of living

U.S. citizens can live modestly on the outskirts of San José for less than 1.5-million colons per year—including the costs of one or two servants. Salaries for live-in maids are about 11,685 colons a month (you must also pay their social security). Part-time maids are a better deal. They charge only 78 colons an hour, and you don't have to pay their social security.

Residential electric bills greater than 2,337 colons a month are rare. Food—especially fresh vegetables and tropical fruits bought at farmers' markets—is an exceptional bargain. Bananas, for example, sell for a few cents per pound. According to the *Costa Rica Report* newsletter, broccoli is 31 cents per pound; onions are 27 cents per pound; oranges, 3.5 cents each; cauliflower, 37 cents per head; pineapples, 64 cents each; strawberries, 68 cents per basket; tomatoes, 19 cents per pound; melons, 35 cents per pound; and eggplants, 25 cents each. Visit the farmers' market, *avenida 10,* in San José, just west of the cemetery.

Entertainment, too, is a bargain by American standards. You can see a first-run movie in San José for 154.20 colons or enjoy a steak dinner at a good restaurant for 771 colons. A haircut is less than 154.20 colons.

The State Department's per-diem rate for an official visiting San José is $88, which is intended to cover lodging, meals, and incidentals, such as tips, dry cleaning, telephone calls, and local transportation. This should give you a good idea of what you can expect living expenses to be.

Of course, not everything is a bargain. Gasoline is expensive. Because of high tariffs, most imported goods, such as electric appliances, machinery, and automobiles, cost up to twice as much as in the United States. You may be better off purchasing locally manufactured goods instead. In general, the high prices of imports are more than offset by the inexpensive costs of food, clothing, and housing.

The drawbacks

The advantages to foreigners of living and doing business in Costa Rica are obvious and plentiful. The country remains a model democracy. It offers a good climate, friendly people, and civil rights for foreigners. Foreign income is not taxed. Prices are low. And the country is easily accessible. In Costa Rica, you can be a gentleman farmer without losing your shirt.

Despite all this, the number of American retirees seeking resident status in Costa Rica has been declining recently, because of the political situations in other Central American countries. Considering Costa Rica's somewhat shaky economic situation, the country's continued political stability and social harmony are surprising. Most people seem to forget that Costa Rica's foreign debt is huge. Inflation is 11.2%, and export earnings are declining.

San José has been plagued by an increase in petty theft. It is best not to carry your wallet in your hip pocket or to use a shoulder bag unless you sling it across your chest. Gringos are targets. However, the city is not plagued by violent crime. Thieves want only your money—if you fight back, they run.

But the quality of life enjoyed by Americans living in the country has scarcely been affected. San José is much less violent than American cities of comparable size, and you still can walk the streets after dark without fear of attack. The cost of living remains low for Americans. All in all, the advantages seem to outweigh the drawbacks.

Vital statistics

Costa Rica, about the size of West Virginia, is bordered by Nicaragua to the north and Panama to the south. It is cradled between the Pacific and the Caribbean. It is the second smallest Central American republic, after El Salvador.

About 60% of Costa Rica is covered with forest; 30% is used for agriculture.

The Costa Rican people are overwhelmingly of European descent. Although predominantly Spanish, many have German, Dutch, Swiss, French, or Belgian ancestry. The language is Spanish.

About 96% of the people are white, primarily Spanish or mestizo, a mixture of Spanish and Indian. Two percent of the population is black. (These people, of Jamaican descent, live on the Atlantic coast.) The population is only 2% Indian.

The Costa Rican government has accepted many thousands of refugees from other Central American countries. The influx of Nicaraguans has seriously stretched national resources.

Temperate tropics

While Costa Rica lies entirely within the tropics, its climate is tempered by the altitude. The weather is hot and muggy on the coastal lowlands, temperate in the highland plateau, and cool in the mountains. Most people live at altitudes of 3,000 to 4,000 feet, where the climate is spring-like year-round.

The average maximum temperature on the coast is 95 degrees Fahrenheit. San José escapes the crucifying heat of other Central American capitals; the temperature in the capital city ranges from 58 degrees Fahrenheit to 80 degrees Fahrenheit.

The country has 177 microclimates (even San José includes many microclimates), so you should be able to find one to your liking. In general, the Costa Rican climate is wet, which is why the countryside is so lush and green. While San José averages less than 1 inch of rain in February and only 12 inches in September, other parts of the country average 75 inches of rain per year.

During the rainy season, from May through November, mornings are generally sunny, while afternoons are interrupted by brief showers—not unlike the weather in Florida. In the fall, rain falls continuously for two weeks, turning roads into rivers. The rainfall is heavier throughout the year on the Caribbean side of the country. During the summer or dry season, from November to April, hardly a cloud passes overhead.

The lay of the land

Costa Rica has rich volcanic soil and a climate suited to growing anything from coffee (which likes cool weather) to bananas (which like a steamy environment).

A brilliant green dominates Costa Rica from November through May, a time when other Central American countries fade into a dusty tan.

San José, the capital, is a cosmopolitan city, filled with art galleries, bookstores, theaters, parks, fountains, trees, and gardens. The well-educated Costa Rican populace—almost everyone is literate—likes to keep up with the outside world. But old customs are preserved. While a band plays in the Parque Central, for example, young men and women walk around the park in opposite directions, keeping a speculative eye on the opposite sex.

San José sits in a beautiful and fertile valley, the **Meseta Central,** where two-thirds of the country's population resides. This 1,800-square-mile highland valley is also the center of most of Costa Rica's economic activity.

Turbulent rivers—such as the Reventazón—tumble down from the volcanic mountains of the Cordillera. The climate of the central plateau is spring-like year-round. Northeast of San José in the Meseta Central are four large volcanoes, two of which, Irazu and Poas, are intermittently active.

The Costa Rican city of **Liberia** sits in the foothills of the Rincón de la Vieja and Miravalles volcanoes. Known as the White City, its streets and walls are white from limestone. All houses in this 218-year-old town have two doors—one to the north, another to the east—to allow the maximum amount of sunlight to enter. Liberia is the capital of the agricultural province of Guanacaste. It has reasonably priced hotels, most with pools, and is a good place to stay while exploring the Pacific coast beaches, national parks, and volcanoes.

Just a few miles from Liberia is **Santa Rosa National Park,** where 20,000 parrot turtles spawn between July and December. The park also has beautiful white sand beaches: Playa Naranjo, Estero Real, Nancite, and Tule.

The jungles surrounding the Meseta Central harbor monkeys, parrots, iguana, scorpions, and 600 varieties of snakes. The giant leaves of the Gunnerainsignis measure six feet across and mingle with 1,000 different species of wild orchids clinging to every conceivable kind of tropical tree and shrub.

The coastal areas are hot, humid, heavily forested, and sparsely populated, with areas of low-lying swamps. The near-tideless Caribbean brushes the tropical beaches in the east. Most of Costa Rica's Caribbean coastline is covered with dense tropical forest. In places, you will feel as if you are in the islands—the culture is Caribbean, and the population is largely black. While the Caribbean lowlands comprise one-fourth of the country, they contain only 6% of the population. Most of the country's banana plantations are here.

On the Pacific coast are miles and miles of sheltered and unspoiled beaches.

Southern Costa Rica, with about 9% of the population, receives heavy annual rains. After a prolonged workers' strike, the banana plantations in the south rotted, and the United Fruit Company pulled out of the country.

A massive chain of rugged volcanic mountains rising more than 12,000 feet crosses Costa Rica from northwest to southeast. Cold and windswept **Chirripo Grande,** Costa Rica's highest peak, lies no more than 50 miles from either coast. Within the mountain areas are depressions (of which the Meseta Central is the principal one).

The government respects the natural beauty of Costa Rica and has set aside large areas as natural reserves. These areas attract scientists and researchers from all over the world. The entire **Osa Peninsula** near the border of Panama is one such area. It remains wild and primitive.

Is it healthy?

Costa Rica has a longer life expectancy—74 years—than several major European nations. And the medical facilities in San José outrank those in most other Latin American cities. There is 1 hospital bed for every 289 people.

Medical and dental facilities are excellent, and care is inexpensive. Malpractice insurance in unknown here. An eye examination costs less than 234 colons, and you can have a cavity filled by a dentist for 389 colons.

When you need medical care in San José, you can go either to one of the several good hospitals that are part of Costa Rica's national health-care system or to a private hospital. The former are substantially less expensive. American retirees can take advantage of the savings if, through membership in the **Associacion de Pensionados y Rentistas de Costa Rica** (Association of Pensionados and Rentistas), *Apartado 700-1011, San José,* they belong to the country's social security program. Family membership in the program costs 19,475 colons per month. Association dues are also 19,475 colons per year.

According to an article in the *Costa Rica Report* (February 1988), "As one who has a social security card, the patient gets free care, on the same basis as a Costa Rican citizen. This means a ward room and on-duty personnel. However, at modest added cost (5,453 colons per day), he can have a private room with a bath and a day-bed for a family member. All ancillary services (operating room, anesthesia, drugs, dressings, X-rays, pathology) are free."

The San José telephone directory lists no less than 40 categories of doctors, ranging from neurosurgeons and gastroenterologists to proctologists. Many of the country's doctors are trained at the Costa Rica University Medical School, then work as interns and residents in U.S. or European hospitals. Most speak fluent English.

Most of the hospitals that are part of Costa Rica's national health-care program—including San Juan de Dios, México, and Children's Hospital (all in San José)—are equipped with modern and sophisticated equipment that enables them to perform such operations as bone marrow transplants and the installation of cardiac pacemakers.

Private hospitals are also top-drawer, according to the *Costa Rica Report*. The Clínica Bíblica and the Clínica Católica are both equipped to perform a wide range of services, including surgery. At the latter, the first kidney transplant in Central America was successfully performed some years ago.

In the outlying areas, some 20 regional hospitals in the population centers are backed up by more than 60 local clinics.

Facilities for dental care are also good. And the cost of service is a fraction of what you'd pay in the United States. A subscriber to the *Costa Rica Report* wrote that when he was having dental problems, his U.S. dentist quoted him $7,000 for the necessary work. Instead, he took a three-week vacation in Costa Rica with his family, had the work done there, and returned home having saved about $3,000 after paying the dentist and the costs of the trip, including lodging, tours, meals, and entertainment!

Costa Rican plastic surgeons are world-famous for their expertise, and costs are only a fraction of U.S. prices. Many Americans needing plastic surgery go to the Clínica Bíblica, which is staffed with American nurse supervisors and local nurses.

Even Costa Rican's poor population was healthy until recent years, when refugees flooded across the border, bringing tuberculosis and malaria. Health authorities are working to combat the diseases. Costa Rica has one of the highest rates of stomach cancer in the world. The medical community is performing studies to see if this is related to the population's high intake of beef.

While malnutrition affects small segments of the population, Costa Ricans are well-fed compared with other Central American people. The most prevalent diseases, which include gastroenteritis and tuberculosis, are related to a lack of sanitation.

If you suffer from sinusitis, hay fever, or asthma, you may not want to retire in Costa Rica, because of the altitude and humidity. Even if you don't have any of these ailments, if you have not lived at high elevations before, you may experience a general slowdown at first. This usually passes within a few days.

The general level of sanitation and health controls in San José is comparable to that in most American cities. But you should avoid eating uncooked food as a precaution against intestinal disorders. Although malaria has been largely eradicated, it's a good idea to take anti-malarial drugs, if you plan to visit the lowlands.

Following is a list of Costa Rican hospitals:
- **Clínica Bíblica,** *tel. (506)21-54-22.*
- **Clínica Católica,** *tel. (506)25-50-55.*
- **Clínica Santa Rita,** *tel. (506)21-64-33.*
- **Hospital México,** *tel. (506)32-61-22.*
- **Hospital Nacional de Niños** (for children), *tel. (506)22-01-22.*
- **Hospital San Juan de Dios** (takes only local calls), *tel. (506)22-00-88.*

Dr. Oscar Ortiz, internist, *tel. (506)22-01-74,* and **Dr. Federico Sosto Peralta,** *tel. (506)22-81-90,* work as medical advisors to the U.S. embassy in Costa Rica.

No economic extremes

The extremes of wealth and poverty so prevalent in most of Central and Latin America are not evident in Costa Rica. Most residents own their own homes, although land in the city is expensive. Homes are typically constructed of concrete or weather-worn wood and have steep roofs and balconies. Most are decorated with flowering plants that frame the windows and doors.

President Oscar Arias, as part of his political platform, promised to overcome the dire housing shortage by constructing 80,000 housing units. Many thought this would be impossible, but construction is ahead of schedule. The little tin-shanty village that you would have seen on the road from the airport to San José five years ago has been replaced by a village of small cement houses, each with its own front yard and flower garden. Hundreds of these villages are scattered throughout Costa Rica. Families cannot rent homes in these villages; they must buy them, no matter how modest the payments. This creates a pride of ownership. In many cases, the residents themselves help with the construction.

Only about 8% of the population lives in absolute poverty. On the other end of the scale, the wealthy are not generally ostentatious in their way of life.

A stable government

Costa Rica is one of the few Central American countries where the form of government doesn't change with the tide. It holds the record for democratic transfer of power in a part of the world where government by coup is the rule rather than the exception.

Only 3 of Costa Rica's 50 presidents since independence have been military men, and the country has never suffered a major invasion or occupation by a foreign power.

A successful democracy since 1949, Costa Rica is neutral, does not have an army, and has a free-market economy. The army was abolished in 1949 and replaced by the National Guard. The nation practices non-intervention in the affairs of foreign governments.

President Arias was awarded a Nobel Peace Prize in 1987 for his efforts to find a peaceful solution to the troubles in Central America. His work culminated in the signing of the Esquipulas Agreement by five area presidents, which set up the mechanics for amnesty and cease-fires in Nicaragua and El Salvador in November 1987.

Costa Rica was one of the first countries to ratify the American Convention of Human Rights and continues to be a strong supporter of international and domestic human rights. The Inter-American Institute of Human Rights Court is based in San José.

The biggest cloud over Costa Rica is the threat to its stability from the war in Nicaragua. Since 1984, the Costa Rican government has forbidden Contra guerrillas to train behind the Costa Rican border.

In the event of foreign attack, Venezuela, Mexico, and Panama have promised to come to Costa Rica's defense, as has the United States.

However, few Costa Ricans express concern about invasion from Nicaragua. When Ambassador Jeanne Kirkpatrick suggested that the United States provide military aid rather than loans to Costa Rica, the Costa Rican government firmly declined.

173

Costa Rica probably will continue to be plagued by annoying incidents along its northern border, but the country should remain otherwise undisturbed.

Paperwork

As an American citizen arriving by air, you need proof of American citizenship, a passport with a Costa Rican visa (for longer visits), a ticket for onward passage, a tourist card (which can be purchased for $2 from airlines), and sufficient funds for your planned stay in the country. As an overland traveler, you need a passport and a visa.

Visas are valid for up to 30 days. If you stay longer, you must get an exit permit from the Department of Migration in the Ministry of Public Security in San José and pay an emigration tax of about 350.55 colons.

If you want to take your pet to Costa Rica with you, you must obtain an importation permission form for pets. Contact the **Jefe del Departamento de Zoonosis,** *Ministerio de Salud, P.O. Box 10123, San José.* Your pet must have certificates showing that it has been vaccinated against rabies, distemper, hepatitis, and leptospirosis, as well as a health certificate testifying that it is free from external and internal parasites. This must be signed by a registered veterinarian, notarized, and stamped by the clerk of your U.S. county. The rabies shot must be more than 30 days old but no more than 3 years old. If you don't follow the rules, your cat or dog could be held in quarantine for six months.

To import an animal other than a dog or cat, you must contact the Department of Agriculture in San José. Check with the nearest embassy or consulate for more information.

Money matters

Costa Rica's monetary unit is the colon, which is divided into 100 centimos. Bank notes are divided into 5, 10, 20, 50, 100, 500, and 1,000 colons. Coins come in units of 25 and 50 centimos and 1, 2, 5, and 10 colons.

The colon is devalued about once a month. Costa Rica has brought its inflation rate down to about 9%, and the dollar holds its own because of these mini-devaluations. However, wages for Costa Ricans are declining in real terms along with the devaluations, causing some discontent.

The average middle-income Costa Rican family earns 38,950

colons to 46,740 colons per month. So if you live like the local residents, you can do very well on 46,740 colons per month and extremely well on 93,480 colons a month.

Because of the slow devaluations, the street and bank exchange rates differ little. And the 5% difference is not worth risking the possibility of getting stuck with Colombian-made counterfeit colons.

When traveling in Costa Rica, carry traveler's checks and U.S. currency, which is the most acceptable foreign currency. However, don't exchange more than you expect to use, because it is sometimes difficult to exchange colons for dollars. The central bank, the **Banco Central de Costa Rica,** *Apartado 10058, San José,* has a currency-exchange office at the San José International Airport. *La Nación,* a local newspaper, prints the unofficial top currency-exchange rate every day.

A good way to ensure that you don't exchange more currency than you'll use is to change money daily rather than in one lump sum. Tourists can change a limited number of dollars at their hotels. You need a passport to exchange currency.

A cashier service for receiving deposits and cashing checks operates at most banks in San José Monday through Saturday from 8 a.m. to 7 p.m. When a foreign check is deposited into a Costa Rican account, it is automatically frozen for one month before the funds are credited to the account. One way around this is to cash foreign checks on the black market, then deposit the cash, which is credited the next day.

In 1982, the Costa Rican central bank not only prohibited the purchase of goods and services with U.S. dollars, but it also banned the quotation of prices in dollars or any other foreign currency. Even hotel rates must be quoted in colons. So memorize the currency-exchange rate before you go—it will save you time and frustration.

Change your colons back to dollars at airport banks, but remember that they will not exchange more than 3,895 colons. Another word of advice about banking: Be patient. Lines can be long. Banks are open Monday through Friday from 8 a.m. to 11 a.m. and 1:30 p.m. to 3 p.m.; Saturday from 8 a.m. to 11 a.m.

Only the four state-owned banks offer checking and savings accounts: Banco de Costa Rica, Banco Crédito Agrícola de Cartago, Banco Nacional, and Banco Anglo-Costarricense.

Buying property in Costa Rica

Property in Costa Rica is a real bargain. Although prices have increased now that the fighting around Costa Rica has cooled down some, most homes remain reasonably priced compared with homes in the United States. This is an excellent time to acquire a Costa Rican farm, a beach retreat, or an elegant house in one of San José's upper-class neighborhoods. You can buy an acre of planted coffee for about 1.2-million colons. Good farmland starts at 31,160 colons an acre.

Costa Rican law protects the private ownership of land. For the most part, foreigners have the same rights as citizens, but some restrictions are imposed. One restriction concerns land given or sold to a citizen by Costa Rica as part of a land distribution program—this land is not initially transferable to foreigners. Another restriction, which applies to all, is that most coastal land 200 meters inland from the high tide line is state-owned and cannot be sold. (Some of this beach land can be leased.)

Red tape

To own property in Costa Rica, you do not have to be a citizen, a formal resident, or even present in the country.

The country's real estate profession is at an early stage of development. The best brokers can supply copies of land titles, registered plot plans, and sometimes photographs of the property. They should also be able to answer questions about possible squatter problems, the water supply, and any plans for building roads near or on the property.

Sales contracts are not standardized; therefore, your lawyer should check all contracts carefully. Costa Rica Escrow S.A. is the only escrow company in the country.

Acquiring the title to a piece of property is not as routine as in the United States. But the title registration is usually protected against hidden claims. Titles are inscribed at a central national property registry, and any legal change in the status of a title must be recorded at the registry as well. Titles are handwritten in a lawyer's protocol book and then in the county court's book.

Although the local attitude toward title searches may seem relaxed, you should give your full attention to the writing of a title. Whatever is recorded in the protocol book is fixed, so be absolutely sure that boundaries, rights of way, and all other details are written down accurately. Costa Rica has no title search companies and no title insurance. To protect yourself, retain your own lawyer to perform a complete search for you. And remember that checking on titles takes time.

When you're interested in buying a piece of property, make an offer in writing, including a description of the property and all details of the transaction. This is usually accompanied by a cashier's check for 10% of the purchase price, which is held in escrow by the real estate company. You have 30 to 90 days from the date of the offer to complete the purchase. If you back out of the deal, the escrow is forfeited. Usually, you must expect to pay cash or to arrange your own financing—although in some cases you may find two- to eight-year owner financing.

Banks do not finance the purchase of land, except in a few cases. And if they do agree to provide financing, they charge extremely high interest rates—as much as 31% per month. Home loans can be obtained more easily from the national insurance company and the finance companies of the national banking system. Arranging a loan is an extremely long process, and interest rates are high.

If you don't plan to live in your house year-round, consider renting it out when you are away. Costa Rica has rent control laws, which prohibit rent increases for five years if the same Costa Rican tenant is inhabiting the property. After five years, however, rent can be increased as much as 50%. Costa Rica has no fair-housing laws.

If you buy property in a good area and then rent it out, you can expect low vacancy rates—about one month or less. People stay in hotels waiting for houses to become available. Rentals in the western suburbs get top dollar and have tripled in price over the last five years.

The market is tight for building expensive houses, so higher priced homes are becoming even more expensive. Appreciation is difficult to define, because of the devaluation of Costa Rican currency. Real estate taxes are low, but they are being upgraded.

An important first step to a successful real estate investment in Costa Rica is enlisting the services of a real estate agent licensed by the Chamber of Real Estate Brokers. Beware of the taxi driver or intermediary who says he can get property for you cheaper. Also beware of those who charge fees, generally about $100 a day, to help you find a house. You'll come across two or three phony agents for every licensed agent you find.

One reliable, knowledgeable real estate agent is Irma Morice de Petersen. She and her American husband Al own **Find-A-Home,** *Apartado 444, Centro Colón, San José; tel. (506)33-52-15.* They deal in beach and farm properties, as well as property in San José. Many of their remote and isolated listings are on video. Find-A-Home has been in business for eight years and serves a clientele that is 95% expatriate, including many Americans.

Another real estate agent is Margaret L. Sohn, with Aria Fraenkel S.A., a leading San José firm specializing in properties for foreigners. She can be reached at *P.O. Box 981, Centro Colón, 1007 San José.*

Where and when to buy

Exceptional deals are often found when an owner is forced or anxious to sell. A common example is the American retiree who moves to Costa Rica when he's 50 years old, stays 10 or 20 years, then suddenly decides to return to the United States. A person in this situation is usually more concerned with making the sale than with getting the best price. And he often wants to sell lock, stock, and barrel, so you can pick up everything you need at a good price.

Although you can find a pleasant, middle-class house built for a local resident for much less than you'd pay for a comparably sized house in the United States, a large bathroom and an efficient, modern kitchen may not be part of the package. You may prefer to buy from an American who has renovated or built his own house.

The western suburbs of San José are considered *the* places to buy. Most expatriates and diplomats live in these areas. **Escazu** is especially attractive. Because such a large number of diplomats live here, security is tight—a benefit for residents. And the American, German, and English schools are in this area.

Once a small, rural settlement, Escazu has seen a building surge in recent years. Elegant Spanish mansions and tiny *peón* houses mingle with modern bungalows. Escazu has three modest shopping centers and several supermarkets. A new highway puts the community within reach of the business district. You should be able to find a three-bedroom house in Escazu for as little as 4.3-million colons, but most sell for between 11.7-million colons and 46.7-million colons.

Another elegant and even newer community surrounds the Cariari Country Club. Houses here start at 7.8-million colons and go up to 779-million colons. This is an elegant community, with an 18-hole golf course, tennis courts, and a first-class restaurant.

Other neighborhoods to consider in San José include **La Sabana** and **Los Yoses**. Both are near the university and popular among Americans. Unfortunately, Los Yoses is becoming a neighborhood of offices rather than homes. La Sabana is nice, but **Rohmosser** is now the in place, because of the gorgeous new American embassy being built there, and housing prices have shot up.

Some find Escazu too windy and Los Yoses too rainy. If you

agree, consider **San Isidro,** on the other side of the city from Escazu, instead. This suburb is known for its mild climate.

Moravia, farther away from San José, also attracts Americans.

At the **El Bosque** development in San Francisco de Dos Ríos, San José, small but comfortable two- to three-bedroom houses go for about 1.9-million colons. Amenities, such as water heaters, tiled bathrooms, and kitchen cabinets, can be added for less than 779,000 colons. Many expatriates find this development attractive.

The farther you go from San José, the more land you can get for your money. The best deals are the isolated properties, which allow you to leave hectic urban living behind. But remember, when you decide to sell the property, it probably will be a great deal for the next purchaser, too.

In the countryside a half-hour from San José, a two-bedroom furnished house with maid's quarters, verandas, gardens, a lawn, a fence, trees, and a pool on five acres of hillside costs about 9.8-million colons.

For a fraction of East and West coast prices in the United States, you can buy a palatial beach house on Costa Rica's lovely Caribbean shore. Beach houses here sell for between 3.1-million colons and 14-million colons; beach condos are available from 61-million colons.

Nicoya Peninsula, on the Pacific coast, is an up-and-coming area. Although it takes two to five hours of driving on bumpy roads to get to Nosaro or Tamarindo, you can fly to these places from San José in only 20 minutes. **Flamingo** has a new marina, a plush new hotel, and excellent condo apartments—all of which are helping to make this area a good sailing and fishing center.

Farther down the Nicoya Peninsula, **Tango Mar,** a beautiful private community, is developing as a beach and riding club. It boasts fine horses, including a couple of paso finos. If Tango Mar's cook stays, all of San José will be knocking at the door. He is terrific.

Development is also picking up near **Quepos** and **Mañuel Antonio Beach and National Park,** also on the Pacific coast. Prices are especially reasonable in these areas, where real estate dealing is relatively new.

Renting

If you are looking to buy property, Costa Rica is a buyer's market. If you want to rent, it's an owner's market—many people moving to Costa Rica are choosing to rent rather than buy. However, you still can find a rental for less than you'd pay in the United States.

Apartments in San José rent for about 17,527 colons to 31,160 colons per month.

Apartment complexes in San José include **Apartamentos Van Fossen,** *P.O. Box 7428; tel. (506)53-16-86;* **Apartamentos Escazu,** *Aptdo. 258, Centro Colón 1007; tel. (506)28-26-11;* and **Residencias de Golf,** *P.O. Box 5548; tel. (506)39-10-20.*

Buying a piece of land

Buying land is a good way to go. You can buy cattle pasture land for 7,011 colons to 21,033 colons per acre; timber land for less than 7,790 colons per acre; and dairy land and mechanizable crop land for 14,022 colons to 42,066 colons per acre.

Beach acreage is about 27,265 colons to 77,900 colons per acre, with lots running from 311,600 colons to 2,726,500 colons per quarter-acre.

While you can find land for 77,900 colons to 311,600 colons per acre in the Central Valley, prices skyrocket the closer you get to San José. Quarter-acre lots in prime areas start at 5-million colons.

Outside the San José area, lack of highway access, electric power, and municipal water can cause problems. However, the time to buy this kind of property may be before these improvements are made and the prices go up.

Most land is financed by the seller. Usually, you'll have to make a large down payment and agree to terms of two to five years and high interest rates.

Land involved in a land redistribution program by the government is not initially transferable to foreigners. It may be acquired after the original owner has held it for a specified period. In cases where the government has expropriated land, the courts tend to be more sympathetic to the owner than to the government. And such expropriation must be by due process of the law.

Certain land areas are reserved for ownership by nationals, including Indian reserve lands and other areas bought from private owners to be redistributed to the poorer segments of the population.

The government owns all coastal land to 200 meters inland from the mean high tide line. The first 50 meters are considered public land and inalienable. The remaining 150 meters can be bought for private use from the nearest municipal government.

The tourist bureau has special powers in areas thought to be of particular national interest for tourism and recreation.

Under the Beach Law of 1977, you can obtain a lease for beach property if you are a Costa Rican citizen, a foreigner with five years' residence, or a Costa Rican corporation with 50% Costa Rican shareholders. The leases are inexpensive, run for one year, and can be renewed 10 times before being renegotiated. A lease gives the lessee exclusive use of the property.

A few places, including Samara Bay, sell lots that are actually in the maritime lease zone. Prices run from 155,800 colons to 779,000 colons per half-acre.

Some areas along the coast offer title up to the 50-meter line. These deals are exceptions to the rule, and you should be wary of them. Most land with title up to the 50-meter line is in Junquillal, Tamarindo, and Playa del Coco. Developed quarter-acre lots range from 623,200 colons to 1,947,500 colons.

Building a home

If you plan to build your dream house in Costa Rica, expect to spend about 1,550 colons to 2,726 colons per square foot on construction and materials. Construction costs in San José are generally half those in the outlying areas, but this is balanced by the higher price of property near the capital.

Local engineers and architects are competent and can take care of obtaining the necessary permits. They must sign off on the design to assure that it conforms to code and anti-earthquake design standards. Employ only professionals who are locally licensed.

If you bring building plans with you from the United States, make certain the measurements are translated from feet into meters by someone who really knows math and building techniques. The best way to find a contractor is through word-of-mouth; ask for—and check—references. And plan to be on-site to oversee the job's progress.

The typical construction is steel-reinforced cement block on top of reinforced concrete footings. Popular roofing materials are galvanized corrugated iron and corrugated asbestos cement roofing. A Spanish-tile roof is expensive and requires a lot of maintenance.

The hardwoods that grow in Costa Rica are excellent for both decorative and structural purposes. They are expensive by local standards but much cheaper than in the United States.

Where to stay while you're looking

The **Ambassador,** *Paseo Colón; tel. (506)21-8155,* is a first-class hotel with rooms for 2,331 colons to 5,063 colons per night. The

181

Gran Hotel Costa Rica, *tel. (506)21-4000,* downtown opposite the National Theater, is a local meeting place. Rooms are 2,802 colons to 4,050 colons. **Bougainvillea,** *tel. (506)33-6622,* across the river and five minutes from the city, has lovely decor and great food. Rooms are 1,947 colons to 2,331 colons per night. The **Plaza,** *avenida Central; tel. (506)22-5533,* is small and clean, with rooms for 1,502 colons to 2,103 colons per night. **Pensión Otoya,** *avenida Central; tel. (506)21-3925,* a quiet place with big rooms, charges 428 colons per night for a room with bath.

Finding friends

The Kiwanis Club is popular among American retirees. And the Club Amateur de Pesca, Costa Rica's International Game Fishing Association affiliate, is active. Other social and service clubs in San José include the Rotary, the Lions, and the Jaycees.

Touring Costa Rica

Before you settle in Costa Rica permanently, visit the country to make sure you like the lifestyle and to determine where you want to live.

Retirement Explorations, *19414 Vineyard Lane, Saratoga, CA 95070; (408)257-5378,* leads tours to Costa Rica for Americans interested in retiring there. Tours include inspections of real estate and information seminars conducted by government officials, doctors, lawyers, businessmen, realtors, and cultural experts. You'll also visit with Americans who live in Costa Rica and can tell you firsthand what it's like there.

Central American Tours, headed by Jorge Taylor, *Apartido 531, San José; tel. (506)23-08-50,* is a good tour company.

If you'd like to explore Costa Rica on your own—and you have a taste for adventure—consider taking the Atlantic Railroad (also known as the Jungle Train), which cuts through treacherous jungle and steep mountain passes on its way from San José to the coast. Four-thousand men died building this engineering feat. The entire trip takes 8 hours, with 52 stops.

The most spectacular part of the trip is through the **Cordillera Central,** a majestic dormant volcanic range often shrouded in mist. The train stops here in Cartago, the original capital of Costa Rica, destroyed by earthquakes in 1841 and 1910. This city's most famous sight is the white Basilica of Nuestra Señora de Los Angeles, which houses La Negrita, an Indian image of the Virgin, who is said to have

182

appeared in this city in 1810. The basilica also has a bubbling spring believed to have healing powers. Believers from all over Central America make pilgrimages here.

The train also winds its way through coffee plantations in the Meseta Central. It then follows the rushing Reventazón River through the Orosi Valley. Tiny villages break the wilderness. In places you'll see ox carts.

Near the coast, the atmosphere is Caribbean. The weather is hot and humid. Black women carry baskets on their heads. Houses are built on stilts. As the train nears Limón, its final destination, you'll pass palm trees rustling in the breeze and the glimmering blue sea.

For more information on the Atlantic Railroad, contact the **Costa Rica Tourist Office** in the United States or Costa Rica, *addresses below*.

If you don't have time for the entire train trip, you can still get a feeling for Costa Rica by taking part of the trip and returning by bus or plane. Twice a week, the train features a special car with a guide, soft seats, and liquor (other cars in the train have hard wooden seats and few amenities), for those who want to sample the ride in comfort for just a few hours.

A bit of history

Columbus discovered Costa Rica in 1502 on his fourth and final voyage. He named it Costa Rica, meaning rich coast, believing that is was rich in gold.

Costa Rica is one of the few countries in the Americas that can count its revolutions on only one hand. That may be because the country has no impoverished *campesino* (peasant) class trying to live off meager plots of land, as in Mexico and elsewhere in Latin America.

Costa Rican lore claims that the arriving Spanish found the native Indians so dangerous that even the governor of the colony tilled his own garden rather than relying on enslaved Indian labor.

Little evidence remains of the Spanish-American hacienda system, under which large plantations were farmed by poor tenants. In part, that is because the most fertile land is in mountainous areas best suited for small farming units rather than big plantations.

Because of the country's apparent lack of minerals, Costa Rica was not particularly interesting to the original Spanish government, so the colony developed without the influence of Spanish grandees and the class distinctions they would have emphasized. Costa Rica was not affected by the pomp and circumstance of Spanish lords. It developed autonomously, with fewer outside influences than any other Central American nation.

In 1821, Costa Rica declared independence from Spain in a non-violent revolution. In 1824, it became a state of the Federal Republic of Central America. The republic collapsed 14 years later—after a series of revolutions—and Costa Rica resumed its independence.

The current Costa Rican government is a republic with seven provinces. Every four years, Costa Ricans vote for a president, 2 vice-presidents, and 57 deputies of a unicameral assembly. Neither the president nor the deputies may succeed themselves. Restraints are placed on the president that limit his functions and authority more than in most Latin American countries.

The constitution provides for a free, open, and competitive electoral system. No political party is outlawed or excluded from the process.

Personal experiences

While Costa Rica is an attractive place to retire, not all Costa Rican retirees report pleasant experiences. Paul Goodyear wrote the following letter to *International Living* newsletter (**Agora Inc.,** *824 E. Baltimore St., Baltimore, MD 21202*) in January 1987:

"Having lived in Costa Rica for five years (1971 to 1976), I feel that I have had experiences that would be helpful to your readers.

"The Costa Ricans do have a wonderful pensionado program—on paper! Friends built a luxurious, beautiful home in Carriaci and brought in new and expensive furniture on their pensionado papers. It took several months for the furniture to clear customs. Then, when released, there was a hole in each and every pillow and the backs of the sofa and chairs, as well as the overstuffed arms. Inquiry as to the reason for the damage brought the answer that officials were searching for dope. So they had rammed a half-inch rod through everything. Duty-free? Yes, but the repairs were exorbitant and amateurish. And because only one set of furniture can be imported, the couple had no choice but to have the damaged pieces repaired.

"Another friend brought in his car duty-free. When he went to Puerto Limon to pick it up, the tires were thin and treadless, although he had purchased a new set in anticipation of exporting his car to his new home. The spare was missing, as were all the tools he had stowed in the trunk. Again, the costs of the replacements made the duty-free label a joke.

"When we left in disgust in 1976, Americans were leaving in hordes. Many people who had invested in homes sold them at distress prices. Everyone felt lucky just to get out of the country."

On the other hand, Lawrence Martin, an American living in Alajuela, Costa Rica, wrote a letter to *International Living* (April 1986) highly praising his new home:

"Having only left the United States 1 1/2 years ago, I find the cost of living in Costa Rica about 50% less than back home. Our bank pays all our bills, taxes, and employees automatically every month without service charges. As a fledgling gourmet, I find the food...to be some of the best anywhere in the world.

"True enough, taxes on many goods are extremely high, but foreigners...are provided special benefits that make the maximum tax payable 15% on most goods."

Jim Fendell, an American businessman in Costa Rica, says that Americans must leave their conventional attitudes behind when they move to Costa Rica. Clenched fists and a raised voice will get you nowhere. Costa Ricans are polite and respond best when treated similarly. He notes that Americans often forget that a card of thanks or a bouquet of flowers is greatly appreciated in return for a favor. (Whereas you pay your way in Mexico, for example, money is an insult in Costa Rica.)

Getting there

Miami is a 2 1/2-hour flight from San José. Connecting services are operated from Miami by Eastern, PanAm, and LACSA (the major Costa Rican airline). TACA flies to Costa Rica from Houston.

Miscellaneous notes

In San José, garbage is collected regularly, and there is a central sewer system. Sanitary regulations, however, are not always rigidly enforced.

Because the waiting list for a telephone is long, it is best to purchase or rent a home with a phone already installed.

Air conditioners and central heating are not necessary in most homes. But an electric heater is nice for chilly days. Dehumidifiers also are a good idea, because humidity averages about 78%. Mildew and mold can be problems during the rainy season.

Electronic water filtering systems are available in San José at reasonable rates.

Colds and flu are common, because of the dampness during the rainy season and the quick change of temperature from midday to evening.

Flower gardens decorate practically every home in Costa Rica, and gardeners are inexpensive.

For more information

Contact the following organizations for more information on retiring in Costa Rica:

• **Asociacion de Pensionados y Rentistas De Costa Rica,** *Apartado 700, 1011 San José,* or *Apartado 6386, 1000 San José; tel. (506)23-1733.*

• **Center for the Promotion of Exports and Investments** (CENPRO), *Apartado 5418, 1000 San José.*

• **Costa Rican Coalition for Development Initiatives** (CINDE), *Apartado 7170, 1000 San José.*

• **Costa Rican Embassy,** *2112 S St. N.W., Washington, DC 20008; (202)234-2945.*

• **Costa Rican Tourist Board** in California, *3540 Wilshire Blvd., Suite 707, Los Angeles, CA 90010; (800)762-5909* or *(213)382-8080.*

• **Costa Rican Tourist Board** in Costa Rica, *Apartado Postal 777, 1000 San José.*

• **Costa Rican Tourist Board** in Florida, *(800)327-7033 or (305)358-2150, extension 200 in Florida.*

• **FIABCI** (the International Real Estate Federation), *777 14th St. N.W., Washington, DC 20005; (202)383-1032.*

• **LACSA** (the Costa Rican airline), *c/o Victor Vidal, Room 242, 630 Fifth Ave., New York, NY 10111; (212)245-6370* or *(800)225-2272.*

• **Retirement Explorations,** *19414 Vineyard Lane, Saratoga, CA 95070; (408)257-5378.*

The following books and publications are also good sources of information on living in Costa Rica:

• *Costa Rica Report, Apartado 6283, 1000 San José* ($39 for 12 issues).

• *Costa Rica Traveler,* by Ellen Searby, available from **Windham Bay Press,** *P.O. Box 34283, Juneau, AL 99803* ($11.95).

• *New Key to Costa Rica,* by Beatrice Blake, available from the *Costa Rica Report, Apartado 6283, 1000 San José,* or **Bookpeople,** *2929 Fifth St., Berkeley, CA 94710; (800)227-1516* ($11.95).

• *Tico Times, Apartado 4632, San José* ($16.50 for three months).

Chapter 9

Ecuador

E̲cuador may not strike you as a perfect retirement haven. You may not even be sure exactly where Ecuador is located (it's between Columbia and Peru on the Pacific Coast of South America). But because it is little-known, Ecuador is all the more attractive. This lovely little country has not been invaded by tourists, despite its ideal climate, mountain scenery, and incredibly low prices.

Although it lies on the equator, much of Ecuador has springlike weather year-round, because of its high altitude. The climate along the coast and in the eastern jungles is hot and humid. But temperatures in the Andes are cool, and rain usually falls in the evening. The highest recorded temperature in Quito is 86 degrees Fahrenheit. The lowest is 32. Not very taxing by U.S. standards! Temperatures usually range from 45 to 73 degrees Fahrenheit.

Ecuador is a politically stable and relatively crime-free country. Quito is safe, unless you are traveling through the Old City at night, when you should look out for pickpockets. Be cautious in Guayaquil, however, which is notorious for its thieves and pickpockets. Outside the cities, crime is rare. And the entire country is virtually free of violent crime.

Ecuador surfaces in the headlines only on those rare occasions when an earthquake occurs, a volcano erupts, or the ancient border war with Peru flares momentarily. It is a country of breathtaking scenery and amazingly varied terrain—from lush tropical rain forests to stark deserts, from sparkling sandy beaches and tourist resorts on the west coast to towering snow-capped Andean peaks. One peak, Chimborazo (20,500 feet), is almost as high as Mt. Everest.

Conquering the paperwork

To visit Ecuador as a tourist, you must have a valid passport and a round-trip ticket. A tourist visa is not required if you are staying 90 days or less. For longer stays, obtain a visa from immigration authorities upon arrival in Ecuador.

If you wish to live in Ecuador, you must request a visa from the nearest Ecuadorean consulate or the Ecuadorean Embassy in Washington, D.C. Six visas are offered—retirees are most likely to apply for visas I, II, or VI.

Visa I

This visa is for immigrants who can support themselves from bonds, stocks, or any permanent income coming from overseas. Applicants for this visa must prove a monthly income of $1,000 per person ($350 per dependent over 18).

To get this visa you must show the original, permanent copy of your federal income tax return. It must be notarized, legalized, and authenticated by an Ecuadorean consul and the Ministry of Foreign Relations with jurisdiction in Quito. Or you can submit an original deposit receipt showing you have $5,000 (enough money for five years) at the Central Bank of Ecuador.

Visa II

This visa is for investors in Ecuadorean real estate, money certificates, stocks, or security bonds (from the state or national credit institutions) worth a minimum of $50,000.

To get this visa, you must show copies of property deeds and registered stocks, bonds, or trusts. If your investment has not yet been finalized, you can obtain a provisional visa by depositing 25,000 sucres at the Central Bank of Ecuador (arrange the deposit through the General Foreign Relations Officer). You must finalize your investment within 90 days, or you lose your deposit and your visa is canceled. When your investment is finalized, you receive your residence permit and your deposit is returned.

Visa III

This visa is for responsible individuals (it excludes partnerships or corporations with stockholders) investing in industry, agriculture, cattle farming, or export commerce for a minimum of $75,000.

Visa IV

This visa is for those performing administrative or technical functions in general or specialized industries; institutions; private lenders; and judicial or civil service people in the country through powers of attorney or working contracts.

Visa V

This visa is for diverse professions, technical professions exercised within accordance of the Law of Superior Education or by international contracts or international treaties.

Visa VI

This visa is for the dependents of residents of Ecuador (Ecuadorean or foreign).

Additional information

Wives and husbands of residents of Ecuador must show a marriage certificate or certificate of kinship that has been notarized, legalized, and authenticated by an Ecuadorean consul. This document must be translated into Spanish. You'll also need a notarized guarantee of solvency from your sponsor (husband, parent, or close relative) and a copy of your sponsor's Ecuadorean identification card and voter's registration certificate.

When applying for all six visas, the following are required: a passport valid for at least six months from the date the visa is issued and a copy of your police record.

An individual visa also covers your husband or wife, father, mother, children, brothers, sisters, and grandchildren. Sons, brothers, and male grandchildren may live as dependents only until they are 18. Daughters, sisters, and granddaughters may live as dependents as long as they remain single.

A word to the wise: Before applying for a visa, brush up on your Spanish. We found embassy and consular officials friendly and helpful, but their English was rudimentary at best.

Looking at real estate

In Quito, you can rent a new, beautifully furnished two-bedroom, two-bath apartment in the posh Avenida Gonzalo Suarez area, near the Intercontinental Quito Hotel. These apartments have fantastic views of the surrounding mountains and cost between $500 and $800 a month. However, if you want to live just as luxuriously for less, you can rent the same apartment for between $300 and $400 in other residential areas that are just as pleasant and offer the same breathtaking views.

You can buy an unfurnished two-bedroom, two-bath apartment with a kitchen, living room, dining room, and servants' quarters for as little as $30,000, just minutes from downtown. Most affluent Ecuadoreans own both an apartment or house in the city and a hacienda in the countryside. The Valley of Chillos, just 20 minutes from Quito, is ideal. So is Conocoto.

It is best to rent through a real estate agency, such as **Cobira,** *Ave. Republica 189, Almagro;* **Servimandato,** *Juan Rodriguez 159;*

or **Lucy Pita,** *Carlos Montufar 380, Quito.*

Or, if your Spanish is good, you might look through the classified ads in one of the local newspapers (prices are sometimes lower this way): *El Comercio, El Universo, Mercurio,* or *Telegrofo.*

Living costs in Cuenca are even cheaper than in Quito. A Spanish-style house with a red-tiled roof and a patio and garden can be rented for as little as $250 to $325 a month. The local tourist office, Dituris, can provide you with the name of a real estate agent.

Ecuador's low cost of living

Prices are low in Ecuador. Dinner for two at a good restaurant is only $7. A double room in a deluxe hotel is about $65. A taxi ride from the airport to downtown Quito is $1. Gas is 40 cents a gallon. A finely woven Panama hat can be purchased for $15 to $30. And a bus ride almost anywhere in Quito is never more than 8 cents.

Americans and other foreigners living and working in Ecuador (including embassy personnel, petroleum executives, and missionaries) hire multiple maids: one to do the cleaning, one to take care of the children, and another for kitchen duties. And why not, when Indian help can be had for as little as $40 to $50 a month? Agencies for hiring maids include **Agencia de Empleos San Cayetano,** *Sucre 544,* and **Agencia Comercial de Colocaciones,** *Benalcazar 418, Bolivar.*

No restrictions are placed on foreign currency in Ecuador. You can buy or sell any amount. Local banks offer savings accounts with interest rates that are currently as high as 25% (for sucre, not dollar, accounts).

The Ecuadorean lifestyle

Ecuadoreans (especially in Quito) love to go out in the evening to dine and dance. Hotels throughout the country feature gambling casinos, entertainment, and orchestras for dancing. *Peña folkloricas* are nightclubs with folk music and dancing. Audience participation is encouraged. The **Pacha Mama** is one of the most popular in Quito.

Restaurants, bars, and hotels automatically add a 10% service charge to your bill, but an additional moderate gratuity is expected if the service is good.

Not all taxis have meters, but drivers are usually honest and rarely overcharge.

Siesta is observed throughout Ecuador. Shops, banks, and other places of business generally close from noon until 3 p.m. As in Spain, it is fashionable to dine late—about 9 p.m. But you should always be able to find one restaurant in every deluxe or first-class hotel that stays open all day.

Soccer, or *futbol,* is a national passion. Most towns in Ecuador have a team, and games are played on weekends in Quito and Otavalo. Bullfights are also popular. *Pelota de guante* (gloveball), a peculiar Ecuadorean game, is played with a leather glove and ball. And marlin fishing is popular off the country's coasts.

Indian markets

Ecuador probably has more Indian markets than any other South American country. They offer bargains on shawls, ponchos, blankets, scarves, woodcarvings, wall hangings, jungle fruits, and such oddities as *cuy* (roasted guinea pig), a delicacy among the Indians dating back to the Incas.

Our favorite marketplace is the one at **Otavalo,** a two-hour drive from Quito. Every Saturday morning the Otavalo Indians set up their wares in the public square and quickly dispose of farm products, hand-crafted pottery, and hand-loomed woolens ranging from ties to ponchos. The industrious Otavalos are descendants of the Incas. They have kept the ancient method of dying and weaving woolens alive for centuries, and their handwoven products are among the finest in the world. A sweater that might cost $150 in Los Angeles can be bought here for $20. An imported rug that would sport a $600 price tag in New York City goes for just $50. Handwoven wall hangings with vibrant Inca designs are about $14.

If you're interested in leather goods, stop at the village of **Cotacachi,** near Quito, where every store in town sells clothing, handbags, luggage, shoes, hats, and ponchos made from the finest hand-crafted leather. A coat sells for $50 or $60, a purse for less than $10.

A look at the country

Conquered by the Spanish Conquistadors in 1534 in their quest for Inca gold, Quito was once the northern capital of the vast Incan Empire. During the reign of this incredible civilization, asphalt-covered roads and llama trails were constructed, linking Quito with the city of Cuzco, the Inca's southern capital in Peru.

Because of its inherent beauty, Quito attracted Spanish artists, architects, writers, and intellectuals, who immigrated to the New World seeking the opportunity to put their creative skills to work. They educated and trained the mountain Indians, who in less than 15

191

years supplanted the Spaniards as instructors. Classic examples of Indian primitive art can be found in the city's 87 churches, monasteries, and other religious buildings dating from the Colonial era.

The focal point of the city is its main square, the **Plaza de Independencia,** an ever-changing kaleidoscope of activity, filled with Indian women in colorful skirts and shawls toting huge bundles on their backs, artisans displaying their crafts, and businessmen carrying attaché cases. A blind musician plays a melancholy Inca tune on one of the hand-carved flutes he sells for a living. On park benches old *caballeros* relax over cigarettes as they discuss politics, while children play hide-and-seek among the flowering trees.

Quito is filled with excellent restaurants serving every type of cuisine—Italian, Spanish, French, and typical Ecuadorean dishes. The **Excalibur,** *Calle Calama,* is superb. As is the **Rincon de Francia,** *Roca 779.* Quito also has its share of fast-food restaurants, including King Chicken, Pollo Kentucky, and McDonalds.

The **Big Ben Bar** in the Hotel Alameda Real, *Avenida Amazonas,* is a pleasant meeting place. But be careful—at this altitude (9,300 feet), 1 drink can have the effect of 10.

Ecuador's third-largest city, **Cuenca** (population 275,000) feels like old Spain. The Tomebamba River skirts the old section of this charming colonial city. Ancient ochre-colored wooden buildings cling precariously to a high bluff, while just below clusters of Cuencanos wash their clothes in the river, spreading them to dry on the emerald-green grass.

You'll notice that most of the Indians wear straw hats. These are the famous Panamas, the best of which are so skillfully woven that they can be rolled up and drawn through a ring. The Panama hat originated not in Panama, but in Ecuador, in the coastal town of Montecristi. When the Panama Canal was under construction, thousands of the hats were exported to protect the laborers from the searing heat; eventually they became known as Panamas.

Hat making is a cottage industry in the area around Cuenca, and you can watch craftsmen working with native straw. A superior Panama is creamy white, almost like linen, and malleable enough to spring back to its original shape even after being rolled into a tight ball. A deluxe chapeau costs about $45.

Because many consider it inaccessible, Cuenca has been overlooked by the average tourist, making it all the more attractive. Its skyline is not cluttered with high-rise buildings or condominiums. Rather, it gleams with church domes. Cobblestoned streets wind around colorful flowered plazas lined with red-tiled adobe buildings.

Cathedral Nueva dominates Calderon Park in the heart of the city. Construction of this tremendous church began in 1880, but the building remains unfinished. Due to an architectural miscalculation, the bell towers were made too heavy for the gigantic structure, so the bells from West Germany still stand dismally at the entrance of the nave.

Nonetheless, the cathedral is beautiful. The altars are fashioned from pink and white marble, most mined nearby, and the stained-glass windows are impressive.

The flight from Quito to Cuenca on TAME Airlines takes only 35 minutes and costs $18.

Ingapirca, the only major ruins of the Incan Empire found in Ecuador, is a two-hour drive from Cuenca through a beautiful Andean setting of velvety green mountains with snow-capped peaks. Once the residence of Emperor Huayna Capac, Ingapirca was built during the 15th century. The significance of its site remains a mystery, but it is believed to have been a religious center as well as a fortress.

Well before the arrival of the Incas, Cañari kings worshipped the moon in Ingapirca. The region's topography made it possible for them to observe with precision the movements of the stars in relation to the earth. Later, Inca sun worshippers took full advantage of the locale and constructed additional temples on top of the Cañari settlement.

The gigantic diorite stones that make up the ramparts were cut along the same pattern used by the ancient architects of Cuzco in Peru.

Until 1966, when a dirt road was built, Ingapirca remained almost completely cut off from the rest of Ecuador, accessible only by foot. This enabled treasure hunters to plunder many of its valuable gold statues, artifacts, and precious jewels. And peasants living in the area used many of the rocks to build their homes.

En route to Ingapirca, stop off at the village of **Chordeleg,** famous for its exquisite gold jewelry—available at prices you won't believe—and **Gualaceo,** an arts and crafts center.

The Galápagos—an escape from civilization

The **Galápagos Islands,** the 13 desolate Pacific lava piles where Darwin confirmed his theory of natural selection, have long attracted illustrious scientists and adventurers. They are famous for their large tortoises (weighing as much as 500 pounds), flightless cormorants, and other wildlife arrested at various evolutionary stages. And divers love the waters off their shores.

These islands also have attracted colorful individuals who want to leave the civilized world behind and make this South American netherworld their home.

The most famous of these escapees of civilization is a German baroness named Eloisa de Wagner Wehrborn. In 1932, she arrived on **Floreana** with three lovers: Rudolf Lorenz and Robert Phillipson of Germany and José Valdevieso of Ecuador. The foursome wanted a remote hideaway where they could unleash their violent passions. The lovers quickly shed their clothes and proceeded to lead an uninhibited existence. But one by one they vanished. José grew tired of the *ménage à quatre* and headed back to the mainland. Later the body of Lorenz washed ashore on nearby Marchena Island. The sexy baroness and her remaining paramour were never seen or heard from again.

The spell of the uninhibited baroness lies heavily over these misty volcanic islands. As the tales of her debauchery traveled to the far corners of the world, others made their ways to the Galápagos seeking unfettered existences.

Writer Jane Dolinger recently spent time on Floreana and met some of the people who live there today.

Roberto Costanza is an artist from Milan who lives in a cave. "I used to work in a shoe factory," he told her. "It was the most boring job in the world. One day I decided to take off. That was five years ago, and I haven't regretted it for a moment."

Roberto spends several hours each day painting scenes of the islands. He hopes one day to have an exhibit of his work in Quito. He lives simply. "I don't need much money over here," he said. "But who knows? I may become famous one day—the Gauguin of the Galápagos."

Kathy Baastrup, a native of Denmark, came to the island with her parents when she was 16. When her mother died, her father became homesick and returned to Copenhagen. Kathy stayed behind.

"I don't think anything could draw me back to my country," she said. "Here in this tropical paradise I've rediscovered the true meaning of life—simplicity and nature."

Bernice Newman is 40 years old. She came to the islands from Minnesota two years ago, cleared a portion of the jungle, dug a well, built her own palm-thatched house, and planted a garden. She spends her days roaming the island with her machete, clearing trails and gathering firewood.

Before moving to the Galápagos, Bernice worked with a rodeo out West, was a fashion model in New York, and later bought a banana plantation in Ecuador. "I've always been restless," she said, "and I love the unstructured lifestyle here. I wanted to find my own Shangri-La, and this is it."

How healthy is Ecuador?

Inoculations against typhoid, polio, tetanus, and hepatitis are recommended throughout the country. Malaria suppressant and yellow fever inoculations are recommended in the lowlands. You must be careful about the food and water you consume. Tap water is not drinkable in most areas. The high altitude of the Sierra might cause problems, especially for elderly people and those with heart problems. And precautions must be taken against sunburn.

While health care for Ecuador's poor masses and rural population is poor (only 18% of the population has access to health services, according to *The State of the World's Children 1987*), fairly good health care is available to city residents and those with money (Americans live like royalty in Ecuador). Many of the doctors in Quito have been trained in the United States or West Germany, and Quito has good hospitals.

Make sure your U.S. insurance company will cover you in Ecuador. One company that will is Bankers Life and Casualty.

The political scene

Ecuador is a constitutional republic with three branches: executive, legislative, and judicial. The country has 16 political parties representing a variety of views. Literate citizens between the ages of 18 and 65 are obligated to vote. Voting is optional for others who are eligible.

The constitution provides for concurrent 4-year terms for the president, vice president, and 12 congressmen (of a total 71), who are elected as national (at large) legislators. The remaining 59 legislators, representing the country's 20 provinces, serve 2-year terms. No president may be re-elected, and outgoing legislators must sit out a term before running for congress again.

The Ecuadorean government has good relations with the United States. It also maintains good relations with Eastern and developing nations. Relations with Peru are not as good. One of Ecuador's basic foreign-policy objectives is a revision of the 1942 Rio Protocol of Peace, Friendship, and Boundaries, which ended a short war between Peru and Ecuador. Ecuador holds that the protocol unfairly awarded to Peru territory that rightfully belongs to Ecuador. A revision of the protocol would give Ecuador access to the Marañon River, a tributary of the Amazon. This long-running border dispute occasionally has erupted into armed hostility. The most recent episode was in 1981.

Who are the Ecuadoreans?

Half the population of Ecuador is Meztizo (mixed Indian and Spanish). The other half is made up of pure Indians (25%), Spaniards (10%), and Africans (10%). The majority of Ecuadoreans are Roman Catholic. Spanish is the official language, although Indian languages, especially Quechua, are spoken frequently. About 88% of the population is literate.

The original residents of Ecuador were the Incas, who were conquered by the Spanish Conquistadors in 1532. In 1822, the Incas won their independence from Spain with the help of Simon Bolivar, only to become part of the Republic of Greater Columbia. In 1830, Ecuador seceded and became a separate republic.

Where to stay while you settle in

Visit Ecuador several times before settling in permanently. Deluxe hotels are inexpensive; moderate hotels are cheap.

The **Intercontinental Quito** is deluxe, with double rooms for about $75. It is elegant but not centrally located.

A double room at the deluxe **Alameda Real,** Avenida Amazonas, Quito, is only $50. This hotel is located conveniently, near shops and banks.

Medium-priced hotels in Quito, such as the **Chalet Suisse** and the **Inca Imperial**, charge $40 for double rooms.

In Cuenca, **La Laguna** is deluxe but a little too far from town. It offers comfort and tranquility for $50 a night. A better bet, however, is **El Dorado,** in the heart of the city, with excellent cuisine, for just $30.

How to get there

Fly Ecuatoriana or Eastern from most major U.S. cities.

For more information

For more information on travel to or through Ecuador, contact the nearest Ecuadorean consulate, an office of Ecuatoriana Airlines, or Metropolitan Touris (the U.S. representative is **Adventure Associates,** *5925 Maple, Dallas, TX 75235*).

The **Ecuadorean Tourist Office,** *(800)553-6673,* is helpful. For information on visas, contact the **Embassy of Ecuador,** *3535*

15th St. N.W., Washington, DC 20009; (202)234-7200, or the
Ecuadorean Consulate, *18 E. 41st St., Room 1800, New York, NY 10017; (212)683-7555.*

Chapter 10

France

If you love impressionists, pastoral or Alpine scenery, good wine, gourmet food, high fashion, sophistication, and the French language, retirement in France will bring you one step closer to paradise. The French value life's necessities: food, wine, Sunday strolls. They squeeze pleasure from every aspect of living.

Regardless of your tastes, you should find what you're looking for in France. Paris is vibrant and sophisticated. The French Riviera attracts the jet set and sun worshippers. The Alps are a skier's heaven. The Pyrenees are rustic. And Normandy is verdant and peaceful.

A mild climate

Both winters and summers are mild in France. In the winter, the average daytime temperature is 40 degrees Fahrenheit throughout most of the country, but as high as 55 degrees Fahrenheit along the Riviera. Of course, it is much colder in the Alps. In Paris, winter months are gray and rainy. Spring can also be cool and damp. Late summer and early fall bring the nicest weather.

Visit France in winter as well as summer before taking up permanent residence. Paris may be gay in the warm season, when café tables are set up outside and the streets are filled with vendors and performers, but it can be wet and miserable during the winter, when pale Parisians shuttle from metro stop to home, huddled beneath umbrellas. The countryside is always idyllic and lovely, but you may find it tiresome after eight months.

Parts of France change radically when vacation time comes to an end. The areas around St. Tropez, Antibes, Roquebrune-Cap Martin, Cannes, Nice, and Monte Carlo are totally different during the off season (this can be good or bad, depending on your preferences).

Red tape

To live in France for more than three months, you must apply for a *carte de séjour*. The permit is issued for one year. At the end of that year, you must apply to the local prefecture of police for a renewal (you must produce a certificate from your bank in France and pay a fee of FF120).

If you wish to retire to France permanently, you must show proof that you have sufficient resources to live there without working. You must submit, in duplicate and in French, proof of pensions, dividends, savings, or social security benefits. For more information, contact the **Embassy of France,** *4101 Reservoir Road N.W., Washington, DC 20007; (202)944-6000.*

Always carry your papers with you when traveling in France—it's a law.

In general, you may bring into France all the contents of your home or apartment (that you have owned for at least six months) free of import duty. Select your moving company with care, and distrust any firm that claims it can avoid customs formalities.

Because of recent terrorist bombings in France, rules on immigration are being made more stringent. Americans, for example, must have a visa to enter the country. For details, contact the **Embassy of France,** *address above.*

Where should you live?

Even if you choose to live in the country, you'll probably want a place that's easy to get to. The areas around Toulouse in the southwest, Montpellier in the center, Lyons in the Rhône Valley, and Aix-en-Provence are all easy to reach by fast train or plane.

Other questions to consider when shopping for a home include whether or not you want to be near a big city or a small town. Are you looking for culture (shops, theaters, movie houses) or tranquility?

Before you buy property, find out if your access road is private or belongs to the community. In the latter case, road maintenance is the responsibility of the entire village (if you don't vote in local elections, you may be overlooked when the repair bills are due). Also, if your access road is owned by the community, you'll have mushroom seekers, hunters, and strollers passing your way every day—which is a good way to meet the neighbors if that's your desire.

If you're considering buying property in the country, find out if there is a legal right of passage that allows sheep or goats to cut across your land. This is the case for many rural French properties.

Although it is difficult to find affordable housing in Paris or the Côte d'Azur, good buys exist throughout the rest of France. The best deals are away from the large cities, particularly Paris, and in the beautiful country in the south (away from the coast).

A special government tax on people who own more than one house has forced many country homes onto the market. And, because of the tax, demand for these homes among the French is low. This has created a great market for foreign buyers.

About 85% of all foreign residents live in the south of France. A British colony has formed in the northwest and in the area from Bordeaux to the Spanish border. The Dordogne is also popular among foreigners.

In the **Côte d'Azur**, the greatest number of non-French buyers is along the eastern part of the coast, from Marseilles to Menton in the *département* of the Alpes Maritimes and inland about 20 miles. St. Tropez east (including Cannes and Nice) is the most expensive and most developed region. Finding affordable property here is next to impossible (prices are even higher than in Paris). However, because of the large concentration of wealthy foreign property owners, real estate values here do not bear much relation to those in the rest of the country. In general, a studio apartment in the best part of Cannes costs as much as a five-bedroom house in Languedoc-Roussillon.

The Beaulieu area is also popular among retirees, but it, too, is expensive. And farther inland, prices are creeping up in sleepy farming villages, as the simple life and Provençal farmhouses become trendy.

The least expensive property along the Mediterranean is from Perpignon to Nîmes in the **Languedoc-Roussillon.** This area is beautiful but undeveloped, with few restaurants or shops. But you can find ancient farmhouses at rock-bottom prices. One reason the prices are so low is that these farmhouses generally don't have insulation, which makes for chilly winters. And this area is tormented by the frigid *mistral* (a dry, cold northerly wind that blows in squalls through the Rhône Valley and the Mediterranean coast of France) from November through March.

You can also find inexpensive old houses in the **Alpes-Maritimes.** This area, like the Languedoc-Roussillon, is undeveloped—and cold.

The next cheapest region is from **Marseilles to St. Tropez** in the *départements* of the Bouches du Rhône and the Var. This is an agricultural, wine-growing region with lovely Provençal villages, where you can buy a vineyard or an old farmhouse for restoration. Development reaches only about 10 miles inland. During the summer, it's quiet, hot, and slow. During the winter, the *mistral* blows, and the region becomes even quieter and slower. If you want a truly quiet village, investigate **Normandy** or **Brittany**, picturesque coastal areas with lots of peace and plenty of rain.

If you have ever dreamt of buying a vineyard and spending your retirement years as a viticulturist, consider the Hérault, Gard, Var, and

201

Vaucluse wine-growing regions. (The wine-growing regions around Bordelais and Burgundy are more expensive.)

The **southwest** of France is known for its spas (it has about 30 major ones) and the rough shores of the Atlantic. Prices are highest along the coast.

In the **Loire Valley,** where châteaux are as common as schools, prices are high—especially the nearer you get to Paris. But the soil is fertile, and the scenery is beautiful.

The people and architecture in the villages in **Alsace-Lorraine,** the *département* bordering Germany, have a Germanic flavor. Compared with the cost of property across the border, real estate here is a bargain.

Perigord, a verdant agricultural region in southwest-central France, has rolling farms, historic châteaux, quaint old villages, and scrumptious truffle-topped gourmet delicacies. What's more, the price of property in Perigord is favorable for buyers with dollars.

Hunters may find their happiest hunting grounds in the **Sologne, Landes,** or **Auvergne** areas. And anywhere in central France is good hunting territory.

The **Alps** may seem like paradise to skiers, hikers, and those who enjoy incredible vistas and the pure Alpine air. However, property here is incredibly expensive. The **Pyrenees** are lower, but ruggedly beautiful—and much more affordable.

How to buy property in France

No restrictions are placed on foreign purchase of real estate. However, funds used to purchase property must come from abroad— in other words, dollars must be converted to francs. Few owners offer mortgages, and French banks never finance more than 50% of the cost of property purchased by a foreigner. More than 70% of all property transactions are made in cash. If you eventually sell your French property, you must pay French capital gains tax.

Houses and apartments in France are commonly purchased *en état future d'achèvement*—or in the building stages. When the property has been completed and inspected, the buyer makes his final payment of 5%. The law provides guarantees against building defects for up to 10 years.

Apartments are purchased *en copropriété* (joint ownership), which means you must contribute to the costs of building maintenance. Make every attempt to find out what the service charges will be. A concierge or shared heating system can raise the costs considerably. If buying from an existing owner, ask to see records of the service charges he has paid.

When buying property, you must engage the services of a *notaire*, who acts as both a government official and a legal advisor to both parties involved in the transaction. The *notaire* is responsible for making sure that the vendor has full and clear title, that the vendor is paid, and that stamp duties and registration fees are paid. The *notaire* collects the purchase tax and the capital gains tax. (Some Americans claim that it is impossible to find an honest *notaire*, but that may be an exaggeration.)

If the seller does not agree with the buyer's choice of *notaire* (it is the buyer's prerogative to choose), two *notaires* can be used. If two *notaires* are used, the buyer and the seller split the fees between them. If there is only one, the buyer usually pays the fee (although this varies regionally).

Finding a good *notaire* is no easy matter if you do not have previous connections in France. For recommendations, ask the local consulate or bank.

Upon purchase, you must pay a tax on the value of your new property. If built within the last five years and sold by the builder or first buyer, the tax is about 2.5% of the purchase price. If the property is more than five years old or has already been sold once, the tax is between 8.5% and 11.5% of the purchase price, depending on the region.

Don't leave loan details until the last moment. And don't allow property developers, sellers, or their agents to negotiate a loan for you. Get advice from your bank.

You do not have to have a bank account in France to purchase property, but it helps. All payments must be accompanied by a certificate from a French bank assuring that the money came from non-French sources. If this is not done, you may not be able to export the proceeds when you eventually sell the property.

Commission fees to real estate agents are not uniform. In most parts of France, the seller pays the agent's fee. However, in certain *départements*, including the Dordogne, it's the other way around. Negotiate. If you are purchasing property in a *département* where the buyer must pay the agent, you may be able to strike a deal.

Transfer taxes are high unless you qualify for some of the exceptions. When it's time for the transfer of title to take place, both parties must be present at the signing. Foreigners who want to avoid the boredom of this rather lengthy transaction can appoint a representative with the power of attorney (called a *procuration*). In France, a separate power of attorney is required for each transaction. For example, you'll have to get another one to have your representative get cash from your bank for you.

The French do not always disclose the total cost of real estate in the records of the sale. This system applies especially to older properties. If the buyer pays part of the purchase price in cash, a lower price can be recorded. This allows the seller to reduce his capital gains tax liability and the buyer to pay less transfer tax. However, this practice is not abused as much in France as in Italy.

Upon completion of a real estate transaction, the buyer must make three payments (in addition to the purchase price of the property): the fees of the *notaire,* the stamp duty, and the land registration fees.

The *notaire's* fees for the preparation of the *acte de vente* (including the TVA, France's value-added tax) are charged on a sliding scale according to the purchase price of the property.

The stamp duty (*enregistrement*) includes several taxes, which are recovered by the central, regional, and local governments. In all, it may reach 17% of the purchase price (in Paris and most regions of France it is lower). Exceptions to this very high duty include:

• Recently built property for which you have already paid tax on the purchase price.

• A house or apartment purchased as a private residence only. If you break this agreement, the balance of the full duty must be paid along with a 6% penalty.

• Land bought for construction, as long as building is begun within four years.

• Agricultural land and buildings, which are subject to a basic stamp duty of 14.6%. In this case, the duty can be reduced to 0.6% if you farm the land for at least five years.

As a rough guide, *notaire* fees, stamp duties, and other charges can be assumed to be about 2% of the purchase price for new houses and about 9% of the purchase price for older houses. Consult a lawyer or tax expert to be sure you don't pay more stamp duty than necessary.

Land tax, or *taxe foncière,* is quite low. It is the estimate of the local rental value of the property. You do not have to pay this tax the first two years following the completion of a new building or the restoration of an old building.

It was possible at one time to avoid French taxes entirely by buying property in the name of a non-French company. The government has cracked down on this, but you can still get around the restrictions. However, property belonging to a company registered in a tax haven now is subject to an annual tax of 3% of its market value.

(To avoid this, make sure the company is incorporated in a country that has a tax convention with France.)

Finding a Paris pad

If you want to buy an apartment in Paris, find an area you're interested in, spend some time there, and look for a reasonable seller. Prices vary greatly. Location is the primary criterion—the prestige of an address carries a lot of clout with Parisians. The view is also a deciding factor—properties overlooking greenery or the Seine command the highest prices.

The most expensive areas in Paris are the fashionable 5th, 6th, 7th, and 16th *arrondissements*, the Marais, the Ile St. Louis, and the Champs Elysées.

Rents in the 17th *arrondissement,* which were once inexpensive, are inching up as the area is becoming more and more trendy and popular among artists.

The lowest prices are in the 10th, 11th, 12th, 13th, 18th, 19th, and 20th *arrondissements.*

However, these guidelines are just that—guidelines. Prices in any section of town vary 30% to 50% from one street to another, from one side of a street to the other, and from one floor to another in the same building. Apartments on busy or noisy streets lined with junk-food stands or restaurants, for example, are less expensive than apartments on other streets in the same neighborhood.

Most of the properties available are six- and seven-story structures erected after the reconstruction of the city under Napoleon III in 1850. The typical building is dressed up with balconies and cornices rimmed with wrought-iron railings and ornamental stonework. Inside, the apartments usually have high ceilings, small rooms, and long hallways.

The renovation boom has hit Paris, and many of these 19th-century buildings have been completely modernized. Many are being converted into New York-style lofts. However, the French have not yet fully embraced this concept, so most of these lofts are being snatched up by foreigners, especially Americans. The lowest-priced lofts are in the working-class 18th, 19th, and 20th *arrondissements.*

A good way to find a Paris apartment is to read *De Particulier à Particulier, 8 rue du Général Delestraint, 75016; tel. (33-1)46-51-01-11,* a weekly real estate ad sheet that puts buyers in direct contact with sellers. It is available on newsstands and comes out every Thursday. Another good place to look for listings is **Indicatueur Bertrand,** *11*

rue du Louvre, 75001, which appears on the 1st and 15th of each
month.

Renting in Paris

Finding a suitable, affordable rental in Paris takes time and hard
work. If your time is limited, you may want to enlist the services of an
international rental agency. **Families Abroad,** *194 Riverside Drive,
New York, NY 10025; (212)787-2434,* and **Relocation Services,** *17
rue de Colée, 75008; tel. (33-1)4-289-09-15,* can save you the trouble
of having to research the housing market and can help you understand
your rights as a tenant. Families Abroad specializes in short-term
rentals (three months to a year) and deals primarily with the owners of
apartments or houses. Relocation Services works directly with
companies that are transferring families for much longer stays.

Both agencies help with the nitty-gritty aspects of moving—they'll
find a school for your children, a garage for your car, and insurance
for your new quarters. The flat fee for these services is about FF590.

Unlike most private real estate agencies, Relocation Services and
Families Abroad are willing to explain the complicated French lease
law. It may be useful, for instance, to know that you can't be evicted
without a court order—and you can never be evicted in winter
(October through March), even if you don't pay your rent. Once you
have signed a lease and moved in, you don't have to give up your
unfurnished apartment or house unless you want to. (Furnished
apartments are excluded from this law.)

All these pro-tenant benefits have created a tight, expensive
market. However, they can work to your advantage. Landlords often
prefer to rent to foreigners, because the high turnover allows them to
raise the rent more often.

Another good way to find a rental in Paris, or anywhere in France,
is to contact the **Fédération Nationale des Agents Immobiliers et
Mandataires** (FNAIM), *129 rue du Faubourg St. Honoré, 75008; tel.
(33-1)4-225-24-26,* which can give you a list of agents in the area
where you hope to settle.

The least you can expect to pay for a three-bedroom house in the
fashionable western suburbs of Paris (where most of the international
schools are located) is FF10,000 a month. Prices are about the same
for a two-bedroom apartment in the chic 16th *arrondissement.* Be
prepared to pay three month's rent up front. You'll also have to pay
service charges (central heating, hot water, and so on), which can run
as high as 10% to 20% of a month's rent.

If you go through a real estate agent, you'll have to pay a finder's fee. You may also be asked to pay key money. This is compensation to the previous tenant for any improvements he made to the apartment.

If you elect to find your own apartment, set your alarm for the crack of dawn. You'll need to see the listings in the daily papers before the other 1,000 homeless people in Paris beat you to it. The best listings are in *Le Figaro*. The *Free Voice,* a monthly English-language paper, is another good place to look for rental listings. Pick it up free at the **American Church,** *65 Quay d'Orsay, 75007; tel. (33-1)4-705-07-99.* (This church is a good place to meet fellow expats and to make connections. A flea market is held here every Saturday afternoon from 3 p.m. to 5 p.m., and spaghetti dinners are organized occasionally.)

Passion, *18 rue du Pont-Neuf, 75001; tel. (33-1)4-233-00-24,* also has property listings. This English-language magazine can be found on most Paris newsstands and in many major cities throughout the world.

Also check the classifieds in the ***International Herald Tribune,*** 181 ave. Charles-de-Gaulle, Neuilly-sur-Seine, 92200, and ***International Living,*** *824 E. Baltimore St., Baltimore, MD 21202.* The bulletin boards at the **American College in Paris,** *31 rue Bosquet, 75007; tel. (33-1)4-555-91-73,* are also good places to look.

Once you've found a Paris rental that interests you, you'll be asked to prove that your monthly income is four times the basic rent in francs. If you are unemployed, you'll have to produce a bank guarantee (it can be from a foreign bank with a branch in Paris) that states the bank will pay your rent in case of default. Alternatively, you can get a guarantee from a reputable French citizen (although you'll have difficulty finding someone who'll stand up to a French landlord's inspection).

All leases must be made in writing. Oral agreements, as someone once said, aren't worth the paper they're not printed on. As a potential tenant, you are entitled to receive, before signing anything, written information about the property that includes a complete description of fittings and fixtures, the length of the letting (if the landlord is a company, the lease must be for six years or more), the monthly rental charge, and a record of the previous year's service charges along with an estimate of the current year's charges.

You don't need a notary to witness the signing of a lease.

Sample Paris rentals

The following apartments were advertised recently in *De Particulier à Particulier, address above.* (Keep in mind that by the time you read this, these apartments will have been rented. For current rental listings, consult the sources listed above.)

• A quiet and luxurious studio apartment in the 7th *arrondissement* near the Quai d'Orsay is available for FF4,900 a month.

• A furnished 20th-floor studio of 30 square meters near the Eiffel Tower is available for FF3,500 a month. The apartment complex has a pool and a solarium.

• A modern two-bedroom, two-bath apartment, fully furnished, is available for FF1,350 a month, not including utilities. The rental is in the 6th *arrondissement.*

• A furnished, one-bedroom apartment with a den and a well-equipped kitchen is available for FF8,000 a month. The apartment is in the quiet 7th *arrondissement* near the rue du Bac.

• A two-bedroom apartment with a kitchen, bathroom, and balcony is available for FF5,000 a month. This rental is in the 11th *arrondissement.*

• A quiet, three-room apartment in the 16th *arrondissement* is available for FF1,500 a month, including utilities.

• A beautiful, furnished flat in the 16th *arrondissement* is available for FF25,000. The apartment has an enormous living room, a big dining room, two bedrooms, and an American-style kitchen.

• A studio apartment with all the amenities in the 19th *arrondissement* is available for FF2,950.

• A two-bedroom apartment in a renovated building with an elevator and a concierge is available for FF6,000 a month, plus a deposit of FF900. This apartment, in the 1st *arrondissement* near Châtelet and Les Halles, has a large living room, a fully equipped kitchen, and a bathroom.

• A two-bedroom apartment with a living room, a bathroom, five closets, a kitchen, a maid's room, and a wine cellar in the 16th *arrondissement* is available for FF6,800 a month, plus a deposit of FF900.

A country house in the south of France

Because the working rural population has dropped dramatically in the last century in the south of France, houses here are available at low prices—so low, in fact, that artists and writers have been snapping them up. You can find a house in the south of France for as little as FF200,000. This region of France is many countries in one.

Provence is glamorous, with expensive homes. During the summer, it is culturally active, with concerts, theater, and lectures. The southwestern valley of the Dordogne has prehistoric grottoes and charming hill towns—not to mention truffles and *foie gras*.

Between the two regions lies Massif Central, which has national parks, excellent terrain for cross-country skiing, and low property prices.

Some of the most charming houses in southern France are in the region's hill towns. Called *villages perchés* by the French, some of these communities date back to prehistory. Each is grouped around a church and a castle and lies beneath the crest of a hill. The narrow houses form circles of ramparts. The small winding streets were designed to keep the villages cool in the summer and sheltered from the cold in the winter.

Hill-town houses are built onto each other; your terrace may be your neighbor's roof. But don't worry about disturbing your neighbors. Your walls may be as much as a yard thick. Many of these homes have vaulted ground floors, where animals once were kept. They are dark but cool and elegant (many have been transformed into boutiques and galleries). The Roman-tiled roofs often have fine chestnut beams. Some of these houses have small walled gardens once used to grow the family vegetables—today, they're perfect places to relax and enjoy the views over the valley below.

Keep in mind that these houses are narrow, with rooms on each level built one behind the other. But if one house seems too cramped for you, you could always buy two and redesign the entire inside.

However, before you fall in love with these ancient villages, consider the potential problems. Who will your neighbors be? How close are they? Are the adjoining houses occupied year-round? (This is good theft protection, if you plan to be away often.) Where will you shop?

The south of France offers other property options as well. Most villages have outlying hamlets where you might be able to find a house for sale. And in the valleys are the famous *mas*, or sprawling farmhouses.

Water is an important element to consider when purchasing any property in the south of France. (In Provençal literature, murders were committed for water rights; read Marcel Pagnol's *Jean de Florette* and *Manon des Sources*.) If you choose a village, make sure it has water piped in from a nearby reservoir or lake. Otherwise, your water may be rationed during the summer. If you purchase a farm, make sure it has a well, springs, or a cistern. Or find out if it can be connected to a water network.

When trying to find properties for sale in the south of France, consult the classified ads of national newspapers, such as *Le Figaro* and the *International Herald Tribune*. But don't take the ads as gospel. They don't mention that the next-door neighbor has a smelly hen house, for example, or that a cement electric pole stands three feet from the living room window.

A Belgian psychiatrist and his wife bought an inexpensive house through an ad in *Le Monde*. When they arrived, they found the house much as expected—with one exception. They were surprised to find the neighbors were not simple local peasants as the agent had promised. They came from four other countries. The story points out the importance of inspecting a property in person before signing on the dotted line.

Take time to explore—either with a local realtor or notary or on your own. Each small market town has at least one realtor. However, keep in mind that if you buy through an agency, the seller pays the fee but jacks up the price of the house accordingly. It's cheaper to deal directly with the seller.

If you can explore in the autumn or early in the spring, when few other foreigners are around, you may be invited to meals with the local residents, which will give you the opportunity to find out what property is for sale.

Once you have decided on a house, you and the seller sign a *promesse de vente* (promise of sale), which obliges the seller to you and you to him. At this time, you must put up 10% of the sale price.

Many property sales are concluded with money exchanged under the table. The seller may propose that you provide a substantial sum in cash. This is, of course, illegal. But it's common practice. Be prepared for the issue to arise.

Rising from ruin

Many houses in the countryside of southern France need extensive repair and renovation. You can buy a fine ruin with everything but the walls to redo, a recently inhabited farmhouse with primitive lighting and plumbing, a house that's renovated—but not to your taste—or a place you can move into right away.

Of course the price varies according to the amount of work that must be done. The general rule for a ruin is that restoration costs at least as much as the purchase price of the house. But don't follow this rule religiously. Rules come cheap, but work does not. One real estate company estimates that you should plan to spend one to two times the purchase price on restoration. Ask your real estate agent for help locating qualified but affordable local craftsmen, architects, and builders.

In addition to being costly, property renovation is time-consuming. Most people who have redone a ruin will tell you that they had no idea what they were getting into. Projects can drag on for 3, 5, even 10 years and can cost much more than originally planned. Those who have completed the task tend to relay these facts with an air of smug satisfaction.

Before beginning your project, get free estimates from at least two masons or construction firms. This, too, takes time. But it will save you both time and money in the long run.

One of the best-known and most well-established French construction and renovation companies is **Propinter,** *10 rue des Cordeliers, 24103 Bergerac; tel. (33-53)57-53-75.* (The company also has other offices located throughout France.) You can find other renovation companies through local real estate agents.

A renovation expert speaks

When Maj. Roderick Galloway worked for the Ministry of Defence at Whitehall, his superiors would joke about finding him asleep at his desk on Mondays. However, Galloway's weekends were not spent in the midst of wine and roses. Rather, he spent his Saturdays and Sundays restoring tumble-down cottages in the European countryside.

Maj. Galloway is the owner of **Casa Antica,** *24130 La Force; tel. (33-53)57-32-58,* a firm that finds, sells, and restores properties in southwest France. Properties range from magnificent historic châteaux to modest cottages. With the exception of large projects that involve the historic buildings department, Galloway undertakes all the restoration work himself, using a team he has built up over the years.

"Finding a team can really hold you up," he says. "You have to bully and bully to get anything done. Workmen are notoriously prone to promise and then never show up."

Galloway recommends that, if you want to handle your own restoration, you set aside up to nine months to oversee the work (for a farmhouse). And understand that specialized skills are called for. The unusual stone roofs in Sarlat, for instance, are costly to fix and require a skilled mason.

Another obstacle you'll encounter if you try to handle your restoration yourself is locating the historic materials you'll need. "I had to go all the way to Burgundy to find tiles to cover the roof of a farmhouse we were doing," Galloway says.

Interior restoration also calls for special materials, such as authentic *terre-cuite* tiles and flagstones, and special skills, such as *chaux gras*—plastering to cover stone walls.

Although Casa Antica's crew does not handle large, historic restorations, Galloway will manage them—hiring and overseeing craftsmen and crews and working with architects and the French historic buildings department.

Galloway's recent projects include the restoration of a château that had been sacked by Simon de Montfort in the 13th century and left to crumble since the 15th century; building a stone spiral staircase in an old tower; replacing a steeply pitched château roof; rebuilding vaulted ceilings; and even dismantling and rebuilding a dome.

Reconstruction by Casa Antica follows traditional methods whenever possible, using oak beams instead of metal girders and dowels and pegs instead of nails.

Galloway's Périgord

Galloway's territory consists primarily of the old *département* of Périgord, which includes the modern *départments* of Dordogne, Gironde, Lot, Lot-et-Garonne, Tarn-et-Garonne, and Gers. The rivers Dordogne, Lot, Garonne, Tarn, and Gers bound the region and give it a distinctive topography. Perigord is a harsh and rocky area similar to New England. The principal towns are Bordeaux, Périgueux, Cahors, and Toulouse.

Périgord is renowned for cuisine, wine, and history. Prehistoric artists painted caves in Les Eyzies. Sarlat retains its medieval layout and houses, and Rocamadour was the center of 12th-century pilgrimages to see the Black Virgin.

Périgord is adjacent to and part of the old duchies of Aquitaine and Gascogne, lands that went back and forth between the French and English and were heavily contested during the Hundred Years War. As a result, Périgord is full of 13th- and 14th-century châteaux and fortified villages.

When traveling through this region, orient yourself by observing the materials used to build houses. In the Dordogne, houses are built of wood and granite in the northern part of the *département* and of granite and limestone that gradually darkens from gold to brown in the south near Sarlat.

In Lot, you'll see farmhouses of white stone. And in the southern reaches of Périgord, where stone is difficult to find, the châteaux are built of brick.

Tips on buying French property for restoration

Buying property in a foreign country—especially property that requires restoration—is fraught with potential obstacles and unexpected expenses. To keep both problems and expenditures under control, Roy Veatch of **Period Houses,** *(301)229-4514 in the United States,* has the following suggestions:

• Hire someone to do a structural survey of the property before you buy it. If you are calling in an architect for renovations, he will take care of this. He should also provide you with a list of problems that need to be corrected and the estimated cost of doing so.

• Use an attorney skilled in the real estate business to handle the purchase and transfer of the property. Expect to pay much less to a lawyer in France than you would in the United States.

• Arrange to make your down payment through a branch of an American bank. That way, if anything goes wrong, you will have a better chance of recovering your money. Use an American bank when you finally sell your property, too.

• Remember, it is the buyer, not the seller, who pays the commission to the real estate company. And the government expects more than 8% of the total (official) price—which also must be paid by the buyer. Mentally add this tax into the price of any property you consider. Sellers in Paris and most of France (except Dordogne) are responsible for the real estate commission.

• French land is measured in hectares. One hectare equals 10,000 square meters, or 2.471 acres. One acre equals 4,047 square meters.

Buying your own castle

If you've always dreamt of owning your own château, contact **Period Houses,** *address above,* or Maj. Roderick Galloway of **Casa Antica,** *address above.*

The average price of a fully restored château without farmland is about FF3 to FF3.5 million.

One château recently on the market in France was built in the 19th century by an American. David Haviland, an American shopkeeper who moved to France to set up his porcelain manufacturing business, decided that he wanted to live the good life in France and that the way to do this was to buy a château. But he couldn't find one that suited him, so he built his own and called it Le Reynou. It's in a secluded valley near Solignac, about five miles south of Limoges.

Le Reynou is not classified as a historic property, because it's only about 100 years old. But in many ways, it's superior to older châteaux in both design and quality of materials. For example, each step of the main staircase is one centimeter less tall than the previous step, making the climb to the top less tiring. The exterior stone is a durable rose-colored granite. Limoges porcelain and oak woodwork adorn the building, which is huge. The main floor alone is almost 10,000 square feet.

The château sits on 188 acres, part of which has been made into a park and planted with trees from North America. More money was spent on the park than on the building. It has three man-made lakes, a trout stream, and a footbridge and fallen trees molded from concrete.

Le Reynou was advertised for FF4.5 million. For more information, contact **Richard Abel,** *P.O. Box 4944, Santa Rosa, CA 95402; (707)539-4036.*

Recently advertised French properties

The following properties were advertised recently in France. (Keep in mind that this list is meant only as a guide; for more current listings, consult *De Particulier à Particulier, address above.*)

• A totally furnished, spacious one-bedroom apartment in Paris, with a living room, a dining alcove, a kitchen, a bathroom, a cellar, an elevator, and a concierge, is available for FF1.2 million.

• A two-bedroom apartment in Paris' 16th *arrondissement,* with a kitchen, a bathroom, and a wine cellar, near the metro, is available for FF620,000.

• An apartment in a historic building with beamed ceilings and stone walls is available for FF1.1 million. The apartment is located in Paris' 5th *arrondissement.*

• A three-room apartment on the fourth floor with an elevator, a bathroom, and a kitchen, located in Paris' 5th *arrondissement,* is available for FF1.1 million. The apartment is in perfect condition.

• A renovated building near the Arc de Triomphe, with two bedrooms, a kitchen, a bathroom, and a wine cellar, is available for FF690,000. The building is in the 17th *arrondissement* of Paris.

• A one-bedroom apartment on the fifth floor of a stone building in Paris' 11th *arrondissement* is available for FF450,000. The apartment has a kitchen, a bathroom, a cellar, and a watchman.

• A two-room apartment in the 2nd *arrondissement* of Paris, *49 rue d'Aboukir,* is available for FF385,000. The apartment has beamed ceilings and a kitchenette.

• A recently renovated independent duplex in Paris near the Bastille, with three bedrooms and a living room, is on the market for FF2.1 million.

• A stone house 12 miles north of Soissons in Aisne with a living room with a fireplace, three bedrooms, central heating, a garage, outbuildings, and an orchard is available for FF350,000.

• A country house in St. Vincent sur Jabron, in need of restoration, is available for FF349,000. The house, private but not isolated, borders a river and fields. It is available for FF349,000.

• A two-bedroom apartment in the pedestrian district of Nice, with a living room, a kitchen, a bathroom, and a large balcony with a view of the sea and a garden, is on the market for FF700,000.

• A recently built three-bedroom villa 10 miles from Nice is available for FF950,000. The villa has two bathrooms, shaded terraces, a cellar, a wood shed, and a workshop.

• A fifth-floor apartment in Cannes with panoramic views, a balcony, two bedrooms, a living room, a fully equipped kitchen, and a private swimming pool is selling for FF995,400.

• Situated in Ardennes nine miles from Belgium, between Hirson and Charleville, this five-bedroom stone house with a vaulted cellar, a large attic, a barn, stables, and timbered ceilings and walls is selling for FF160,000.

• This regional house near Carcassonne in Aude has a living room with a monumental fireplace and a marble staircase, as well as a kitchen, a living room, an entrance hall, a storage room, a huge bedroom on the second floor, and a bedroom with a balcony on third floor. The price is FF400,000.

• A two-bedroom home in Villers sur Mer in Calvados, with a kitchen, a bathroom, and a balcony, is on the market for FF160,000.

• A 15th-century country house in Dordogne near Bergerac, situated on one-third acre with an orchard, a fish stream, and views of a 12th-century château, is available for FF690,000. The house has three bedrooms, two bathrooms and has been restored to include all the modern conveniences.

• A large one-bedroom penthouse in the residential center of Toulon, near Nice, Marseille, and Monaco, is available for FF371,200. The penthouse offers a spectacular panoramic view of the harbor, the hills, and the city from its balcony.

• Two hours from Paris, this 200-year-old farm on 18 acres is available for FF466,100.

- A large château situated on 625 acres in Dordogne is on the market for FF5.6 million.
- A shepherd's cottage in the countryside near Grasse on 171,200 square feet of land is selling for FF350,000.
- A stone chalet in the hills 30 miles from Nice with a sitting room, a kitchen with a fireplace, two bedrooms, and one bathroom is selling for FF400,000.
- A historic stone farm manor house in Monestier in Dordogne, in need of restoration, is on the market for FF250,000. A huge barn is attached to the house, which features a bread oven and a courtyard. The house has neither water nor electricity.
- An impressive 12th-century stone house near Bergerac in Dordogne is selling for FF400,000. Located in a quiet square, the house has a magnificent hall/living room, a huge terrace, an attractive garden, and a large first-floor bedroom. The house was once used as a restaurant, but it is suitable for a private residence.
- A small farm in Vaucluse in need of some restoration is selling for FF270,000. Located near a small town, the farmhouse has a courtyard, three bedrooms, and 31,742 square feet of land.
- A ruined farm on 111 acres in Drôme is selling for FF535,000.

French real estate agents

Consult the following real estate agents for help locating and purchasing property in France:

- **Agence Largier,** *L'Agence des Ambassades, 32 blvd. Malesherbes, 75008 Paris; tel. (33-1)4-265-1883.*
- **Agence Bassanelli,** *8 blvd. Elemir Bourges, 04100 Manosque; tel. (33-92)876-409.*
- **Cabinet Daniel Houdiard,** *La Grande Roche, 53260 Entrammes; tel. (33-43)566-160.*
- **Continental Immobilier L. Raynaud,** *32 ave. de l'Ope'ra, 75002 Paris; tel. (33-1)4-742-6834.*
- **Demeures & Châteaux du Soleil,** *Jean Pierre Fougeirol, Immeuble Carré Bleu, Route de Marseille, 26200 Montélimar; tel. (33-75)01-66-33.*
- **France Sterling Estates,** *Michael Bret, B.P. 212, 06508 Cannes Cedex.*
- **Gunst Immobilier,** *11 ave. Jean Medecin, 06000 Nice; tel. (33-93)82-33-44.*
- **Hampton & Sons,** *19 ave. Franklin-Roosevelt, 75008 Paris; tel. (33-1)4-225-5035.*

• **Michel Hulot de Tocqueville,** *18 rue Perpignan, 75007 Paris; tel. (33-1)4-783-2013.*
• **Sepco Central Bureau,** *Bretelle Autoroute, 06110 Le Cannet.*

A sailor's delight

If you are a boating buff, consider living on a boat along the Côte d'Azur rather than in an apartment or house. Between Marseilles and Menton, you'll find a marina every few miles.

Prices vary according to the size of the boat and the facilities of the port. The high season cost ranges from FF400 in Menton to FF3,500 in Beaulieu. Annual rent in Cros-de-Cagnes is FF1,689; in Juan-les-Pins it's FF21,360. Ask the *capitaine de port* (harbor master) for prices. Rent usually includes water, electricity, and telephone service.

Strict customs laws restrict the activities of non-French boats—and not following these rules can lead to impoundment of your vessel. You may dock your boat in France free of TVA if it is not used for more than six months a year. You will have to pay the TVA if you become a resident of France, charter your boat, or use your boat more than six months a year.

For up-to-date information on customs, consult a *transitaire* (customs clearing agent). When your boat is not being used, your ship's papers must be held at the local customs office.

Special services for seniors

France takes services for seniors seriously and has created a new Secretary of State for Senior Citizens, the goal of which is to expand services to retirees and to keep the elderly out of institutions. The government has increased home nursing services and has improved the quality of home care. Housing has been expanded, including winter housing in mountains and rural areas, where isolated older persons have a difficult time surviving the winter alone; summer housing to enable families caring for older people to go away on vacation; and transition housing, providing housing for older people after they've been hospitalized.

In addition, the government helps finance and arrange vacations, set up and organize senior citizens clubs (which now number 15,000), provide low-cost meals at special restaurants, and provide household help.

Retirees in France are entitled to many privileges. For instance, the *carte vermeil* (senior citizen card) provides half-fare train travel for seniors during off-peak periods. Men over 62 and women over 60 can buy the pass for FF85 . The card is valid for one year with proof of age. Application forms are available at most train stations in France or from **SNCF,** *Paris Tivoli, 20 rue de Longchamp, 75016 Paris.* The card is also available through the **French National Railroad,** *610 Fifth Ave., New York, NY 10019.*

Seniors (with identification) also are entitled to a 50% reduction on most museum entrance fees. And they are exempt from certain taxes.

Air France and Air Inter offer discounts for seniors on domestic flights that range from 25% to 50%, depending on the time of year, the day of the week, and the time of day.

Health matters

You won't have trouble locating English-speaking doctors in Paris or the larger towns. Contact the American embassy or consulate for advice. If you need a continuous supply of any drug, ask your U.S. doctor or an international pharmacy whether it is available in France and, if so, under what brand name. And have the dosage translated into the metric system.

At the **American Hospital,** *63 blvd. Victor Hugo, Neuilly sur Seine; tel. (33-1)4-747-53-00,* in a suburb of Paris, you'll find friendly English-speaking doctors and nurses. And care here is covered by Blue Cross-Blue Shield and Aetna insurance. Paris also has the **British Hospital,** *48 rue de Villiers, 92 Levallois-Perret; tel. (33-1)4-757-24-10.*

The cost of living

Overall, the cost of living for Americans in France is low. Paris is slightly more expensive than Washington, D.C., but most of the rest of France is a bit cheaper. A couple needs from $25,000 to $35,000 annually to live moderately well in France. A single person needs $8,000 to $26,000.

However, it has become difficult to find inexpensive housing in France. The State Department estimates that an average-size middle-income family must spend $1,200 a month on housing; a single person should expect to spend $850 a month.

Food in restaurants throughout France tends to be inexpensive (steak with french fries is FF20.65; an omelette is FF12), and staples are cheap in the markets (baguette is FF1.8 francs; a liter of milk is FF3; a liter of peanut oil is FF8). However, big-ticket items, such as

218

cars, sofas, and appliances, are expensive. So are hot water and electricity (the French limit the number of showers they take because of the cost of hot water).

One way to save money in Paris is to purchase the book *Cheap Eats in Paris,* which is available for $8.45 from **Cobble & Mickle Books,** *P.O. Box 3521, San Diego, CA 92103-0160.* Author Sandra A. Gustafson guides you past the bad food you often get when trying to each cheaply in the city. She offers in-depth reports on 104 restaurants, brasseries, and bistros. Prices range from FF30 to FF380.

Money

There are 100 centimes to a franc (centimes are rarely used in amounts less than 10 at a time). Bank notes are issued in denominations of FF10, FF20, FF50, FF100, FF200, and FF500. Coins are issued in denominations of 5, 10, 20, and 50 centimes and FF1, FF2, FF5, FF10, and FF20.

For the best deals on exchange rates, change your currency at a *bureau de change* run by a bank. These *bureaux* are everywhere in Paris; the easiest places to find them are railroad terminals. Avoid changing money at hotels, restaurants, or shops, which overcharge.

In general, Paris banking hours are Monday through Friday from 9 a.m. to noon and 1:30 p.m. to 4:30 p.m. Banks close at noon the day before official holidays. On weekends, go to Crédit Commercial de France on the Champs Elysées just east of the Arc de Triomphe. This is where you'll find the best rates.

Americans can keep up to $5,000 in a foreign account or financial instrument without having to make a declaration to the Internal Revenue Service (IRS).

Banking

Should you open a bank account in France? If you're going to do business or make investments there, yes. However, France does not have attractive banking laws, so it's a good idea to keep only the necessary minimum in a French account.

Following are additional reasons you should not do your banking in France:

• France has no bank privacy. The opening of every account is reported to the government.

• The clearing system for checks can be slow, and bank statements are not always accurate. It takes longer to order a checkbook than in the United States. Interest is never paid on checking accounts.

- You cannot endorse a check except to a bank or similar institution.

- A *chèque sans provision* (bounced check) can bring sanctions much more serious than in the United States. This is especially so with a non-resident account; if you overdraw, you are illegally borrowing French francs without the Bank of France's consent.

On the other hand, checks are accepted virtually everywhere in France, whether they are drawn on a resident or a non-resident account. Cash withdrawal Visa cards (which you can apply for through your bank) also can be used throughout the country.

To deposit more than FF5,000 in a non-resident bank account, you must show that the money was imported from outside France. The bank will handle the paperwork for a fee of about $12.

If you become a resident, your account becomes subject to foreign exchange control laws. This means that you must have permission from the Bank of France to transfer out of France funds in excess of FF10,000. You may not draw checks on your French account outside the country.

For exchange control purposes, you are treated as a non-resident for two years following your arrival in France. If your visits to France are irregular or if you don't need a residence permit, you can probably keep a non-resident bank account indefinitely. It is up to the bank to discover whether you have become a resident.

The following large French banks maintain correspondents or representatives in the United States: Société Générale (known as the European American Bank in the United States), Crédit Lyonnais, Banque Nationale de Paris, Crédit Industriel et Commercial, and Crédit Agricole.

U.S. banks maintaining branches or subsidiaries in France include the American Express Company, Bank of America, Bankers Trust Company, Chase Manhattan Bank, First National Bank of Chicago, Citibank, and Morgan Guaranty Trust Company of New York.

Taxing matters

Taxes are high in France, ranging from 5% to 60%. However, many deductions can be taken. Management Center Europe, a business research center, estimates that a married couple in France with two children earning $100,000 is left with $64,000 after tax and social security deductions.

Foreigners not living or spending more than 183 days a year in France are taxed only on their incomes from French sources or on the basis of three times the rental values of their residential premises in France, whichever is greater.

If you live in France year-round and it is considered your fiscal domicile, you must pay tax to the French government on worldwide income. Your fiscal domicile is considered to be in France if your *foyer* (home or principal place of residence) is in France or if you spend more than 183 days in the country in any tax year. You are also considered to have a permanent residence in France, even if you do not actually spend that much time in the country, if your spouse or children are living there; if you carry on an occupation in France, either salaried or self-employed; or if you have financial interests, such as collecting rent from French property or royalties from patents, centered in France.

If you are an American citizen domiciled in France with world-wide total income of more than $70,000, you will have to pay U.S. as well as French taxes.

You file your *déclaration de revenu* (tax return) with the local *inspecteur*. The *déclaration* includes income, capital gains, and VAT. Tax payments are due in three installments: Feb. 15, May 15, and Dec. 31. The tax year begins on Jan. 1. You pay the year after the money was earned. Tax is collected by the local *recette du trésor*.

French tax returns are simple—the government works out your tax for you. Local tax offices can be helpful, but you should obtain the services of a good local accountant or one of the large international accounting firms, such as Price Waterhouse or Arthur Andersen.

Learning the language

If you plan to live in France, you should attempt to learn the native tongue. The French are proud of their language. They haven't accepted the dominance of English as an international language and can be quite defensive on the subject. You'll find them much friendlier and easier to get to know if you at least try to use their language, rather than expecting them to use yours.

If you live in Paris, finding French language lessons is easy. The Alliance Française, the Institut Catholique, and the Sorbonne all offer French classes for foreigners at reasonable rates.

Throughout France, you will find that French people are delighted to exchange French lessons for English lessons. Find a partner by placing advertisements on bulletin boards in local schools.

Customs

When moving to France, you can bring free into the country
anything intended for personal use and not for resale. Americans may
bring 400 cigarettes, 100 cigars, or 500 grams of pipe tobacco duty-
free. Also allowed are 2 used cameras with 10 rolls of film and a
movie camera with 10 reels of film. You can bring in as many French
francs and foreign bills as you wish.

When leaving the country, you can take with you up to FF500
francs without making a declaration. No restrictions are placed on
traveler's checks or letters of credit obtained outside France. All
currency declared upon arrival can be taken out with you when you
leave.

Animals less than three months old are not allowed into France.
To bring other pets into the country, you need a recent certificate
stating that your animal is free from disease and has had rabies shots.
(Double check these regulations with the **Ministère de l'Agriculture,**
*Direction de la Qualité, Bureau de la Reglementation Sanitaire, 44-
46 blvd. de Grenelle, 75732 Paris Cedex 15; tel. (33-1)4-575-62-25.*
They change often.)

Transportation

Unless you live in a rural area, you can get by in France without a
car. The Paris metro can get you anywhere in in the city quickly and
cheaply. The country's train system is extensive and efficient. And
every sizeable town has a good trolley or bus system.

The Paris metro runs until 1 a.m. and is easy to use. Large maps at
each stop show the routes. The cheapest way to travel on the metro is
to buy a *carnet* of 10 tickets or a month-long pass called the *carte
orange.* (You need a passport-size photo to purchase the pass.)

Known as the SNCF, the French railroad covers 22,000 miles. All
lines radiate from Paris, where there are six train stations. Go to the
Gare de l'Est for eastern France, Switzerland, and Germany; to the
Gare de Lyon for the Riviera and Marseille; to the Gare d'Austerlitz
for central France and Spain; to the Gare Montparnasse for Brittany
and the outskirts (*banlieue*), such as Chartres; to the Gare Saint
Lazare for Normandy and St. Germain en Laye; and to the Gare du
Nord for the north coast, Denmark, Holland, and boats to Great
Britain.

The French National Railroad offers several economy-priced train
tours and tickets. Round trips of more than 900 miles cost less than
one-way fares. And you can buy rail passes valid for one to four

weeks through the **French National Railroad office** in New York, *610 Fifth Ave., New York, NY 10020; (212)582-2110* (these are not available in France).

A *carte d'abonnement* (season ticket) may be well worth the cost. You can also purchase a *carte à libre circulation* (unlimited mileage), which costs a bit more.

A *carte couple/famille* (family card) is issued free to married couples and families at most of the larger railway stations. (You must present photographs and proof of relationships.) This pass permits a 50% reduction during non-peak hours for family members traveling together and is valid for five years.

If you plan to drive in France, purchase *Le Permis de Conduire Français* from any bookshop or driving school. This will teach you how the French should drive. Keep in mind as you taste the delights of French vineyards that the *alcooltest* or *dépistage* (breathalizer test) is used throughout the country.

The equivalent of the American Automobile Association is **Touring Secours,** sponsored by the Touring Club of France. The cost is about FF100 a year for coverage of simple repairs and towing.

One couple's Paris retirement

Annette Lyons wrote the following article about her experiences in Paris for the June 1988 issue of International Living. *She and her husband retired to Paris in 1987.*

Retirement in Paris is not for everyone. But for those who want the stimulation of a culturally rich city, it can be rewarding.

When my husband and I decided to retire here, I didn't speak a word of French. We had only one family friend and no other acquaintances in the city. Immediately after we moved to Paris for our first six-month trial stay, I enrolled in an intensive French course at the Sorbonne.

We had found an apartment on a previous trip and had purchased it for vacations. Initially, we decided to spend six months each year in Paris and six months in New York. But by the second year of our plan, having made many acquaintances and grown comfortable and happy in the city, we decided to leave New York completely and move to Paris for good.

Being a retiree in Paris has many advantages. Almost all movie houses offer 20% to 30% discounts to senior citizens. Some live theaters offer discounts of as much as 50%, and all museums give 50% reductions. A few museums, including the Carnavalet Museum in the Marais section of the city, give free admission to the third age (as Parisians refer to seniors).

The metro is another bargain. It's only half the price of the New York subway. And it's much more efficient, better lit, cleaner, and safer.

As for safety, I am comfortable in Paris day and night—whether traveling on public transportation or on foot. Parisians think nothing of walking the streets or riding the metro alone at midnight. That's a good feeling, particularly as you get older. I feel completely safe walking along the Seine at night, for example.

We have found no need to have a car. Public transportation, the occasional taxi, and car rentals for extended trips serve us much more economically than the bother, responsibility, and expense of a car.

One of the best parts of living in Paris is the food. The preparation of food is an art form in France, and the abundant choices of fresh delicious fruits, vegetables, cheeses, and breads, not to mention all those desserts, make every meal a special treat. Shopping for groceries is an experience rather than a chore, with numerous market stands and individual food stores in every neighborhood, in addition to the usual supermarkets.

Medical care in Paris is a bargain. It's both inexpensive and excellent. To maintain the residence card required for living here, you must show proof of private insurance coverage or buy French personal health insurance. We chose the French insurance. It's much less expensive than Medicare (which doesn't cover Americans overseas), and the coverage is much better. Payment is generally 75% of doctor and dentist charges, 40% to 70% of prescriptions, and a small percentage of optical bills. Hospitalization is fully covered, and there is no deductible.

This insurance does impose limits on allowable procedures, but the services in the clinics of the large teaching hospitals are usually within the limits. We have found these clinics, where we have regular appointments with the same doctors every visit, to be excellent. Preventive medicine is practiced, and the staff is courteous.

For more information

The following organizations and publications can help you prepare for your French retirement:

• **Air France,** *(800)237-2747.*

• **Chambre de Notaires de Paris,** *Marché Public Immobilier, 12 ave. Victoria, 75001 Paris; tel. (33-1)4-236-2626.*

- *De Particulier à Particulier,* 8 rue du Général Delestraint, 75016 Paris; tel. (33-1)46-51-01-11.
- **Embassy of France,** 4101 Reservoir Road N.W., Washington, DC 20007; (202)944-6000.
- **Federation Nationale d'Agences Immobilière (FNAIM),** 129 rue du Faubourg St. Honoré, 75008 Paris; tel. (33-1)4-225-24-26.
- **French Government Tourist Office,** 610 Fifth Ave., New York, NY 10020; (212)757-1125; 9401 Wilshire Blvd., Beverly Hills, CA 90212; (213)272-2661; 645 N. Michigan Ave., Chicago, IL 60611; (312)337-6301; World Trade Center 103, 2050 Stemmans Fwy., Dallas, TX 75207; (214)742-7011; and 360 Post St., San Francisco, CA 94108; (415)986-4161.
- **French National Railroad,** 610 Fifth Ave., New York, NY 10020; (212)582-2110.
- *Indicateur Bertrand,* 11 rue du Louvre, 75001 Paris.
- **International Real Estate Federation,** 777 14th St. N.W., Washington, DC 20005, (202)383-1033.
- **Société Anglo-Française Immobilière,** 10 ave. de la Libération, 06600 Antibes, Alpes-Maritime; tel. (33-93)336-033.

Chapter 11

Greece

To visit Greece is to see the inspiration from which its great civilization grew. It is a beautiful country—breathtaking—of mountains and islands and sea. Its special light gives a sharp clarity to the blue sky above and the colors below, colors that include a happy profusion of wildflowers in early spring. The Greek climate is gentle, the air smells of the sea. Life somehow seems more poignant in Greece than it does anywhere else on earth.

This land inspired the colorful myths and legends upon which much modern day poetry and art are based. It is the land of the Greek gods. What better place to retire?

On a more down-to-earth level, Greece is also cheap. With a U.S. salary or pension, you can live like a god. Apartment rents in Athens, for instance, are less than half those in New York City.

Choose your paradise. Greece is made up of 1,452 islands and islets; 166 are inhabited. It is Greece's close companionship with the sea that has always attracted the outside world.

Red tape

Visas are not required for U.S. citizens who plan to stay less than three months in Greece. For a residence permit, you must apply in person at the **Alien's Bureau**, *173 Alexandras Ave., Athens 11522; tel. (30-1)646-8103.*

Buying Greek real estate

Greek real estate is attractive for foreigners—if the property is bought for personal use and not for speculation. Outside Athens there are some real bargains—beautiful land at attractive prices. But there are some drawbacks.

Should you decide to sell your Greek property, the proceeds cannot be taken out of Greece. There is one way around this regulation, however. If you are a permanent resident of another country, the Greek government will allow you to sell your property to another person who also has a permanent domicile outside Greece. If you can find another American to buy your property, a deed of transfer can be executed before a Greek consul in the United States and the amount agreed upon can be paid to you in dollars, minus the Greek transfer tax (about 12%, paid to the consul). As long as both parties are permanent residents of another country, the transaction is legal and the Bank of Greece need not approve it.

However, if you have taken up permanent residence in Greece, you will have to deposit the proceeds from the sale in a blocked account in a local bank. These accounts earn interest of about 11.5% annually. Money can be taken from the blocked account only to invest again in Greece: for the purchase of more property or Greek stocks, to repair Greek property, to establish a business, to pay Greek taxes, or to support you and your family in Greece. Withdrawals can be made only with the permission of the Bank of Greece. A maximum of 100,000 drachmas can be released per month.

Banking may be easier in the future, however. Greece is moving toward full liberalization of capital movement.

Permission to transfer money out of the country from blocked accounts must be requested from the Bank of Greece, which usually refuses. Normally, the only exception to this is if the owner, residing outside Greece, is unable to support himself because of ill health or old age. The owner's petition for a transfer of funds must be accompanied by an official statement attesting to his difficult circumstances, signed by a Greek consular officer in his country of domicile. The request to the consular officer must be accompanied by medical bills or other evidence. Once the request is accepted, the official statement of recommendation is valid for one year and will cover any number of requests for transfers filed within that period of time.

Money from the rental of foreign-owned property also must be deposited in a blocked account. It can be transferred abroad if the owner permanently resides outside of Greece. An annual statement has to be sent to the Greek bank stating that the owner still maintains his permanent domicile outside of Greece. It has to be signed by the Greek consular officer in the owner's country of domicile. A maximum of $2,000 per year may be transferred abroad.

Where to buy

Foreigners are free to own property in about 95% of Greece. For national security purposes, Greek law forbids foreign ownership of land in frontier regions, which rules out Crete and the choice islands of Rhodes and Corfu, along with a few smaller islands along the coast of Turkey. Some foreigners get around this ruling by setting up limited liability companies that own the property for them. Greek real estate agents estimate that as many as 1,500 holiday homes in frontier regions may be owned this way by foreigners.

If you do not wish to run the risk of owning property in the frontier regions, there is a lot of land left to choose from on the mainland and throughout the islands.

Living in Athens

Athens has a large expatriate community made up of multinational businessmen, diplomats, the U.S. military establishment, and foreign teachers and students connected with several U.S. colleges and the TASIS international boarding school. Real estate prices here are the highest in Greece, partly because of the increased demand from the international community.

The selling price for a one-bedroom apartment in Athens is between 5,095,500 and 8,285,000 drachmas. Garden houses fetch the biggest prices—two-bedroom houses were advertised for sale in a recent Athens newspaper for about 13,095,000 to 14,550,000 drachmas.

Rents for four-bedroom apartments in the best neighborhoods run around 43,650 to 87,300 drachmas per month. Larger apartments in these neighborhoods range from around 72,750 drachmas to more than 116,400 drachmas. Houses of equivalent space in posh suburbs are more expensive, running from 145,500 drachmas to 291,000 drachmas. Luxury apartments rent for 101,850 to 174,600 drachmas; luxury houses, 189,150 to 319,100 drachmas. Unfurnished accommodations are slightly lower, but "unfurnished" often means one has to provide all kitchen appliances.

Rents in Greece can be substantially lower for those who shop carefully, especially without a real estate agent, and especially if you avoid the expatriate ghettos. In Athens, an independent search can turn up very nice, spacious apartments for one or two, for as little as 17,000 drachmas per month in rent. Agents take big cuts from both parties in a real estate deal, and are best avoided if possible. However, they are clued in to the turnover of nicer properties, usually speak English, and alleviate headaches for those who'd rather pay the extra expense.

Those searching without an agent will find plenty of leads in English-language newspaper ads. But even these will quote high prices, as they are aimed at expatriates. The best leads are through local contacts. Just about every Greek has an uncle who has property for rent or sale. The Greeks are amiable, accessible people, easy to talk to, and eager to make introductions. All you need to do is ask everyone you run into if they know of a place for rent or sale.

Utilities are not included in Greek rents, and renters often contribute to the salaries of apartment building employees. Monthly utility charges run from about 7,275 to 29,100 drachmas—more if heating oil is needed. Central heat is provided only in new apartment buildings.

Getting a telephone is not easy because there are not enough lines. One young American living in Athens waited six months for a phone. There were 7,000 people on the list ahead of her. Telephone installation costs about 4,000 drachmas; monthly phone rental is about 100 drachmas.

Home away from home

The Athens residential areas of most interest to foreigners are the wealthy northern suburbs; the more centrally located and posh **Kolonaki Square**, within walking distance of Constitution Square (Syntagma); and **Glyfada**, an eastern suburb along the beach that grew up as a bedroom community for the nearby U.S. Air Force base. Diplomats and executives live in the northern suburbs; Kolonaki Square is for rich artistic and avant-garde types; Glyfada's lifestyle is the most relaxed and probably would seem most like home to Americans. One disadvantage to Glyfada, however, is that parts of it are under the direct flight path of aircraft landing and taking off from the international and domestic airports, as well as the Air Force base.

The sleeper of Athens' residential areas is the **Plaka**, the old market area below the Acropolis, in the heart of downtown. Still somewhat cheap, its real estate values have risen, thanks to a govern-ment effort to renovate the area and preserve its historical character. The Athens government has offered low-interest credit for restoring old Plaka houses and facades. Buildings not conforming to a new Land Use Law have been shut down, and police monitoring of the local criminal activities has been stepped up. Young artistic types are moving in to bring new life to the old buildings. The program has been successful, and much of the area had been restored.

For many, Athens is not the best place to live unless they have business in the city. It is noisy, busy, and not very attractive. Its pollution is the worst in Europe. But beneath the big-city surface is a lifestyle that appeals to many. There are those who love its night life, ancient ruins, access to the sea and numerous islands, and location as a communication hub connecting Europe and the Middle East.

And don't forget its fascinating archaeological sights. The ancient **Acropolis** stands on a hill overlooking the city, a constant reminder of the wonders of the past. In the same area is the ancient **Agora**, or marketplace, of the old city. Around town are other ruins, including **Hadrian's Wall**, built during the days of the Roman Empire, and numerous Byzantine churches. North of the city is **Delphi**. South of Athens is the temple of **Poseidon**, at Cape Sounion.

The islands have better beaches

If your idea of paradise is retiring by the beach so that you can swim every day, head for the Greek islands. According to a recent report of the Panhellenic Center for Ecological Research, the greater Athens area is polluted far beyond the most reasonable limits for health safety. In fact, the entire Saronic Gulf coast may prove hazardous. Chemical and microbial pollutants are in such high concentrations that one would be well-advised to avoid any type of water sports on the shores from the Corinthian Isthmus to the tip of Cape Sounion.

Signs have been posted in some areas by the government ministry, but they do not appear in all polluted areas. Government figures on pollutants differ from those of the environmentalist group. (The seriousness of Athens' air pollution is likewise played down by the government so as not to ward off the tourist influx.)

In short, if you want to swim in Greece, either find a swimming pool or take off for the islands.

The islands also offer more beauty, a more relaxed lifestyle, and lower prices. Of Greece's many islands, we picked two most favored by foreigners to highlight—**Skiathos** and **Mykonos**. They already have foreign residents and basic facilities (access to water, communications, roads, etc.). Here, accommodations are the most similar to U.S. standards. And there is easy access to the outside world— efficient communications, banking, and transportation.

Although the smaller islands offer more bargains, the physical as well as cultural isolation they impose make life more difficult, especially if you don't speak Greek. Not only do many of these islands lack such amenities as electricity, but their societies are often more conservative, which can make a foreigner's life lonely and difficult. And many smaller islands do not have medical facilities.

Keep in mind, as you look for a home in the islands, that Greeks do not respond well to aggressive behavior from foreigners. Personal relationships are important. If they develop a respect and liking for you, they will go a long way toward giving you a "Greek" price. The best way to shop for property in the islands and in the countryside is to spend several months in a community and become acquainted with the locals. Spring and fall are the best times to search, as room rentals are cheap enough to allow a long stay. Winter is cheapest and it is easier to get into the local community when there are no tourists. The Greek winter, however, is overcast, damp, and cold (especially on the islands). Many businesses, including restaurants, close for the season.

Skiathos: a British retreat

Skiathos, the tourism center of the Sporades, has a large British expat community, which colors its cultural atmosphere. The British accent can be heard behind the cash registers of several of the town's shops, and English pubs are sprinkled among the alleyways of the old town.

To get to the Sporades, you cannot simply pick up a ferry in Piraeus, the port of Athens. Piraeus is on the wrong side of Greece for the Sporades. You have to depart from eastern provincial ports such as Aghios Konstantinos, or Volos. Or you have to make your way to Kimi Harbor on the largest Sporadic island, called Evia (or Euboea) and ferry on from there. Or you can simply fly via Olympic Airways to Skiathos.

As villas are the major form of vacation accommodation on the island, there appear to be more families and older expats on Skiathos than on Mykonos, for instance. The offerings include country villas as well as flats in town, and there are many deluxe homes on the island.

Skiathos is a beautiful island with many sandy beaches, a rare occurrence in Greece, where most beaches are pebbly. The Sporades islands are covered with pine trees and olive groves and are particularly gorgeous in spring when splashed with the colors of wildflowers—mostly bluebells. Water skiing, windsurfing, and boating are popular here. Yet there also is a sense of privacy for those who want to get away from it all.

One good way to find peace is to take a 40-minute walk to **Mandraki**, the most unspoiled bit of the Skiathos coast, the port of the invading Persians under Xerses. Or you can take the two-hour climb to the **Kastro**, the fortified center of the old walled town of Koukounaries (which, like other Greek villages, turned its back on the sea). You can only reach the town through a series of steep steps that replace the ancient drawbridge, which used to provide the only access.

Real estate agents in Athens as well as international agents in the United States can help you buy or rent on Skiathos, but an independent search for property on the island is easy and will save you money.

The community is small and friendly. If you wish to launch a really low-profile search, take a room in a family home where you can make local contacts. Small shops in town that advertise themselves as tourist agents are usually multiservice businesses dealing in real estate as well as room and auto rentals. All are within a few short blocks of each other, and they might compete for your business if they know you're doing a careful job of comparison shopping and are not gullible. Friendly, patient insistence on a lower price is the key to a good offer.

According to local sources on Skiathos, the selling-price for a 100-square-meter plot of land in the countryside averages between 800,000 and 2,000,000 drachmas, depending on location and available facilities, such as water supply and road access. Less expensive plots can be found, usually where an access road and/or a well must be constructed. A plot in the countryside with a deluxe villa can cost 12,240,000 to 15,300,000 drachmas. A villa with a sea view and accommodations for up to 12 people, with three to four bedrooms, two baths, living room, and dining room, would cost about 5,092,500 drachmas. This price and others, however, were quoted by local agents, so some freelance shopping might turn up considerably lower prices.

A season's rental of a larger, four-bedroom villa (based on 100 days) would cost about 509,250 to 640,200 drachmas, or about 5,092 to 6,547 drachmas a day. With an extended family or friends to share the rent, a luxurious summer on Skiathos can be quite cheap per person.

The most luxurious place to stay in Skiathos, while you are looking for a more permanent residence, is **Skiathos Palace** on Koukounaries Beach, *tel. (30-427)22-242* and *22-243*, which costs 17,000 drachmas for a double room in June, and 20,000 drachmas for demi-pension (including breakfast and one meal) in July and August.

The best deal, if you think you'll be in a hotel for a while, is the **Xenia**, *tel. (30-427)22-041* and *22-042*, which has doubles for 3,900 drachmas.

Book far in advance, though—it can be almost impossible to find a room in Skiathos between June 1 and Sept. 1.

Mykonos: a Cycladic refuge

While Skiathos is the tourism center of the Sporades islands, **Mykonos** is the tourism center of the Cyclades. Famous with the jet set, it has a reputation for being wild and flashy. It is more open, vivacious, and relaxed than Skiathos. In the height of the summer season Mykonos is crowded with fun-loving tourists, and its charm makes even the crowds exciting. A small community of U.S. expats and artists have made Mykonos their home. The lifestyle is free-spirited—it is a place for lovers of all persuasions.

Unlike Skiathos, but like other Cyclades islands, Mykonos is dry, with few trees. However, it is just as beautiful in its own dramatic way. It is covered with red poppies in spring. Mykonos is famous for its whitewashed windmills and miniature whitewashed port town. The Greek community is more tight-knit and warmer here than perhaps anywhere else in Greece, and the residents are committed to hospitality. Mykonos also features a modern hospital.

There are a few real estate agents with signs in town, but here again, it is better to make friends with some locals—the agents take a big cut. Making friends is easy; just sit in the open-air tavernas for a few evenings. Or ask the tourist police about local real estate.

There's a lot of attractive land on Mykonos. It is shaped like a small mountain, and almost all countryside plots have a gorgeous view of the sea. Many overlook the harbor, with its pretty little town and big passenger ships, both gaily lit at night.

Selling prices for 1,000-square-meter plots are quoted at about the same as on Skiathos (765,000 to 2,142,000 drachmas), although everyone says land is cheaper here. One source says 6,120,000 drachmas will fetch a luxurious home—half for the land and half to build the house. The minimum size plot you can buy for building is 4,000 square meters. On Mykonos, building is zoned to preserve historical character—you had better be sure the plot you covet is zoned for a house. You must also adhere to height limits.

Many villas are rented in the countryside as well as in town. Those in town are more expensive. You can rent a house in the countryside for as little as 61,200 drachmas for two weeks during the low season. In town, a one-room flat with bath rents for about 10,710 drachmas a week during the high season. Season rentals should be reserved early in the spring and are almost impossible to secure once summer has started.

The Peloponnese—a monumental retirement

If archaeology fascinates you, try taking up residence in the **Peloponnese**—this area features the greatest number of archaeological sites in all of Greece. **Corinth**, known for its luxury and decadent lifestyle during ancient times, is here. The Peloponnese also includes **Mycenae**, featuring the tombs of Agamemnon and Clytemnestra;

Nafplion, a pretty Venetian town, site of a Venetian fortress; **Epidaurus**, where Greek plays are performed in an ancient theater; and, of course, **Olympia**, site of the ancient games. Actually, the whole peninsula is full of ruins; these are just a few of its offerings.

For the beach life, try the town of **Tolon**, near Mycenae. **Patras** is the site of the biggest carnival celebration in Greece.

Thessaloniki, popular with Yanks

About 1,500 Americans live in **Thessaloniki**, including employees of Ethyl Hellas, Goodyear, five U.S. banks, and a U.S. tobacco company, teachers at three U.S. schools, and Fulbright scholars.

Thessaloniki is Greece's second major city, and the only other large metropolis in the country. It is primarily an industrial and trade center, more modern and richer than Athens. There are several interesting things to see, but the most outstanding are near **Pella**, the former capital of Alexander's Macedonia, still being excavated; and **Vergina**, where several tombs, one thought to be that of King Philip, are being excavated. Also nearby is the town of **Veria**, with its many mosques and its Turkish atmosphere.

Cycladic charms

The Cyclades islands are located south of Athens, between Attica and Crete, and offer 17 inviting refuges. The most famous members of the group are **Mykonos** (described above), **Santorini**, and **Delos**. **Tinos** is visited by pilgrims of the Greek Orthodox faith. **Ios** is dramatically beautiful, with a town built on the side of a mountain. **Paros** is lovely and a favorite getaway spot for vacationers.

Little-known **Naxos** is lovely. This is where Theseus rested after slaying the Minotaur and where he abandoned Ariadne. In the 16th century, Naxos was ruled by a Jewish refugee from Spain, named Duke of Naxos by the Turks. As you sail into the island's tiny harbor, you will pass a spit of land topped by a perfect yellowed marble arch, gateway to a temple to Apollo that has since sunk into the waves. Balancing it, on an island on the other side of the harbor, is a tiny white stucco Orthodox church with a belltower.

The vista of Naxos Town is perfect. Along the harborfront are steps of worn marble and stone where the local women do their laundry in the sea. A bit higher up is a street with a row of buildings that look out to the sea. Here, each evening, local youths circulate, boys walking one way, girls the other—until they reach the end of the street and turn around.

Along this promenade are tavernas serving the abundant food of the island. It is customary to walk into the kitchen and point to what you want. Choose between ubiquitous shish kebabs and stuffed peppers, eggplant casseroles, and fish specialties such as grilled tuna and squid. With the exception of what you order from the grill, most food is served lukewarm rather than hot or cold.

Islanders make a special lemon brandy that is potent and unpleasant, but you can get non-resinated wine if you insist. And the lemon trees that grow throughout the countryside give the island a pleasant lemony smell.

Just a short walk north of the harbor village is a very good beach. On the north coast of the island is **Apollonas**, which has an extraordinary amateur museum with a statue of a naked youth (*kouros*) that lies lifeless and unfinished in the middle of the stone quarry where the carver abandoned it a few thousand years ago.

Santorini (or Thera as it is called by the Greeks) is the most beautiful Greek island, possibly the site of the mythical Atlantis. This island is more sophisticated and wilder than Naxos. English is widely spoken here. The island is so barren and poor that its sons have gone off to America to earn their ways. Tourism is the major trade.

Le Corbusier's concept of architecture supposedly changed dramatically after he visited Santorini. The buildings here are curving and fluid.

To get to the island, sail into the **Kaldera**, the mouth of a huge sunken volcano that last erupted in 1956. The Kaldera was created about 1500 B.C., when the volcano, which had been in the middle of the island, blew up so fiercely that three sides of it fell into the sea. Because much of the volcano sank, Santorini may have been the Atlantis of antiquity.

Santorini is famous for its archaeological finds. Explore the island's archeological dig at Akrotiri—but be prepared for a long climb. As in Naples, the best work of Akrotiri has been carted off to museums, but you can still get an idea of what a Minoan town was like. This was a metropolis, not a backwater. The large city has municipal buildings decorated with frescoes (now in Athens), a pottery factory, mosaic floors, and stone walls. As in Pompeii, the sudden volcano froze the town in time, leaving an eerie slice of life 3,500 years ago. For more information on the Akrotiri site, call *tel. (30-286)22-217.*

Climb to the Acropolis for a remarkable view. These remains are more recent than those of Akrotiri, a mere 2,200 years old. Here are carvings and bas-reliefs of the gods of classic antiquity—Zeus,

Apollo, and Poseidon. The island's main town is **Thira** (also known as Fira), which has lovely churches. Landing at Thira is dramatic. A sheer black volcanic cliff rises above the narrow quay.

To get to the top, where the town is, you can climb, take the cable car, or (more fun) ride a donkey. Outside Thira are beautiful beaches. On the southwest coast there are the black sand beaches at Kamari, Monolithos, and Perissa. Several castles guard the island. And the Nea Kaimeni volcano on the small island in the harbor is active.

The best way to see Santorini is by jeep, which you can do for $35 a day.

There are several apartments and villas for rent on Santorini—ask one of the tourist agents on arrival, or the Greek National Tourist Organization (EOT) before embarking for Santorini. There are traditional settlements in **Oia**, on the northeastern tip, restored by the government and run by the EOT, for use as inexpensive tourist accommodations.

Santorini also has wonderful little out-of-the-way country restaurants and isolated beaches.

The atmosphere on Santorini is more formal than on other Greek islands. It has several monasteries and grandiose churches, and the islanders seem to take their religion more seriously. Shop-owners here are not as friendly and appear reluctant to let you view their wares. Santorini is famous for its wine, which is quite good. Tasting is free at **Canava Roussos**, in Kamari.

The **Phinika Restaurant**, on the road to Oia, serves Nychteri (night wine), which is never exposed to daylight before being served.

Delights of the Dodecanese

Rhodes is the prime destination in the Dodecanese island group. Not far from Turkey, it has a slightly Turkish character. The city of Rhodes is located in and around the walls of the medieval Fortress of the Knights of St. John. Wandering among the shops and restaurants inside the fortress is a little like visiting Disneyland. There are sound and light shows and six outdoor movie theaters, costumed Greek dancers, and painting and handicraft exhibits. Outside the walls is a gambling casino in the Grand Hotel. There's also an 18-hole golf course at Afandou.

Rhodes is a free port and has shops ranging from those that sell Greek handicrafts to those that sell Gucci and Yves St. Laurent items. As the prime Greek island for European tourists (mostly beautiful blond Scandinavians), Rhodes offers a number of good restaurants and lively night life. The tourist police and the EOT, both just outside the walls in the market area, can provide suggestions on where to live.

There is a small U.S. community on Rhodes—philanthropists, artists, and retirees (mostly Greek-Americans). The U.S. government has a Voice of America relay station there.

About 13 of the Dodecanese islands are suitable places to retire. **Patmos** is considered one of the most beautiful in the Aegean. **Kalymnos** has a busy harbor town and peaceful countryside.

The Ionian islands

The most popular of the Ionian islands is **Corfu**, sometimes called the most beautiful island in Greece. Covered with lemon, orange, cyprus, fig, and olive groves, it is a lush semi-mountainous island. Corfu was the setting of Homer's *Odyssey*, Shakespeare's *Tempest*, and Henry Miller's *Colossus of Maroussi*. Many of the island's beautiful villas belong to British expats. The main port, **Kekira**, is a town of Venetian elegance, almost more Italian than Greek. Corfu is geared for tourists and offers many shops, hotels, restaurants, and good night life.

Sadly, you may not buy property in Rhodes if you are not Greek. But you can rent there.

The southern and western coasts of Corfu have the most striking scenery. Eight miles south of the port is the impressive **Achilleon Palace**, *tel. (30-661)38-629*, once the summer residence of Kaiser Wilhelm II of Germany, now a gambling casino. The jet set hangs out in **Paleokastritsa**, on the west coast. The northern coast is the most touristy area, with several resort towns. **Kassiopi** is one of the least spoiled and most reasonably priced places to stay.

Zante is an island whose charms are known by few Americans. Green and relatively unspoiled, it was called the "flower of the Levant" by the Venetians. Today it is known for its relaxing pace and good food. It has a Venetian fortress and some lovely beaches, but the main port town of Zante is not especially spectacular.

Crete: a land unto itself

Crete, a mini-country with its own lifestyle, is a huge island of over 5,000 square miles. It has some of the world's most interesting ruins and arresting scenery. **Iraklion**, on the north-central coast, is near Knossos and other Minoan ruins to the east. **Hania** is the busy capital of Crete, situated on the northwestern coast.

The ancient capital of Minoan civilization, **Knossos** is the main destination for tourists. Iraklion, the closest thing to a modern-day city, is not attractive. To the east of this city is the tourist belt of Crete, where there are beaches and hotels. The most "swinging" area is around **Elounda**, a completely preserved Minoan town; and **Zakros**, another Minoan palace.

The southern and western coasts of Crete are the least developed, while the interior is virtually unspoiled. Phaistos, also a palace, is inland from the central southern coast. Gortys, an old Roman town, is nearby, and Agia Triada, another Minoan site, is on the coast to the west. Limnes, a picturesque fishing village, and Matala, where there are ancient cave tombs overlooking a beach, are two modern-day resort areas near the ruins.

The natural pièce de résistance of Crete is the **Samarian Gorge**, located in central western Crete. It is the largest—and many think the most beautiful—gorge in all of Europe, and provides a popular jaunt for hikers.

Hania has a picturesque Venetian harbor and narrow streets. The Venetian quarter is the most interesting area. The city has lots of handicraft shops. Accommodations are reasonable and easy to find, all on the modest side.

Warning: Foreigners have lost property on Corfu

Seventeen years ago, British banker Jacob Rothschild bought a dilapidated olive farm on Corfu. That was before tourists discovered the island en masse and land prices soared—tenfold in the last 15 years.

Rothschild invested time and resources in his property, which is now a magnificent villa. The heirs of the former owner thought so, too. Using a Greek law of 1927 that forbids foreigners to hold Greek land near borders, they sued to declare Rothschild's purchase illegal. They won.

The Greek Supreme Court voided the purchase, deciding that since the Greek holding company that Rothschild had set up to purchase and own the property was controlled by a foreigner, it could not hold Greek border land. (Corfu is near Albania.)

It is now open season for locals who want their property back. And the rise in property values makes the prospect of doing so extremely tempting.

Not all of the approximately 1,000 foreigners who own land in Corfu bought it through a holding company. Another method is to use a Greek nominee, often a property lawyer, to circumvent the restrictions. Caveat emptor: Current legal opinion is that nominee purchases also would be voided in a court challenge.

Sources for buying real estate

If you're doing an independent search, check the classifieds of the daily *Athens News*, sold on every street corner. Buy a copy of the *Athenian*, an English-language monthly that carries a directory of telephone numbers useful for expats. The directory includes numbers for utility companies. OTE offices, Greece's combination post office/telephone centers, carry the *Blue Book*, which lists telephone numbers in English and has a section like the U.S. yellow pages that list real estate contacts.

For names of international real estate agents specializing in Greek property, check with the **Federation of International Real Estate Agents (FIABCI)**, *777 14th St. N.W., Washington, DC 20005; tel. (202)383-1167/1032.* The FIABCI office in Greece is at *24 Charilaou Tirkeopi St., Athens; tel. (30-1)562-1930.*

One agent they recommend is **Peter G. Manners,** *Sheldon Green & Associates, 1720 Kennedy Causeway, Miami, FL 33141.*

The following real estate agents were listed in the Athens *Blue Pages*:

•**Dianas Athanassios,** *50 Liassion and Epirau Streets; tel. (30-1)881-3364;*

•**Fatsis George,** *13 Loucianou St., Kolonaki; tel. (30-1)722-5050;*

•**Andreas Hassapis,** *36 Sina St., Kolonaki; tel. (30-1)363-4504;*

•**Martin Charles,** *3 Kapsali St., Kolonaki; tel. (30-1)721-2229;*

•**Orfandis Char. Petros,** *19 Herodotou St., Kolonaki; tel. (30-1)722-0386;*

•**Papaevagelou Nikol.,** *64 Nea Vouliagmenis Ave. and 100 Karapanou St.; tel. (30-1)894-1402;*

•**Papazoglou George,** *186 Kifssias Ave., Psyhico; tel. (30-1)672-2786;* and

•**Sotiropoulos Spiros and Sons,** *5 Zalakosta St., Syntagma; tel. (30-1)363-5184.*

For legal advice: Contact the **U.S. Embassy,** *Vas. Sofias 91, Athens; tel. (30-1)721-2951,* for its list of attorneys.

Banking and money

One Greek-American who has returned to Greece to retire tells us that with a $40,000 stake, an American can live like a prince in

Greece on the 25% interest offered by Greek banks, and never have to touch the principal.

Greek banks are regulated by the government. The Bank of Greece manages the nation's money through a complex system of reserves designed to control the supply of money and finance public spending. In other words, money is tight in Greece. Don't expect a mortgage.

There are 33 domestic commercial banks in Greece, but due to indirect government control, only six are truly private. There are also three special banks, three investment banks (including the Hellenic Industrial Development Bank), and the Postal Savings Bank.

U.S. commercial banks with facilities in Greece include Citibank, Bank of America, Continental Bank, American Express, Chase Manhattan, and Bank of Chicago. Each has an office in Athens, and several have offices in Thessaloniki. American Express, Bank of America, Chase Manhattan, and Citibank also have offices in Piraeus. Manufacturers Hanover has a representative office in Athens.

Banking hours are from 8 a.m. to 2 p.m., Monday through Friday. The branches of many banks stay open in the afternoon and on Saturdays. For a list of these banks, contact the **E.O.T. Information** *Bureau, 2 Karageorgi Servais St., Syntagma Square, Athens; tel. (30-1)322-2545.*

Greeks gladly accept most traveler's checks and credit cards. Outside Athens there is often no check on one's credit card number, which can work to your advantage if you have a limit (or are behind on your payments)—and against it if your card is stolen. If you run out of money, Greek banks will advance up to 10,000 drachmas on a major U.S. credit card.

The Greek monetary unit is the drachma, made up of 100 lepata.

Where to find money

•**The AMEX Bank,** *17 Panepistimious St., GR 102 26 Athens; tel. (30-1)323-4781.* The travel, tourism, credit card, and traveler's check departments are at *2 Ermou St., GR 102 25 Athens (or P.O. Box 3325, Athens); tel. (30-1)324-4975.* In Thessaloniki, the commercial bank is at *19 Tsimiski St.;*

•**Bank of America,** *39 Panepistimious St., GR 105 64 Athens; tel. (30-1)325-1906; 116 Kolokotroni St., Pireaus; tel. (30-1)452-7251; 34 Tsimiski St., Thessaloniki; tel. (30-31)268-021;*

•**Chase Manhattan,** *3 Korai St., GR 102 49 Athens; tel. (30-1)323-7711; 87 Akti Miaouli, Pireaus; tel. (30-1)411-3711; 6 Aristotelous St., Thessaloniki; tel. (30-31)236-221;*

•**Citibank,** *8 Othonos St., GR 103 92 Athens; tel. (30-1)322-7471;*

•**The National Bank of Greece,** *86 Aeolou St., Athens; tel. (30-1)321-0411.* Hours are until 9 p.m. weekdays, 8 p.m. weekends. In the United States, the **Atlantic Bank of New York** is a subsidiary of the National Bank of Greece. It's at *960 Avenue of the Americas, New York, NY 10001; tel. (212)695-5400;*

•**Merrill Lynch,** *17 Valaoritou St., GR 106 71 Athens; tel. (30-1)361-8916;* and

•**Paine Webber,** *4 Koumbari St., GR 106 74 Athens; tel. (30-1)362-8037.*

Transportation

If driving, keep in mind that Greece has the second highest accident rate in Europe (Portugal is the worst) and that many of the roads are very dangerous, particularly if you are unfamiliar with them.

Greek public transportion is among the cheapest in Europe. Streetcar, bus, and subway tickets cost 30 drachmas and are free before 8 a.m.

Greek Railways offers substantial reductions for seniors. You can get a senior card if you are over 60 and present an identity card or passport. The card costs 5,500 drachmas first class; 3,980 drachmas second class. It is valid for one year and it entitles the holder to make five single voyages free of charge any time except the 10 days before and after Easter or Christmas or from July 1 to Sept. 30. It also allows a 50% reduction on any number of trips in excess of the initial five free trips within a year.

If you are not over 60, the tourist card is a good deal. Tourist cards are granted to individual passengers, families, and groups of up to five persons. They are valid for 10, 20, and 30 days and entitle the holder to make unlimited trips on every route served by the railway (second class) and on certain buses. Tourist cards for two people are 8,500 drachmas for 10 days, 13,850 drachmas for 20 days, 18,800 drachmas for 30 days.

For information on railways, contact the **National Tourist Organization of Greece,** *Information Department, 2 Amerikis Str.; tel. (30-1)322-3111.* To purchase tickets, go to *1-3 Karalou St.; tel. (30-1)522-2491* or *6 Sina St.; tel. (30-1)362-4402.*

Communicating

The Greek public telephone system is cheap. Direct-dial calls, both to destinations within the country and overseas, can be made at the OTE offices (as mentioned earlier, Greece's combination telephone-telegraph-postal offices), located in most villages and big cities. They are generally open from 6 a.m. to midnight. In larger cities, there is usually one OTE office open 24 hours.

If calling from a private phone, dial 161 to get the overseas operator. Dial 162 for an English-speaking operator. It's about 70 cents per minute to call the U.S. East Coast. The direct-dial prefix from the United States is 011-30-1 for Athens; other towns will usually have double-digit city codes (instead of the final 1). From Greece, the direct-dial code for the United States is 001. Public phones are located at some newspaper kiosks. To send a night letter or telegram, stop at an OTE or dial 165.

Mail takes five to six days between the East Coast of the United States and Athens. Service within Greece is slow and irregular, and sometimes unreliable. Mail boxes are small and yellow, usually attached to a building wall at eye level. And post offices change money as well as sell stamps.

Medical facilities

Medical facilities in Greece are government-run. In Athens there are many U.S.-trained doctors and dentists. Several hospitals provide competent care. Dental care is more expensive than in the United States. Local eyeglasses are neither fashionable nor cheap. Outside Athens, medical facilities are scattered—some isolated islands have none.

For information, contact **The Medical Association,** *61 Akadinias St., Athens; tel. (30-1)361-7141.*

The telephone number for the **Athens First Aid Station** is *166.*

Greek spas

Greece has always been known for its thermal spas, even in classical times. Today 20 spas are located at summer resorts in picturesque parts of the country. Many are on the sea. Each spa specializes in a group of ailments.

The **Greek National Tourist Organization,** *645 5th Ave., New York, NY 10022; (212)421-5777,* has a list of spa resorts and their specialties.

Greek food

Greece has some of the best food in the world. Although simple, its very simplicity and ultimate freshness are what make it so good. Except during the height of tourist season, when busy resort areas may import vegetables and fish to take care of the volume, you can rest assured that the Greek food you eat is grown or caught nearby and is almost always of same-day freshness.

The staple may be the best Greek dish of all: the Greek salad, with chunks of fresh red tomatoes, cucumber, feta cheese, slices of fresh onion, and big Greek olives. A real Greek salad is topped only with Greece's aromatic olive oil (among the world's best). Along with the peasant bread served with it, a Greek salad is big enough to make a cheaper-than-cheap lunch or light dinner.

A Greek salad with fried squid makes a delicious meal that costs only a dollar or two. Grilled octopus is also tasty and chewy, especially when grilled over an open fire and topped with olive oil.

A favorite Greek pastime is to sit in an outdoor café and munch on hors d'oeuvres with a glass of Greek beer, wine, or ouzo. Ouzerias (ouzo bars) are devoted to Greek samplers. These snacks, called *Mezze*, when served with Greek bread, are filling enough to make a light meal. Among the many temptations are fried eggplant served with garlic sauce; stuffed grapevine leaves (*dolmades*); Greek "caviar," a fish roe dip (*taramasalata*); cucumber, yogurt, and onion dip (*tsatziki*); and olives. Try a different one each time.

Other than fish, main entrees are *souvlaki* (grilled shish kabob—either meat, fish, or chicken) with rice, grilled chicken, or *moussaka* (eggplant and cheese casserole). Lamb is the favorite meat used in Greek cooking.

Greek-made Amstel is the best beer. Domestica is the all-around favorite Greek wine, while retsina (resinated wine) is an interesting Greek specialty. The pine flavor of retsina comes from the fact that it is stored in barrels made of pine rather than oak. Santorini is known for its domestica, while retsina comes from the north. Licorice-flavored ouzo is the most famous Greek alcoholic beverage. It is more potent than it tastes, and is always served with a glass of water for mixing. Sanka means U.S. coffee, and by the way, it is not decaffeinated.

Greek restaurant and bar bills usually include a service charge. (In Athens, many cafés charge an extra service charge around Christmas.) If the service is particularly good, leave an additional 15% to 20%. The Greek custom is to leave loose change on the plate and an equal amount on the table. The change on the plate is for the waiter; the change on the table is for the busboy. Busboys work for tips alone.

Breakfast is early, sometimes over by 9 a.m. Lunch is usually served from 1 p.m. to 3 p.m. Cocktails begin at 7:30 p.m., and Greeks dine around 9 p.m.

Shopping in Greece

Clothes are cheap and fun to buy in Greece. Each little Greek shop sells its own along with factory-made pieces. You'll find lots of embroidery and handmade lace. Handknit sweaters of all types are a real buy. Peasant skirts and blouses, as well as fashionable resort wear are abundant.

Furs are a real buy. Greeks are the world's specialists in fur cutting. Prices here are about 50% lower than anywhere else. Kastoria and Siatista are famous areas for furs. Greek leather is also cheap. You can get good sandals for a little over 765 drachmas. Greek rugs are another good value. Among them are furry *flokatis*, which are usually white. *Flokatis* are pure lambswool from the mountains of northern Greece, originally used as wall hangings to keep out the cold and damp—5-foot-by-7-foot rugs cost about 9,975 to 13,300 drachmas. Woven Greek tapestry rugs are colorful and extremely cheap—small throw rugs can be bought for under 4,000 drachmas.

One couple's happy retirement

Stuart M. Hunter describes his Greek retirement.

Retire a little early, put our U.S. affairs in order and spend the next two to four years living, traveling, painting, and writing in Europe. That was our plan.

We are now into the second year of our sojourn abroad. What's it been like? Strenuous in almost every respect—and we have no regrets. So far, this has been a fabulous experience.

We spent winter and spring this year in Greece, living on Crete and another island in the Aegean, Paros.

Finding a habitat

It took us about eight or nine days to find the place we wanted to rent on Crete. Leads came through the Tourist Police in Aghios Nikolaos in Crete and through word of mouth from asking at shops and tavernas. Everybody knows of just one place and there is no listing center (at least, in the off-season) except for a listed one at the Tourist Police. That, plus a tough language barrier, made checking out possibilities a laborious and time-consuming process.

The two places we did finally rent, the one over the winter and

the other during April, came to our attention entirely through acciden-
tal, round-about referrals.

Our three-month winter place was a very large, one-room "villa"
part way up a steep hillside, overlooking a beautiful bay and an island
eight miles north of Aghios Nikolaos.

Weathering Greece

Winter weather in Crete is similar to North Carolina's (they're on
the same latitude): warm, bright, and beautiful when it's sunny, quite
chilly (35 to 50 degrees Fahrenheit) and windy when it's cloudy. It
was about 60% cloudy in December, January, and February and about
35% in March.

At least two electric heaters are a must, and a fireplace is extremely welcome and enjoyable. A three-month supply of firewood
cost us about $80 and a source was difficult to locate. A man at the
Tourist Police found it for us finally through a friend of a friend of
whom he said, "I know him. He's good boys."

A matter of trust

Trust. That's what our sojourn in Greece has been all about. And
great natural beauty, warm and friendly people, and a lifestyle we
never imagined back home in Minnesota.

When we put our car in a garage once for several days for
safekeeping, I had a long, mutually incomprehensible conversation
with the garage attendant about getting a claim check. He finally
dragged me down the street to our hotel where the man at the desk
could translate. The upshot: It's hard to lose something as big as a car,
but it's easy to lose a small slip of paper—and, the garageman added,
if you lose your claim check, you've lost your car! It seemed to make
sense to both of them.

So we shook hands all around to seal the deal—and off the
garageman drove with our car. Retrieving it three days later only
required our pointing to it, smiling, digging through a stack of car
keys, paying the fee, and leaving with another cordial handshake.

When we opened our Greek checking account we had to sign a
long bank form, all in Greek. No one could find a translation—so we
just signed.

At the laundry we were given two laundry lists, one in English,
which they couldn't read, and the other in Greek, which we couldn't
read, and which, of course, was the control list. We'd ask for our
laundry two days ahead of when we expected to be in town again in

hopes it would be ready. But nearly always they hadn't yet started it and would ask us to come back in two hours, at which time most of it would be in dryers and ready in a half-hour—if they could find it all.

Our landlord, the local communist mayor, said it was a good laundry, but totally disorganized and had once lost a pair of his trousers. Another victim of capitalism.

He was some communist: owner-manager of a thriving dry-goods store, a superbly located large tourist gift shop, a string of high-class tourist villas rented through an agent, and, before becoming mayor, president of the local chamber of commerce. Small wonder he also had an ulcer.

Postal problems

Dealing with the post office in our little town in northeastern Crete was an experience. Our postmaster was a short, wiry man with a huge, black, turned-down moustache, a dour, expressionless face, and fierce, dark eyes.

We frequently had to send complicated overseas mail that would send him furiously digging into postal regulations and folders of stamps of various denominations—all the time darkly muttering to himself.

Occasionally the postmaster would have to call up the post office in the larger city a few miles away for information, and here again he would become embroiled in a shouting telephone match, which never ended, so far as we could determine, with "Good bye" or "Thank you."

Our fearsome postmaster quickly came to know who we were and for some reason always seemed to be "on our side." When we came in to ask for our mail he would brusquely wave us back to the bin to look through the stack of general delivery mail for ourselves.

More than once as we drove slowly through the village square we would find the little post office closed and the postmaster, in his long leather coat-jacket, out on his appointed rounds. Usually this included having coffee on the square with a group of equally dark and dour-looking men. If he would see us at such times, he would break routine, stride over to our car, motion towards the post office, march over to open it up and give us our mail.

One Sunday morning early in the winter we went to the village church (a totally unfamiliar Greek Orthodox service) and there he was—our gruff little postmaster in charge of selling candles to the worshipers. We bought a candle from him, lit it, and placed it in the large holder with all the other candles. Our postmaster only glowered at us and yet we sensed that we had cemented our relationship. In a strange land you can't be in too well with your postmaster.

The fruits of the earth

The oranges of Crete, available only in the wintertime, are fantastic: huge, easy to peel, uniformly sweet and juicy, plentiful, and cheap. They are trying to grow bananas as well in Crete, but so far without much success. The homegrown black or bing cherries are simply out of this world. And in March the markets are full of artichokes.

In January and February almost the entire population is out harvesting olives from the trees that have been nurtured, some for centuries, in large groves and in small clusters, or even singly, wedged into nearly any awkward, craggy spot where a tree could possibly take hold. In that season the valleys, hills, and mountainsides come alive with the sights and sounds of the olive harvest.

Families and groups of families, representing three or four generations and nearly all states of physical condition, will work on a cluster of olive trees—or even just one tree that may be hanging its laden branches out over a road.

A large net or tough plastic drop cloth is laid around under the tree and the olives are then shaken and beaten into it. The men get into the tops of the trees and shake them, while the women and children beat at the middle and lower branches with long, thin sticks. Other children and the very elderly gather up stray olives and branches and help with sundry other chores.

The sights and sounds present an unbelievable scene of quiet serenity and harmony: muffled voices, the swish-swish of sticks beating in the trees, a carpet of yellow wild flowers underfoot, a backdrop of snow-covered mountains, a rooster crowing far off somewhere, and the rasping bray of a nearby mule.

Making friends

In June we had a milestone wedding anniversary and decided to drive back into the mountains south of Iraklion to visit several reportedly picturesque villages that feature special weaving and needlework. The one that impressed us most was Anogia and we decided to have our picnic lunch there.

In a very pretty little square at the center of this mountainside village is a small "kafenion." We asked the elderly man and woman in charge if we could have some coffee and a sweet and use of their few small tables for our picnic.

Once our coffee and sweet were served, the woman disappeared. But the old gentleman sat out in front of his kafenion a short distance away and curiously watched us as we unpacked our small lunch.

In a few minutes he disappeared inside and emerged with his own cup of coffee, some nuts and olives, and slowly walked over to our table, put down his things and pulled up a chair to help us celebrate.

We offered him some of our wine, bread, cheese, and fruit, which he accepted, and we shared his nuts and olives and, later, a small glass of powerful *raki*.

At nearly every drink of wine we toasted each other with a clink of glasses and "yah-sahs!" and we carried on our usual, garbled conversation by furiously thumbing through our English-Greek phonetic dictionary and digging up all the "shepherd Greek" we'd learned over the winter.

It worked quite well in this case, because this wonderful old gentleman, with his traditionally huge, beautiful moustache and nearly expressionless face, proved to be a retired shepherd himself.

He was dressed for it: black headband, a dark threadbare suitcoat, hugely bloused out jodhpurs and elegant, knee-length heavy leather boots, and gnarled olive-wood cane. It was strenuous and faltering conversation, but altogether a thoroughly enjoyable and delightful lunch.

When we rose finally to leave we shook hands all around, and this almost teetering old man nearly broke our hands with his grip, still powerful from decades of milking sheep. As we walked back in the direction of our car, we noticed growing in a corner just behind our table a stand of beautiful calla lilies. My wife had carried a simple bouquet of these lilies at our wedding on this day many years before. It was a perfect note to a wonderful day in our sojourn abroad.

For more information

•**Embassy of Greece,** *2211 Massachusetts Ave. N.W., Washington, DC 20008; (202)667-3168.*

•**Greek National Tourist Organization,** *Olympic Tower, 645 Fifth Ave., Fifth floor, New York, NY 10022; (212)421-5777; 168 N. Michigan Ave., Chicago, IL 60601; (312)782-1084; 611 W. Sixth St., Suite 1998, Los Angeles, CA 90017; (213)626-6696.*

•**The American Women's Organization of Greece (AWOG)** publishes *Hints for Living in Greece*, which you can buy at the Family

Liaison Office at the U.S. Embassy, or at the American Club.

•**The Greek Handbook—An A-Z Practical Guide to Almost Everything You Want to Know About Greece,** by Tom Stone, is published in Greece by Lycabbetus Press and is available in local bookstores. Useful.

•**The National Geographic Society** publishes several maps, "Greece and the Aegean" and "Historic Mediterranean Sea," and a special-interest chart, "Mythical Realm of God and Heroes," all for $4. Write the Society at *P.O. Box 2806, Washington, DC 20013.*

For anything you might want to know about the capital of Greece, dial the office of the **Mayor of Athens;** *tel. (30-1)324-2213.*

Chapter 12

Ireland

Fifteen-thousand Americans open their social security checks in Ireland (Eire) each year. Foreigners began retiring here in great numbers in 1969, when the Dublin government offered tax exemptions to professional artists and writers. American celebrities who have chosen Ireland as their retirement home include John Huston, Burl Ives, Angela Lansbury, Gregory Peck, and Peter Ustinov.

Outside Dublin are peaceful country retreats, beaches, ancient villages, and resorts. Kerry, on the southwestern tip of the country, has a beautiful coastline. About 7,000 lakes surround Killarney, and the Aran Islands (Inishmore, Inishmaan, and Inisheere) are rugged and romantic.

Ireland's temperatures are consistently mild, ranging from 40 degrees Fahrenheit in the winter to 65 degrees Fahrenheit in the summer. Because of the heavy rains that fall here (80 inches a year in some places), the country really is emerald green. Soft mists and gentle breezes roll across the green countryside, and lovely blue skies hang above it.

However, one of the best things about Ireland is that real estate is downright cheap. You can buy a cottage on the scenic Dingle Peninsula for less than $15,000—a price unheard of in Britain.

Taking up residence

If you were born in Ireland, or if you can show that at least one parent or grandparent was born in Ireland, you are free to live in Ireland without restriction.

If neither of these situations applies to you, request information on residency from the **Department of Justice,** *72 St. Stephen's Green, Dublin 2; tel. (353-1)789711,* or the **Consulate General of Ireland,** *580 Fifth Ave., New York, NY 10036.*

Approval for permanent residence is usually granted if you can prove financial independence. Once you are a foreign resident of Ireland, you can vote in local, but not national, elections.

What you can bring with you

When you take up permanent residence in Ireland, you can

251

import duty-free used personal belongings and household effects (including cars), as well as any belongings used for your business, trade, or profession. Usually, importation must take place six months before or after the date on which you move to Ireland.

For detailed information on the steps involved with importing your goods, including which papers you must fill out, contact the *Secretary,* **Office of Revenue Commissioners,** *Dublin Castle, Dublin 2; tel. (353-1)792777.*

Health care

People who make less than 12,500 punts per year are eligible for free medical care in Ireland. If your income is greater than that, you can join a medical insurance system for less than 138 punts per year. Doctors charge half what they do in the United States, but you may have difficulty finding one outside the major cities. For more information on health care, write the **Department of Health,** *Dublin 1.*

Money matters

Property is inexpensive on the Emerald Isle. But inflation is high, so goods and services can be expensive. And taxes are astronomical, bringing cigarettes up to 1.80 punts ($2.52 in the fall of 1988) a pack.

A single person could live in Ireland on an American pension of $10,000 a year; a couple could live on $12,000 a year. (The average income in Ireland is 8,000 punts per year.)

A look at taxes

A double-taxation agreement between Ireland and the United States assures that you will not pay income taxes twice. Irish residents are taxed at 35% on the first 4,700 punts of their income; 48% on the next 2,800 punts; and 58% on the remainder of their income. However, generous tax breaks are available. All taxpayers are entitled to a 2,000-punt personal allowance; taxpayers with dependent wives are entitled to a 4,000-punt allowance. Those over 65 are entitled to an age allowance of 200 punts; married couples over 65 are entitled to an allowance of 400 punts. In addition, you can write off medical insurance premiums, life insurance premiums, health expenses, interest on loans, rent if you are over 55, some charitable contributions, and some investments.

Tax exemptions (on the basis of individual applications to the **Office of Revenue Commissioners,** *address above*) are available to artists, writers, and composers who produce original and creative works generally recognized as having artistic merit. This exemption applies to non-nationals as well as nationals, provided they are residents in Ireland for purposes of income taxes and are not residents elsewhere. Works that may be claimed include books, plays, other writings, musical compositions, paintings, sculpture, and other visual arts.

If you buy property in Ireland, beware the residential property tax. This is payable if your household income exceeds 24,468 punts a year and your residence is valued at more than 68,728 punts. The tax for any property valued at more than 68,728 punts is 1.5%. (It is adjusted each year.) Property taxes must be paid by Oct. 1 each year to the **Revenue Commissioners,** *Collector-General, Teach Earlsfort, Hatch Street, Dublin 2.*

Buildings that are of significant historical, architectural, or aesthetic interest and are open to the public may be exempted from property taxes. Application for the exemption should be made to the *Secretary,* **Office of Public Works,** *51 St. Stephen's Green, Dublin 2.* Even if the building is not exempt from taxes, the garden may be if it is of national, scientific, historic, or artistic interest.

For more information on taxes, contact the **Office of Revenue Commissioners,** *Dublin Castle, Dublin 2; tel. (353-1)79-2777.* Or send for copies of *A Home of Your Own* and *The Quarterly Bulletin of Housing Statistics,* both published by the **Department of Local Government,** *Dublin 2.*

Where to live

Where should you live on the Emerald Isle? If you enjoy good restaurants, museums, and concerts, you should probably settle in Dublin. If you prefer peace and quiet and long walks in the country-side, get as far from Dublin as possible. Try Sligo, with its dramatic scenery, or peaceful Killarney, with its many lakes.

Counties Clare and Galway

Ireland's most unusual and dramatic scenery is in counties **Clare** and **Galway.** Between Limerick and Galway Bay, the black **Cliffs of Moher** in County Clare rise a spectacular 700 feet from the ocean. This county is also a center for traditional Irish music.

Ennis in County Clare is the best base for exploring the west of Ireland, from which many Americans stem. The old market town (population 20,000) has escaped relatively unscathed by tourists, even though Shannon Airport is nearby. The main street in Ennis is lined with shops selling genuine (if pricey) antiques and good crafts. But the town's gem is its monastery—a roofless, weed-covered Gothic ruin.

County Kerry

County Kerry's Inveragh Peninsula is encircled by a 110-mile drive called the **Ring of Kerry.** You can make the drive in a day. You'll see **Skellig Rocks,** where cells were carved from solid rock by monks escaping the Vikings; **Ballaghisheen Pass,** which passes through scenic mountains; and, along the southern half of the ring, peaceful beaches.

County Kerry's wild and Gaelic **Dingle Peninsula** makes for another beautiful drive. Begin in **Dingle,** on the ocean. Surrounded by hills, this fishing town is protected by an ancient wall. From Dingle, take the road to **Ventry,** which has an inviting beach. Outside Ventry are beehive huts built long ago by Irish monks. **Slea Head,** at the tip of the peninsula, offers a view of the seven Blasket Islands and a beach with water warm enough for swimming, thanks to the Gulf Stream.

Northeast of Slea Head is **Gallerus Oratory,** an unmortared stone building from the ninth century. After 1,000 years, it is still watertight. From the Conair Pass you can see the lakes and Brandon, Tralee, and Dingle bays. At **Sybil Head** you'll see high, green cliffs topped by thatched cottages and washed by the Atlantic below.

The main tourist center in County Kerry is **Killarney.** Surrounded by deep blue lakes and green hills, Killarney is the place for boaters, fishermen, and hikers.

County Wicklow

Known as the Garden of Ireland, **Wicklow** is incredibly green. At the heart of this county is **Wexford,** a small Viking-founded seaside town. It's been said that Henry II repented at the nearby abbey for the assassination of Thomas à Becket, and Oliver Cromwell's troops massacred the townspeople here in 1649 in an anti-Catholic rage. The Kennedy family homestead is in **Dunganstown,** a small town nearby.

The other place to visit in Wicklow is **Glendalough,** a deep valley in the Wicklow Mountains. In the sixth century, St. Kevin took refuge in this peaceful glen between two lakes. However, his refuge didn't remain secret. His disciples followed him and founded a monastery and a famous center of learning here. You can see the remains of the medieval round tower, as well as buildings from the

9th through 13th centuries. Hike the nature trails that lead through the valley.

Dublin

Dublin's most famous resident was the writer **James Joyce,** born at *41 Brighton Square W.* He lived in Sandycove (as did his characters in *Ulysses*), and he frequented **Mulligan's Pub,** *Poolbeg Street.*

Dublin is a city that begets poets. Percy Bysshe Shelley and George Bernard Shaw also live here.

In addition to its literary history, the city boasts the *Book of Kells,* the most intricately illuminated manuscript in the Western world. It is kept at Trinity College, Eire's ancient and revered center of learning. Dublin also has its own castle. A remnant of the days of royalty, it now houses government offices.

To see the rowdier side of Dublin, visit the **Guinness Brewery,** which produces Ireland's rich and frothy national stout, or the **General Post Office,** *O'Connell Street,* the scene of the 1916 uprising against the British.

Phoenix Park, a stretch of green at the heart of Dublin, is both the official residence of the Irish president and the city's playground. It has a race course, a soccer field, a zoo, sports grounds, gardens, a lake, and a monument to Wellington.

Kilkenny

Slightly inland, **Kilkenny** has medieval buildings, cobblestoned streets, pleasant walkways by the Nore River, and a grand castle. The seat of the kings of Ossory, Kilkenny was the site of parliaments and assemblies in the 14th, 16th, and 17th centuries.

Kinsale

A yachting center, **Kinsale** overflows with gourmet restaurants frequented by boat owners from all over the world. The *Lusitania* was torpedoed off the coast of Kinsale by a German sub in 1915. This was also the site of the 1602 Battle of Kinsale, when the English defeated the northern chieftains, establishing English domination of Ireland.

Sligo

Sligo is the dramatic countryside where the poet Yeats spent his childhood summers. He asked to be buried in **Drumcliffe Church-yard,** five miles north of Sligo proper. At the summit of the nearby

Glen of Knocknarea is said to be the grave of the legendary Maeve, queen of the immortal faeries. It is also the site and source of Yeats' poem "The Lake of Innisfree."

Sixty years ago, Sligo was the center of the Irish literary revival. The area also claims one of the largest concentrations of prehistoric graves and monuments in Western Europe. You won't find them listed in tourist brochures—you must discover them by word-of-mouth. And then you may have difficulty locating them—most are not fenced off.

Buying a piece of the auld sod

Property in Ireland is amazingly inexpensive by American standards. You can buy a seaside cottage in good condition with a view of the Blasket Islands for 18,000 punts.

In general, older cottages in the countryside go for 15,000 punts to 25,000 punts, while newer bungalows in the countryside go for 30,000 punts to 35,000 punts. If you were to draw an imaginary line from Dublin to Galway, the most attractive places to live would be north of the line, or along the seacoast. The heart of Ireland, south of this imaginary line, is largely industrial.

Dublin

The most expensive places to buy real estate are Dublin and County Dublin. However, even in these areas prices are low compared with prices in major U.S. cities. In general, houses go for 50,000 punts to 70,000 punts. Properties in southern Dublin are usually $10,000 more than those in northern Dublin. Hamilton and Hamilton recently listed a three-bedroom bungalow in Castlemark for $39,250.

Western Ireland

The counties in the west are the least expensive places to buy property. Estate agent and auctioneer **William H. Giles & Company,** *23 Denny St., Tralee; tel. (33-66)21073* or *(33-66)22277,* recently listed the following properties on the spectacularly beautiful Dingle Peninsula.

• A roadside cottage with a tiled fireplace, two bedrooms, a bathroom, a yard, and a garden is selling for 8,000 punts.

• A cottage beside Slea Head overlooking the Blasket Islands with three bedrooms, a bathroom, and a living room fireplace is available for 18,000 punts.

• A cottage overlooking the bay in Fenit with a marble fireplace, timber ceilings, two bedrooms, teak windows, a bathroom, and a garden is on the market for 25,000 punts.

• A thatched cottage in Taulaght with two bedrooms, a bathroom, and a yard is available for 20,000 punts.

• Inchaloughra Cottage, Castlegregory, a modern furnished dormer residence with panoramic views is selling for 60,000 punts. The cottage is located near the beach.

• A dormer cottage on five acres in Castlegregory is selling for 20,000 punts.

Michael McMahon & Son, *O'Connell Square, Ennis, County Clare; tel. (353-65)28307,* recently listed the following properties in County Clare.

• A two-bedroom semi-detached house in Riverdale is available for 34,250 punts.

• A new five-bedroom, two-bathroom home with a large 17-foot entrance hall is selling for 105,000 punts.

Red tape

To buy property in Ireland, contact a house agent, an estate agent, an auctioneer, or a solicitor. Estate agents charge a commission of 1.5% of the purchase price. The **Irish Auctioneers' and Valuers' Institute,** *38 Merrion Square E., Dublin 2; tel. (353-1)611-7947,* and the **Incorporated Law Society of Ireland,** *Solicitors Building, Four Courts, Dublin 7; tel. (353-1)784533,* can provide lists of agents and solicitors.

Non-citizens can purchase up to five acres for private residential use. To do so, you need the permission of the **Land Commission,** *Agriculture House, Kildare Street, Dublin 2,* which can be obtained quickly and simply. You'll have to make a down payment of 10% to 20% of the purchase price.

Buying farmland is more difficult than buying private residential property. An outsider is still viewed suspiciously in some areas in the countryside. What's more, Protestant farmers tend to sell to Protestants, Catholics to Catholics. So you should hire a solicitor of the same persuasion as the farmer you hope to buy from. The best way to find property for sale in the countryside is to ask around at local shops and pubs.

Traditionally, houses in Ireland are sold at public auctions. (However, because the market is low, this is becoming less popular.) Irish auctions can be cutthroat, so we suggest hiring a solicitor or estate agent to do the bidding for you. A solicitor will charge 300 punts to 400 punts.

The government takes its share of the action when you buy property in Ireland. You must pay a stamp duty on the price of the property. This tax fluctuates with each year's budget, but it usually ranges from 3% to 6% of the purchase price.

Irish banks and building societies do not approve mortgages for retirees and non-residents, so you will have to pay cash or get a loan from an American bank.

Irish estate agents

For help purchasing property in Ireland, contact one of the following estate agents:

• **Brendan Tuohy & Company,** *Ballintubber, Caremorris, County Mayo; tel. (353-98)25613 or (353-98)25111.*

• **Hamilton & Hamilton,** *15 Molesworth St., Dublin 2; tel. (353-1)765-501.*

• **Marsh & Sons Ltd.,** *19 Cook St., Cork; tel. (353-21)270347.*

• **Michael McMahon & Son,** *address above.*

• **Murphy & Sons,** *12 Castle St., Sligo; tel. (353-71)2118 or (353-71)85068.*

• **Osborne, King & Megran,** *11 South Mall, Cork; tel. (353-21)271371.*

• **Palmer McCormack & Partners,** *Canada House, 65 St. Stephen's Green; tel. (353-1)784744.*

• **Sean Meehan,** *Main Street, Bundoran, County Donegal; tel. (353-72)41351.*

• **William H. Giles & Company,** *address above.*

Where to find listings

When looking for property in Ireland, consult the following Irish newspapers:

• The *Cork Examiner* and the *Evening Echo, 95 Patrick St., Cork; tel. (353-21)26661.*

• The *Irish Press* and the *Evening Press, 46-47 Lower O'Connell St., Dublin 1; tel. (353-1)741871.*

• The *Irish Independent* and the *Evening Herald, 90 Middle Abbey St., Dublin 1; tel. (353-1)746841.*

• *Irish Property News, 26 Clare St., Dublin 2.*

• The *Irish Times, 11 D'Olier St., Dublin 2; tel. (353-1)722022.*

When it's time to sell

Any property sale of more than 50,000 punts must be referred to the tax authorities for capital gains clearance. This can cause a delay of about a month in finalizing the transaction—even if no tax is due.

Ireland has strict exchange control regulations, so don't be tempted into any under-the-counter transactions. It is essential to keep everything clear and aboveboard from the time of purchase so that you will be able to export funds if you later sell your property.

Renting in Ireland

It's a good idea to rent a house in Ireland before actually buying property there. And, to be sure you're prepared to take up permanent residence, rent a house during the winter, when it's cold and damp, not just during the summer, when it's gloriously green.

Dublin is the easiest place to find rentals. Expect to pay at least 300 punts per month. Leon, Bagnall, Deering recently listed the following Dublin rentals:

• A two-bedroom apartment in Palmerston Park with a shower, a living room with a balcony, and a kitchen is available for 375 punts per month.

• A furnished house on Ragland Road in Ballsbridge with two bedrooms, a lounge, a kitchen, and a bathroom is available for 400 punts per month. (This rental is near the American embassy.)

Contact the following Dublin estate agents for additional rental listings:

• **Keane, Mahony, Smith,** *tel. (353-1)779446.*
• **Leon, Bagnall, Deering,** *tel. (353-1)774323.*
• **Lisney and Son,** *tel. (353-1)682111.*

Renting a house in the Irish countryside is more difficult than renting one in Dublin. The best way to find a house to rent outside the city is by word-of-mouth. Generally, two-bedroom furnished houses in the countryside can be rented for 250 punts to 300 punts per month and up. Two-bedroom unfurnished houses can be rented for 175 punts to 220 punts per month. Before signing a lease, find out exactly what amenities are available. In the countryside, modern amenities taken for granted by Americans—such as telephones, central heating, dishwashers, washing machines, and freezers—are often not available.

The **Irish Tourist Board,** *757 Third Ave., New York, NY 10017; (212)418-0800,* publishes a guide that lists cottages, castles, houses, chalets, and apartments for rent throughout the country. However, because the the guide is aimed at the holiday market, the rentals listed are expensive and usually for two-week periods. Sometimes, though, the owners of these properties are willing to rent for longer periods and at better prices, especially if you are willing to stay during the off season (October through May).

One retiree's experience in Ireland

Jack G. Wilson wrote this article for International Living *(**Agora Inc.**, 824 E. Baltimore St., Baltimore, MD 21202) after trying out the Irish lifestyle for a year. He highly recommends it.*

I'd spent years at staff meetings, board meetings, and labor meetings; so many, in fact, that I began to suspect my tombstone might read, "Off to Another Meeting." The time finally came when my wife and I could leave all that behind, and we began searching for a place where an unhurried life of peace and relaxation would be possible.

It was then I remembered the often-repeated Irish saying, "When God made time, He made plenty of it." Knowing that the words *hurry* and *rush* are barely part of the Irish vocabulary, we decided to try Ireland.

Our budget was tight, so every move had to be made with caution and careful preparation. The plan was first to rent in Ireland for six months. This would give us a chance to get to know the country and to decide if and where we wanted to put down roots. Establishing a banking connection was our first priority upon arrival, which we did with the help of a letter of introduction from our bank at home. We brought a draft in American dollars for our initial deposit and received an excellent exchange rate.

Our next need was transportation. Because new automobiles in Ireland are expensive, we looked for a used car. We found that owners frequently display them as is, making no attempt to clean or polish them. We chose one covered with mud from the farm and showing obvious traces of hay hauling. But it had an engine that hummed with perfection.

After intensive bargaining, which the Irish seem to expect, we made our purchase. I am happy to report that the car has served us faithfully for thousands of miles.

Gas is expensive in Ireland, but maintenance costs are cheap. When we took our car to a garage for some adjustments and a general checkup, we were happy to learn that the bill was less than 7 punts.

House hunting

We wanted to live the rural life, so we chose County Kerry. It has miles of rolling meadows and fields, lakes, mountains, rocky shores, and sweeping beaches along the Atlantic Ocean.

We inquired at local post offices and soon had a number of houses to choose from. They varied from ancient gate houses furnished with a bare minimum of old, decaying furniture to modern four-bedroom homes with slick interiors. In some, the only heat came from the fireplace and turf-burning stove, while others had central oil heat and every modern convenience.

Common rental prices are less than 70 punts a week. In some cases utilities (electricity is expensive) are included.

We chose a typical Irish country farmhouse with a view of the River Shannon and the glorious solitude available only when your nearest neighbors are cows and birds. Our three-room home is long and narrow, with chimneys rising from each end of the roof. The structure is more than 200 years old and only in the past few years has the thatched roof been replaced with slate.

For this our rent is 25 punts a week, which includes electricity and the most wonderful family of four elderly landlords anyone could dream of. The frequent appearance of a fresh apple tart or a delicious porter cake is an example of Irish hospitality.

The country life

Typically, we begin each day by gathering enough fresh turf to rebuild the fires. Turf, or peat, is cut by hand from the bogs. It is made of ancient twigs and leaves that have been compressed over the centuries into a highly efficient and burnable fuel. After drying, turf, which is cut into blocks the size of bricks, is a clean, economical source of heat.

During our breakfast (usually of porridge), the electric water heater is preparing for our baths and maybe some laundry. While I retire to my typewriter in front of a cozy fire, my wife Jeanne bakes up a fresh batch of scones or a loaf of tasty brown soda bread.

The rain and sun take turns hour by hour in Ireland. We are usually able to hike during the afternoon, but we always carry raincoats in the backpack just in case.

Our walks have given us an intimate view of this country. We always find a farmer along the way to talk with or a friendly driver who stops to offer a ride. When we hike through the nearby small villages, the people are interested in us because we're strangers, but they never ask personal questions. That is a delightful trait, typical of a country where friendship is based on deeds, not wealth or status, and where the teapot is always warm and ready for neighbor and stranger alike.

The local pubs are the center of our social life. Farmers gather in them in the morning, friends meet in them in the afternoon, and seemingly everyone stops in from about 10 p.m. until closing at 11:30 p.m. Traditional Irish music is usually played on Thursday, Saturday, and Sunday nights. A few miles away, in the tiny hamlet of Finuge (pronounced fin-noog), the only pub is packed each Saturday with farmers and their wives, who come to dance.

Sunday night in nearby Tarbert offers music of a different kind. This is when men from the area gather informally with their instruments at Miss Mina Coolahan's pub. Button accordions, hand-held drums, guitars, and an occasional concertina bring friends together for a session of jigs, reels, hornpipes, and waltzes. Someone is bound to produce a set of goat bones from his pocket and add to the rhythm, while someone else always starts clacking away with a pair of spoons. Frequently, a customer lends a beautiful Irish, offering renditions of favorite local songs such as *Dingle Bay* or the *Rose of Tralee*.

The closest village is Moyvane, about three miles away. It has a population of 400, 5 pubs, 8 small groceries, a butcher, a hardware store, and a post office. We do a lot of our shopping in Moyvane but drive five miles in the other direction to Tarbert (where the car ferry crosses the Shannon) for fresh fruit and a larger selection.

Listowel, which boasts more than 9,000 residents, is 10 miles away. Thursday is market day there, when farmers come from miles around to buy and sell cattle. Stalls are set up, where you can buy vegetables and other produce—as well as shoes and hardware.

The cost of living in Ireland is expensive. Appliances, cleaning supplies, clothing, and almost everything but fresh food is heavily taxed and almost double the price of the same goods in England. Alcohol is particularly expensive; a bottle of whiskey costs more than 13 punts. Ships from Cork City and other ports are booked with people who go to England and back in 24 hours to shop for major purchases. And special buses take shoppers on one-day excursions to Northern Ireland, where prices are much lower.

Buying a house

Purchasing a house in Ireland takes time, patience, and attention to detail. As might be expected, houses in the suburbs of Dublin are more expensive than those in the countryside. However, the housing market is depressed at the moment, and with careful searching you can find good buys.

We find the west coast of Ireland, from Donegal in the north to Kerry in the south, the prettiest and the most typically Irish. Reputable real estate agents are located in almost every town.

In the village of Loughill on the south shore of the Shannon I spoke with Paddy Barrett, who has a small real estate business (**J.C. Barrett & Sons,** *Loughill, County Limerick*). At the top of his listings was a four-bedroom bungalow with a dining room, a living room, a kitchen, a utility room, and two bathrooms, one with a shower. The house was situated on a quiet half-acre lot in the countryside. The asking price was 28,000 punts, but he told me that was "adjustable."

On the other end of the listing scale was an old Irish cottage with a basic kitchen, two tiny bedrooms, and a small sitting room. It had electricity, but no water, thus no indoor plumbing. The only heat came from the stove. The cottage was on one acre of land and had a magnificent view of the Shannon. The asking price was 9,000 punts.

A winning bet

Our time in Ireland has been like winning a bet—the Irish Sweepstakes, perhaps. We've been happy here.

If you are considering a sojourn in Ireland, here is one suggestion that may make your stay as happy as ours: When in Ireland, do as the Irish do. This is particularly true in rural Ireland, where city ways and things foreign are greeted with suspicion. Prepare to enjoy evenings at the pub and impromptu songs and music. Be willing to talk about dairy farming and the weather—even when what you really want is a pair of shoelaces. Take time to savor the pace of local life, and you will find yourself, as we have, happily embroiled in Ireland and the warmth of the Irish.

A tale of two couples

Two American families with little Irish lineage gave up their comfortable lives in the United States in exchange for life on the southern coast of County Cork. They now live close to the sunny, sandy beaches near Kinsale, a cosmopolitan yachting town with a mushrooming gourmet reputation. One family brought its familiar comforts to Ireland, while the other adapted to the local, rural Irish lifestyle.

Donald and Mary Grant, two former American journalists, put their savings into a five-acre farm, the legal limit for non-citizens. They found property prices comparable to those in the American Midwest. A small pension and Mary's income from her homemade goat-milk cheese help pay for life on the farm. The couple chose a two-cylinder car to keep the cost of gasoline down and have come to prefer wool clothing to the 276 punts per month it costs to heat the drafty farmhouse.

"The average gung-ho American doesn't fit in," Mary says. "But, for the sort who likes nature, wants a mild climate, doesn't need the social structure of the States, and has a good marriage, it's the ideal place. It's a question of values."

Donald (who died in 1983) wrote a book about the couple's adjustment to retirement in the Irish countryside called *White Goats and Black Bees* (Doubleday & Company, New York, 1974).

Harry and Rosemary Casler, a couple from Washington, D.C., visited Ireland for the first time on a golf vacation six months before retiring from publishing. Ireland's beauty and real estate opportunities captured their hearts.

They investigated housing with the help of a surveyor and decided on a spacious 200-year-old home that once housed a church rector and his servants. Any hint of rustic discomfort vanished with the appearance of dishwasher, gas stove, oil heater, and shower—still a luxury in rural Ireland.

Harry, a former photo editor for the *International Herald Tribune,* found the peace of southern Ireland particularly appealing.

"We lived all over the world—Saigon, Malaysia, Panama City, Caracas, Ghent. But we chose Ireland as our hideaway," he says. "Here, the pace is slow, so there's minimal friction. We don't discuss religion or politics with our neighbors."

Once a year, the expatriates return to Washington, D.C. to visit their doctor. This is a personal preference, as Irish medical services are respected and free to all residents who earn less than 100 punts per week per couple.

Transportation throughout Ireland is free to all residents over 66, but the Caslers say they rarely venture beyond the nearby town of Clontakilty, population 1,500.

What do they do with their time? They call themselves "creative putterers." Eighteen-hour summer days leave plenty of time for mowing the lawn and rotating the donkeys, whose appetites trim alternating fields. Harry prunes the flowers near their bamboo grove and occasionally searches for ancient artifacts in the fields. Rosemary, a former cover girl and fashion designer, paints.

They say Ireland has a knack for making time stand still.

For more information

For more information on retiring in Ireland, contact the following agencies:

• **Embassy of Ireland,** *2234 Massachusetts Ave. N.W., Washington, DC 20008; (202)462-3939.*

• **Irish Tourist Board,** *757 Third Ave., New York, NY 10017; (212)418-0800.*

• **Aer Lingus,** *(800)223-6537,* has flights to England and Ireland.

Chapter 13

Israel

If you like the idea of retiring on the Mediterranean, but dislike the crowds of France and Italy, consider Israel. Despite the violent pictures of Israel we see on the nightly news, the country is largely peaceful. And while Israel's southern half is desert, the fertile northern half has typically Mediterranean weather, with sunshine, mild winters, and long summers.

Where to settle

Israel has a climate to satisfy just about everyone. If you prefer ocean breezes and mild winters, settle close to the beach in **Natanya** (the Pearl of the Sharon Plain), **Herzliya** (the Riviera of Israel), or the port city of **Ashkelon.**

Israel's most beautiful coastal city is **Akko,** which is surrounded by sea walls, fringed with palm trees, and punctuated with minarets. Only 14 miles north of Haifa, it was an important Phoenician port and later served as a capital for the Crusaders. Akko is the holiest place on earth for people of the Baha'i faith, because their prophet, Bahaullah, is buried here.

On the southern edge of Akko is the **Argaman,** or Purple Beach, the most beautiful on the coast, with crystal-clear water.

If you prefer mountain air, settle in walled **Jerusalem,** a holy city for Jews, Moslems, and Christians. Jerusalem's temperatures range from 41 degrees Fahrenheit to 55 degrees Fahrenheit in January and from 64 degrees Fahrenheit to 87 degrees Fahrenheit in August. While most new buildings in the city have central heating, they may be heated for only a few hours per day—you might want a space heater.

Haifa, situated on Mt. Carmel and overlooking the Mediterranean, offers both ocean breezes and mountain air. A natural harbor on a deep bay ringed by steep hills, Haifa has been compared to San Francisco and is one of the most beautiful cities in Israel. The temperature here ranges from 49 degrees Fahrenheit to 65 degrees Fahrenheit in January and from 76 degrees Fahrenheit to 90 degrees Fahrenheit in August.

The **Dead Sea,** which is 400 meters below sea level, is the lowest point on earth. As a result, it has one of the driest climates in the world. Its pure and pollen-free air is wonderful for people with allergies or respiratory problems.

Because this region has the highest atmospheric pressure on earth (which reduces the chances of sunburn), it is one of the most relaxing places to sunbathe—and it has more than 300 cloudless days a year. (People with skin disorders come here to take advantage of the therapeutic ultraviolet rays.) The swimming is enjoyable, too. And you don't have to worry about drowning—the salt-laden water makes you float like a cork. (The Dead Sea has 20 times as much salt as any ocean in the world. Its mineral-rich waters have been known for their therapeutic values since ancient times.)

The shores of the Dead Sea are lined with resort hotels and historical sites, but you won't find any residential housing in the area. The only places to settle in the area are in the nearby mountain towns, which are about 40 minutes by car from the shores of the sea.

Green, pastoral **Galilee** in northeast Israel borders the sea of the same name and is dotted with small cities and historical sites. **Tiberias,** the largest city on the shore, is famous both for its therapeutic hot springs and as a winter resort. A holy city, it is filled with synagogues and churches. It was founded 2,000 years ago in honor of the purity of Caesar Tiberias (who turned out to be an extremely decadent ruler). For 200 years after the fall of Jerusalem, it acted as the center of Jewish learning.

The hillside town of **Safed** (Zefat), also in Galilee, is another good retirement spot. Jewish refugees expelled from Spain during the Middle Ages took refuge here on the steep slopes of Mt. Canaan. Safed became a center for the study of Cabala—Jewish mysticism and magic. Narrow streets wind through the centuries-old Synagogue Quarter, and painters and sculptors inhabit the former Arab Quarter.

Red tape

If you are Jewish, retirement in Israel is an easy prospect. The Law of Return allows every Jew who wishes to settle in Israel to do so. You can obtain citizenship upon arrival in the country. For information, contact the **Ministry of Immigrant Absorption,** *Department of Aliyah and Absorption of the Jewish Agency, P.O. Box 13061, 91130 Jerusalem; tel. (972)2-91-130,* or the Aliyah (emigration) office in the city nearest you. Keep in mind that if you accept Israeli citizenship, you must pay high Israeli taxes.

Non-Jews, too, can retire in Israel, but the procedure is more complicated. If you are not Jewish, you can enter Israel on a tourist visa, which you can renew every 3 months for up to 27 (consecutive) months; on a B-1 visa, which is a tourist visa with a working permit; on a temporary resident's visa, which is good for up to 3 years; or on a permanent resident's visa. Any of these visas is relatively easy to obtain, unless you are a Christian missionary, an Arab, or a member of the Black Israelite sect in the United States. Israel is one of the few countries that welcomes foreigners who want to take jobs.

The best way to go about settling in Israel if you are not Jewish is to visit first on a tourist visa. This way you can explore a bit to make sure you like the country and to find the area best suited to your lifestyle. When you're sure you want to settle, go to the **Ministry of the Interior,** *General Building, 1 Rehov Shlomzion HaMalkah, 94 146 Jerusalem; tel. (972-2)245561 or (972-2)228211,* to apply for a temporary resident's visa. If you do not have a criminal record and can support yourself, you should have no problem obtaining the document. After living in Israel for a number of years, you can apply for a permanent resident's visa.

Buying a home

Foreigners can buy property in Israel. A two-bedroom apartment costs 128,880 shekels to 144,990 shekels, depending on the size, the location, and the state of the market.

Senior citizens' apartment buildings, in which most housing units are sold individually, are being built in some Israeli cities. Many offer nursing services; most have security systems. Other services include a kosher cafeteria, a library, a synagogue, transportation, parking, cleaning, laundry, cultural programs, trips, lectures, and telephone.

For more specific information on retirement communities in Israel, contact the **Tefahot Bank,** *Heleni Hamalka Street, Jerusalem;* **Arnold Druck,** *attorney at law, 12 Moshe Hess St., P.O. Box 4252, 94185 Jerusalem;* or **Yehoshua Raveh,** *attorney at law, Herbert Rubenstein and Associates, P.C., 1818 N St. N.W., Washington, DC 20036; (202)857-0870.*

When you first arrive in Israel, you'll probably want to stay at a hotel while you look for more permanent accommodations. If you make arrangements with an Aliyah office in the United States before leaving for Israel, you may be able to stay in a hotel at a reduced rate until you find a permanent home.

Mortgages are available from the Ministry of Housing to men

under 65 and women under 60 at the time of immigration. Older immigrants can get mortgages of 20,000 shekels, and couples are entitled to mortgages of 24,800 shekels. Down payments must be made in cash. Lawyers handle most of the necessary transactions.

Tour Va'Aleh, *12 Rehov Kaplan, Tel Aviv; tel. (972-3)258311,* offers free guidance to senior immigrants on all aspects of housing in Israel.

The cost of living

With an income of $700 to $900 (1,127 shekels to 1,450 shekels) a month, a couple can live comfortably and maintain a moderate standard of living. However, a large initial outlay of cash is needed for buying household appliances.

For a rough idea of the cost of living in Israel, consider these ballpark figures: groceries for a family of three cost about 193 shekels a week; dinner for two at an average restaurant is 48 shekels to 65 shekels; doctors' fees vary, but 80 shekels for a visit is considered reasonable; clothing costs about twice as much as in the United States; a bus ride within a city is about .64 shekels, and a bus from Jerusalem to Tel Aviv is about 5 shekels; theater tickets are about 48 shekels; a movie is 14 shekels; gasoline is about 3.20 shekels a gallon.

Immigrants may keep any amount of foreign currency or foreign securities, whose source is from abroad, for 20 years from the date of their arrival. They may also hold tax-free foreign-currency accounts in Israel for 20 years.

Historically, inflation in Israel has been as high as 500%, but it has been brought down in recent years. The average inflation rate in Israel from 1980 to 1986 was 182.9%.

Taxes

American retirees' Social Security checks are tax-exempt in Israel, as are government pension payments from Israel and other countries. However, payments that are taxable in the United States are not exempt from taxes, including pensions paid out by private employers. One way around this tax is to deposit the payment first in a U.S. bank. When the money is later transferred to Israel, it is not considered direct income, but simply a capital transfer, which is not subject to tax.

A major element in the process of retiring to Israel is *hondling* (bargaining). No good Jew would go to Orchard Street shops and pay the asking prices; neither would he simply up and retire as a resident taxpayer in Israel without a bit of *hondling* beforehand. Once you have emigrated to Israel, you cannot renegotiate the terms, so it's important to do so in advance.

As a retiree in Israel, you'll want to shelter your wealth from the country's prohibitive taxes on worldwide income, as well as from its hefty inheritance taxes. So you must bargain. Demand in advance assurances of special tax treatment different from that of the native Israeli. In compromise, the government official probably will brush off some of the special social aids that Aliyah Israel offers. (Most of these aids are aimed at working folks or those too poor to afford medical insurance.) To help your cause along, you might mention that you do have other retirement options, that you have raised large sums of money for the United Jewish Appeal, or that your presence in Israel would be an asset to the country (an argument Einstein or Kissinger could have used if he had decided to settle in Israel).

Healthy living

Medical care in Israel is expensive (although less expensive than in the United States). Israel does not have a nationalized health insurance program, so we recommend that you take out medical insurance. Israel's health services include *kupat holim,* which are health funds for workers largely run by their unions, and government and private programs.

Although private medicine is marginal in Israel, it is gaining in popularity. Dental care, on the other hand, is almost all private. Even patients who consult a doctor privately generally belong to a *kupat holim.*

For more information, consult a health affairs coordinator at a regional office of the **Ministry of Immigrant Absorption,** *address above.*

All immigrants, including temporary residents, are eligible for free health insurance for the first six months after their arrival in Israel. This coverage is offered by the four main *kupat holim*: Klalit (also known as Kupat Holim Histadrut), Maccabi, Meuhedet, and Leumit.

After six months, the *kupat holim* covering you might require you to undergo a medical examination before accepting you for regular membership. However, medical tests are generally required only when it is suspected that you suffer from a chronic illness or that you may require regular hospitalization, heart surgery, or some other serious medical care. The exam is usually waived if you did not require any special treatment during the first six months of coverage.

The *kupat holim* may refuse to accept you on a permanent basis or offer you only limited coverage if your health is poor, you are elderly, or your ability to pay premiums is uncertain. If you have a chronic health condition, it is a good idea to check your eligibility for health insurance prior to immigrating. The procedure takes about two months.

In some cases, the Ministry of Immigrant Absorption can arrange to extend your coverage for an additional 2 1/2 years if your health fund is unwilling to extend your coverage beyond the initial six-month period.

Obtaining medical insurance is sometimes easier if you have children already living in Israel. Klalit and Leumit both have plans for parents of members; Meuhedet accepts parents of members on a case-by-case basis.

Is it safe?

Israeli cities are significantly safer—for pedestrians in general and for the elderly in particular—than some of the crime-ridden cities of the United States. The stone-throwing incidents seen on television are generally limited to specific localities that are easily avoided.

Volunteering

You should have no trouble finding a volunteer position in Israel. You can tutor Israelis in English or volunteer to work for a service organization, a hospital, or an institution for the handicapped. Or perhaps you'd rather welcome new immigrants or give museum tours. Whatever your interests, you should have no trouble filling your time.

Getting-acquainted tours

Many Jewish organizations sponsor three-month programs for active retirees in Israel in conjunction with Tour Va'Aleh. These programs offer a living experience in Israel, usually during the winter months. Participants work at volunteer jobs in the morning and study Hebrew in the afternoon. Cultural and educational activities are offered in the evening—lectures, folk dancing, home hospitality. Tours of the country are also part of the programs.

To be eligible for an active retirees program, you should be 50 years old or older, in good health, and physically capable of working.

Two-week seminars are offered by Tnuat Aliyah of the World Zionist Organization (WZO), the Aliyah Department, twice a year.

Participants take extensive tours of the country, meet other retirees, and attend workshops of interest to retirees in Israel.

For more information

The following agencies can help you plan your retirement in Israel:

• **Association of Americans and Canadians in Israel,** *21 Washington St., 94187 Jerusalem; tel. (972-2)248823 or (972-2)240445.*

• **Embassy of Israel,** *3514 International Drive N.W., Washington, DC 20008; (202)364-5500.*

• **Israel Aliyah Center,** *515 Park Ave., New York, NY 10022; (212)752-0600; 8730 Georgia Ave., Silver Spring, MD 20910; (301)589-6136; or 6505 Wilshire Blvd., Suite 516, Los Angeles, CA 90048; (213)655-7881.*

• **Ministry of Immigrant Absorption,** *Hakirya Building 2, 91006 Jerusalem,* or *P.O. Box 13061, 91130 Jerusalem; tel. (972-2)661171.*

• **Ministry of the Interior (MISRAD HAPNIM),** *General Building, 1 Rehov Shlomzion HaMalkah, 94 146 Jerusalem; tel. (972-2)245561 or (972-2)228211.*

• **Tour Va'Aleh,** *12 Rehov Kaplan, Tel Aviv; tel. (972-3)258311,* or *3 Rehov Ben Yehuda, Jerusalem, Israel; tel. (972-2)246522 or (972-2)202346.*

Chapter 14

Italy

Knowst thou the land where the lemon trees bloom,
Where the gold orange glows in the deep thicket's gloom
Where a wind ever soft from the blue heavens blows,
And the groves are of laurel and myrtle and rose?
                —Goethe, translated by Thomas Carlyle, 1824

Italy has beckoned outsiders for centuries with its beautiful landscapes and vast cultural heritage. This was the site of the awakening of Europe after the Dark Ages. Dante, Petrarch, Leonardo da Vinci, Botticelli, and Michelangelo flourished in Italy. What better company can you find?

Of course, Italy is not all fine art and fine living. It is a predominantly rural country, with one of the lower per capita incomes of Europe. But Rome, Florence, and Venice are beautiful and cosmopolitan. Once you get there, you will understand why so many non-Italians have stayed. Today, Italy is a wonderful country for those seeking a rich and diverse experience at bargain prices.

Some 43,000 Italian-American retirees live in Italy. But you don't have to be Italian. Anyone (with a bit of capital and courage) can take up residence here.

Many retirees prefer to live in the Lake Country in northern Italy in the summer and go south to Sicily in the winter. Florence and Rome are also popular.

Red tape

You will need a valid passport to enter Italy, but a visa is not required for stays up to three months. If after entering Italy you decide you would like to stay more than 90 days, you can apply, once only, at any police station (*questura*) for an extension of an additional 90 days. You will have to prove you have adequate means of support and that you do not want the extension for study or employment. As a rule, permission is granted immediately.

Tourists are supposed to register with the Italian police within three days of their arrival. Usually this is taken care of by your hotel.

If you are staying in a private home, you will have to register in person. And you are supposed to register again each time you change guesthouses. (Not many people do, though, and enforcement is lax.) In Rome there is a special police information office to assist tourists (with available interpreters), *tel. (39-6)461-950* or *(39-6)486-609*.

If you plan to live in Italy for more than six months, get a visa from the Italian Embassy or one of the Italian Consulates in the United States before departure. You'll need two passport photos.

In theory, foreigners living in Italy must report to the local police every three months. However, many people ignore these regulations. So, the official number of retirees reported in Italy might reflect only half the number actually living there.

You can import personal belongings duty-free, including clothing, books, household equipment, a typewriter, and a record player, as long as they are only for personal use.

If you plan to bring a pet with you to Italy, you must have a veterinarian's certificate stating that the animal is in good health and has been vaccinated against rabies between 20 days and 11 months before entering Italy. The forms are available from all Italian diplomatic and consular representatives and from the Italian Government Travel Offices. A dog must be on a leash and sometimes muzzled when in public.

For more information, contact the **Italian Government Travel Office,** *630 Fifth Ave., New York, NY 10111* or the **Embassy of Italy,** *1601 Fuller St. N.W., Washington, DC 20009; (202)328-5500.*

Cost of living

Americans can live well in Italy. A single room in a pension costs 12,000 lire per night; a double is 18,000 lire per night. A double room in a standard tourist-class hotel averages about 50,000 lire. In a small, simple restaurant, a three-course menu with a liter of wine ranges from 20,000 to 30,000 lire. Seats for open-air opera at the Baths of Caracalla cost 8,136 lire. A movie costs 5,000 lire. A woman's shampoo and set costs 20,000 lire.

Inflation is high, however. The government plans to cut spending and raise taxes to reduce inflation. Value-added taxes (VATs) have increased 2% to 3%.

A small, two-bedroom villa in Tuscany or Sicily can be rented for about 271,200 lire a week. You can buy a vacation home in the Lake Country for about 10,000,000 lire. A restored castle on 15 acres of land in Umbria may be found for 115,260,000.

Money matters

Italian currency is the lira. Notes are issued for 1,000, 2,000, 5,000, 10,000, 20,000, 50,000, and 100,000 lire. Coins are 10, 20, 50, 100, 200, and 500 lire.

You may not take more than 500,000 lire in or out of the country without official clearance. Italy has no restrictions on the amount of foreign currency imported. However, everyone entering Italy should declare the amount he is carrying so that the same amount may be exported.

You can change foreign money for lire through any bank or exchange office (Ufficio di Cambio). A limited amount of lire can be obtained from conductors on international trains and at certain stations within Italy.

The lira remains fairly steady against other European currencies, but not against the dollar. You'll probably get a better exchange rate for your traveler's checks than for cash.

Taxing matters

Italy has no wealth tax. But real estate capital gains are taxed at 3% to 30%, depending upon time held. Worldwide income is taxed from 10% to 72%, with assorted credits, including local taxes paid. (Note: The Italian government is really cracking down on tax evasion.)

There are two income taxes on individuals in Italy: personal income tax (IRPEF) and local income tax (ILOR). Residents are taxed on income from any source. Non-residents are taxed on income produced in Italy. Local tax does not apply to income from abroad.

For tax purposes, a resident is anyone inscribed in the record of the office of resident populations; anyone who has his or her principal offices or interests in Italy; or anyone who lives there more than six months a year.

Tax rates are progressive and range from 10% on taxable income of 3-million lire or less to 72% on the portion of any income in excess of 500-million lire.

Price Waterhouse, *Via Aniene 30, 00198 Rome; tel. (39-6)844-01-51,* has information on taxation in Italy.

Banking matters

A recent cartoon in the British magazine, *The Banker*, shows three chefs marching into an Italian bank—ready to spoil the "financial broth." Although the Italians are said to have invented double-entry bookkeeping, the opinion of the banking community today seems to be that they are too inventive. Italian banks have had a practice of shifting funds in and out of subsidiaries and fellow banks, so that everyone shows a paper profit. (Key to this practice was that few concerns shared the same fiscal year.)

While the Bank of Italy is trying to put a stop to such shenanigans, at the same time it has been freeing its control over individual banks. Italy's premier merchant bank, Mediobanca, has recently been sold to the private sector (the Agnelli family). And the commercial banks are being allowed to set their own interest rates and compete for customers as they please. The Bank of Italy's control comes from the interest rates it charges and from reserve requirements.

With the huge public debt to service, funds are tight in the lending sector. The prime rate is about 17%, and small businesses typically pay 20%. Venture capital is almost nonexistant.

The high interest rates benefit savers, who typically earn from 15% to 16% on deposits. Italy's savings rate, not surprisingly, is even higher than Japan's—22.7% compared to only 17% for the Japanese. Banking customers get other conveniences as well. Most Italian banks are part of the Bancomat system. Customers receive a card they can use to withdraw money at member banks.

Some of Italy's big banks with branches in New York are: **Banco di Roma,** *(212)952-9300;* **Banca Nazionale del Lavoro,** *(212)581-0710;* **CARIPLO,** *(212)541-6262;* **Banco di Napoli,** *277 Park Ave.;* **Allgemene Bank Nederland,** *335 Madison Ave., New York, NY;* *(212)503-2400;* and **Credito Italiano,** *(212)546-9600.*

Other Italian banks are the **Banca del Monte di Milano** and **Banca Commerciale Italiana**.

U.S. banks with branches in Italy include: American Express International Banking Corp.; Bank of America NT & SA, San Francisco; Bankers Trust Co., New York; Chase Manhattan Bank N.A., New York; Chemical Bank, New York; Citibank N.A., New York; First National Bank, Chicago; Irving Trust Co., New York; Manufacturers Hanover Trust Co., New York; and Morgan Guaranty Trust Co., New York.

About health

Health care in Italy is plentiful, good, and reasonably priced. There are plenty of hospital beds—about 10 per 1,000 residents. And there are more doctors per 100,000 residents than in the United States. A visit to a doctor costs from 27,120 to 67,800 lire, and a hospital room is around 135,600 lire a day.

Italy has no medical program covering U.S. citizens, so make sure your U.S. insurance will cover you abroad.

At every drug store (*Farmacia*) there is a list of those open at night and on Sundays.

First Aid Service (*Pronto Soccorso*) with a doctor on hand is found at airports, ports, railway stations, and in all hospitals.

In case of emergency, telephone *113* or *112* for the State Police or the Immediate Action Service. (These numbers are *only* for emergencies).

Italy is also blessed with numerous thermal baths, many of them of volcanic origin. They have been known for their restorative powers since Roman times. The spas are located in some of the most beautiful areas of the country. **Montecatini** and **Chianciano** are in Tuscany near Florence. The baths of **Abano** and **Grado** are near Venice. **Fiuggi** is a short distance from Rome, in the midst of the medieval town of **Latium**, while Levico is in the Dolomites.

Parla Italiano!

While the Italians aren't as defensive about their language as the French are, you will find it easier to meet them if you speak their native tongue. While urban and educated Italians often speak good English, country and common folks do not.

Italian language, literature, history, and culture courses for foreigners are offered in major cities. Following is a partial listing of schools:

•**Dante Aligheri**, *Piazza Firenze 27, Rome*;

•**Centro di Cultura per Stranieri**, *Via Vittorio Emanuele 64, Florence; tel. (39-55)472-139;*

•**Dante Alighieri**, *Centro Linguistico Italiano, Via dé Bardi 12, Florence; tel. (39-55)284-955;*

•**Eurocentro**, *Piazza S. Spirito 9, Florence;*

•**Direzione dei Corsi presso l'Università degli Studi**, *Via del Perdono 7, Milan* (courses held at Gargano on Lake Garda); and

•**Scuola di Lingua e Cultura Italiana per Stranieri**, *Università degli Studi, Siena.*

Buying your Italian home

Real estate has appreciated less in Italy than in most Western countries. Foreign buyers are finding restorable farmhouses on Italian hillsides, just as these markets are drying up in France and Spain.

Italians tend to live in apartments rather than houses. And although Americans can buy apartments, they are expensive. In a resort area, apartments sell for 135,600,000 to 406,800,000 lire. For example, a two-bedroom apartment in San Remo was recently advertised for 271,200,000 lire.

It's almost impossible to rent on a yearly basis. Landlords prefer to rent on a seasonal basis, with prices beginning at around 406,800 lire a month. Housing is less expensive outside the resorts. You can get a two-bedroom apartment for 67,800,000 lire.

Properties are cheapest south of Rome, where the land and the people are poorer. Farmhouses in the south of Italy can be quite cheap. But expect to pay as much for restoration as you do for the house.

If you decide to buy a home, you must deal with a notary public, an Italian government finance office, a seller, and an agent. You should list your investment with the government finance offices so that you can take money out of the country later.

Slow money

One problem peculiar to Americans buying property is fund transfer. In Italy, exchange control regulations are very strict and for a foreigner to purchase property it is essential that the necessary funds come from an external source. Often money transfers are not executed quickly enough and the property and initial deposit are lost. At present, U.S. banks are not very efficient at transferring funds to Italy. It's a good idea to use a U.S. branch of an Italian bank.

When the final transfer of property is made, Italian law requires that all parties fully understand the details of the contract. Foreigners must show that they have good command of Italian or hire an interpreter. Another alternative is to go through a realtor whose representatives can be given power of attorney to act on behalf of the purchaser.

Sample properties

The following old farms were advertised for sale in the summer of 1988. The buildings are original structures that have been either partially or completely restored. For more information, contact **Cuendet Spa,** 1742 Calle Corva, Camarillo, CA 93010; (805)987-5278.

•Two stone farmhouses in **Bovana**, Tuscany, are selling for 300-million lire. Both completely restored farmhouses are in the hills of Mugello, about 24 miles from Florence. One house has a living room with a fireplace, a small kitchen/dining area, three bedrooms, and one bathroom; the other house has a loggia with an archway, a parlor, a kitchen with a fireplace, three bedrooms, and one bathroom. Water and electricity are connected.

•A 200-million lire castle apartment is for sale in **Torre**. This apartment is located on the top floor of a castle that has been converted into four apartments. It features a living room with a fireplace and terrace, a kitchen, two bedrooms, and one bathroom. The apartment has been completely restored, with wood beams and brick floors throughout. Gas heat, water, electricity, and a telephone are supplied. The castle is about 15 miles from Florence and has a great rental potential.

•A partially restored farmhouse in **La Vigna** costs 200-million lire. Located 36 miles south of Siena, this house sits among vineyards and olive trees. Its second floor has been completely restored and features a living room with a fireplace, a kitchen, two bedrooms, and one bathroom. Below are four unrestored rooms. The property also includes a two-car garage, a storeroom, and a small hayloft. Heat, water, electricity, and a telephone are supplied.

•A large farmhouse selling for 115-million lire is in **Caggiolle**. Situated on 75 acres south of Siena, this farmhouse is in good condition. It includes five rooms, a large kitchen with a fireplace, a storeroom, a cellar, a stable, and an old bread oven. The property is peaceful and remote. Water and electricity are connected.

•A luxurious **Pozzo** farmhouse is priced at 200-million lire. This beautiful, completely restored farmhouse is nine miles from Arezzo in the Chiana Valley. It has two living rooms (one with a fireplace), a kitchen, three bedrooms, three bathrooms, and a dressing room. The extensive restoration work includes spectacular arches and brick floors. Water, electricity, central heat, a telephone, and a television antenna are supplied.

•In **Bianca**, a restored portion of a farmhouse sells for 95-million lire. Ready for occupancy, this completely renovated farm townhouse has a living room with an arched ceiling, a kitchen with a fireplace, two bedrooms, a shower, a storeroom, and a garage. It is situated about 15 miles south of Siena. Water and electricity are connected.

•A restored farmhouse in **Ghita** is available for 240-million lire. Completely restored, this farmhouse comprises a living/dining room with a fireplace, a kitchen, three bedrooms, and three showers. It's located about 17 miles from Volterra, close to the sea.

The following apartments in the area around Florence were advertised in La Pulce *in August 1988. While they may have been*

281

sold, *properties like them will be on the market.*

•An elegant apartment in **Via Dello Statuto, Florence,** on the top two floors, with five ample bedrooms, a balcony, and a pretty view of a park. 290-million lire. **Cisco Casa,** *viale Machiavelli 2/A, Florence; tel. (39-55)222-333, (39-55)22-95-91,* or *(39-55)22-30-72.*

•A two-room apartment with garden in **Via Calatafimi, Quinto,** sells for 135-million lire. **Cisco Casa,** *address above.*

•A two-bedroom apartment in a restored period house is available in Val di Pesa, Mercatale, for 110-million lire. **Cisco Casa,** *address above.*

•A small apartment in good condition in a typical **South Florence** building is selling for 88-million lire. **Istituto Fondiario Immobiliare,** *Viale Fratelli Rosselli 69, Florence; tel. (39-55)35-77-31.*

•In **Scandicci,** 135-million lire will buy a three-room apartment with bathroom, balcony, on top floor. **Istituto Fondiario Immobiliare,** *address above.*

•In the historic district of **Prato,** a four-room apartment with a bathroom is selling for 85-million lire. **Livi Immobiliare,** *Via Fra Bartolomeo 118, Prato; tel. (39-574)59-58-26.*

•A restored period house with nearly six hectares of land is available in **Montevettolini** for 350-million lire. **Livi Immobiliare,** *address above.*

The following property was advertised recently in International Living, *824 E. Baltimore St., Baltimore MD 21202.*

Outside **Perugia,** is a charming 10-acre hilltop farm with a restored nine-room stone farmhouse plus modern studio/apartment. It is completely furnished with all utilities and phone—and no property taxes. It is good rental property, and is selling for $135,000. **Raphael,** *2413 Brentwood, Alexandria, VA 22306; (703)768-8863.*

Finding property

Some real estate agents who deal in Italian properties:

•**Begg International, Inc.,** *2121 Wisconsin Ave. N.W., Washington, DC, 20007; (202)338-9065;*

•**Scai,** *Via F. Turati 86, 00185 Rome;*

•**Cuendet Spa,** *1-53030 Strove, (35) Siena;*

•**Organizzazione Immobiliare COVA,** *Piazza Colombo 32, San Remo, Italy;*

•**Agenzia Flora,** *Piazza Colombo 10, San Remo;* and

•**Eurocessioni,** *Via Cioberti 30, San Remo.*

One good place to find property in Northern Italy is in the classified section of **La Pulce**, *tel. (39-55)679-341*. Advertisements are in Italian, however.

Your best sources, however, are people. Printed information may be up-to-date and helpful, but you still need the perspective on "best bets," or traps to avoid, which people alone can provide. So try to establish relationships wherever you begin your information hunt.

Some Italian cities have American Women's Clubs. Contact them—they specialize in helping newcomers with housing and settling in. You may even be able to sublet a house or apartment from a family about to return to the United States.

Sources of real estate information

•**Italo Ablondi**, *Ablondi and Foster, PC, 2100 Pennsylvania Ave., Suite 720, Washington, DC 20006; (202)296-3355.*

•**Oliver Harris**, *Worldwide Relocation Assistance, P.O. Box 1402, Madison Square Station, New York, NY 10159; (212)465-0990.*

•**Avocati Ughi E Ninziante**, *via Sant' Andrea 19, Milan, Italy; tel. (39-2)79-3951.* Partners Giovanni Ughi and Gianni Nunziante speak English. This office also has corresponding offices in other major cities.

You can get more referrals from the offices of the major U.S. accounting firms. Begin by contacting the U.S. offices of **Peat Marwick Mitchell**, *(212)758-9700*, or **Price Waterhouse**, *(212)489-8900*. Each has branches in Italy. They can suggest further steps.

Renting in Italy

Housing is in short supply in Italy. But, oddly enough, foreigners have an easier time finding a place to live than Italians do. Italy imposes strict rent controls on landlords renting to Italians. Consequently, many landlords would rather leave a property vacant than let it out at a fixed low price, under laws that make it difficult to evict tenants.

But rent control laws do not apply to foreigners, which makes them attractive tenants. Landlords also figure that foreigners won't stay long, so the rent can be raised as soon as they move out. Because of this last factor, don't expect to find great bargains. Even so, properties can be found in Italy for half the rent of comparable U.S. units.

The best sources of rental information are the schools and universities in the area where you want to live. Newspapers are often good sources as well. Make lots of contacts, too. Some of the nicest rentals are found through word of mouth.

You may want to go through a rental agent, called an *immobiliari*. There are many of these agencies throughout Italy, handling properties of all types and prices. *Immobiliari* also handle sales of apartments, houses, and land in Italy. For addresses of *immobiliari*, contact the **Italian Embassy**, *1601 Fuller St. N.W., Washington, DC 20009; (202)328-5500.*

Also worth a look are a number of residences and pensiones that rent attractive apartments and rooms for extended periods of time. Listings can be found in the local *Pagine Gialle* (Yellow Pages) under *Case albergo e appartamenti ammobiliati, Pensione,* and *Camere ammobiliati.*

You will find apartments far more quickly than you'll find houses in Italy. Because of rent control laws, few houses ever reach the rental market.

In Florence, the **Agriturist Office**, *via del Preconsolo 10, 50123 Florence,* has information about old houses for rent or sale. If your interest is Rome, the U.S. Embassy's **Commercial Office** there may help, *tel. (39-6)4674.* The regional U.S. Consulates, of course, have their own sources.

As is generally true worldwide, renter beware: Agents and landlords tend to be high-handed. You should allow four to six weeks to find an appropriate unit. Above all, begin your search well before summer—many landlords vacation during July and August.

Be prepared to pay two to three months' rent as deposit and an additional two to three months' rent in advance. Afterward, you're likely to pay rent on a quarterly basis. Security deposits, sad to say, you may never recover. Be sure to identify a number of landlord candidates, then do your homework on each.

Some average rental costs include: a furnished, three-room apartment in Rome, about 881,400 lire per month; a six- to nine-room, luxury apartment in Rome's best residential neighborhood, about 2,983,200 lire a month; a seven- to nine-room house in a residential area of Rome, about 2,467,920 lire a month.

Be sure to sign a lease only after consulting a lawyer you trust in order to avoid any trick items. This is where contacts with accounting firms may prove worthwhile, especially if you intend to purchase real estate for investment purposes.

In some heavily industrialized regions, the need for telephones has outstripped the available supply. If you want one where you live, you might have to find a residence that already has one.

Besides being careful when signing contracts, take time to do a careful inventory—even in unfurnished houses. Landlords take this seriously, even if you don't. Check for cracks, scratches, chips; test the appliances and locks; flush some paper down the toilet—in short do a full "walk through" together. And be sure you have all the keys. Otherwise, you may have unpleasant surprises and charges later.

Below are a few good residences in Florence where you can rent a room for an extended period.

•**Residence Porta al Prato**, *16 Via Ponte al Mosse; tel. (39-55)47-60-71;*

•**Residence Ricasoli**, *8 Via Ricasoli; tel. (39-55)21-52-67;* and

•**Pensione Geneve**, *43 Via Mattonaia; tel. (39-55)247-79-23.*

Short-term house rentals

One way to sample life in Italy before moving there is to look for a short-term house rental. These tend to be at the top of the market and aimed at vacationers, however. **Cuendet Spa** is a vacation real estate rental agency specializing in short-term accommodations. Cuendet can help you rent a villa, farmhouse, castle, or apartment in Tuscany, Umbria, Veneto, or Sicily. All are rated, indicating the degree of luxury.

All letting periods begin and end on Saturdays. The minimum stay is two weeks for most properties, although some have a one-week minimum. Bookings can be made through a Cuendet agent or an authorized travel agency. Prices begin at less than 27,120 lire a week in low season.

For a color catalog listing 1,500 properties, send $10 to **Suzanne Pidduck,** *Cuendet Agent, 1742-A Calle Corva, Camarillo, CA 93010; (805)987-5278.* She can also send you a free brochure describing Italian farmhouses for sale.

Hidden in the classified section of *International Living* recently was a tempting ad for short-term renters: Italy—Between Florence and Rome. Restored farmhouse, sleeps six. Day trips to Assisi, Urbino, San Marino, more. From $300 weekly. Also studio sleeps two. From $125. **Hanes Corposano #4**, *San Giustino, 06016 Italy; tel. (39-75)856-9150.*

Other rental agents that handle properties in Italy include:

•**At Home Abroad**, *Sutton Town House, 405 E. 56th St., Suite 6H, New York, NY 10022; (212)421-9165;*

•**Villas International**, *71 W. 23rd St., New York, NY 10010; (212)929-7585;*

•**Resort Villas International**, *30 Spring St., Stamford, CT 06901; (203)965-0200, ext. 260;*

•**Posarelli Vacations**, *180 Kinderkamack Road, Park Ridge, NJ 07656; (201)573-9558;*

•**Families Abroad**, *(212)787-2434;* and

•**RAVE (Rent A Vacation Anywhere)**, *328 Main St. E., Suite 526, Rochester, NY 14604; (716)454-6440.*

Swapping homes

Regular housing and car swaps may be best for extended stays overseas. These can be arranged informally or through advertising in travel publications such as *International Living, Town & Country, Travel & Leisure*, or even the *New York Review*.

Using a home-swapping service is relatively simple. For a small fee (usually between $25 and $100), you'll be listed in a directory prepared by the service. Once on the list, write a brief letter describing your location and home. This letter should include information about when you would like to travel and where. You can send copies of your letter to the list of members whose time and location suits you best.

Some of the details can get sticky, but a little common sense will solve most of the problems. Since every home and auto has its own idiosyncrasies, you should list such things as important phone numbers, how-to hints, points of interest, and directions to food stores and gas stations. Just to be safe, put breakables and heirlooms away, as well as other personal items you might feel nervous about leaving around.

For more information on home-swapping, there are quite a few agencies you can contact. **Vacation Exchange Club** is the oldest, established in 1960, and is at *12006 111th Ave., Unit 12, Youngstown, AZ 85363; (602)972-2186.* Also try **InterService Home Exchange**, *Box 87, Glen Echo, MD 20812; (301)229-7567*; **Loan-a-Home**, a mail inquiry outfit only, *2 Park Lane, 6E, Mount Bernon, NY 10552*; and **International Home Exchange Service**, *P.O. Box 3975, San Francisco, CA 94119; (415)382-0300.*

A geography lesson

Italy is a 116,000-square-mile finger pointing toward Africa and dividing the Adriatic and the Mediterranean seas. Much of the Italian peninsula is mountainous. More than a third is spiked by ranges of more than 2,300 feet, most is hilly, only a quarter is flat plains. The two major mountain ranges are the Alps and the Apennines, which form the spine of the entire peninsula and the island of Sicily.

The most important and extensive plain in Italy, the **Po Valley**, flattens more than 17,000 square miles. Through it runs the Po River and its tributaries, and the rivers Reno, Adige, Piave, and Tagliamento. Intensive agriculture is practiced in its fertile lower plain.

Italy is divided into 20 administrative regions called *compartimenti*. They vary greatly in size and geography and correspond generally with historically unified regions. Regions in the north include: the castle-studded Piemonte, which reflects some French influence and is the seat of united Italy's former royal dynasty; the mountainous Valle d'Aosta, a winter-sports paradise; Lombardy, where mountain-mirroring lakes relieve the industrial landscape around Milan; Trentino-Alto Adige, dominated by the Dolomites, where winter and summer resorts attract throngs; Liguria, an inexpensive Riviera wedged between the Mediterranean and the Alps; and the Veneto, once the territory of the Venetian Empire.

The center regions include: medieval Emilia Romagna, which has prosperous farms; Tuscany and Umbria, with their vestiges of Etruscan civilization and Renaissance art and culture; the Marches on the Adriatic side; Latium (Lazio) and the Campania, whose hills circle Rome; and the Abruzzo and the Molise regions of the harsh central Apennines.

The south has the poorest regions: Apulia, which overlooks the southernmost part of the Adriatic Sea and flourished under the ancient Greeks; ancient and rocky Basilicata; and the southernmost province, Calabria, which was once haunted by brigands.

Sicily and Sardinia, Italy's two Mediterranean islands, are also considered *compartimenti*. Remnants of Greek and Roman civilization can be found throughout Sicily, as can Roman remains. Sicily's climate is temperate, making it a popular resort. Mountainous Sardinia has been inhabited since prehistoric times. Throughout the island are ancient nuraghi, cone-shaped fortification/dwellings. Sheep and goats are raised here.

Today, the north of Italy is heavily populated and has industrial cities and intensive agriculture. Southern Italians are migrating steadily to the north. Italy's center, which focuses on Rome and Florence, is also becoming industrialized, growing away from its agriculture-and-craft traditions. The south, with the two ports of Bari and Naples and some recently developed industry, still preserves some of the traditional Italian way of life. Sicily and Sardinia are extensively cultivated with citrus fruit and vineyards, pasture for sheep, fisheries, and a shrinking mining industry.

The country has more than 4,800 miles of coastal shoreline—from the northern Riviera to the famous beaches at Amalfi, Taormina, and Sardinia's Emerald Coast.

Italy's climate varies widely. While usually mild, the northern and central regions have a cold January, and a rainy, chilly November, February, and March. But Christmas travelers can sunbathe anywhere in Sicily. The hottest months are July and August. (Italy undergoes a vacation exodus during these months.) The average temperature in Rome in January is 49 degrees Fahrenheit; in July, the average is 82.

Italy has the fifth-highest population density in Europe, with 57,886,000 people. The nation is mostly Roman Catholic.

Portraits of the cities

Rome is the embodiment of ancient and modern Italy. Here the ancient Romans rose and fell. And here the most outrageous fashions and contemporary ideas live on. The ruined Roman Coliseum stands at the center of a mad whirl of traffic, an example of the juxtaposition of eras.

For more than two millennia, Rome has been the world's most celebrated city. Before Christ was born, Romans watched gladiators fight lions in the Coliseum. For 1,500 years, Rome has been the center of Christianity. Today, Rome is one of the biggest tourist attractions in the world. It has some of the world's most exclusive shops and the best restaurants.

Vatican City, within Rome but politically separate of the city, represents the grandeur of the contemporary pope and the impact of Roman Catholicism. Typically, 300,000 people gather at St. Peter's to hear the pope's blessing on holy days. Among the Vatican's many attractions is the Sistine Chapel, a marvel of the Renaissance frescoed five centuries ago by an unwilling Michelangelo at the order of Pope Julius II.

Pillars and columns are all that remain of the great Roman Forum. They provide a peaceful and historic setting for a picnic.

In contrast, the Piazza di Spagna (Spanish Steps) are a living work of art, jammed with tourists, students, beggars, and merchants selling colorful clothing, flowers, and trinkets.

Florence, as much a work of art as the famous works of art it contains, lies in the most pleasant region of Italy, Tuscany. The hill towns surrounding Florence are full of charm. Food is extremely good, particularly meats. Chianti is the regional wine.

This Renaissance city is where art was reborn around 1500. Remarkable figures such as da Vinci, Michelangelo, Botticelli, Machiavelli, and Cellini got their inspiration in Florence. That spirit remains, making Florence a fascinating city to explore and absorb.

The Uffizi, an amazing museum featuring the works of Botticelli and his fellows, is at the artistic heart of Florence. The Duomo (S. Maria del Fiore) is one of the world's largest churches, containing frescoes illustrating Dante's *Divine Comedy*. And the Pitti Palace houses works by Rubens and other masters.

Milan is a rough, industrial city. It is also one of the world's fashion capitals. The Duomo, in the heart of Milan, is spectacular. Begun in 1386, it is covered with some 3,000 statues. Leonardo da Vinci's *Last Supper* can be viewed in the Church of Santa Maria delle Grazie, for which it was painted. The Certosa de Pavia near Milan is a 600-year-old Carthusian monastery worth visiting.

Venice is famous for its canals and gondolas. Water is used more often than land for transportation. Pedestrian streets are connected by ornate footbridges, giving the city an ethereal appearance. The Piazza San Marco at the heart of the city attracts throngs of people and huge flocks of pigeons. The Basilica of St. Mark, begun in the ninth century and later rebuilt, is on this central plaza.

The islands of the lagoon—the Lido, Burano, and Torcello—can be reached by *vaporetti* (water taxi) from the Fondamenta Nuove, near Campo dei Gesuiti. They offer beaches, fishing villages, small art museums, and relief from the frenzy of Venice itself.

Mantua has the charm of Venice without the crowds. The River Mincio wraps around the ducal city like a cloak and threads its way through the city via little canals. Graceful bridges cross the winding waterways. Once the seat of one of the most brilliant courts of Europe, today it is one of the best-preserved medieval cities in Italy. It has no modern industry and no high-rise buildings. The city's most famous sight is the Ducal Palace, built in the Middle Ages. It has 500 rooms, seven gardens, and eight courtyards. Frescoes by Pisanello decorate the Hall of Dukes.

Naples has a reputation for crime, although the crime here is actually no worse than that of New York and other major cities. Because of its undeserved bad reputation, Naples has fewer tourists than other Italian cities. There is a U.S. Naval base nearby, however.

A huge, hilly town in the shadows of Mt. Vesuvius, Naples is cooled by the breezes of the Gulf of Naples. The city's waterfront is lined with booths where you can buy drinks.

Neopolitans have a lugubrious interest in the macabre. In the Cappella Sansevero, for example, is the 16th-century corpse of a family servant mysteriously preserved by the alchemy of the Duke of Sansevero. The chapel is hidden on a small side street off Piazza San Domenico Maggiore. The National Archeological Museum in Naples houses one of the most important collections of Greek and Roman antiquities in the world, including many of the treasures excavated from Pompeii and Herculaneum, which are nearby.

Siena is the provincial capital of Tuscany—Italy's wealthiest and loveliest region, blessed with golden hills, rich soil, and a treasure-trove of antiquities. Pass through the ancient city gates, and you're thrown back in time. Cobblestoned streets snake between turret-towered buildings. Streets twist up in sensuous curves, then plunge down in parallel lines. The Campo (main square) is a breathing space for the monochromatic pink buildings that surround it. If you are fortunate enough to be there in July or August during Il Palio, a centuries-old bareback horse race, you'll never want to leave.

Mountain resorts

If you like hiking or skiing, you might enjoy retirement in the Dolomite Mountains of northern Italy. The area has charming Tyrolean villages near ski slopes and mountain hiking trails. The best known is Corvara, which is also the largest. Others include Colfosco, La Villa, Pedraces, and San Cassianto.

Cortina d'Ampezzo, in the eastern Dolomites, is Italy's most popular ski resort. Although it is crowded, it has some of the best ski facilities in Italy. The area is huge—you can ski for days without doubling back to the same runs. When you tire of skiing, you can ice skate in the remnants of the Olympic Stadium, shop in the town's many boutiques, or dine in one of its many restaurants.

In **Courmayeur** and **Cervinia** you can ski in the summer as well as the winter. These towns are well-known—and pricey for Italy. The Val d'Ayas is undiscovered and has lower lift prices (and more challenging runs).

Colfosco, a small, quiet ski village with numerous runs, is great for beginning and intermediate skiers. It offers little cross-country skiing and no deep-powder skiing. Its major advantage over the large, more crowded resorts is that it is part of the Alta Badia, a five-village ski association. With a Colfosco lift ticket (which costs about 134,500 lire a week), you have access to 75 miles of trails and 53 lifts. For an additional 6,725 lire you can buy the Super Dolomite lift pass, which gives you access to 10 major ski areas that include 650 miles of trails and 430 lifts (not all of them easily accessible).

Hiking is terrific in the Dolomites, which are crisscrossed by trails. The best time for hiking is August and September, when the snow has completely melted. Don't hike in April and May unless you are an expert. The melting snow causes avalanches.

Pedraces, near the Austrian border, is one of the best places for hiking. The National Park of Abruzzi, near Pescasseroli, is another beautiful place to hike. The trails wander through a forest of pine trees blanketed with snow.

Lake Country

Italy's Lake Country has steeply rolling hills and a Mediterranean touch. Olive groves and palm trees surround the warm waters. This region has always attracted the famous (Flaubert, Dickens, Dumas, Hemingway) and royalty.

Stresa, a mere hour from Milan's Malpensa Airport, offers fishing, swimming, strolling, and steamer rides on the Lago Maggiore. This misnamed lake 48 miles northwest of Milan is neither greater than the other lakes (as its name suggests), nor deeper. But its appealing western shore is less-touristy than virtually any of the other lakes. Its key attraction is the Borromean Isles, especially Isola Bella.

Lago Garda, the easternmost lake, is the largest and most frequently visited. It has Mediterranean scenery—olive groves, lemon trees, and palms. And it is ringed by four cities known for art: Mantua, Verona, Trent, and Brescia.

Torbole, at the far end of Lake Garda, is the windsurfing capital of Europe. (The steady breezes that blow across the lake create perfect conditions for this sport.)

Lake Como, Europe's deepest lake, is too polluted for swimming. But it is bordered by two lovely towns: Como and Bellagio. **Como** is worldly, wealthy, and refined. Its Duomo (cathedral) is one of the most famous churches in Italy. Built between 1457 and 1485, it has a spectacular rose window and houses Bernardino Luini's *Adoration of the Magi.* **Bellagio,** the lake district's art center, invites artists to spend a month or more there developing works in progress. Located at the point where Lake Como intersects with Lake Lecco, Bellagio has narrow streets and ancient buildings.

Campione d'Italia is located on the banks of Lake Lugano. This enclave of 2,000 inhabitants is part of Italy but has a Swiss economy. Unlike many parts of Switzerland, however, foreigners can buy real estate. (A two-bedroom apartment with a lake view sells for 135,600,000 lire.) And it is a tax haven with fluid borders—there's free access to Switzerland and Liechtenstein. Corporations formed here can take advantage of Italy's relaxed laws while operating with Swiss efficiency. The lake resorts of Como, Lugano, and Maggiore are nearby; the big city amenities of Milan are just 45 minutes away.

The Italian Riviera

The Italian Riviera, which stretches from the French border to Tuscany, is less expensive than the French Riviera and just as pretty. It is divided into the Riviera di Levante (coast of the rising sun) southwest of Genoa and the Riviera di Ponente (coast of the setting sun) southeast of Genoa.

The character of the land changes when you cross the border from Menton, France, into Italy. Where the French roads perilously cling to the side of the Alpine hills that drop into the Mediterranean, the Italian roads, triumphs of engineering, use bridges and tunnels to zoom east, away from France and Monte Carlo, toward Genoa, toward the well-known resort towns around Portofino, toward Rome.

In the little villages below the great viaducts are beaches, fishing ports, cheap hotels, restaurants, all forgotten in the autostrada rush. Tiny beaches and fishing ports fill the valleys running north to south between the mountains and the sea. They are sheltered from the east and west winds and open to the sun from the south. Geography favors these villages; fashion and the speeding Legionnaires and Alfa-Romeos of the highways above have passed them by.

Where the French part of the Riviera, the Côte d'Azur, has made a nightmare of an authentic old fishing village like St. Tropez—stuffing it with high-rise buildings, exhaust-spewing cars, beautiful people, glitzy shops, and foul restaurants—a dozen miles away Italy's equivalent remains authentic. The stucco is peeling, the awnings are patched, the cars are Fiat 500s instead of fat Peugeots and BMWs. But beautifully tended flowers bloom, palm trees line the boardwalk, and the prices are affordable.

Bordighera is the second resort in Italy as you come from France; the border town is Ventimiglia, a center of market gardening, cactus and flower production, smuggling, counterfeit French and Italian "label" merchandise, and financial *combinazzione*.

The hills of Bordighera and Ventimiglia are covered with scrubpines and cypresses, olive and citrus groves—and fields of cultivated flowers. Here carnations, jasmine, hyacinths, narcissus,

292

violets, tulips, mimosa, and roses are grown for European buyers and the perfume industry. The gardens are full of bougainvillea, palm trees, and roses. It is at Bordighera that the best palms in Italy are grown, supplied to the Vatican itself for Palm Sunday. The old town, still enclosed by walls, with steep streets and winding alleys, white stucco houses and old chapels, topped by red-tile roofs, is full of good seafood restaurants.

Although summer is the high season, Bordighera is a year-round resort because it is sheltered from cold. And the sea breeze keeps it from being too hot in summer.

In **Ventimiglia**, a bit more down-market because it is right on the border, there is a real business in rental cottages and apartment-hotels. **Holidays Beach,** *Strada Romana; tel. (39-184)39-508*, rents apartments with kitchens from May to the end of September for 300,000 lire per week (500,000 in July and August). If you really want to rough it, there is **Villeurope,** *Cabo So Mentone 55; tel. (39-184)38-057*, which has bungalows with kitchen facilities but centralized bathhouses. The high-season rate for a bungalow with sink and kitchenette for up to four people is 350,000 lire per week.

Better-known **San Remo** is pricier. It is the oldest resort on the Riviera and has been overbuilt. But it has a casino and a yacht basin, and the hotels are affordable despite their Edwardian elegance (inexpensive ones are located along the via Matteotti). This resort town of some 70,000 is only 21 miles from Monte Carlo and not much farther from Nice. San Remo is a prime example of just what retirement in Italy has to offer: hundreds of hotels and pensiones of every category, facilities for all kinds of boats, miles and miles of beaches, lavish public gardens, a 14th-century cathedral, swimming pools, and a nearby ski resort.

Italy's crème de la crème surfaces in **Portofino** during the summer. Very private and romantic, Portofino is one of the most photographed places in the world. Its remarkably deep natural harbor attracts yachtsmen from all over the world. Among the celebrities who have stayed here are Lauren Bacall, Humphrey Bogart, Aristotle Onassis, and Ernest Hemingway.

The most charming town on the coast is **San Fruttoso.** You can get there by boat from Camogli—it is accessible only by sea. The town is surrounded by pines, olive trees, and oaks that lead down to the sea. Walk through the cloisters and corridors of the Benedictine Abbey of San Fruttoso di Capo di Monte, which consists of a 13th-century palace, an 11th-century church, and a Romanesque cloister.

At the southern end of the Riviera is one of the least crowded, most picturesque areas: **Cinque Terre**. The mountains, woods, vineyards, and hilltop villages of the Cinque Terre cover 15 miles of coastline. The area's five villages—Monterosso, Vernazza, Corniglia, Manarola, and Riomaggiore—are perched on the rocky coast north of La Spezia.

Monterosso is the largest and most crowded of the five towns. But it has a beautiful beach at the southern end of the cove. You can rent boats here. Climb the hill to the Convento dei Cappuccini, which houses Van Dyck's *Crucifixion*. Hiking trails lead from Monterosso to Cinque Terre's quaint towns. A 1 1/2-hour hike along a goat path leads through vineyards and olive groves to Vernazza. Another hiking trail leads to Corniglia, which has a long pebbly beach. If you're up to another hour's walk, follow the trail along the jagged coast to Manarola, the most beautiful of the Cinque Terre towns. Here, yellow houses balance on cliffs and artists and writers seek their muses.

To get to the Riviera, fly to Nice or to Genoa, and then rent a car or take a bus or train. The train is slow but the scenery is stunning.

The Amalfi Coast

The **Amalfi Coast**, a mountainous peninsula between the Gulf of Naples and the Gulf of Salerno, is a land of legends. Pirates once used the secluded inlets as hideouts. Spectacular views can be enjoyed from the dizzying summits of the mountains. Serpentine roads wind through cliff villages. Olive groves and grape vines dot the plains.

In July and August, the Amalfi Coast becomes a madhouse, and it is nearly impossible to drive. The spring and fall are idyllic—warm and uncrowded.

Positano, a hill-climbing village with a single road, is on the western strip of the Amalfi Drive. It looks out onto the Tyrrhenian Sea and its storybook islands of sirens. Nearby is the Green Grotto, even more beautiful than the more famous Blue Grotto in Capri.

Another spectacular view is from the little town of **Ravello**, above Amalfi. A bus will take you to the summit via narrow, twisting roads. The cathedral of Ravello has sculptures of strange-looking animals and contains a reliquary with the skull of Saint Barbara.

Island living

Capri is a beautiful but crowded island that can be reached by hydrofoil from Naples, Sorrento, or Pozzuoli. Capri is also the name for the crowded main town. The island's most famous sight is the Blue Grotto. But more spectacular is the view from the top of Mt.

Solarno, where an old monastery stands. And the pagan shrine of the Matromonia Cave is interesting, not to mention the ruins of 12 villas built by Roman Emperor Tiberius to honor the 12 Roman deities.

Sardinia is the land of *banditti*, family clans, and blood vengeance. Movie stars and royalty are attracted to its luxurious Emerald Coast. Ship service is available from Genoa, Civita Vecchia, and Naples. This overnight trip takes 14 hours. House rentals are available throughout the island. The Italian Government Travel Office has a list of agents. A small house that sleeps four and overlooks the sea costs about 2,700,000 lire per month.

Enna, picturesquely situated on a horseshoe-shaped plateau in the center of Sicily, has aptly been called the belvedere of the island. This provincial capital of 30,000 is rich in history and pageantry. The week before Easter it is ablaze with colorful parades. The altitude (about 3,500 feet) provides cooling breezes in summer. Costs are delightfully low.

Finding *la dolce vita*

Stuart Rabinowitsh first visited Florence in 1985. Enchanted by the city's beauty and serenity, he decided to make it his home. He described his life in Florence in the February 1987 issue of International Living.

What brings people from all around the world to live in Florence? It's hardly the land of golden opportunity. Italy's economy is terrible, and even Italians can't find jobs. But any artist or art lover would sell his soul to live in Florence. This Tuscan city is a magnet for students, artists, and writers. It is a city of great, almost unreal beauty.

Florence offers foreigners a pleasing alternative to Rome or Milan. Centrally located between these two giants, it is small enough to feel at home in. Expatriates can become very much a part of its vibrant culture. And its proximity to Pisa, Siena, Bologna, and Venice adds to the city's appeal.

For all its 15th-century heritage (the city was substantially developed by the Medicis during their reign), Florence has a young heart. Young people dominate the squares and streets, their hip styles contrasting with and complementing the city's neoclassical grace.

While Florence's metropolitan area houses more than a million people, it is a surprisingly peaceful city. There is no international airport nearby. You never hear the roar of jets zooming overhead, as you would in Rome or Pisa. Instead, you hear church bells. Depending on your location, you can be awakened by the sweet peal of one angelic bell, or, in the city center, by the drone of some 15 different bells, none in tune with another. This clangor is what I hear from my bedroom window every morning.

Central to the lively daily life of the city are the piazzas sprinkled throughout the town. Piazza del Duomo, surrounding the Duomo (Florence's red-domed cathedral, formally known as Santa Maria del Fiore), is the main landmark and center of town. Piazza de la Republica is the business center of town. Its arcaded buildings house the central post and telegraph offices. These are always crowded. It's best to do your business at smaller branches, such as those located on Piazza del Olio, near the Duomo.

A short walk past the fashionable shops of Via de Calzaiuoli takes you to the historic Piazza Signorina. Here is the Palazzo Vecchio (which now houses the seat of government for the state of Tuscany) and the entrance to the Uffizi, Florence's fabulous art museum, which features works of Michelangelo, Leonardo da Vinci, and other Renaissance artists.

Here's a tip for Americans coming to Florence: Don't drive. It's not a city to make American drivers at ease. Florence's convoluted streets are a navigational nightmare. Parking is even worse. Spaces are hard to find, and tickets are a way of life. Good garage space could solve that problem, but it's ridiculously expensive. (The center of Florence is closed to traffic now in any case.)

You don't really need a car in Florence, anyway. Most everything is within walking distance. In fact, it's a magical city for walks, with surprises around every corner. A bicycle is a good way to get around. Used ones can be bought in many small stores around town. You can rent a bike for a few dollars a day. Public transportation is good, too, and quite cheap.

Florence is the center of Tuscany, the region of Italy famous for Chianti wine. This wine is part of a revered Italian tradition: eating. Tuscan cuisine stresses cheese and light sauces, rather than the tomato and cream sauces of southern Italy. One staple of the region is steak Florentine—a robust, well-seasoned cut of meat thick enough for a Texan's appetite.

The Mercato San Lorenzo, the bustling central market of Florence, is the best place to go for your groceries. On the street level is a wide variety of good meats, fresh and frozen fish, cheese, fresh pasta, and pre-packaged goods. Upstairs, the market offers fresh fruit and vegetables. Everything is prime quality, and the prices are great. The Mercato San Ambrosio is another marketplace, also housing a good, inexpensive eatery. And should you become weary of Tuscan food, you can give your palate a change at one of the many Chinese restaurants in town.

If you are a latent artist, take advantage of Florence. Many art schools here are open to foreigners. Below are three of the most accessible. All are fine schools and are relatively inexpensive.

•**Centro di Cultura Lorenzo di Medici,** *1 Piazza delle Pallattole, 50122 Florence; tel. (39-55)28-31-42;*

•**Scuola Leonardo da Vinci,** *4 Via Brunnelesci, 50123 Florence; tel. (39-55)29-42-47;* and

•**Scuola Dante Alighieri,** *12 Via dei Bardi; tel. (39-55)28-49-*55.

For more information on Italy

•**The Italian Embassy,** *1601 Fuller St. N.W., Washington, DC 20009; (202)328-5500.*

•**Italian Government Travel Office,** *630 Fifth Ave., Suite 1565, New York, NY 10111; (212)245-4822; 500 N. Michigan Ave., Chicago, IL 60611; (312)644-0990; 360 Post St., San Francisco, CA 94108; (415)392-6206.*

•**U.S. Embassy,** *Via Vittorio Veneto 121, 00187 Rome; tel. (39-6)46741.*

•**U.S. Consulate,** *Lungarno Amerigo Vespucci 46, 50123 Florence; tel. (39-55)298-276.*

Chapter 15

Mexico

Retirement south of the border is becoming increasingly
popular for at least two reasons: the dollar goes a lot farther in Mexico
than it does in the United States, and the climate is marvelous along
the coasts. More than 100,000 U.S. retirees are taking advantage of
Mexico's values.

John Howells, author of *Choose Mexico* (Gateway Books, San
Francisco), vouches for the fact that it is still possible (in 1988) to live
in Mexico on $400 (about 918,400 pesos) a month. He and his wife
spent a month in San Miguel de Allende last year for just under $400.
This included 460,000 pesos for the rental of a new, two-bedroom,
two-bath apartment, the costs of a cleaning woman three mornings a
week, and food. Had the couple taken a one-year lease, their rent
would have been 344,400 pesos a month!

What's more, Mexico gives retirees credit for foreign income
taxes paid, and it has no inheritance taxes.

Those who are happiest with their retirement to Mexico seem to
have followed several rules. First, they traveled extensively throughout the country, investigating possible sites, before deciding on a
place to settle. Second, they learned to be patient with the slow tempo
of Mexican life. Third, they kept funds in U.S. banks to avoid suffering from the devaluation of the peso.

Retirees to Mexico can choose from houses near empty, idyllic
beaches; villas in the undiscovered countryside; apartments in
sophisticated Mexico City; or ranches near pre-Columbian ruins. The
most popular areas among Americans are the Guadalajara/Lake
Chapala area, which has a large U.S. colony with its own newspaper;
Acapulco; Ixtapa/Zihuatenejo; Cuernavaca; and most of the cities
within a day's drive of Mexico City.

Living for next to nothing

Life in Mexico can be so inexpensive that it's almost embarrass-
ing. Two Americans reported going to Mexico recently and sharing a
multicourse lobster dinner, including wine and dessert, for 18,368
pesos. They left an 11,480-peso tip for the waiter, who was so grateful
that he followed them all the way to their car showering them with
thanks.

Another American recently stayed in a simple hotel in Chihuahua where a double room was 9,185 pesos. Double rooms with private baths in three-star hotels outside resort areas range from 48,216 pesos to 96,432 pesos a night.

In Tapachula, Chiapas, you can buy a 16-ounce Coke for about 15 cents and a beer for 75 cents.

Throughout the country, resident seniors are entitled to discounts on train travel.

But best of all, property is dirt-cheap. The Mexican peso has plummeted to such lows that real estate prices are cheaper than ever. Elegant houses go for the price of tiny condos in the United States. In Mexico City, for example, a two-bedroom duplex with a garage was advertised recently for 5-million pesos. Also in Mexico City, a four-bedroom house with a pool and landscaped gardens was on the market for 68-million pesos. (Keep in mind, however, that prices in the popular beach resorts are much higher. A condominium in Acapulco, for example, might cost as much as 200-million pesos.)

The vital signs

Mexico has a population of 79,662,000. (The population is increasing at an annual rate of about 3.3%, one of the highest in the world.) Three out of four Mexicans live in the cities. The capital of this 760,373-square-mile nation is Mexico City. About 75% of the country is arid or semi-arid; only 15% of the land is arable.

The country is bordered by mountains to the south, east, and west. Mexico City, at an altitude of 7,500 feet, is the cultural population center.

In the south, the rainy season lasts from May to October. Except in the coastal areas, little rain falls during the rest of the year. The east coast is hot and humid. The west coast beaches (San Lucas, Guaymas, Las Mochis, Mazatlán, San Blas, Puerto Vallarta, Manzanillo, Playa Azul, Zihuatanejo, Acapulco, and Puerto Escondido) are seldom humid, although they can be hot. The central regions are temperate and semi-tropical, and the north is arid or semi-arid.

Where to live

Below are short descriptions of places in Mexico popular among American retirees.

Mexico City: Mexico's heart and soul
Mexico's capital is the place for city lovers and archeology buffs.

It has lively night life, scores of restaurants, cultural events, artists and intellectuals, and some of Mexico's most interesting archaeological sites.

Mexico City has been the head and heart of Mexico for centuries. It was already a metropolis when the Spanish conquistadors arrived. From this city, Aztec ruler Montezuma held sway over vast tracts of present-day Mexico, most of Central America, and a good chunk of the United States.

The center of the city is the Zócalo and the Zona Rosa, where you'll find hotels, restaurants, embassies, the National Cathedral, the stock exchange, and the National Palace.

At the edge of the Zócalo, archeologists have discovered the ruins of an Aztec temple and aqueduct. Called the Templo Mayor, it served as the focal point of life for the people of Mexico from at least the founding of **Tenochtitlán** (the Aztec name for Mexico City) in 1325. This temple site once consisted of two pyramids and a building where ceremonies were held. The monks who accompanied Hernan Cortés destroyed much of the site, which was rediscovered in 1913. Major excavations date back only to 1978. The dig is accessible to visitors thanks to a system of ramps and staircases.

The **Palace of the Spanish Viceroys,** which later became the presidential palace, was built on the site of Montezuma's palace. Early in this century, President Lázaro Cárdenas (father of the defeated 1988 candidate) moved out of the Chapúltepec Castle (the royal summer palace), now the Museo Nacional de Historia. (However, he kept the Mexican white house on the Zócalo.) The museum displays famous murals.

Chapúltepec Park is popular among local families. It has a pleasant lake for rowing, a zoo, picnic areas, and a half-dozen museums to explore. However, activities in the park become less wholesome at night.

If you have even a slight interest in Mexican culture, visit the **Museo Nacional de Antropología** (National Museum of Anthropology), which houses most of the country's excavated treasures. A half-day here is equivalent to a complete course in Mexican history and civilization. The ground floor exhibits include some of the most striking works of art anywhere. Statuary, carvings, pottery, artifacts, murals, bas reliefs, frescoes, panels, idols, drawings, jewelry, utensils, furniture, tools, and documents—a magnificent hoard of remains of the pre-Columbian Indians—have been gathered here.

About 35 miles north of Mexico City is **Teotihuacán,** the largest and most impressive urban site of ancient America. The size of a dozen football fields, it is graced by the Pyramid to the Moon (which is difficult climbing); the Pyramid to the Sun (which is higher—217 feet—and larger than the Pyramid of Cheops in Egypt, but easier to climb); and the stone, stucco, and paint Temple to Quetzalcoatl, the plumed serpent god. The Indian builders of these huge edifices cut their stones with obsidian so cleanly that they were fitted together without mortar.

The **National Cathedral** in Mexico City was built over the site of an Aztec temple. Construction began in 1525 and was completed 250 years later. The cathedral is open at all times for worship; visitors are encouraged to come between 10:30 a.m. and 12:30 p.m. Women should dress modestly.

The **Ballet Folklórico,** a cultural display of regional costumes, dances, and music, is presented every Wednesday at 9 p.m. and every Sunday at 9:30 a.m. and 9 p.m. at the National Palace of Fine Arts.

You'll find excellent restaurants in the downtown and Zona Rosa areas. Try **La Fonda el Refugio,** *166 Liverpool;* the **San Angel Inn,** *Palmas and Altavista*; **Alfredo's,** *Pasaje Jacaranda;* and **Les Champes Elysées,** opposite the Maria-Isabel Sheraton.

The best ways to get around Mexico City are taxis (which are inexpensive), buses, and the metro. Rental cars are expensive. And using your own car subjects you to parking problems and rip-offs at gas stations. Furthermore, if you have an accident while driving here, the police are likely to assume it is your fault, simply because you're the foreigner.

While Mexico City is one of the most expensive places to live in Mexico (after Acapulco and Cancun), prices here are low compared with the rest of the world. An average monthly rent is 688,800 pesos, less than one-third the average rent in New York City. And you can rent a four-bedroom house for 3,444,000 pesos a month.

Cuernavaca: city of eternal spring

Cuernavaca, in the heart of Mexico, is known as the city of eternal spring, because of its perfect climate. Temperatures rarely vary more than 10 degrees from an average of 75 degrees Fahrenheit. The city is extremely popular among well-heeled expatriate Americans. In fact, it has been a popular resort and refuge from Mexico City since the days of the Aztecs.

Cortés had intended to retire to Cuernavaca. His palace is now an archeological museum housing murals by Diego Rivera, Siquieros, and Orozco. Cuernavaca is also the site of the summer palace of the luckless Emperor Maximilian, behind which grow the beautiful Borda

Gardens. Cortés founded a cathedral here in 1529 (on top of an Aztec temple).

The best place to eat in Cuernavaca is the restaurant at Las Mananitas. The Posada Jacaranda has an unusual restaurant called the Nido de Amor, a romantic treehouse with good food.

Morelia: heart of the handicrafts

Morelia—about midway between Mexico City and Guadalajara—is a picturesque national landmark with spectacular 17th-century buildings. It is also the place to shop for handicrafts (try the **Casa de Artesanías,** near the cathedral). Morelia can be used as a base for exploring the surrounding villages, each of which has its own handicraft specialty. The Tarascan Indians sell their crafts at Independence Market.

Guadalajara: a Mexican tradition

Guadalajara, popular among U.S. retirees, is the cradle of mariachi music, the Mexican hat dance, and the Mexican rodeo. The city is divided into four sections: **Libertad,** which contains the main market, bull rings, the mariachi plaza, and the red-light district; **Hidalgo,** a swanky residential section with a huge shopping center called Plaza Patria; **Juarez,** the downtown financial and governmental center; and **Reforma,** with the Technical Institute and a lovely public park. Through the city runs the Zona Chapúltepec, a wide, tree-lined promenade—Guadalajara's answer to the Champs Elysées.

Nearby (really a suburb of Guadalajara) is the village of **Tlaquepaque,** famous for its handicrafts. It is filled with artisan's shops selling textiles, silver, blown glass, brass, leather goods, and antiques. The main plaza is called El Parian.

Guadalajara has so many good restaurants that it would be hard to have a bad meal here. The style is informal.

The coastal resorts

Everyone who has seen *The Night of the Iguana* has seen **Puerto Vallarta**. That was 20 years ago, though, and Puerto Vallarta has quadrupled in size. While this is still an unpretentious and charming resort, property in Puerto Vallarta can be expensive. A three-bedroom villa with a pool was advertised recently for 757.7-million pesos.

During high season (December through May), rentals in Puerto Vallarta range from 803,600 pesos to 1.4-million pesos a month. (Often, payment must be made in dollars.) For help finding a rental, contact **Puerto Vallarta Homes,** *Paseo Diaz Ordaz 82, Puerto*

Vallarta, Jalisco.

Puerto Vallarta is mainly beach and jungle. You can arrange a tour on horseback into the jungle (bring mosquito repellent), parasail on the beach, or play polo—on the back of a burro.

Puerto Vallarta is the place to eat seafood and fish. You can buy it from a local fisherman (who probably will grill it in front of you if you ask) or enjoy it in one of the city's many good restaurants, where lobster can cost as little as 11,480 pesos. Restaurants with good views include Señor Chico's, which overlooks the bay, and Chico's Paradise, which overhangs a waterfall. Both have delicious food for low prices, but, as in any Mexican restaurant, the service is anything but quick.

Acapulco is crowded, smoggy, and overdeveloped. But it has fantastic night life. The main drag is Costera Miguel Alemán, with beaches and big hotels on one side and boutiques on the other.

If you are interested in buying a condominium in Acapulco, the following classified advertisement ran recently in *International Living, 824 E. Baltimore St., Baltimore, MD 21202:* "Acapulco: Two beachfront one-bedroom condominiums. Furnished. All facilities. Gorgeous views. Full hotel management and services. Takeover corporate ownership. $110,000 each."

San Blas is one of the newest of Mexico's west coast resorts. The tiny port, filled with brightly colored colonial houses, is guarded by the ruins of a Spanish castle. Down the bay is one of Mexico's most beautiful beaches, with yellow powdery sand and great surfing, windsurfing, and scuba diving.

San Blas remains undiscovered, primarily because it's not easily accessible. The nearest airport, at Puerto Vallarta, is 160 miles away. It is a much better idea to take a train or to drive the 150 miles along the gorges of the Rio Conde de Santiago from Guadalajara to Tepic, the state capital of Nayarit. From there it is 40 miles down the coast to San Blas. Accommodations in San Blas include three hotels (Los Amigos, Posada Bucanero, and Las Brisas) and an apartment complex called **Suites San Blas,** *A.P. 12, Apicama and Las Palmas, 63740 San Blas, Nayarit; tel. (52-321)50047* or *(52-321)50505.*

Cabo San Lucas, located on the tip of the Baja California peninsula, is where the Pacific meets the Sea of Cortés. This area is a paradise for those who enjoy fishing, diving, and water sports.

Mazatlán, one of the best harbors in Mexico, is a popular stopover for cruise ships. Marlin and sailfish can be caught in the waters off its beaches, and between December and April, whale watchers make their way here. Mazatlán is the resort for those who like to fish, relax, and watch the sun set.

The following classified advertisement appeared recently in *International Living:* "Mazatlán Mexico—Las Casitas. Luxurious condo located adjacent to Balboa Club, two large bedrooms, two bathrooms, swimming pool, beautiful gardens, daily maid service. Contact **B.H. Wilson,** *(206)588-7773."*

Ixtapa is a resort area newly created by the Mexican government. It includes 16 miles of beach and several new hotels, including the $65-million futuristic Camino Real.

Many people say that **Zihuatenejo** is the Puerto Vallarta of 20 years ago: quiet, picturesque, and *tipico* Mexican. Development is encroaching, but as yet Zihuatenejo is a laid-back fishing village.

Retirement in the Yucatán

The still-developing resort of **Cancún** on the Caribbean Coast of the Yucatán Peninsula is a good base for snorkeling, scuba diving, and visiting Mayan ruins. The area has been attracting tourists only since 1976, and construction is still in progress. Cancún is actually a sand spit washed on one side by the aqua waters of the Caribbean, on the other by the calm Bahía de Mujeres. It has talcum-soft beaches shaded by coconut palms.

While the hotel strip is luxurious and expensive (for Mexico), with elaborate pools and lovely gardens, downtown Cancún and the Yucatán inland are fairly poor and inexpensive. Away from the resort, on the road to Chichén Itzá, you can see the humble homes of the descendants of the Maya Indians. They live in one-room, palm-thatched huts with unscreened windows and little furniture other than a table and some hammocks. The floors are earthen, and spaces are left between the wood slats that make up the walls. The Mayans speak their own language and live off the land.

What little we know about Mayan civilization (a highly developed, pre-Columbian Indian culture) has been inferred from the numerous ruins of the Yucatán Peninsula. The sites are filled with awe-inspiring buildings and intricate carvings: plumed serpents, jaguars, pictures showing human sacrifice. As you drive along, you'll see tangled vines rising in a pyramid shape from the scrubby jungle. Explore—it's probably a half-excavated ruin you can wander through with nothing but bats, birds, and iguanas to watch.

Chichén Itzá is worth the three-hour bus ride from Cancún. El Castillo, the Mayan pyramid pictured on Mexican pesos, is an accurate calendar. The 91 steps to the top of each of the pyramid's four faces, plus the one step to the temple at the top, add up to 365, the number of days in a year. Fifty-two panels decorate the sides of the pyramid, one for each year of the Mayan century. The 18 terraces add up to the 18 months of a Mayan year.

At the ballfield where Mayan warriors played, winners were sacrificed to the gods. Sacrificees were given hallucinogenic drugs and wine before they were dropped down the 390-foot sacrificial well. There was one consolation—they were guaranteed a place in heaven.

Closer to Cancún is **Tulum**, a walled Mayan city on a cliff overlooking the sea. The piles of ancient rock are brightened by flowering trees. Parts go back to A.D. 500. Five-hundred narrow, steep steps lead to the top of the pyramid. Below, white-sand beaches stretch in either direction. Human sacrifices were once pushed over this cliff.

Downtown Cancún (the hotel strip is outside the center of town) is not picturesque. However, it does offer some interesting shopping, if you can drive a hard bargain. The town's major market area is downtown along Avenue Tulum. As you walk by this open-stall market, which stretches for about two blocks, the shopkeepers call to you—some even reach out to grab you by the arm. The blankets, sweaters, silver bracelets, and straw hats in these stalls are thrown across boxes and tables, and nothing is marked with a price. Feel free to rummage, but wait to ask for help until you're sure of what you want to buy. Once you have the attention of a salesperson, you won't get rid of him easily. Ask the price of something, then offer half as much. The shopkeeper probably will say that it is not enough. Walk away—he probably will follow you. One U.S. visitor bought herself a handmade wool cardigan sweater here for 91,840 pesos after hard bargaining. Heavy Mexican blankets can be found for 18,368 to 27,552.

The best way to get around Cancún is by taxi, which is cheap. Most rides within town are under a dollar.

Buying your hacienda

Under Mexican law, foreigners cannot own real estate within 31 miles of any coast or 62 miles of any border. However, foreigners can buy beach-front property by setting up trusts at Mexican banks or fiduciary institutions, which offer the advantage of 30-year leases at favorable rates. After 30 years, they must sell to a Mexican national or corporation. Most foreigners get around this rule by forming corporations owned 51% by Mexican nationals, and continue to enjoy ownership rights.

Also restricted is any area designated as *ejido* (common land granted to peasants in agrarian reforms). About half Mexico's cultivated land is *ejido*. This land can only be disposed of by the Agrarian Reform Secretariat. There have been some sensational scams in recent years in which shady Mexican corporations have illegally leased *ejido* land to Americans for building homes. The Mexican government confiscated the homes as well as the land.

Foreigners may acquire property directly if they have immigrant status—however, the property is supposed to be used primarily for residential use, not for renting out. Also, foreigners must agree to consider themselves Mexican nationals in regard to the property and not invoke the protection of their government if it should be expropriated.

Just as you would in the United States, have the title investigated and hire a reputable lawyer. Names of lawyers can be obtained from the U.S. Embassy, the American Society of Mexico, or the American Chamber of Commerce in Mexico.

Most popular properties range in price from 114,800,000 pesos to 344,400,000 pesos. The higher prices will be found in Mexico City and resorts such as Acapulco. Undeniably, the quality you get for these prices would cost you many times as much in the United States. But you should weigh that against the limited duration of ownership and the somewhat risky nature of obtaining a title.

For further information, contact the following banks, which have large real estate departments:

•**Banco Nacional de Mexico, S.A.,** *Departamento de Bienes Raices, Balderas 33, Mexico 1, DF;* or *Isarl la Católica 42, Mexico City;*

•**Bancomer, S.A.,** *Departamento de Bienes Raices, San Juan de Letran 9, Mexico 1, DF;* or *Universidad 1200, Mexico City 03339;* and

•**Secretaria de Turismo,** *Direccion General de Tenencia y Uso de la Tierra, Mazaryk No. 172, Mexico 5, DF.*

One Mexican real estate agency is **Ideal Real Estate,** *Juarez 18-102, Mexico DF, Mexico.*

The **U.S./Mexico Chamber of Commerce,** *1900 L St. N.W., Suite 612, Washington DC 20036; (202)296-5198,* might be able to answer some of your questions about buying property.

Properties for sale are listed in two Mexico City newspapers: *El Universal, Vucareli 8, Mexico 06040 DF; tel. (52-5)588-3955;* and *Excelsior, Paseo de la Reforma 18, Mexico 06040 DF; (52-5)566-2200.*

An argument for renting

John Howells, author of Choose Mexico, *argues in favor of renting rather than buying in Mexico. Below, he tells why.*

For one reason or another, we North Americans think we have to own a house. Of course, during the past few years in the United States, home ownership has been a way of keeping ahead of inflation, and in many parts of the country, achieving generous appreciation. We write the loan interest off our income before taxes, and overall we come out pretty well financially.

But things aren't the same in Mexico. For one thing, nobody sells with bank loans—you pay cash—so you have no interest payments to deduct from your income. Also, since you're retired, or perhaps living on savings, you probably won't have much income tax to pay in the first place. Yet, doesn't property ownership protect you from inflation?

Not necessarily. Surprisingly, during hyperinflation, property is not a hedge against falling purchasing power. With hyperinflation, property doesn't rise in value with the economy, instead it drops. Why? Because playing the inflation game requires hard currency (dollars) to manipulate and invest in things that go up in value. Real estate prices are set by how much rental income a property might bring in if it were rented. So, when inflation eats into tenants' income, it erodes their ability to pay higher rent. Therefore, property becomes a poor investment. This is one reason rents and housing are so reasonable in Mexico.

Even though property ownership isn't as attractive in Mexico, many people find great joy in buying old colonial homes and restoring them. Others build their own homes, doing their own designing and testing their artistic abilities as architects. Fortunately, with the low cost of labor and the availability of unusual building materials such as custom-made tiles and hand-formed bricks, the cost of re-doing a home is certainly reasonable.

Legal technicalities

The matter of buying a house, however, is not as simple as in the United States or Canada. There are Mexican laws, strictly enforced, concerning property ownership. Except for those people with immigrant standing, it's illegal for foreigners to own property in their own names. Don't listen to glib salesmen who say, "There are ways to get around that; we'll take care of it after the money changes hands." If you've heard horror stories about people losing property in Mexico, it's because they've done something illegal. The government has never, to my knowledge, arbitrarily moved against anyone who handled a transaction legally and properly.

But property ownership is possible. You do it by setting up a bank trust account to own the property. The trust then leases the house back to you for a dollar a year. Inasmuch as you have control over the property and pay taxes on it, it's virtually the same as outright ownership. When you sell, you have the buyer purchase the property from the bank, who remits the cash to you. Have a lawyer set this up.

Particularly dangerous are *ejido* lands. *Ejidos* are communal agricultural projects the government started years ago as a way of redistributing land ownership to the poor. The land is farmed in common. The farmers, as long as they work the land, continue to be tenant-owners of the communal plots, but they cannot sell. *Never*, regardless of what some smooth-talking real estate salesman may hint. Once a family moves away from the land, their plot reverts back to the *ejido* and the communal organization. Often these restricted lands are on choice beachfront locations and look quite tempting.

These laws aren't always understood even by the people living on these plots. After all, when a family lives on a plot of ground for several generations, they can't understand why the land isn't theirs to do with as they please. There have been cases where the bureaucracy has permitted long-time settlers to file for ownership. But the process is so complicated and spotted with legal pitfalls that seldom does anyone know what's going on. I'm quite skeptical about the process.

If you are one who insists on home ownership, and you decide on living in Mexico, by all means go right ahead and make the arrangements. (Myself, I prefer to rent.) When you do buy, be sure to obtain a competent attorney. I don't recommend going through real estate agents in Mexico. Many either don't know what they are doing or they are crooked. Look around for yourself. Talk to the North American community in Mexico—ask for advice about who is reliable and what's for sale.

If you decide to buy, please do yourself a favor and rent for a period of time to make sure you want to live in Mexico. It's not everyone's cup of tea. Rental agencies (*agencias de renta*) and real estate agencies (*agencia de bienes raices*) can help you in large towns and cities. But in smaller towns, you'll have to do your own hunting. A good way to begin is to ask Americans living in the area. Or just walk around the neighborhoods that interest you, looking for signs saying *Se Alquila* or *Se Renta* (for rent). Houses that are for sale (*Se Vende*) are often for rent if you ask.

Immigrating

There are at least 15 categories of visas for foreigners entering Mexico. Those entering Mexico for more than 72 hours need a tourist card, which is free from Mexican Consulates, Mexican Tourism Offices, at the border, and from airline offices. This allows one entry and one exit from Mexico in a six-month period. Citizens of the United States don't need a passport, but some proof of citizenship is required, such as a birth certificate or a voter's registration card.

Foreigners who receive a pension from a foreign government or receive income on a permanent basis from investments (abroad or in Mexico) may qualify for an immigrant entry permit. Some people prefer to deposit or purchase certificates of deposit in a Mexican bank or *Nacional Financiera S.A.* (development bank) for an amount that renders a minimum of interest sufficient to cover living expenses and support family dependents. As a rule, *rentistas* (pensioners) are not permitted to work in Mexico. Under this visa, the retired person may leave and re-enter Mexico as many times as desired.

To apply for an Inmigrante Rentista visa, you must be at least 50 years old and have an established and dependable income of at least $1,000 a month, plus $80 a month for each dependent (including spouse) over 15 years old. This can be proven through Social Security records, a statement from a corporate pension fund, or evidence of a bank trust. Proof must be submitted to the Mexican Consulate nearest the retiree's home in the United States.

Once five years have passed, the Immigrante Rentista visa may be changed to Immigrado, which gives the right to work and to own other types of property in Mexico.

The Visitante Rentista visa is available to retired people who do not wish to immigrate. It requires less income than is required for an Inmigrante Rentista visa. The visa allows a stay of six months, renewable for three additional periods of six months each. After two years, the retired person must leave the country and begin the process again. Under this visa, multiple entrances and exits from Mexico are permissible but are taxed.

To enter Mexico, all immigrants must obtain a permit from the **Secretaría de Gobernación,** *Subdirección de Inmigrantes e Inmigrados, Morelia No. 8, Colonia Roma, México, DF.*

Send the application through the Mexican Consulate in the area where you live since it must be accompanied by other documents, some of them to be legalized by the consulate. Documents must be translated into Spanish, including the application. The Consulate does *not* do translation work, although it will give advice.

Immigrants may be admitted into Mexico for one year, to be extended on a yearly basis for up to five years provided the conditions under which they were originally admitted continue. After five years they may apply for the status of permanent resident (*Inmigrado*).

The fee for the entry permit is $68.40. Each extension is $102, subject to change without notice. Legalization of documents should be enclosed with the application, along with $15.80. The visa on the passport is also $15.80.

During the first two years, immigrants may not spend more than three months a year outside Mexico. During the next three years, absences are computed cumulatively as a whole including those of the first two years and cannot exceed a total of 18 months for the five years. Permanent residents cannot stay out of Mexico for more than two consecutive years without losing their status, nor for more than five years in a period of 10 years.

Immigrants (primarily American and European) make up 3% of the Mexican population.

For more information contact the **Consular Section,** *Embassy of Mexico, 2829 16th St. N.W., Washington, DC 20009; (202)293-1711;* or the **Mexican Tourist Bureau,** *405 Park Ave., Suite 1002, New York, NY 10022; tel. (212)755-7261.*

Banking secrets

The two largest banks in Mexico are **Banco Nacional de Mexico** and **Banco de Comercio.** (Banco Nacional de Mexico has a branch at *375 Park Ave., New York, NY; tel. (212)838-8300.*) Exchange rates vary slightly, but are always better at banks than at hotels and shops. Go to a large office and say that you want a *cuenta* (an account). And open your account in dollars, not pesos. The procedure is simple and most offices have someone on staff who speaks English. Bank hours are 9 a.m. to 1:30 p.m.

Taxing situation

During the first year of residence, there is a one-time exemption from the General Import Tax on household goods, automobiles, and personal effects. Pensions and other funds received from abroad are exempt from Mexican income tax (but may still be liable for U.S. income tax). And there is no inheritance tax.

Medical information

Major cities, particularly those with large foreign colonies, usually have good health care. In fact, some Americans prefer to go to Mexico for dental work, because it's much cheaper and is said to be just as good as in the United States. Mexico has many medical and dental schools that are staffed by U.S.-trained doctors and dentists. Remote areas of Mexico, however, don't offer extensive medical care. Medical evacuation services can be hired to transport the very ill back to the United States, but costs are enormous. Also, note that Medicare and Medicaid will not cover illnesses treated in Mexico. You must have other types of insurance.

By the way, it is possible to visit Mexico and not get *turista*. There are all sorts of possible explanations for the stomach bugs that plague tourists in Mexico: the use of human waste as crop fertilizer; bacteria in the water; the way the water is stored (in tanks on hotel roofs); or what your digestive tract is accustomed to—Mexicans get sick in the United States. Some visitors eat what they please and never experience any distress. Still, it is wise to avoid fruits that cannot be peeled, raw vegetables, tap water, food from street vendors, and drinks with ice (the drink may be okay but not the ice). Brush your teeth with mineral water.

There is anecdotal evidence that prophylactic doses of Pepto-Bismol, begun before departure, may help. Don't try this without consulting your doctor. And one of our readers insists that the best way to prevent *turista* is to eat yogurt.

You can purify your water by boiling it for 20 minutes or adding *yodo* (iodine) or water purification tablets. Treated water should be allowed to stand for at least 30 minutes before drinking. Liquid bleach can also be used to purify water, but it tastes bad.

Bottled water is sold in five-gallon bottles, which can be refilled by water vendors, who have regular delivery routes. If you live in a house, you can have bottled water delivered. Gas stations also sell water.

Mexicans often consult a *curandera*, or healer, when they are sick. There is a Mexican saying that goes, "When a rich man is ill he goes to a doctor; when he's desperate he goes to a *curandera*. When a poor man is ill he goes to a *curandera*, when he's desperate he goes to a doctor." *Curanderas* (herbologists, witch doctors), *brujas* (witches), and *espiritualistas* (spiritualists) probably outnumber doctors and nurses in Mexico. Some of the plants they use appear to produce surprisingly helpful results.

Mexican entertainment

Nearly every town of any size has a bullfight on Sunday. In Mexico City, bullfights are at 4:30 p.m. at the Plaza Mexico. They are not for the squeamish. Tickets cost anywhere from 500 to 3,000 pesos.

Jai alai (pronounced HIGH-a-lie) is a popular ballgame similar to lacrosse but played at breakneck speed. Gambling on the outcome is done at breakneck pace, too. Games are held at the Frontón Mexico in Mexico City most evenings. Even small towns have a *jai alai* court for local play.

Mexico also is one of the few countries where you can see cockfighting legally. Guadalajara's Plaza de Gallos is the most colorful arena.

Food: not just tamales

While most Americans are familiar with Tex-Mex style of cooking, the Mexican kitchen varies greatly by province. Although the principal grain is corn (as in tortillas and tamales), the popular meats or seafood and the common sauces change from region to region. Although chiles are a staple seasoning, there are over 100 different kinds of Mexican cooking. Many ingredients are unfamiliar: *huitlacoche* mushrooms, acitron cactus, banana leaves. Not all food is fiery, and much of it requires great skill to make. The cooking in the coastal resorts and Mexico City can be very elegant; food in the Oaxaca area is more Indian than Spanish. In the Yucatán, look for *sopas*: usually rice and some other food, like a fried egg, in a little bit of broth.

Working south of the border

Don't expect to take a part-time or easygoing retirement job in Mexico. This poor country has a high unemployment rate. The law protects employment for Mexican nationals. Only where no Mexican national is available are foreigners permitted to fill jobs. Of course, you can try working off the record.

Business hours and holidays

Businesses and government offices generally open around 9 a.m. and close around 1 p.m. or 2 p.m. for a siesta. They reopen again from 4 p.m. until 7 p.m. However, in major tourist areas such as Acapulco, many shops are open all day, and remain open until late at night.

National holidays when banks, government, and offices are

closed include: New Year's Day; Constitution Day (Feb. 5); Birthday of Benito Juárez (March 21); Labor Day (May 1); Anniversary of the Battle of Puebla (May 5); President's Report to the Nation (Sept. 1); Independence Day (Sept. 16); Columbus Day (Oct. 12); Anniversary of the Mexican Revolution (Nov. 20); and Christmas Day.

Mexicans celebrate a variety of saint's days, fiestas, and religious holidays that vary from village to village. Three that are widely celebrated are All Saints Day (Nov. 1-2), the feast of Our Lady of Guadalupe (Dec. 12), and Three Kings Day (Jan. 6). During All Saints Day, families visit cemeteries to remember their departed relatives. Candies and pastries in the shape of skulls and skeletons are sold everywhere—it's a Mexican version of Halloween. The Guadalupe holiday includes elaborate religious processions and services. Three Kings Day is the main day for holiday gift giving (Christmas is a strictly religious holiday), especially for children.

Transportation

Numerous airlines fly to Mexico from the United States, including Mexicana, Continental, Eastern, and American. Most flights to other destinations in Mexico connect through Mexico City, although some flights from the United States go directly to Cancún and Puerto Vallarta.

Five main routes that lead into Mexico are:

•**Constitution Highway 57** is the fastest, from Piedras Negras on the Texas border. It bypasses most major cities and is 823 miles long.

•**Pan American Highway 85**, from Laredo, Texas, covers 765 miles and is the most beautiful route.

•**Pacific Highway 15**, the longest route, covers 1,796 miles from the California border at Tijuana to Mexico City.

•From El Paso, Texas/Ciudad Juárez, Mexico City is 1,300 miles away via **Central Highway 45**.

•**Highway 1** runs 1,000 miles from Tijuana down the length of Baja California.

The Mexican Tourism Secretariat operates a motorist assistance patrol along main highways known as the "Green Angels." If you have car trouble, pull off the highway, lift your hood, and tie a white cloth to your antenna or door handle. The Angels will help you between 8 a.m. and 9 p.m.

You are better off driving a car that takes leaded gas—it is difficult to find gas stations that sell unleaded gas.

It is unwise to drive outside of cities at night; there are too many trucks, donkeys, and cows on the road. And on certain routes, there have been instances of banditry and violence associated with drug smuggling. Make thorough inquiries concerning the safety of any route that is off the beaten track. Also, *do not drive unless you have insurance that will cover you in Mexico.* The Mexican police will put you in jail if you have an accident in an uninsured vehicle. You won't get out without bail until a settlement is determined. Accident insurance can be purchased at border entries and from car rental companies. Do not go anywhere by car without your policy in hand.

Driving within the cities can be an adventure and a real test of courage. Mexico City traffic is a gridlock for most of the day— bumper to bumper and in suffocating pollution. Mexican drivers seem to have taken Driver's Ed in the bull ring. Also, some cities with cobblestoned streets and many hills (Taxco, for example) are unsuitable for driving.

The major car rental companies are all in business in Mexico. Try to get a good map before you leave the United States, because maps are hard to find once you are there, particularly in places tourists don't usually go.

Do not get into a taxi unless you have agreed on a price in advance. When you ask a cab driver for a price, cut it in half, and be prepared to haggle (politely, of course).

Buses are incredibly cheap and incredibly crowded. They are also slow and somewhat reckless. Long-distance trips tend to turn into parties, with passengers sharing food, drinks, and candy. Watch out for pickpockets.

Train travel is a better choice. It is cheaper and more comfortable than bus trips. Routes can be extremely scenic. For those with time and patience, trains are a great way to see the country.

One expat's paradise—Baja California

The following article was written by Lois Lucas, a U.S. citizen living in Rosarito Beach, Baja California, Mexico. She says fellow-expats who manage to keep most of their money in U.S. banks have a high standard of living in Mexico.

Good news for retirees living in Rosarito. Living costs can be much lower than in the United States. It all depends on the way you want to live. Some North Americans say it costs as much as 60% less. Some say 30%. The cost of living will be much lower if you buy Mexican, rather than U.S., products. Many international companies, such as Kraft and Kellogg, manufacture in Mexico as they do in the

United States. If you want to live as if you are still stateside, using U.S. products and services, then you won't realize as much benefit as if you use and enjoy Mexican things.

It is best to buy pesos at banks, which have better exchange rates than merchants.

A word of caution: Many groceries, including dairy products, meats, fresh fruits, and vegetables, are subsidized by the Mexican government and are for consumption in Mexico only. These items may not be exported from Mexico without a special permit.

The monthly utilities charge for a two-person home: 80,360 pesos.

The Cruz Roja Mexicana Emergency Hospital offers a variety of services to Americans in Rosarito. A MedicAlert program is being established, offering a physical that includes EKG, urinalysis, blood pressure, and complete blood tests. The results are recorded on a card you carry with you. The card tells about allergies, medications, and whom to contact in an emergency. The cost is 114,800 pesos.

The Cruz Roja Mexicana provides ambulance service to the border or to a hospital in the United States. The cost is about 229,600 pesos from Rosarito to a hospital in Chula Vista. The ambulance can be met at the border by an ambulance from Chula Vista, but the cost of a U.S. ambulance ride from the border to a Chula Vista hospital is about 195,160 pesos.

Private physicians are on call 24 hours a day. And they make house calls. Dental services are a real saving in Mexico.

Many drugs sold by prescription in the United States are available over-the-counter in Mexico at considerably lower prices.

If you are considering buying property in Baja California, the following advertisement appeared recently in *International Living*: **Mexico's Baja Coast**—Ideal year-around ocean-front living, close to San Diego military facilities. American colony, pool, jacuzzi, tennis, surfing, and golf nearby. Sales and rentals to meet any budget. For details write **Captain Norman D. Champlin,** *Box 16D, San Ysidro, CA 92073.*

What to do if you're cheated
The Mexican Federal Government and the Baja California State Government have set up offices to handle and arbitrate consumer complaints. If you feel you've been cheated while traveling in Baja, the Mexican authorities want to hear about it.

The **United Mexican States Office for the Protection of the Consumer** has offices throughout the country to handle complaints of every kind regarding services and providers of goods—that includes producers, distributors, and advertisers. Goods that are covered include furniture, houses, land, automobiles, clothes, food, electrical items, and more. The office is under the direction of **Mexican Attorney General Jorge Palacio**. In Baja California, look for it at *Third Street, No. 1336, Tijuana; tel. (52-66)83-16-16, (52-66)85-59-03,* or *(52-66)85-59-04.*

The **State of Baja California Norte Office for the Protection of the Tourist** handles problems or misunderstandings with shop owners, translations, or explanations of Mexican law. It also helps in obtaining medical aid, legal assistance, etc. The office is in the *State Government Building, Number 1, Second Floor, Río de Tijuana, Tijuana; tel. (52-66)84-21-81* or *(52-66)84-21-38.*

The difference between the state and federal consumer offices is that the state services are confined to Baja California, while the federal consumer bureau has branches throughout Mexico. This means that if you have a problem in another Mexican state, such as Guadalajara, you can file a complaint with the United Mexican States' office in Tijuana. They will adjudicate it for you without your having to return to Guadalajara.

Both state and federal offices have bilingual attorneys who will assist and advise you free of charge. Before signing any important contract, consult them.

Americans in Baja California

Americans living in Baja California have formed a "non-political, non-racial, non-sectarian, non-profit" association to foster friendly relations between Americans and Mexicans. The American Society teaches Americans about Mexican culture, language, and laws—helping Americans avoid trouble while living or traveling in Mexico, and offering help if one runs afoul of the Mexican legal system. The Society also plans theater parties, square dances, and chili cook-offs.

To find out more about the Society and its functions, write the **American Society of Baja California,** *c/o Robert Lucas, Apdo. Postal 506, Playas de Rosarito, B.C.N., Mexico.*

Life in the Guadalajara area

John Howells, author of Choose Mexico, *wrote the following rave review of the Guadalajara/Lake Chapala area for us.*

Where do North Americans go for Mexican retirement? The list of potential paradises is long, so let's just look at the most popular:

the area around Guadalajara.

No part of Mexico attracts more long-term residents than Guadalajara and the nearby little towns of Lake Chapala and Ajijic. Current estimates of its U.S. and Canadian expatriate population range between 25,000 and 30,000. More than 80 North American social, religious, civic, philanthropic, and special-interest organizations serve this huge and diverse collection of individuals who find Mexico's "second city" irresistible. There is also an excellent English-language weekly newspaper, the *Colony Reporter*, to keep you up-to-date on events affecting the North Americans.

Particularly convenient is the large number of North Americans already there, allowing an easy transition. However, residents we've interviewed list a number of other equally valid reasons, not the least of which is the superb perpetual-spring climate. The weather, they insist, is the finest in the world. Averaging only one day per month without at least some sunshine, and with an average temperature ranging from 61 in January to 77 in May, the Guadalajara boosters may not be exaggerating.

Another plus enumerated by gringos living in Guadalajara is the quality of medical care. Its two medical schools, excellent hospitals, 24-hour emergency pharmacies, and other medical care services are comforting factors. Frequently mentioned is the fact that Guadalajara and its environs are convenient to get to from the United States and Canada. Its major airport makes it a transportation hub for much of the country.

Prices here, although fairly typical for Mexico as a whole, are somewhat lower, at least for housing, than some of Mexico's other popular retirement meccas. Below are some examples of real estate offerings selected from recent copies of English-language newspapers in Mexico:

•Rancho Del Sol bungalows—furnished, English-speaking community, five minutes from new Gigante (shopping center), adults only, $85 a month.

•Santa Anita—lovely two-bedroom, two-bath home in American compound, $250 per month.

•Old-style house near downtown area—garden in center, two-bedrooms, one story, furnished, with telephone, only $85 per month.

•Furnished room—gentleman, refrigerator, bathroom, kitchenette, $70 per month.

•Executive suite within magnificent Lomas Mansion—$400 per month, hotel service.

These are representative of housing in typical retirement areas.

You can pay much less and you can pay much more. If you're able to live away from the company of English-speaking neighbors, your chances of buying or renting a house for a fraction of these prices are excellent.

The center of much North American resident life in Guadalajara is the **American Society of Jalisco**, known to its several thousand members as "AmSoc." The new headquarters building in the pleasant Chapalita section of Guadalajara is a regular beehive of activity. They hold bridge games, perform community service, and plan frequent (and very economical) outings all over Mexico. The society provides low-cost medical insurance and helps newcomers feel welcome in their adopted community.

Other attractions of Guadalajara and its nearby towns are multiple recreational and cultural activities. Golf courses, tennis courts, and swimming pools appeal to the sports-minded. The city has many fine parks as well as hanging gardens. One of my favorite little parks is decorated with the busts of Mexicans whose heroic statures were earned in such unmilitary pursuits as poetry, philanthropy, education, and music. Fountains splash at almost every intersection.

Movie theaters with films in English, frequent concerts, museums, and organized trips are ubiquitous. A typical weekly issue of the *Colony Reporter* lists 20 or more activities. There are two libraries with books in English and many bookstores and newsstands with U.S. publications. Cable and satellite television have revolutionized home entertainment and videotapes of American films circulate freely.

Nearly every day there is a new art exhibition or an event at the Institute Cultural Cabás, the Degollado Theater, or one of the city's many other museums and concert halls. A typical weekly issue of the *Colony Reporter* lists 20 or more such activities.

A particularly interesting museum was established in the old studio of Clemente Orozco after the artist's death. Citizens of Guadalajara are proud of this famous native son, whose murals embellish many public places throughout Mexico.

The food here is thoroughly international, and the price is right.

The main drawback to Guadalajara is the terrible smog during the dry season. It is worse than in Los Angeles. Few residents ever mention this problem—it is a conspiracy of silence.

Lake Chapala and Ajijic
An hour's drive from Guadalajara brings you to the shores of **Lake Chapala** and the town of the same name. Together with the nearby villages of Chula Vista, San Antonio, and Ajijic, this is the

"Chapala" district of the Guadalajara area. Lake Chapala is Mexico's largest lake, about 65 miles long. It lies about a half-hour drive south of Guadalajara. Unfortunately, the lake's level is down lately, but plans are underway to increase both its level and its purity. Because of heavy pollution, no one swims in the lake. Several half-day bus tours to the lake leave from the Plaza Principal in Guadalajara.

Ajijic, long famous as a center of both Mexican and foreign artists, is now a fashionable residential community filled with upscale restaurants and boutiques. Some of the homes and landscaping are absolutely breathtaking. Lower-cost housing is also available. This is perhaps the closest you come in Mexico to a North American "enclave." Here you will find an interesting phenomenon: two cultures living side-by-side, seemingly invisible to each other. The local people go about their business with almost no social contact with the northern strangers who live in their neighborhood. In turn, the foreigners seldom bother to "network" with the locals. Yet those who do find a far richer and more interesting life than those who stay strictly within the English-speaking community.

Ajijic has one of the most beautiful cathedrals in Mexico. Begun in 1571, it is topped by two 200-foot towers and has no less than 11 ornate altars. It is surrounded by a cruciform of four plazas, the Government Palace, the city's museum, and other historical attractions.

Why Lake Chapala or Ajijic? The amenities are numerous: a golf course, plenty of good restaurants, and a full social life among expatriates. The area has been the subject of several recent books and videotapes and *Time Magazine* recently headlined an article: "Paradise, Down Mexico Way—Americans who settle near Lake Chapala find the sweet life." Satellite antennas dot the horizon, supplementing the videotapes and cable television services. The links to the United States are numerous and strong. Prices, particularly for real estate, tend to reflect this popularity, yet we have met residents who claim that comfortable living is still possible at the $400 per month level.

One woman's Guadalajara sojourn

Maggi Stewart wrote the following article for International Living *(June 1988) after exploring retirement life in Chapalita for six months.*

For 3,000 American retirees, **Colonia Chapalita**, in the southwestern part of Guadalajara, is home. They move here for the warm weather, active social life, and low costs.

The air in Chapalita is fresher than in the narrow streets of downtown Guadalajara, and it's full of strange sounds. The church bells toll, mailmen blow their *brasuras* (whistles), trash collectors ring cowbells, and knife sharpeners toot their *alfiladores* (flutes). The buildings dazzle white in the relentless sunshine. Yes, rain does fall during the rainy season (June through September), but it's mostly at night. During the six months I lived here, I saw only a couple of rainy days and one storm.

Finding an apartment

I lived on avenida de las Rosas, a street I chose because I liked the name. I was walking along López Mateo, came upon the street, and saw the "For Rent" sign at Jacaranda Suites. Built around a small courtyard of fountains and plants, the building has bright mural-painted walls, stone stairwells, and tile floors. My apartment was a tiny one-bedroom unit with heavy dark furniture and glass-louvered windows protected by Samson-strong iron bars. The rent was 459,200 pesos ($200) a month, including weekly maid service.

I had looked at other apartments in this price range, but I found Jacaranda Suites the best because of the building's location. It's on a bus line and near stores, shopping malls, the American Society, Las Calas Cultural Center, and Sandi's, the English-language bookstore.

Dirt-cheap apartments are available throughout the area. For example, the head of the local Senior Citizen's club, an affable man named Marshall Wright, found a real winner in Ajijic, by Lake Chapala. His one-bedroom apartment, with pool, rents for less than 460,000 pesos a month.

Another alternative is to live in a hotel—which is much less expensive than you might imagine. Before I found my apartment, I spent a month at the **Hotel Calinda Roma,** *Avenida Juárez, Guadalajara; (800)228-5151* or *(52-36)14-86-50.* (Quality Inn chain hotels are known as Hotel Calindas in Mexico.) While the nightly rate for a double is about 115,000 pesos ($50), I got a reduced rate through the Senior Citizens Club of Guadalajara. My total rent was 688,800 pesos for a month. Some retirees live indefinitely in this hotel. To contact the club, write **Marshall Wright,** *Senior Citizens Club, Hotel Calinda Roma, Suite 107, Avenida Juárez 170, Guadalajara, Mexico.* There is no membership fee.

When you arrive in Guadalajara and begin your search for a place to live, your first stop should be the Senior Citizen's Club, which meets every Wednesday at the Calinda. Guest speakers talk about living in Guadalajara. You're bound to meet some real estate agents at these meetings who can help you find an inexpensive place to live.

Acclimating yourself to Guadalajara, especially the downtown area, may be difficult. The traffic patterns are horrifying. Legal left turns are all but impossible to make. And the uniformed traffic directors spit out only top-speed Spanish.

Guadalajara is strictly a leave-the-driving-to-us city. Fortunately, public transportation is plentiful and far-reaching. The bus drivers navigate the roads like madmen, but they know how to get around. And the buses are cheap—the fare for all buses is one *cien*, a brass coin worth 100 pesos.

The bus system comprises several hundred routes. Although they're numbered and named, they may be difficult to understand at first. I walked a lot, observing the numbers, then gradually began boarding buses. At a gathering of Americans, I overheard one man explain how he had learned the bus routes. "I tried every bus in my early days," he said. "And I mapped their routes. This took many days of bus riding, but I had nothing else to do then. I suppose I rode 200 to 300 different buses."

All buses are designed for standing passengers. The drivers will make change and stop to let you off when you yell *"Parada"* (stop) or *"Esquina próxima, por favor"* (next corner, please). Or, if you can pronounce it, mention the name of the street you want.

For the same fare as the buses you can ride the trolley, an electrified bus that runs between downtown and Los Arcos, stopping at key points such as Chapalita hotels, the tourist office, a market, public buildings, and the Plaza Tapatío. The trolley runs every few minutes and stops at marked *parada* (stops).

Another transportation option is the *sitzicombi*. These numbered white vans race through the city. They seat 13 but often become crowded to standing-room only. The fare is 150 pesos.

Of course, taxis will take you anywhere. But set the price before you hop in. I look at taxis as luxuries, to be ridden only when you have heavy baggage to haul.

To keep abreast of what's going on in your town, you'll need the *Colony Reporter* and the *Sunday News*. These English-language weekly papers are available at Sandi's, in hotel newsstands, and on some street corners.

Always among friends
During the time I lived in Chapalita, I met more people than I have anywhere else. The American retirement community is very friendly—almost everyone is on a first-name basis with almost everyone else.

I found living in Chapalita very reasonable. I had no problem living on $400 (about 918,400 pesos) a month—but I did it alone. Most couples said that they needed about $900 a month. Understand also that I lived frugally, foregoing the usual American wants—no car, no telephone, no television. But I didn't miss them.

A Senior Citizens introduction

If you like the idea of retiring in Chapalita, a program to introduce prospective retirees to Chapalita is available through the Senior Citizen's Club (address above). The club arranges an introductory hotel stay for two or three weeks, including use of all hotel facilities. When I wrote to the club for a preliminary reservation for two weeks, I received a confirmed reservation at **Hotel Diana,** *Augustin Yzanez 2760, Guadalajara,* on the edge of Chapalita. The hotel is in a prime spot near the Minerva Fountain, Los Arcos, and the trolley to downtown.

My initial two-week plan included accommodations and gigantic daily breakfasts—all for $200. I extended my stay another week, with the breakfasts, for less than half the original weekly rate. The total bill for three weeks came to 613,032 pesos ($267).

For a good overview of the city, I recommend the Panoramex tours. One free city tour, ending in Tlaquepaque, an artisan center, is included in the senior welcome package. I also went on the Lake Chapala tour, which visits the villages 30 miles south of Guadalajara, and a tour that goes to suburban Zapopen, 10 miles north, then on to a tequila factory. These inexpensive (16,000 to 23,000 pesos) tours depart Los Arcos and downtown daily. You'll find them advertised at most hotels.

The welcome wagon

In addition to the Senior Citizen's Club, several other organizations can help you adjust to life in Guadalajara. Officers and volunteers at **The American Society (AmSoc),** *Avenida de San Francisco 3332, Colonia Chapalita; tel. (52-36)21-23-95,* spend weekdays welcoming, advising, and getting Americans acquainted with life in Chapalita. You can listen to lectures, see films, attend classes, play bridge, go on tours, go to parties, and meet fellow retirees. Dining Discoveries, for example, is a series of outings to various restaurants led by Nellie and Len, two Americans who moved to Chapalita, met, and married.

AmSoc also sponsors a volunteer program (last Christmas I wrapped gifts for the needy) and offers health services. Gilda, a registered nurse from San Diego, will take your blood pressure weekly. You can join the Memorial Society through AmSoc; the 10,000 pesos membership fee gives you a newsletter listing members and coming events. And for 4,000 pesos, you can buy lifetime death-benefit protection in Mexico.

For a more personal orientation to the area, contact Judy and Fran Furton through AmSoc. Retired teachers, the Furtons have lived in Chapalita for more than a decade. They've made a business out of welcoming newcomers. "We open our home on Tuesdays, answer questions, give information, and take you to lunch." The Furtons can help you make sense out of the money aspect of living in Chapalita. They can tell you where to bank and where to invest.

One good piece of advice is to obtain a debit card from **Banamex Bank** (Banco Nacional de México), which enables you to withdraw funds in pesos without paying interest fees. Get to know Banamex. The government-run bank also sells long-term, high-yield CDs, buys property in your name and leases it back to you on long and generous terms, invests your money for you, and acts as an agent for you in government transactions.

If you have served in any division of the U.S. military, you're welcome to join the **American Legion,** *Alvarez Castillo Post 3, San Antonio 143; tel. (52-36)31-12-08.* Annual membership is $18. Members meet monthly and sponsor benefit functions, dances, holiday celebrations, and in January, host the big chili cookoff.

San Juan Cosala Health Spa
About 20 miles west of Guadalajara is the San Juan Cosala Health Spa, with its concentrated mineral hot tubs, Olympic-sized mineral pools, and hour-long massages.

The spa is located in Jalisco in the Sierra Madre mountains at about 5,000 feet, on Lake Chapala. It caters to an international clientele. The owner and some of the employees speak English.

Mineral springs feed the hot tubs and pools. The geyser is a spectacular sight. The thermal waters are recommended for the treatment of arthritis, rheumatism, insomnia, and fatigue. Maria, the masseuse, gives an excellent massage for about 8,000 pesos.

Each hotel room has its own private mineral hot tub and, of course, daily maid service. Some have refrigerators. A mariachi band plays most nights. Heat and air conditioning are not necessary because of the pleasant breeze and low humidity. There is no smog.

Time-share condominiums are large enough for a family or to share with another couple. Some can accommodate three or more couples with privacy. Sitting beneath an umbrella at a poolside table, you have a view of the lake amid flower-covered mountains.

For information and reservations, contact the **San Juan Cosala Health Spa,** *Lago de Chapala, Jalisco, Mexico.*

The good life in San Miguel de Allende

Becky Tozer described her life in San Miguel de Allende in International Living *(June 1987).*

Several thousand Americans live in San Miguel de Allende—a delightful little colonial town in the heart of Mexico. The expatriate community is an eccentric blend of artists, writers, gays, retired folks (who support an American Legion), and others who have paused there. It's an active society that mixes harmoniously with the Mexican culture.

Located on the high central plateau about 250 miles northwest of Mexico City, San Miguel is in the agriculturally rich Bajío region on the colonial route. The entire town is a historic national monument; all architecture conforms to the colonial style.

The town's landmark is the main cathedral, La Parroquia. With its imposing pink facade, La Parroquia is a 19th-century Indian mason's interpretation of a French Gothic cathedral. The steeple bell rings out every 15 minutes.

In addition to its other virtues, San Miguel is an artist's town. You can live there and study painting, sculpture, music, dance, photography, ceramics, weaving, or silverwork. I have taken a class or two while living there, but my greatest art education has come from artists I met at parties, in parks, or in restaurants. Artists are everywhere—it's fascinating to talk to them and watch them work.

San Miguel is also a good place to study Spanish. The best-known schools include the Instituto Allende, Bellas Artes (Centro Cultural El Nigromante), which is housed in an impressive former monastery, and the Academia Hispano Americano.

Though quaint at first glance, San Miguel is best appreciated with time. You can meet fascinating characters during happy hour at La Fragua piano bar or at a late-night jazz or flamenco session at Mama Mia's.

The more time you have to learn the town, the more likely you are to get invited to some of the homes behind the tall, bougainvillea-draped stucco walls. It's the only way to get to know the residents. In no time, you become part of the rhythm and colorful life of the town.

The public library, amply stocked with bilingual publications, organizes weekly home and garden tours—another way to glimpse life behind those walls. The library also helps produce *Atención*, a lively bilingual newspaper of local goings-on. It's required reading for every foreign resident.

On a more serious level, San Miguel has a new hospital, a real plus for foreign retirees.

For such a small town (more like a village, actually), San Miguel is alive with fun and enlightening things to do. Concerts of all musical genres, art shows, theater productions, and poetry readings are always going on. Not to mention the extravagant parades and fireworks that celebrate every holiday (there are many in Mexico).

Another favorite attraction is the hot springs located a few miles outside town. At the resort Taboada you can soak in the steaming water while a waiter brings you drinks. At La Gruta (in El Cortijo) you can swim in an olympic-sized heated pool or get steamed in a cave of hot mineral water.

For me, however, the best pleasures of San Miguel are free: making friends; jaunting up and down the cobblestoned streets framed by flower-laden balconies; and chancing upon mariachi musicians and late-night merrymakers.

For more information

The **Embassy of Mexico,** *2829 16th St. N.W., Washington, DC 20009; (202)234-6000.* Mexico has consulates in Los Angeles, San Francisco, Chicago, New Orleans, El Paso, New York City, and San Antonio.

The **Mexican Tourist Office,** *405 Park Ave., New York, NY 10022; (212)755-7261.*

The **U.S. Embassy** and consulates in Mexico, *Paseo de la Reforma 305, Mexico, DF 06500; tel. (52-5)211-0042.*

Several agencies conduct tours through the prime retirement areas in Mexico. The most experienced is **Jane Parker's Retirement Explorations,** *19414 Vineyard Lane, Saratoga, CA 95070; (408)257-5378.*

Chapter 16

Spain

One of the most beautiful and inexpensive places to retire to in Europe is Spain. While prices here have risen in recent years, Spain is still less expensive than areas in northern Europe and much of the United States. The sun shines most of the year, especially in the southern regions. Few people need central heating or winter coats. Retirees keep busy swimming, boating, fishing, sunning, going to bullfights, and drinking sangría.

About half the 6,400 Americans who have retired to Spain live on the Costa del Sol, a resort area on the southern Mediterranean coast. The largest number of retirees have settled around Marbella. Other popular spots along the Costa del Sol are Fuengirola, Torremolinos, and Benalmádena.

Retirees are also beginning to discover the beauties of Spain's other coastal areas, where beaches are less crowded and prices are much lower.

Cost of living

If you live like a Spaniard, the cost of living in Spain can be low. An American can live well in Spain on 80,000 pesetas a month, excluding housing costs. The cost of living is highest in the larger cities such as Madrid and Barcelona. In the most expensive areas, groceries for two are about 11,400 pesetas a week. A whole chicken is about 456 pesetas. You can save by shopping in "hypermarkets" and eating Spanish dishes such as *gazpacho, paella,* stews, poultry, and fish.

If you decide to go out to dinner, restaurants are reasonable. Some have fixed-price menus for about 800 pesetas. Moderately priced restaurants serve dinner for two for about 3,500 pesetas, à la carte.

A one-bedroom apartment in Barcelona rents for about 52,000 pesetas a month.

In Spain, unleaded gas is triple the cost in the United States, at 85 pesetas a liter (about 342 pesetas a gallon). Imported appliances and clothing are also expensive. Designer jeans are 11,500 pesetas. A sweatshirt costs about 4,000 pesetas.

On the other hand, medical bills are reasonable. A first-time visit to a doctor will cost about 7,000 pesetas; repeat visits about 4,560 pesetas. One American woman had her appendix taken out at a private clinic in Barcelona for 178,410 pesetas, including four nights in a private room, the operation, and anaesthesia. And medicine is cheaper in Spain than in the United States. Birth control pills, for example, are one-third the cost.

Residents older than 60 can ride Spanish trains for half-fare.

Paperwork

You can stay in Spain up to six months with no special visa. If you want to stay longer without a visa, you'll have to cross the border, get your passport stamped again, and then return. Or you can apply for an extension of your stay at the **Dirección General de Seguridad** (Ministry of the Interior) in Madrid, or in the provinces at the civil government office, or the local police headquarters (Comisaría de Policía). You will receive a *Permanencia*, good for a three-month extension of your stay. If you have been granted two of these, and wish to stay on, you must apply for a residence permit (*Autorización de Residencia*, or simply, *Residencia*).

To apply for a residence permit, which allows you to remain in Spain for a renewal period of two, five, or 10 years, you must present a valid passport; three color passport photos; a completed application form in three copies; proof of an annual income of not less than $8,000; and a certificate issued by the authorities of any country in which you lived during the past five years stating that you were not involved in any criminal action. Your spouse must also present these documents, along with proof of at least $1,500 additional annual income.

If you are applying for the residence permit in Spain, take the paperwork to a Spanish lawyer, where you will fill out an application. You will be asked why you are applying. The application must be signed by two Spanish witnesses. Upon approval, you receive a *Tarjeta de Residencia* (residence card).

If you do get the residence visa, you can import household and personal items duty- and tax-free. Washers and other appliances must be used, not new, to escape tax and duty. The only items that may create problems are cars, yachts, or motorcycles. Spain does not quarantine domestic pets.

For more information, contact the **Embassy of Spain,** *2700 15th St. N.W., Washington, DC 20009; (202)265-0190.*

Taxes

Anyone who lives in Spain at least six months in a calendar year must pay Spanish income tax. Although there is no specific tax treaty between the United States and Spain, you will get a credit for U.S. taxes paid. You can deduct either the amount of U.S. taxes paid or the tax that would be payable in Spain if the income had originated in Spain, whichever is less.

Taxes are levied on a progressive scale after applying various deductions (personal, family, mortgage, investments, etc.). People who earn a gross income of less than 600,000 pesetas a year do not have to declare their income. There is a 17,850-peseta general deduction.

Spain *does* have inheritance tax and tax on capital transfers.

For more information, contact the **Financial Office of Spain,** *(202)462-0020.*

Buying your place in the sun

Spain's liveliest real estate market is the **Costa del Sol**, where prices are still cheap compared to prices in U.S. resorts, although they have risen a good deal in recent years. Here, you can expect to pay 11,400,000 to 17,100,000 pesetas for a three- or four-bedroom house. An apartment costs about 5,700,000 pesetas. Studios can be found for about 1,140,000 pesetas. Or you can rent a house or apartment year-round for about 34,200 pesetas a month.

The Costa del Sol also has a healthy rental market. Many Americans live in their Spanish home most of the year to take advantage of mild sunny winters. Then they rent their places to sun-seeking northern Europeans in July and August. One man rents out his villa for 684,000 pesetas a month during those two months. He can do a lot of traveling on that money. Your return is usually 50% of the actual rental price. People who rent their properties full-time generally find tenants for at least 20 weeks of the year. An agency can take care of rental details for you. Or you can run an ad in the *International Herald Tribune* or *International Living.*

Farms can be a good buy in Spain. Most of Spain's flourishing agriculture is centered in **Andalusia**, comprising the eight provinces of southern Spain (and Costa del Sol). Here, you will find large groves of orange, peach, apricot, almond, and olive trees. Cork and chestnut also grow here, as well as sugar beets, wheat, sunflowers, and beans.

Farms may be difficult to buy because of restrictions on foreign ownership of land and a tradition of word-of-mouth selling. One English company, **Fincasol**, handles farmland in Spain. For current property listings, contact them at: *Cortijo Los Canos, Sotogrande, Cadiz, Spain; tel. (34-56)792811.* They offer a tour of Andalusia and its farming areas.

Foreigners may not own land in areas of strategic or defense importance, except in urban or tourist areas. Restricted areas include the frontiers with France and Portugal, the Campo de Gibralto, and parts of Galicia, Cartagena, Chagarinis, and Alhucemas. Government permission, rarely granted, is required for a foreigner to purchase more than 10 acres of irrigated land, or 49 acres of unirrigated land. Some foreigners have bought land through Spanish nominees, an illegal procedure.

Most of the English-speaking agents who deal with Spanish property are located in England or are branches of English firms in Spain. In the United States, firms dealing in Spanish property aim at buyers of million-dollar homes—and they charge higher commissions than British estate agents.

Real estate red tape

It's wise to hire a Spanish lawyer when you buy property. Be sure to find out about taxes.

To purchase property, you draw up a private contract once you have agreed on a price with the seller. Have your lawyer make sure the seller has a *scritura de compraventa*, the formal conveyance deed, registered in his name. If you will be building, register an *escritura de obra nueva* (new building deed). Make sure there are no separate deeds or mortgages on the land or building.

The *escritura* is prepared by a *notario* (notary). He is entitled to a fee for his services, plus a fee charged to register the *escritura*. These fees together usually amount to between 3% and 5% of the purchase price.

Mortgages are not customary in Spain, but it's now possible to get 50% mortgages from banks on fairly new property in good condition. Interest rates average 15% to 16%, depending on the bank and the mortgage. For more information, consult the **Commerce Office of the Spanish Embassy,** *2700 15th St. N.W., Washington, DC 20009; (202)265-8600.*

When you make the full payment, you sign the *escritura*. For tax avoidance, people often put down a lower price than that actually paid for the property on the deed—perhaps 50% less.

Before you sign, your lawyer should also find out if there are

330

building restrictions on the property and if any road projects (or anything similar) are planned that would affect its value.

When you buy in an *urbanización* (planned community) or an *apartamento en régimen de comunidad de proprietarios* (cooperative or condominium apartment), you are liable for fees to a property-owners association. The fees generally cover maintenance of grounds, street lighting, refuse removal, etc. *Comunidades*, or community charges, are paid quarterly. You may also arrange with your association to pay them annually and/or through your bank.

Property taxes

Most foreigners place the time-consuming tax paperwork in the hands of a competent *gestor*, a kind of administrative facilitator, or banker.

A home buyer pays a one-time property transfer tax (generally known as *Impuesto de Derechos Reales*), as well as notary and registration fees and municipal taxes. For an apartment, this tax starts at 22,800 pesetas. Once the *escritura* is signed, it takes two to three months to have the papers filed and registered. You have to wait until all taxes are paid before you take possession. The total cost to get possession is about 6% to 10% of the declared purchase price, including notarial fees.

When the *escritura pública de compraventa* has been signed by both the buyer and the seller, your *notario* submits it to the *Abogacía del Estado* for assessment of the amount of taxes due. This must be done within 30 days of signature. After the 30-day period, there will be a *multa* (fine) or extra cost to you as the buyer.

Usually, the *notario* will ask the buyer to deposit a sum equal to the estimated amount of the tax at the time of signing the *escritura*. Payment must be made (and recorded on the deed) before the *escritura* can be registered and conveyed to the buyer.

The *Plus Valía* is between 10% and 56% of the difference between the official index values of the previous and current transfers. For non-residents it is 35%. For example, if the property was sold five years ago and valued at X, and is now being sold to you and valued at X plus 10,000 pesetas, the maximum tax is paid on the extra 10,000 pesetas. This can add up when property values have rapidly increased.

Plus Valía is not payable at the time of sale. The assessment usually comes three to six months after the transaction has been completed.

In most provinces the *Plus Valía* tax must be paid by the seller, since the increase in value was beneficial to him. It is possible for the contract to contain a clause stating that the buyer must pay the *Plus Valía*. Many sales contracts specify that all taxes levied after the date of sale are to be paid by the buyer.

The authorities will normally send notices of tax due to both buyer and seller. They will look to the current owner of record for payment if the seller does not pay. However, if the officials require payment, and your contract specifically excludes the *Plus Valía* from your obligations, you have the right to take the previous owner to court.

You must report the acquisition of property to the Delegación de Hacienda for assessment of yearly property tax (*Contribución Territorial Urbana*). Assessments of older house or apartment are often lower than assessments for newer ones.

The *Contribución Territorial Urbana* must be paid every year in one payment between Sept. 15 and Nov. 15. You, as owner, must make this payment even without notification. It is your responsibility to find out the exact amount, and pay it within the allotted time period. There is a 10% penalty for late payments made between Nov. 15 and Nov. 30, and a 20% penalty after Nov. 30.

Non-payment of the *Contribución Territorial Urbana* can result in legal procedures leading to embargo and sale in public auction of your property.

Depending on the locale, the average tax is about 0.5% of the value assessed by the tax office, with the official valuation being somewhat less than the actual cost (or market value).

The *Gasto Suntuario-Disfrute Vivienda* is an annual municipal luxury tax levied on homes whose assessed value is over 10,000,000 pesetas. The amount is calculated on the basis of 0.6% of the total assessment.

Ask your lawyer to find out what the current assessment is and when taxes will be assessed next (there's a new assessment every three years). The assessment determines the amount of transfer tax you pay at at the time of purchase and when you sell the property.

Sample properties

Recently, a nicely furnished one-bedroom apartment in a nine-story building high on a bluff was on the market for 5,244,000 pesetas. The building is right on the Mediterranean in a well-kept complex with a large swimming pool, tennis courts, and beautiful gardens. It has a magnificent view of the **Bay of Málaga**.

A few miles up the coast in **Marbella**, a couple, returning to the United States after 13 years, is selling a two-bedroom hillside villa

332

with a large pool and *lanai* for 20,520,000 pesetas. The home commands a breathtaking vista along the Marbella coast clear to the Rock of Gibraltar.

The following advertisements ran recently in the classified section of *International Living*:

•Spain, Costa del Sol, Marbella area—Deluxe villas, townhouses, apartments. Superb Mediterranean and mountain views. Prices $45,000 to $200,000 with financing available. **Iberian Properties**, *1008 Woodbridge Commons, Iselin, NJ 08830; (201)636-7066,* evenings/weekends.

•Spain—vacation on the Costa del Sol. Luxurious villa of 10,000 square feet living area on 10-acre hilltop estate, has swimming pool, fireplaces, unrestricted view of Mediterranean and the mountains, borders and overlooks 18-hold championship golf course and casino. English/Spanish-speaking staff included. From $1,000 per week. For information contact **Lee Setomer,** *Apartado 53, Benalmadena-Costa, Málaga, Spain; tel. (34-52)448098.*

•Spain, Ibiza—Mediterranean view, two bedrooms, two bathrooms, beautifully furnished balconied apartment. Private swimming pool and walk to beach. Available June through August. $1,500 monthly. **Reitman,** *(212)874-0524* or *(212)921-5447.*

The following advertisements appeared in a recent issue of *Lookout* magazine:

•Marbella, Coto Real. Apartment in a complex with a golf course, tennis courts, pool, for 16,758,000 pesetas ($147,000). **Sierra Bermeja,** *Urbanización Lomas del Marbella Club, Marbella, Málaga; tel. (34-52)779154* or *(34-52)823859.*

•Costa del Sol. Secure and comfortable apartment complex for retirees. Each apartment has a kitchen and a view of the sea and the mountains. The complex has a restaurant, mini-market, bus service, alarm system, emergency services, English-speaking nurse. Apartments start at 6,384,000 pesetas ($56,000), with a monthly fee of 36,480 to 58,026 pesetas ($320 to $509), including medical services. **Interpares,** *Cerrado de Calderon, 29018 Málaga; tel. (34-52)290229.*

•Málaga. Small villa. 15,162,000 pesetas ($133,000). **Sango San Pedro Ja Sanchez Gonzalez,** *API 308, Calle Pizarro 36, San Pedro de Alcantara, Málaga; tel. (34-52)781838.*

•Puerto Banus. One-bedroom apartment. 2,964,000 pesetas ($26,000). **Sango San Pedro Ja Sanchez Gonzalez,** *address above.*

•Pueblo los Olivos, Mijas. Two-bedroom apartments with sea views, pool, and parking, for 6,840,000 pesetas ($60,000) and up.

Urbanización Rivera del Sol, *Ctra. de Cadiz, Kilómetro 198, Mijas Costa, Málaga; tel. (34-52)834000.*

•Málaga. Three-bedroom beach villa with a terrace. 24,282,000 pesetas ($213,000). **R. Galvez Cañero,** *API 279, Calle 1B, Nueva Andalucía, Marbella, Málaga; tel. (34-52)812250.*

•Southern Spain. A modest house on a 60.2-million square foot property with Roman ruins, 10 springs, a lake, and hunting. The skyline is the property limit. The property has a view of Africa and Gibraltar. 17,784,000 pesetas ($156,000). *Tel. (34-52)822950; fax (34-52) 824657.*

Property sources

A good source for Spanish property is a magazine called *Lookout*, an English-language magazine about Spain. The classified section is a rich source of real estate information and sales. Write to *__Lookout,__ Puebla Lucia, 29640 Fuengirola (Málaga), Spain; tel. (34-52)460950.* Also keep an eye on classified section of *International Living.*

In England, contact **Homefinder Ltd.,** *10 East Road, London N1.*

Britain has two trade associations that can advise you about purchases in Spain: **The Federation of Overseas Property Developers and Agents,** *55 Sidney St., Cambridge*; and the **Association of British Overseas Property Agents,** *Orient House, 42/45 New Broad St., London EC2.*

In the United States try **Begg International,** *2121 Wisconsin Ave. N.W., Washington DC 20007; (202)338-9065.*

For information on the process of buying property in Spain, read John Rea-Smith's *Living in Spain*, available from *__International Living,__ 824 E. Baltimore St., Baltimore, MD 21202*; or *Living and Investing in Spain*, a booklet from **Nampa SA,** *Apartado 53, Benalmádena-Costa, Málaga, Spain.*

Medical care

Spain has more than enough doctors: 176 per 100,000. But there is a shortage of hospital beds and nurses. Families are expected to care for their own sick in hospitals, and nurses are not trained to U.S. or British standards. However, there are private hospitals in places such as Marbella, as well as privately run nursing homes.

Spain has a national health service, but this is open only to those who have worked and paid social security tax in Spain. Many U.S. retirees use **Sanitas**, a Spanish health insurance plan providing comprehensive coverage at reasonable cost.

Many Spanish insurance companies will pay the full cost of hospital accommodation and treatment without any financial limit—as long as you pay the annual premium. However, coverage is generally limited to specific hospitals and doctors, which can be a problem if you have a medical emergency in the wrong place. Annual premiums are surprisingly low, as little as 20,000 pesetas per person, no matter your age. However, when the premium is this low, the insurance often is limited to certain specific treatments. More complete coverage is available for about 30,000 pesetas per year per person.

Leaving a Spanish will

If you own a home in Spain, it's a good idea to leave a Spanish will. Although the will you write in your home country covers your Spanish property, a special grant of representation will have to be obtained in Spain. Making a separate Spanish will that disposes of Spanish property will make life easier for your heirs. (It is perfectly legal to have two wills disposing of property in different countries.) You can have a *notario* prepare your will, but it is better to first see an *abogado*, the equivalent of a U.S. attorney. An *abogado* provides legal advice and suggestions on how to keep death duties to a minimum. After this preliminary advice, the *abogado* will prepare the will and then arrange for the local *notario* to draw up the formal document.

Political stability

Spain is a constitutional monarchy, with a free and open process of debate and free democratic elections. The Socialist Party of Spain (PSOE) is in power.

Catalonia has a strong regional identity that in the past has been expressed in attempted rebellions against the central government. It is now an autonomous region with its own elected government. Catalonia is also the economic hub of Spain.

The **Basques**, too, have their own language and culture. Their separatist movement is strong, a survival of Franco's ruthless suppression. Basque separatist extremism seems to be in the wane, particularly now that France is cooperating with Spain against the ETA (Euskadi ta Azkatasuna), the terrorist arm of the separatist movement. In September 1984, a month after the separatists had celebrated their 25th anniversary, France agreed to extradite fugitive ETA members who had been protected during the Franco years.

Banking in Spain

Spain's banking system is tightly regulated and banks are audited regularly. **Banco Central**, created when Spain's four biggest banks merged, is the largest, with 2,000 branch offices. Customer deposits worldwide exceed $18 billion. Foreign offices are in New York, Miami, San Francisco, London, Paris, and Frankfurt.

Spain has never been a haven of privacy. Banking secrecy was removed by a 1977 law entitled "Banking secrecy and collaboration with the tax authorities." Spain does encourage foreigners to bank here—as long as you remain a non-resident, you are exempt from taxation on your net capital in Spanish banks.

There are five major types of banks:

• Apart from the Bank of Spain, there are six **public sector banks** under the Ministry of Finance, specializing in construction, agriculture, growth industries, fishing, public services, and assisting Spanish majority-owned companies. These banks charge a favorable interest rate.

•**Private sector banks and savings institutions** are the major source of long- and short-term financing. Most of the principal banks are either commercial or savings banks (*cajas de ahorros*). The latter belong to a national network and provide financing for housing purchases. But the distinction is becoming blurred.

•Banco Exterior de España is principally a **state-owned bank**. This bank operates under private sector rules and controls official export credit funds.

•**Intermediaries** are based on the discount-house concept—the Sociedades Mediadoras en el Mercado del Dinero have been operating since 1981.

•The fifth category includes all **other private financial institutions**, such as finance companies, that mainly finance domestic consumer purchases.

If you are a non-resident, two types of accounts are available:

• A **Convertible Pesetas Account** involves only foreign currency and checks, converted into pesetas on the day of deposit. Any foreign currency can be withdrawn at the exchange rate in effect on the day of withdrawal.

•**Foreign Currency Accounts** handle no pesetas. Foreign currencies can be converted freely. This includes deposit accounts paying interest.

If you are a resident, you can get a normal **Current Account**

(*Cuenta Corriente*), which has no restrictions on the type of currency deposited, but may be withdrawn only in pesetas.

It is impossible to cash two-party checks, except in the branch of the bank on which they are drawn. The banks may charge up to 0.5% of the value of the check. Sometimes checks are made out to *"portador "* (bearer), as we would make them to "cash." Identification is required to cash checks. Banks do not return your cancelled checks; they provide photocopies on request.

Savings accounts are available to all regardless of residence. There are regular and term deposit accounts.

When you make a long-term credit purchase, you will sign a *letra acceptada*, which will be sent to your bank, addressed to your account, thus authorizing your bank to make payments.

The weather

While the Mediterranean coast has a balmy, mild climate, the rest of Spain is less idyllic. A large country, it has a variety of climates, some influenced by the the cold winds of the Atlantic and by the high altitudes. Inland Spain is cold and snowy during the winter, and you can ski in the mountain ranges. The northwest coast, washed by the wild Atlantic, is rainy and cool. It has a short summer season—July through September—when temperatures are mild and the sun shines most often.

Madrid's weather, with hot summers and cold winters, is comparable to that of New York City, although much drier due to the high altitude.

Barcelona is mild and somewhat humid, year round. The Costa Brava north of Barcelona is sunny and mild for the summer season (May to October).

During the winter, the warmest weather is in the **Canary Islands**, where temperatures are 60 degrees Fahrenheit to 70 degrees Fahrenheit. The Costa del Sol—the Mediterranean coast from Algeciras to Málaga—is also popular in winter, with temperatures around 65 degrees Fahrenheit. The **Balearic Islands** are a few degrees cooler.

Where to live in Spain

Spain has beautiful, historic cities—Madrid, Barcelona, Toledo, Granada. They are great for visiting. But it's the beaches that make great retirement homes. Spain has miles and miles of sunny, sandy coastline. The most popular area for retirement is the Costa del Sol, in the south of Spain. But it is also the most expensive. Less developed and in some cases more beautiful are the Costa Brava, Costa de Almería, Costa Blanca, Costa Dorada, Costa de la Luz, Costa del Azahar, and the Costa Blanca. All have exceptionally attractive beaches. Below, we will give brief descriptions of the various coastal areas in Spain. Good luck finding your niche.

Some 3,000 Americans have retired along the **Costa del Sol** between Almería to the east and Algeciras, 236 miles to the west. They aren't the only non-Spanish to be drawn to this sunny, sandy stretch of Spain. The coast has international settlements attracting British, Germans, Dutch, Arabs, and Scandinavians, as well as Americans.

Marbella, on the Costa del Sol, is the most popular town among retirees. Some 1,700 British expats live here. Thirty years ago, when the Rothschilds and Windsors arrived, Marbella was a fishing village with a population of 1,200. It has grown, to say the least. The area between the Marbella Beach Club and Puerto Banús is known as the "golden mile." The latest status symbols are special pools to keep guard dogs cool.

A one-bedroom condominium in Marbella starts around 5,700,000 pesetas; two-bedroom, 9,100,000 pesetas; three-bedroom, 11,400,000 pesetas. A small apartment in Marbella would sell for around 2,850,000 pesetas, with those closer to the beach going to 5,700,000 pesetas. A small house in Marbella would start around 5,150,000 pesetas.

Many retirees have settled around **Sotogrande** (near Gibraltar), which used to be inexpensive. Prices there have risen dramatically, however, since border restrictions between Spain and Gibraltar have been lifted. Once an exclusive, quiet hideout for the owners of large villas, today it is a bustling community with an international school, a hotel, two golf courses, and a commercial center.

Apartments at the Puerto Sotogrande beach-side complex rent for about 30,210 pesetas per week off-season, and 121,000 pesetas per week in August. Condominiums overlooking the marina range from 4,675,000 pesetas for a studio to 48,425,000 pesetas for a four-bedroom penthouse. For information, contact **Puerto Sotogrande SA,** *27 Hill St., London W1; tel. (44-1)491-3665,* or **Puerto Sotogrande,** *Sales Office, Cádiz, Spain; tel. (34-56)795-252.*

Another popular spot is **Fuengirola**, a family resort of seaside villas and campsites. Nearby is the pleasant little town of Be-nalmádena, where you'll find quaint beach cafés, bars, and quiet coves on wide beaches.

The busiest resort, filled with high-rises and nightspots, is

Torremolinos. Housing there tends to be more expensive than in the quieter areas.

Málaga is the major town of the Costa del Sol. Its waterfront is picturesque and the hills behind the town offer spectacular views. Málaga is also the business and commercial center of the area and a good jumping-off place for Africa (ferry and hydrofoil). Housing and living are a bit cheaper here than in other resort areas.

Some American retirees like to settle around **Rota**, the U.S. naval base in the province of Cádiz. Base privileges are coveted for purchase of home appliances, food items, packaged U.S. products, and medical and dental care.

The **Costa Brava** is where Spaniards go to enjoy secluded beaches away from masses of tourists. Stretching from Blanes to the French border, the Costa Brava (Wild Coast) is known for its ferocious, rugged beauty. Pines fringe the rocky cliffs that drop to the fine, sandy beaches. Little towns are sheltered by the coast's protective coves.

Phoenicians, Greeks, Romans, and Arabs all have taken refuge in the Costa Brava's harbors. Ruins left by these early invaders dot the coast, as do fortified villages from the days of pirate invasions. You'll find Phoenician ruins at Rosas, Greek in Ampurias, and a Moorish fortress at Tossa del Mar.

Gerona is filled with dungeons and ramparts, medieval walls and paintings. The old quarter is dominated by the majestic cathedral, built in the 17th century above Roman ruins. Tossa de Mar, a shiny white town by the sea, is the most popular resort along this coast. It has an old quarter that predates even Roman civilization. Within the 12th-century walls of the old quarter is a Moorish alcazar.

Cadaqués, a purely Catalan village whose white houses contrast with the dark mountain backdrop, is where Salvador Dali found his inspiration. His estate is marked by gigantic egg-shaped ornaments and a whimsical garden.

S'Agaro, a contemporary residential community, attracts the crème de la crème of European society. Paseo de Ronda, which leads to the beach, is lined with gardens, fountains, and statuary.

For the uninhibited, the Costa Brava also has a number of secluded beaches for nude sunbathing. It also offers gay beaches.

Spain's most peaceful beaches are along the relatively undiscovered **Costa de Almería**. Stretching 120 miles between Almería and Cartagena on the southeastern edge of Spain, the coast retains much of its original charm and still has reasonable prices. Much of the coastline is dotted with little fishing villages, many still lacking modern facilities.

A short drive north of the town of Almería is Mini-Hollywood, where replicas of American Wild West streets have been built for spaghetti westerns. *Lawrence of Arabia, The Good, the Bad, and the Ugly,* and *Reds* all were filmed on these incredible sand dunes.

The **Costa de la Luz** in the southwest of Spain, from Algeciras to Ayamonte, has breathtaking coves and white sandy beaches. Atlantic winds blow the sands into constantly changing dunes. The best time of year along this coast is from April to June, when the most important festivals are held and nature is at its best. Beaches are crowded in August.

Summer is beautiful along the **Bay of Biscay**, from San Sebastián near the French frontier to the Portuguese border. Tourists neglect this northern coast, called Cantábria. The terrain is rocky, cut off from the rest of the country by the Picos de Europa, which are snow-covered all year. The damp green valleys in the foothills of the mountains are the center of the Spanish dairy industry. Virtually the entire coast is lined with sandy beaches. There aren't enough people around to make a dent in their loneliness, particularly if you get away from the beaches nearest the towns.

The Cantabrian people are down-to-earth and stolid, in the view of other Spaniards. Their culture is strongly colored by Celtic remnants, right down to their custom of playing bagpipes. The area resisted Roman invasion and later became the starting point for the reconquest of Spain from the Moors. The people are often fair-haired and freckled.

San Sebastián, bordered by the Urumea River, Bahía de la Concha, and three hills, is where Europe's wealthiest vacationers play. The town is known for its Basque cooking and its original use of seafood.

Santillana del Mar, 18 miles west of Santander, is a charming medieval fishing village with its own beaches.

Two miles from Santillana del Mar are the caves of Altamira, painted by prehistoric people. While the caves in France are older, these exhibit more artistic talent. Some experts call the Altamira Caves the Sistine Chapel of prehistoric art. The Altamira artists depicted animals that were not hunted (such as horses) and vignettes of life.

Modern-day cultural life in the area flourishes in August when Santander sponsors an international music and dance festival and yacht races and regattas are held. International golf tournaments are held at the 18-hole Royal Golf Club of Pedreña, a course famous for

340

its sand traps. There is also polo in spring and fall. And you can ski in the Picos de Europa or at Alto Campo in the winter.

The mountains contain a series of refuges and national parks protecting animals that exist nowhere else in Spain: ibex, capercaillie (a sort of grouse), and mountain goats. You can hunt bear, boar, deer, wolf, fox, badgers, and mountain goats. Or you can fish for trout and salmon in the mountain streams (licenses required).

Winter is an ideal time to go to the **Balearic Islands** (Mallorca, Ibiza, and Menorca) or the Costa del Sol in southern Spain. The **Canary Islands**, off the coast of Africa, also have their high season in winter, though their climate is mild all year.

Dining in Spain

The Spanish take their dining seriously. You'll find an abundance of fresh seafood, pork, and lamb. Pork is cooked much longer than in America, so that it becomes much more tender. The beef is not as rich as we are accustomed to, and you may not like it. The Spaniards eat a fair amount of rabbit and other game.

Paella de mariscos, served throughout most of Spain, is a seafood casserole with rice. Usually half a dozen different types of shellfish are included. The most authentic *paella* is prepared in Valencia. Wherever you go in Spain, the *paella* will be different.

Jamón serrano, the salty Spanish equivalent of prosciutto, comes from Andalusia. In the north, many varieties of wild mushrooms appear in the fall, including those not available elsewhere. Almonds, which seem to grow everywhere, are found in cookies, flour, and pastries.

The Spanish tend to eat in sequence—first a tortilla (or omelet), then vegetables, then a turkey leg in sauce, then dessert, for instance. In Spanish homes you'll often find yourself sharing a big flat dish of salad greens with everyone else at the table. Bread is served without butter and is so fresh you won't need it. Instead of butter, the Spanish often rub garlic and a little olive oil on their bread.

The main meal is at 2 p.m. Supper is late, after 10 p.m. Breakfast is coffee and a *pastel*, or pastry. To fill in between these times, you can get *tapas* from about noon to 2 p.m. and from 8 p.m. to 10 p.m. *Tapas* may be simple slices of cured Manchego cheese and slices of spicy *chorizo* sausage. In some places they are elaborate: marinated quail, spicy tripe, snails, or sautéed wild mushrooms. The most common *tapas* when you're inland are *tortilla española* (Spanish omelet), *pincho moruno* (marinated pork), and *ensaladilla rusa* (vegetable salad).

Spanish ways

Close male friends often greet each other with an *abrazo* (embrace). Family names and titles are used until people become better acquainted; close friends use first names.

It is polite for a guest to take or send flowers when visiting a home. Food is not usually appropriate as a gift. And if you are offered a gift, open it right away.

At meals, the host or hostess indicates seating arrangements. Ladies are seated first. The fork is kept in the left hand; the knife is often used to push food onto the fork. When finished, the knife and fork should be laid side by side on the plate. Conversation continues after the meal. Do not rest elbows on the table, and rest your forearms on the edge of the table, not in your lap. Toothpicks are not seen in public, and only children eat on the streets. In restaurants, call the waiter by raising your hand.

Although meetings start on time, the attitude toward time in general is relaxed. Businesses are open six days a week from 9 a.m. to 1:30 p.m. and from 4:30 p.m. to 8 p.m. During the break, most people go home for their main meal and siesta. Most stores, museums, and other public places are closed in mid-afternoon.

The family is the center of social activity. Marriages must be approved by parents, and dates were chaperoned until recently. Couples are usually engaged a long time while they save money to buy an apartment.

The Spanish dress quite conservatively. Clothing is an important indicator of status and respectability. Jacket and tie are customary at meetings; a tie is not usually worn without a jacket, and the jacket is usually buttoned except when sitting.

Spain's standard of living is generally lower than the rest of Europe. Many men work two jobs; often boys over 14 and girls over 16 work during the day and attend school at night. Their wages are used to supplement family income. Middle- and upper-income families spend a large proportion of income on education. The literacy rate is high. In cities most people have modern appliances, telephones, small cars, and televisions. In smaller towns these are less common and they are almost nonexistent in rural areas.

Helpful hints

Tax and service charges are always included in hotel and restaurant bills. Nevertheless, a 5% to 10% tip is customary in the larger cities. For taxi rides, a 5% tip is sufficient. In other cases, 50 to 200 pesetas is reasonable. Porters at airports and railway stations charge about 75 pesetas per piece of luggage.

You should give three to five pesetas to anyone who hands you a towel in a washroom or ushers you to a theater seat. Gas station attendants get a small tip, although windshields are usually not cleaned unless requested.

Crime, much of it committed against foreigners, is skyrocketing in Spain. Pickpockets are deft and they frequent crowds. Hold your purse tightly under your arm and keep your wallet in an inside pocket. Close up your purse or wallet before you leave a store. Málaga has the highest crime rate of any Spanish city; Barcelona is also notorious.

In Spain you'll see beggars. They won't give you trouble. But beware of gypsy fortune-tellers. They'll demand handsome payment for releasing your hand.

Money matters

Spanish money is denominated in pesetas. A five-peseta piece is called a duro.

Tourists can bring any amount of foreign money into Spain, but only up to 150,000 pesetas per person. You can take up to 500,000 pesetas in foreign currency and up to 100,000 pesetas in Spanish currency out of Spain. An unlimited amount of travelers checks can be taken out of Spain.

Four times a year, residents can take a vacation allowance in foreign currency equivalent to 80,000 pesetas out of the country. You can also bring out foreign currency equivalent to 200,000 pesetas per trip for business purposes, with a maximum of 1,400,000 pesetas per year.

If you have a bank account in Europe, you may be interested in Eurocheque, a system that links banks around Europe. It has recently installed cash machines in Spain. You can use these machines, provided you have an account in any participating country. The machines give you cash and debit your account. Visa also has cash machines in Spain, which work for you if your card has a coded pass number.

One couple's Spanish summer

Alice C. Fleming describes her experience living for a summer in Cutar, a traditional Spanish village near the Costa del Sol.

Sight unseen, we rented a house in Cutar, where expatriate friends told us we could experience a Spanish village life that would be hard to find anywhere else along Spain's Costa del Sol.

Cutar is one of a score of small wine villages scattered in the Axarquia mountains about 16 miles north of Vélez-Málaga. Its stony, sun-baked slopes produce muscatel grapes for raisins and for the famous Málaga *dulce* (sweet wine). Málaga muscatel has been celebrated since Roman times and the sherry-like versions, such as Virgen de Málaga, became international rages in the 19th century.

Like the nearby villages of Iznate, Comares, El Borge, and Benamargosa, Cutar was once part of Moorish Spain. It is surrounded by carefully terraced fields and irrigation systems hundreds of years old. The mountain towns often have remains of Moorish fortresses, or *alcazabas*, and sometimes bits of Roman and Phoenician ruins. Along the riverbeds below the village grow olives, lemons, oranges, and avocados. Some of these villages are now sparsely populated, and the goats often outnumber the inhabitants. Some, like Triana, have ghost towns nearby.

Close to the beaches, shops, and night life along the Costa del Sol, Cutar sounded like the perfect place—in the mountains where few foreigners venture, yet only 30 minutes from the coast by car. We rented a car for our two-month stay.

Cutar is typical of the brilliant white villages of Andalusia. Its whitewashed houses, with their red-tiled roofs, spill down a mountainside. Patio gardens grow geraniums, bougainvillea, and jasmine. Cutar's streets are narrow, steep, and often stepped. It has two small plazas (the only flat surfaces in the entire village), an Arab fountain, the remains of an ancient mosque, and an undetermined number of dogs.

About 50 families live in Cutar. During our first walk around town we saw several empty, decaying houses now being used as chicken coops or mule stalls. We later learned that one could buy a house with electricity and water for next to nothing. Our house was at the low end of the village and overlooked olive groves and the dry riverbed below. It had three bedrooms, living room, bath, and fully equipped kitchen. The house walls were almost two-feet thick and the clay-tile floors kept the house cool in the summer heat. Although the wiring looked primitive, we lost electricity only once during our two-month stay and that was because lightning struck the village transformer. Service was restored in less than an hour. Although we did not have a telephone, many of the families did, and a public telephone was hooked up to someone's kitchen.

Cutar boasts one general store, one bakery, and two bars. Every morning around 11 o'clock, a fish truck rumbles down the center of the village bringing fresh squid, shrimp, and sardines. The bakery sold loaves of wheat and white bread, rolls, and honey-flavored nut cakes made every day.

The village store was a real surprise. Packed into the front room of the grocer's house, it seemed to have as many goods as the supermarkets in Vélez-Málaga. If our grocers, Antonia and Miguel, didn't have what I wanted, they would get it for me within a day or two. Antonia and Miguel sold fresh fruit, vegetables, meat, and eggs supplied by local farmers.

Our meals were light and simple. I usually cooked what I could buy in the village. Often I'd spruce up a meal with treats from shops along the coast—German cheeses, pickles, lunch meats, and very good, inexpensive Spanish wines. Villagers also sold us local wines. We ate a lot of *gazpacho*—cold tomato soup—and a cold garlic soup Antonia taught me to make.

What social life we had took place either in the store or at the bar, Las Mellizas (The Twins). Owned by Gertrudes and Paco Menez, and run by them and their five sons and twin daughters, Las Mellizas was the village gathering place. Municipal notices were pinned on the wall next to the bar. Although village women did not often frequent the bar, occasionally some would sip soft drinks there in the evening while the men played cards or dominoes.

My social hour took place at the village store. Each morning women crowded in front of the small counter to buy what they needed to prepare the day's meal. My arrival on the scene would initiate giggles from the younger women, smiles from the middle-aged, and suspicious glares from the grandmothers in the crowd. Once, one of the oldest-looking women I ever saw gave me a stiff poke in my side, frowned, and demanded to know who I was.

"Who is your mother?" she asked.

The other women laughed and explained that I was a foreigner living in Cutar for the summer.

"Oh," snapped the old woman. "I knew I didn't know her."

Antonia would suggest that I buy green plums one day rather than purple, "because they are sweeter," or would explain it wasn't possible to buy pork this early in the day, "because the pig wasn't killed yet."

Even though I was quite a curiosity to the village women, their sense of decorum and politesse never permitted them to ask me many questions. We talked about food, weather, walks to take in the mountains or along the river, and how my home in the United States differed from Cutar.

The leisurely pattern of life changed at the beginning of August. First of all, grape harvest time was near, so the men were busy repairing the grape-drying beds that were scattered around the village next to garden plots and at the top of every hillside in sight. And people were on the hillsides collecting almonds in burlap sacks that they loaded on mules to bring back to the village. There they removed the outer shells before selling them. During the first two weeks of August we saw families on their patios circled around enormous piles of almonds and almond shells.

One morning everyone was busy whitewashing the houses and village walls. Even the niche that held a statue of the Virgin Mary over the water fountain had been newly painted and had bright new plastic flowers. A few younger men were sweeping the streets, normally specked with goat and dog droppings and often hairy goat hooves dropped from a butcher's slop bucket.

I found out at the store what the fuss was about. Cutar was having a *feria* (fair) that weekend. We had been to the *feria* in Málaga, to one in Vélez-Málaga, and to one in Benamargosa. All were fun, although they didn't seem much different than a country fair in the United States. But we looked forward to the Cutar *feria* because we felt part of the village and got caught up in the excitement of the preparations. All that week families welcomed relatives back home who had moved away to jobs on the coast.

Cutar's grand fiesta was in honor of its patron, San Roque, protector of dogs and lost children. There were no modern trappings—blaring rock music, amusement rides, or junk food vendors. The streets were laced with paper flags, and the main plaza with the official's stage was lit with two strands of colored lights.

The fiesta began at noon on Saturday with a barrage of bottle rockets and a cockfight. At 4 p.m. everyone gathered on the cliff side of the village for a skeet shoot. After the skeet shoot, two village teams fought a rough and tumble soccer game. Saturday night the fiesta officials introduced the fiesta queen and her maids of honor to the crowd gathered in the main plaza.

Sunday, however, was the big day. After the final match of the soccer tournament, everyone gathered at the top of the village and lined the road for the ribbon race. Twenty silk streamers, each embroidered, initialed, and dated by a village girl, were rolled around spools and slipped on a wire that was strung high across the road. Each streamer had a plastic loop sewn on its end. Young men took turns driving motorcycles toward the streamers. Each carried a kneeling passenger on the back of the bike who tried to poke a stick through a loop as the bike passed underneath the wire. Everyone cheered when a streamer was snagged. The victors wore the streamers around their necks for the rest of the fiesta. The symbolism was obvious; the tradition, chivalric. Our friend Gertrude told us that when she was a girl the race was run on horseback in the riverbed.

After the ribbon race, villagers joined in a candlelight procession honoring San Roque. A float carrying the statue of the Virgin and borne by 12 girls led the way. The statue of San Roque followed, and both floats were gaily decorated with carnations and candles. The bearers stopped at several houses along the route to sing songs and cheer. As the procession moved through the steep village streets, the band played solemn music. Each person carried a candle.

The procession ended at the church square. Once the floats were placed carefully on the ground, Miguel the grocer set off the most rickety, dangerous, and exciting firework display I had ever seen.

The rest of the night was given to music, dancing, drinking, and eating. In the big plaza, people danced to a rock band. Performing in their flat-brimmed hats and red cummerbunds, fiddlers roamed the village, playing in some of the front rooms of the bigger houses before moving to the plaza at one end of the village. Grandmothers sat on stools nearby, tapping their feet while children fell asleep on their laps. It was almost three in the morning before we left for home. No one else budged. The music was still going strong and Cutar was still hopping at dawn.

One writer's winter on the Costa de Almería

Stuart M. Hunter describes the winter he and his wife spent on the Costa de Almería in southern Spain.

Those of you who have given up on the Spanish coast because it's no longer very Spanish, take heart. There's a little bit of unspoiled coastline left. The Costa de Almería, between Almería and Cartagena on the southeastern edge of Spain, is still relatively undeveloped. Even though it has the best year-round weather on the Spanish coast and miles of good beaches, the Costa de Almería has been overlooked by most tourists, allowing its charm to stay intact and its prices to remain low—for a little while longer.

After living and traveling in Crete and Turkey for several months, my wife and I decided to settle down for the winter in Spain. We rented a two-bedroom apartment in an expatriate development outside Garrucha, a busy fishing town near the center of the Costa de Almería.

347

We found the climate pleasantly dry and warm. The landscape is similar to southern Arizona—except that Arizona isn't washed by the deep blue Mediterranean.

Farther inland, the rusty brown of the Costa de Almería's dry, terraced mountains is broken by patches of pear cactus, tidy olive groves, and rows of majestic pine trees. Here and there is a crumbling stone farm building (*cortijo*), its faded tile roof seemingly askew. And now and then a flock of sheep or goats shuffles across the picture, herded by a craggy shepherd and a floppy little sheepdog, stirring up a cloud of dust as they go by. It's a lonesome setting, fit for outlaws and vagabonds.

Much of the coastline, however, is dotted with picturesque little fishing villages, many still lacking in the facilities that would spoil them with too many visitors. Its outstanding ornament is the ancient Arabesque town of Mojácar, nestled on a hilltop just below some sawtooth mountain peaks about three miles from Garrucha.

Spectacularly situated, Mojácar is a tangled maze of small white buildings with cobblestoned streets, alleys, and archways. Although still charming, it now has two large hotels, a parador, several discos, and a multilevel central shopping complex. It also has a growing community of foreigners (*extranjeros*), who have year-round or vacation homes in town.

The effect of growing attention is evident along the northern part of the coast. Garrucha, for instance, seems to be falling all over itself to anticipate the opportunities and problems of rapid tourist development.

Up the coast northeast of Garrucha lies Aguilas, a larger, more modern, up-and-coming port city with high-rise apartments and commercial buildings along its sprawling waterfront. But development has brought little ambience to Aguilas, and therefore few foreigners.

Cartagena, a historic Roman seaport, offers some charm in its old quarter and along part of its waterfront, but is largely an industrial-commercial shipping center. Further north is the Mar Menor, a congested tourist center reminiscent of Miami Beach.

For the most part, however, life along the Costa de Almería has retained the charm and color of old traditions. Each village still has an open-air street market one day of the week.

Market day is different in each village so that merchants can cover several in a week. A large area near the center of each village is set aside for merchant stalls. You can buy hardware, clothing, shoes, dry goods, pottery, music cassettes, jewelry, trinkets, plants, flowers, produce, olives, baked goods, nuts, sweets, and live animals. It's not uncommon to see a shivering lamb with all four feet tied together, or a quaking rabbit in a cardboard box.

In Garrucha the weekly market clusters near the Plaza de Abastos, a permanent outdoor produce market. A nearby outdoor cafeteria is a pleasant place to sit with a *café con leche* while you watch the jostling crowd.

In an open shed on the dockside, a fish market materializes at sunset each weeknight as soon as the fishing fleet comes in. Wearing rubber boots and slickers glistening with fish slime and sea water, the ruddy, rugged fishermen lug huge trays of neatly categorized and artfully displayed fish into the shed to be weighed and offered to the crowd of restaurateurs and wholesalers.

A festive town

Lively fiestas are a big part of the local lifestyle. The biggest is Semana Santa (Holy Week). Lorca, an ancient, picturesque town that is now an agricultural-commerical center, has a Good Friday procession not to be missed if you are in the area. Both sides of Lorca's two principal thoroughfares are lined with six rows of spectator seats. Hundreds of people jam the streets or hang over balconies and rooftops of adjacent buildings.

The procession lasts from 8:30 p.m. to half past midnight and includes lavish floats, often two to three stories tall, and countless marching units dressed in colorful regalia. Most of the floats depict scenes from Roman or Egyptian times. Some are bedecked with flowers and carry figures of the Virgin Mary and the Crucified Christ. These are greeted with respect by the crowd as they pass by. On the other hand, if the Blue or White Virgin appears, bedlam ensues, as the crowd on one side of the street or the other cheers for its champion.

Making friends

The Spaniards on the Costa de Almería are relaxed and hospitable. One day last winter my wife was painting a picture of some men building and repairing boats at a small harbor-front boatyard in Garrucha. In the midst of their work one of the men broke away and began cooking fish over a crudely constructed wood-burning grill. Before long the entire crew knocked off work to join him for their "coffee break" of fish, bread, and wine—and invited my wife to join them.

To get to know the local Spaniards, you'll have to speak Spanish. Almost no English is spoken, a problem compounded by the local, heavily slurred Andalusian dialect. Mercado, for instance, comes out as "makow" here. The locals are friendly, though, and will make an effort to understand and respond to your high school Spanish.

Tourists are often invited to join local Spaniards for a glass of wine, soft drink, beer, or *café con leche* (but never hard liquor—drunken Spaniards are rare), and often *tapas*.

Eating Spanish-style

The Spanish eating schedule is hard to figure out. There appears to be no real breakfast other than coffee. There is a fairly substantial half-hour "coffee break" (not the time to bring your car into the local garage). Then, there is the three-hour siesta, during which *tapas* are consumed or when a substantial meal is eaten. *Tapas* and drinks start again around 10 p.m. and go on until well past midnight, although some eat a substantial evening meal. Entertainment often starts at 11 p.m. and continues until around 3 a.m.

Restaurants—particularly seafood restaurants—abound along the Costa de Almería. The food is usually simple but tasty, although the restaurants offer little ambience and nearly always the same menu. You'll be offered fish, lamb, pork chops, sometimes rabbit, a mixed salad (often a tired one), string beans, french fries, wine or beer, and an ice cream cake (usually freezer-burned). The best pick is fish—the large variety here is excellent. The Spanish hot-weather delight, Andalusian *gazpacho*, is always good, as are the local June strawberries, sweet and served swimming in thick cream.

Some of the better restaurants are located in small family hostels that can be found both in villages and in the countryside. Hostels also have comfortable, low-cost accommodations for overnight visitors. Popular with the Spaniards, they offer individuality and a family atmosphere.

Although this area is still a place apart, it is definitely pushing hard to catch up with the rest of the Spanish Mediterranean coast, and may not be off the beaten path much longer. Everywhere you look, single-unit residential buildings and small multi-unit commercial buildings are going up. Sizable apartment complexes are under construction in Garrucha and the neighboring inland cities of Vera and Turre. Vast amounts of construction materials are being hauled about everywhere via both highway and boat.

Finding your corner of the coast

About a thousand expatriates live along the Costa de Almería. Most—approximately 70%—are British. The others are an equal mix of Europeans and Americans.

It's easy to rent an apartment or house along the coast—except in the high-season months of July and August. But there is no general realtor or clearinghouse in the area where you can find an overview of what properties are available at any given time. The best way to find a place is to inquire from person to person, starting perhaps with one of the four major residential developers (either crooks or heroes, depending on whom you talk to) who speak English. In our case, we were ultimately referred to a developer—who turned out to be from Mason City, Iowa!—who in turn referred us to another developer.

Most expats who buy property start with a parcel of land, often in an established development, then arrange with a developer to build an individually designed house. A typical lot is 2,000 to 4,000 square feet, usually priced at about 855 pesetas per square foot. A house with two to three bedrooms and two bathrooms generally costs about 5,244,000 pesetas. Some of these "spec" houses already built are for sale, but most people build their own.

An unfurnished condo/apartment sells for about 3,420,000 pesetas. Because of resale difficulties, there is no longer a market here for time-share units.

Our rented house is a well-furnished, spacious two-bedroom, two-bathroom villa of Spanish-Moorish design, one of a group of 50. All the villas in our development are attractively landscaped and clustered around a recreation center that has an inviting pool, bar, restaurant, garden, and tennis court.

The development, La Parata, is tiered up along a mountainside with a view out over the sea and a countryside dotted with old stone farmhouses. Nice as it is, however, our development is nothing compared to the slick sophisticated spots in the Marbella area on the Costa del Sol.

Medical care and facilities are adequate, although in an undeveloped area like ours they seem frighteningly haphazard. There are no scheduled appointments, no records kept, and little recollection by nurses and doctors of your last visit. There's a lack of the antiseptic cleanliness required in the United States, no office nurses or staff, and examinations and tests are minimal.

Doctors readily prescribe heavy medication, for instance, as well as a multiplicity of shots to be administered one to three times a day by a *practicante* (medical assistant), usually located miles from both you and your doctor.

The weather is pleasant year-round. The climate is dry with lots of sunshine, although the air can often be quite hazy. When it's perfectly clear, the coastline can be seen trailing away up toward Cartagena 60 miles away. In the winter the temperature ranges from around 50 degrees Fahrenheit at night to 75 degrees Fahrenheit or 80 degrees Fahrenheit in the daytime. In summer it varies from about 65 degrees Fahrenheit to 70 degrees Fahrenheit at night (often with a nice breeze) to around 90 degrees Fahrenheit during the day. Electric heaters, a cheery fireplace, and a good southern exposure warm local houses in the winter, while overhead fans cool them in summer.

One expat's love affair with Ibiza

Susan C. Ellis writes about her love affair with Ibiza, one of the Balearic Islands.

The Balearic Islands—Ibiza, Mallorca, Menorca, and Formentara—peek sleepily out of the Mediterranean, half-hoping no one will notice them. The islands have changed a great deal since the days when Mallorcans stoned George Sand for wearing pants. Today there are artist colonies and open-minded residents as well as a reverence for thousands of years of history.

Against a backdrop of doors splashed with turquoise flowers and shops pushing sandals, an old woman layered in black inches along the cobblestones in Ibiza. Her black form stands out sharply against the island's scape of breezy white and aqua blue. Her lifetime has spanned the island's transformation from forgotten fortress to idyllic retreat.

Before the old woman, Phoenicians, Greeks, Carthaginians, and Romans were all drawn to this strategic but tiny dot of land off Spain's east coast. Centuries under seige by Vandals, Byzantines, and Arabs eventually led to the construction of an enormous fortress. But the forbidding stone embattlement was not enough to keep the most recent invaders away. Ibiza, to the amusement of its residents, was finally overcome by hippies.

The painters, draft dodgers, writers, and society-duckers have redrawn the face of the island. Today's islander is more than likely a hotel owner or a new restaurateur. Only the most stubborn Ibizans persist in working the salt mines, the fields, or the sea. There is only one season (May to October) in modern Ibiza; the rest of the year is simply, "off."

I arrived at Ibiza in March and immediately fell for its sought-after beauty. I quickly developed a rather unreasonable resentment toward the would-be invaders (probably perfectly nice people) who treble the island's population every summer. Orange and lemon trees

352

climb terraces to sturdy farmhouses on hilltops. A grove of fig and almond trees suddenly splits open, and you're blinking at a white-bright beach, one of dozens that you can claim for your very own.

Now is the time to see Ibiza. Despite efforts to enforce zoning restrictions, houses and apartment buildings are going up with a zeal that bodes ill for people who like their beaches uncrowded. Already, hotels line some of the island's most languid beach strips. Ancient olive groves are being razed for golf courses. And the visitors' appetite for night life has made clubs and bars materialize in some of the most out-of-the-way places.

Throughout the Balearics there's a noticeable absence of Americans, however. Tourist officials blame this on a "lack of familiarity."

Also noticeable is the low cost of most food and lodgings once you step off the beaten path. Villas are easy to buy or rent, although foreigners might run into stumbling blocks in the well-populated island of Ibiza.

It's very easy to fly between islands. Flights, which last 15 or 20 minutes, leave eight to 10 times each day.

Sightseeing, sleeping, and supping

The Citadel on Ibiza is a massive fortress built between 1554 and 1885. It is said to be one of the best examples of military building due to its lengthy wall.

The archaeological museum exhibits Phoenician glassware and ceramics. More ceramics can be seen at the ceramics factory, just outside Ibiza.

Vedra, known as the Magic Rock, captures moonlight at timely moments to dazzle lovers on a night walk by the sea.

The **Comida San Juan** is the best and cheapest restaurant in Ibiza. Grilled trout is a couple of dollars. A fruit plate is a few cents. Local patrons swear by it.

La Marina is the second best and cheapest restaurant on the island.

El Caliu, a thick-walled farmhouse/restaurant with an enviable vista of fields and sea, boasts one of the island's best wine cellars. The specialty is grilled food. Prices are modest.

The **Hotel los Molinos** in Ibiza City is one of two hotels open off-season. Rooms look out over the sea and prices are modest.

Hotel Hacienda; *tel. (34-71)33-30-46,* is a luxury hotel at the north end of the island. An executive suite is about 22,800 pesetas. A double room is 8,550 pesetas.

Pensión es Vive is a comfortable and inexpensive place to stay on the outskirts of Ibiza.

La Cala is a small hotel in Santa Lauria, the town where the *intelligentsia* live. The price is only about 1,710 pesetas per person in high season.

A portrait of Mallorca

Neighboring Mallorca is where the rich and famous jet in for a getaway that offers the high-priced comforts of home. It's the biggest island with the starkest contrasts. Office buildings and windmills share the same plain. Highways course through ancient villages. You look out of place in untraditional clothes, and children inherit 1,000-year-old olive trees when the family farm gets passed down.

Mallorca is designed for the restless. From the cities, craggy, snow-topped mountains tower in the distance. An artists' village called Deia, just along the northwest coast, is for those who seek the quiet life. Relentless bargain-hunters can search out the leather goods factories that the island is famous for. There are Roman temples to visit and beaches, mostly unspoiled. About half the island residents live in Mallorca's capital, Palma.

The island might be the ideal environment for a writer or artist who yearns for the romance of the sea, yet despairs of spending too much time alone with blank paper or canvas. For 40,000 pesetas a month, the aspiring painter can rent a small cliffside dwelling in Deia. A quick spin up the road will bring you to a monastery where an ailing Frederick Chopin and his companion George Sand put in one long and dreary winter in 1839. Sand's book, *A Winter in Mallorca*, talks bitterly of the island's inhospitality. But modern-day Mallorcans, who seem to be in on a national campaign to fill the island's abundant hotels, have done everything they can to dispel that reputation.

Inca, a small town toward the center of the island, has leather factories where price tags on most items will please even the most frugal.

The **Pearl Factory,** *Via Roma 52, Manacor,* manufactures the most beautiful deceptions—strings and strings of almost perfect artificial pearls. You can tour the factory.

Santa Maria Cathedral has one of the world's biggest stained glass windows. Construction on this cathedral began the year after the Moors were conquered, 1230. It was finished 300 years later.

For local fare, try the **Cellar Sa Travessa**, just outside of Inca and 40 minutes from Palma. Try fish soup, suckling pig, and *Frito Mallorquin* (liver, trip, red peppers, onion) for 114 pesetas to 684 pesetas, served on orange-checked tablecloths laid across heavy wine barrels.

Hotel Son Vida Sheraton; *tel. (34-71)45-10-11*, is the loveliest, most expensive hotel on the island. **Hotel Formentor** is the other luxury hotel on the island. It's located on its own point in the north. Very isolated.

Hostal Borune in Palma is one of the few hotels open all year round. Built in 1703 around a courtyard, it is modestly priced and offers bedrooms furnished in heavy wood, and marbled baths.

Peaceful Menorca

Menorca is the smallest of the islands we visited and offers more quiet than pizzazz. It boasts gorgeous isolated beaches and dramatic high cliffs. More than 120 beaches and coves make for fantastic water sports.

The tourist trade here is still in its infancy. This is the kind of spot you might want to escape to on your honeymoon, as Princess Grace and Prince Rainier did. Traveling from one end of the island to the other on its narrow, slithering roads, you may encounter absolutely no one, save unobtrusive sheep on the hillside.

Menorca is very lush and hilly, but not mountainous. It's famous for shoes and processed cheese. Sambal is a four-mile beach that is usually deserted. There are said to be 120 coves with beaches on Menorca, most unpeopled.

Six houses on this island are said to have been cave dwellings originally, built by primitive peoples. And the remarkable Taula de Torralba resembles Stonehenge. It was once a funeral pyre.

For a beautiful view with dinner, eat at **Espla**. This restaurant is famous for its breathtaking location on the waterfront. Behind the lace curtains diners spoon up the house specialty—lobster bouillabaise.

Hotel Cala Galdana is one of the few hotels that opens in March, before the season starts. **Hotel Port Mahone** is a four-star hotel overlooking the sea. And the small, charming **Hotel Del Almirante** is stocked with antiques.

Homes are Spanish in character, with bright whitewashed exteriors and tile roofs. And prices are reasonable. A fully furnished, three-bedroom villa with a covered terrace and swimming pool sells for about 11,400,000 pesetas.

Buying in the Balearics

If you're interested in buying a villa in Menorca, contact San Clemente Villas. This company has several different villas to choose from, priced from about 11,500,000 pesetas. Write to *Keith and Liz Trafford*, **San Clemente Villas**, *Sa Vinya, 29 Avenida del Dr. Guardia, Mahon, Menorca, Balearics.*

In England, contact **Property Investments Overseas Ltd.,** *19 The Mall, Bromley, Kent BR1 1TT; tel. (44-1)460-9910.*

The Canary Islands—continents in miniature

Annamarie Gregory wrote the following article about her adopted home—the Canary Islands.

Imagine living on an island where green mountains tower over brown-sugar beaches and sapphire waters. The air is cool and fresh beneath the tropical sun. Brilliant flowers, waving palms, exotic fruits, wonderful food, gentle people. You are picturing the Canaries.

This string of seven islands and several small islets sparkles in the Atlantic some 60 miles off the coast of North Africa. The Canary Islands' location gives them one of the world's best climates. The trade winds blow softly off the Sahara, and the ocean currents keep the water and air at 72 degrees year-round. There are no hurricanes, tornadoes, earthquakes, or electrical storms. The Canaries are called the Islands of Eternal Spring—some believe they were the Garden of Eden.

Each island has a distinct beauty of its own. Gran Canaria and Tenerife have been called continents in miniature. They each have mountain ranges and hidden valleys, sandy deserts and thick forests in a thousand shades of green. With its lunar landscape, Lanzarote is different from anywhere else on earth.

The Canary Islands is a place where contentment still exists. The señorita who weighs our tomatoes at the local market on Gran Canaria tells us she has never been off her island, not even to go to Tenerife, 25 miles away. She sees no reason to go. "I have everything I need right here," she says.

Gran Canaria

Gran Canaria has mountains with peaks that reach a mile into the sky, deserts sprinkled with cactus, massive sand dunes, and ravines where coffee, almond trees, sugar cane, and bananas grow.

Las Palmas, a city of 500,000 people, is the capital of Gran Canaria, with a port that handles the largest volume of traffic of any city in Spain. There are tree-shaded parks, a street of banks from every corner of the world, and wide sun-splattered boulevards lined with designer shops. Close to the ocean are elegant high-rise apartments. Facing Las Canteras beach are fine restaurants sitting next door to tiny down-home places that serve seafood freshly caught that morning.

The southern beaches are wide and long and blessed with over 3,000 hours of sunshine a year. During the 1970s, a group from Germany built the attractive village of Puerto Rico. Small villas encircle two free-form swimming pools, and the entire complex is almost hidden beneath masses of scarlet and purple bougainvillea. Through the center run gardens of red roses, yellow saucer-sized hibiscus, and 40-foot palm trees.

A multilevel shopping center is cantilevered on the hillside overlooking the bay. It houses a medical clinic, bars, and restaurants with names such as Hofbrau Haus and Der Rathskellar. The Spanish have not succumbed to the lure of big money, so Der Big Mac and Der Fried Chicken are not among the choices. There is a liquor store and supermarket with prices from the 1950s. Shops sell complete swimming suits or, as many prefer, just the bottoms.

Farther north on the coast is the community of Maspalomas Beach, which stretches for four miles and then runs into Playa del Ingles, which reaches another mile and a half. Most go topless on all of the beaches. The southern end of Maspalomas is a nudist beach where there is plenty of privacy among the sand dunes—with the exception of an occasional hang-glider overhead.

Prices for two-story, two-bedroom townhouses at Puerto Rico start around 4,500,000 pesetas. Villas run from 9,000,000 pesetas and up. Apartments near the beach in Las Palmas rent for about 35,000 pesetas a month. Houses and apartments are always completely furnished.

For property information on Gran Canaria, contact **Immobiliaria Barber,** *Secretario Arbiles 44-46, Las Palmas de Gran Canaria, Canary Islands, Spain; tel. (34-28)277-613,* or *Administración Canaria, S.A., Avenida de Francia 13, Playa Del Inglés, Gran Canaria, Spain.*

Tenerife

Tenerife covers more than 1,200 square miles. The peak of Teide, the highest point in Spain, rises over 12, 250 feet and is snow-covered in winter. The farmers harvest four crops a year and grow everything found on earth, from cotton and papaya at sea level to corn and artichokes up the mountain. The Oratava Valley near Puerto de la Cruz produces more than 400,000 tons of bananas per year, most of them sent to mainland Spain, along with tomatoes, coffee, flowers, and tobacco (Canary cigars).

Santa Cruz is the capital city of Tenerife, home to over 200,000 people, and the loveliest city in the Canaries. It has lush green parks, elegant stores, and restaurants where gourmet regional cuisine costs as little as a simple lunch back home.

Tenerife has many small towns ideal for a high lifestyle at low cost. Every village has a market where freshly baked bread is bought each morning and where vegetables and fruits cost next to nothing. Local markets are filled with magnificent handicrafts and spectacular bargains.

The sophisticated side of Tenerife is in Puerto de la Cruz, a city that grew up around a fishing port and is now one of the major tourist centers of the island. It has every convenience: a medical clinic, fine food, markets, a casino, and wide boulevards with every kind of store and service. Entertainment ranges from an underwater nightclub to traditional folk dancing.

Puerto Santiago is a good choice for retirement. It is a picture-book village with red-tile roofs and spotless white stair-stepped buildings set among the rugged cliffs of the west coast. There is a yacht harbor and a black sand beach.

The sandy southern coast of Tenerife has been inundated by people from all over Europe, and has suffered the pangs of sudden growth. Much of the building, however, is done tastefully to blend with the landscape. There are retirement villages with medical facilities, food stores, shops, and entertainment.

Houses and apartments can be found throughout Tenerife. Apartments in Santa Cruz, along the Rambla, rent for 11,400 to 28,500 pesetas a month, including electricity. The temperate climate makes heat and air conditioning unnecessary. Everything is furnished, down to the last napkin. Many apartments occupy entire floors of buildings. The small villages have houses for rent from 23,000 to 45,600 pesetas a month.

You will find property ads in the daily Spanish paper. The tourist bureaus in Santa Cruz and Puerto de la Cruz have lists of available housing. Property ranges in price from 2,300,000 pesetas for an apartment to over 11,500,000 pesetas for a villa.

Parque Santiago, in the heart of Playa de Las Americas, is one of the most beautiful spots on the island. It's a self-contained development built in the Spanish Mediterranean style, with white walls and red-tiled roofs. Wood carpentry is visible throughout, and the houses have magnificent views of both ocean and mountains.

Cobblestoned streets and several swimming pools round out the development. Flowers are everywhere.

Villas and apartments, fully furnished and equipped, are priced from 10-million pesetas. This is first-class investment property in a rapidly developing area.

The agent for Parque Santiago is **Teide Sur, S.A.,** *Parque Santiago 2, Playa de las Americas, Tenerife, Spain; tel. (34-28)790559.*

On the mountainside above Playa de Las Americas is an expatriate community called Chayofa. A small villa here rents for about 40,000 pesetas a month. The community boasts swimming pools, tennis courts, gardens, and a marvelous restaurant.

Just north of Playa de Las Americas is Los Cristianos, filled with new construction and a younger crowd. Still farther north is Ten-Bel, an older, more established expatriate community. Many residents are from Britain, Germany, and Scandinavia. If you want to get away from Americans, Los Cristianos is the place to settle; not many Americans are here. Yet.

For more information on property in Tenerife, contact **Melcarmen Services,** *117 Margaritas, Los Cristianos, Tenerife, Canary Islands, Spain; tel. (34-28)791884;* **Immobiliaria Royal, Estate Agents,** *Calle Virtud 3, Puerto de la Cruz, Tenerife; tel. (34-28)385420;* **Immobiliaria Barber,** *Secretario Arbiles 44-46, Las Palmas de Gran Canaria, Canary Islands; tel. (34-28)277613;* or **Chilcott White,** *125 South End, Croyden, N.E. Surrey, England; tel. (44-1)688-4151.*

Lanzarote

Lanzarote is the easternmost island, the one closest to Africa. Palm trees stand tall against the sky, and low white houses give the island the look of Morocco. In the early 1700s, volcanic eruptions created lava fields that are now a tourist attraction. The farmers of Lanzarote dig craters 20-feet wide into the earth, line them with lava granules, plant their crops, and cover the pit with layers of lava. The granules retain the moisture of the night dew and from these fields come the grapes that produce exquisite Malvasia wine. Watermelons, figs, grapes, tomatoes, and onions are raised in the same way. The craters create a moon-like landscape, and if you dare take a camelback ride, you can see more than 300 volcanic cones from the Montaña de Fuego (Mountain of Fire).

The development of Lanzarote is less offensive than on most European coasts. No high-rise buildings are allowed, and tourist ghettos have been kept to a minimum.

Arrecife is the capital city, a happy, clean whitewashed town. Just to the south of Arrecife is the village of Tías, a development of bungalows and apartments next to a sugary soft beach. There are tennis courts, a marina, subtropical gardens, and a golf course. There is an international windsurfing school and a diving school on Lanzarote. The island is rated one of the world's best places to windsurf. So many lovely beaches are on the island that if the swells are too large at one, or there is no wind, you simply move to another.

Many privately owned townhouses, apartments, and villas are available to rent. Get in touch with **Property Managers S.L.**, *Plaza San Antonio, Playa de los Picillos, Lanzarote, Canary Islands, Spain.* A two-bedroom apartment should cost about 40,000 pesetas a month, including utilities.

Canary carrots

If you are feeling hesitant to move so far away from mainland Spain, consider the many carrots the Canaries hold out.

Gran Canaria, Tenerife, and Lanzarote have large international airports, good highways, and well-developed transportation systems. Flights between islands take only 20 minutes and cost less than 3,420 pesetas. A hydrofoil operates twice daily between Gran Canaria and Tenerife.

The Canaries are a sportsman's paradise. Each island has tennis courts, golf courses, hiking trails, and all kinds of water sports. Deep-sea fishing is big on Lanzarote.

A car is not a necessity. Buses run at all hours, stretch to every corner, and are clean and inexpensive.

Medical care is excellent and there are doctors on every island who are multilingual. Farmacías are well-stocked, and one store is always open for emergencies. The cost for a visit to the doctor and for medication is one-fifth that of the United States.

The telephone system is modern; you can call internationally from anywhere. Mail is fast and inexpensive—letters reach California in six or seven days, packages take a few days longer. The Canary Tourist Radio (747 Khz) broadcasts world news and sports, as well as local weather, in English. There is an English magazine, *The Island Gazette*, as well as a newspaper, *Here and Now*, published in Tenerife biweekly.

The standard of living is high, and there is virtually no crime or poverty. Housing is inexpensive. If you buy your food the way the Spanish do—local products rather than imported—living is cheap. A couple can retire in the Canaries with a "cocktails on the terrace" lifestyle and spend no more than 80,000 pesetas a month.

One last carrot—property taxes in the Canaries average only 11,400 pesetas a year.

For more information

•**Embassy of Spain,** *2700 15th St. N.W., Washington, DC 20009; (202)265-0190.*

•**Spanish National Tourist Office,** *665 Fifth Ave., New York, NY 10022; (212)759-8822.*

•**Iberia Airlines,** *509 Madison Ave., New York, NY 10021; (800)772-4642.*

•*Lookout*, a magazine about Spain in English, is available from newsstands in Spain or by subscription from **Lookout Publications SA,** *Puebla Lucia, 29640 Fuengirola (Málaga), Spain; tel. (34-52)460950.*

•*You and the Law in Spain*, by David Searl, is available from **Lookout Publications SA,** *address above.*

•**U.S. Embassy in Spain,** *Calle de Serrano 75, Madrid 28006; tel. (34-1)276-3400 or (34-1)276-3600.*

There are U.S. consulates in Barcelona, Bilbao, Coruña, Fuengirola, Gran Canaria, Mallorca, Seville, and Valencia.

National Tourist Offices (Oficina de Turismo) are at: *Maria de Molina 50, Madrid 28006; (34-1)580-2200; Principe de Vergara, Madrid; tel. (34-1)580-2200;* in the Chamartin Railway Station and in the Princesa Torre de Madrid; *tel. (34-1)314-1000.*

Also, there are Spanish Consulates in Boston, Chicago, Houston, Los Angeles, Miami, New Orleans, New York, San Francisco, and San Juan, Puerto Rico.

Chapter 17

Switzerland

Switzerland is a postcard-pretty paradise at the peak of Europe. Gingerbread chalets laced with flower boxes are surrounded by rolling meadows. And above the whole of the country loom jagged, snow-covered peaks. Tidy streets wander through orderly towns filled with well-mannered people.

Spectacular scenery, skiing, and hiking draw people from around the world to Switzerland. As do Swiss banks, which offer secrecy and stability. Most educated Swiss speak some English, and Swiss health facilities are excellent. Furthermore, Switzerland is centrally located, a perfect hub for exploring Europe (it shares borders with France, Italy, Austria, and Germany). And it is politically and economically stable.

Switzerland is a safe, prosperous country with little crime, reliable and efficient public services, and virtually no unemployment or poverty. And if you're looking for recreation and healthy living, this is the place to come. Switzerland offers cross-country and downhill skiing, hiking, ice skating, therapeutic hot springs, and boating.

One of Switzerland's disadvantages is that it is landlocked and can be dull. Another is that it is expensive. Lunch in an average big-city café costs SFr15 to SFr20. A bottle of beer at a disco goes for SFr12. A Coke is about SFr4.5. And mineral water in a café will cost you SFr3.3! Prices are lower in small towns and during the off season, but they are still quite high by American standards.

Because Switzerland attracts so many foreigners, the Swiss have constructed bureaucratic barriers to protect their land from overdevelopment. It is difficult to obtain permanent residency in Switzerland. And foreigners may not buy property in many areas, including Geneva, Lausanne, Gland, and Rolle. Gstaad, St. Moritz, Davos, and Zermatt have blocked property sales to non-resident foreigners.

Red tape

Immigration, as it is known in the United States, does not exist in Switzerland. A visa is not required for stays of up to three months.

After three months, you can apply to the local police for a one-year residency permit, which can be extended indefinitely with an annual application to the canton. After you have been a resident of Switzerland for a number of years, you can apply for a permanent domicile permit. These permits are contingent upon substantial means or sought-after skills. Consult a Swiss lawyer for more detailed information.

To retire permanently in Switzerland, you must be 60 or older, have a yearly income of $20,000 from sources other than regular employment, no longer be employed by anyone, and have an "interest in Switzerland." The fourth stipulation is left deliberately vague to allow discretion in deciding difficult cases. You are most likely to be allowed to reside in Switzerland permanently if you have relatives in the country or have lived there for at least one year.

You can apply for residency to the **Embassy of Switzerland,** *2900 Cathedral Ave. N.W., Washington, DC 20008; (202)745-7937,* or directly to the canton in Switzerland where you want to live (the individual canton has the final say as to whether or not you can become a permanent resident). You must submit a resume, two passport photos, and documentary evidence showing that you have sufficient financial means to support yourself in Switzerland.

Tips on taxes

As an American retiree living in Switzerland, you are exempt from taxes on U.S.-source dividends and interest income. However, if your principal residence or business is in Switzerland, you are subject to federal, cantonal, and municipal taxes. The amount of these taxes varies. For example, while residents of Vaud Province pay a 13% cantonal tax on SFr50,000, residents of Zug pay only a 7% cantonal tax on the same amount. The highest cantonal and local taxes are in Vaud, Geneva, Berne, and Lucerne; the lowest are in Zug, Zürich, and Graubünden.

In general, income taxes in Switzerland are comparable to those in the United States. The federal government levies an additional income tax, ranging from 0.31% on SFr30,000 to 4.30% on SFr100,000. Usually, cantons with the lowest income tax rates have the highest housing costs.

To your health

The ratio of the number of doctors in Switzerland to the country's population is excellent: 164 to 100,000. And there are 1,125 hospital beds per 100,000 inhabitants. Medical costs are high, but medicine is cheap and easy to obtain. Dental work is expensive—a filling costs at least $90.

Doctors charge SFr25 to SFr55 for a first house call, depending on the canton. (The cost, based on a sliding scale, also depends on the patient's income.) Hospital rooms are SFr200 to SFr230 per night.

The high cost of living

Following is a list of what you can expect to pay for the necessities in Switzerland:

Liter of milk (roughly one quart)	SFr1.65
1 kilogram beef steak (2.2 pounds)	SFr45.00
1 kilogram pork cutlets	SFr17.86
1 kilogram chicken	SFr9.00
Loaf of brown bread	SFr75.00
250 grams of coffee (about one-half pound)	SFr4.67
Pack of cigarettes	SFr2.53
Man's suit	SFr330.00
Woman's suit	SFr423.00
Local telephone call	SFr.40
Liter of gasoline (about one-quarter gallon)	SFr.96

Banking on Switzerland

Switzerland is famous for its banking system, which allows secret transactions. Swiss banks break secrecy only in criminal and inheritance cases and only when ordered to do so by a Swiss court. Authorities have agreed to exchange bank information with U.S. authorities in cases involving violation of criminal laws in both countries. Banks are required to check the identities of clients who ask to transfer large sums from one currency to another, to verify the identities of clients seeking to rent safe-deposit boxes, to discourage the use of safe-deposit boxes for storing items obtained illegally, and to prohibit the transfer of funds from the account of one foreign client to another if such transfers are illegal in the client's country.

The U.S. government requires that U.S. taxpayers report Swiss accounts of $10,000 or more. And the transfer out of the United States of $10,000 or more must be reported to customs.

Swiss banks offer checking and savings accounts in Swiss francs and other currencies. They allow you to buy and sell securities with your deposit account, and they offer safekeeping and custodial services, portfolio management, fiduciary time deposits, trading in commodities, and safe-deposit boxes.

A common minimum for an account is $5,000. However, the **Migros Bank,** *Seidengasse 12, CH-8023 Zürich,* accepts amounts as low as $100 to $200. It's easy to open a Swiss bank account. Just write to the bank in English explaining your interest.

Following is a list of large Swiss banks:
- **Swiss Bank Corporation,** *Aeschenvorstadt 1, 4002 Basel.*
- **Union Bank of Switzerland,** *Bahnhofstr. 45, CH-8021 Zürich.*

The following small banks specialize in English-speaking clients:
- **Bank Indiana (Suisse),** *50 ave. de la Gare, CH-1001 Lausanne.*
- **FOCO Bank,** *Bellariastr. 82, 8038 Zürich; tel. (41-1)482-6688.*
- **Swiss Credit Bank,** *Paradeplatz 8, CH-8021 Zürich.*
- **Ueberseebank,** *2-K Limmatquai, CH-8024 Zürich.*

Buying Swiss real estate

As a foreigner, you need permission from the government to buy land in Switzerland. It's easiest for foreigners to buy land, a free-standing home, or an estate in rural areas; it's more difficult to obtain permission to purchase property in cities, such as Zürich and Geneva. In recreational regions, condominiums are the only properties readily available.

However, the laws are not nearly as limiting as they may seem, because many areas considered rural are within a few miles of ski resorts and spas. And the condos are attractive and spacious, many with traditional Swiss architecture, mountain views and privacy.

Foreigners may not buy property in Gstaad, Saanen, or Schönried in the canton of Berne. However, Rougemont, in the canton of Vaud, only five minutes from Gstaad, has a small quota of properties available to non-Swiss buyers.

The laws governing the resale of foreign-owned properties have changed in recent years. Prior to January 1984, foreign-owned property could be resold only to Swiss citizens and only after a five-year period of ownership. In addition, a maximum of only 65% of the available apartments in a given condominium unit could be sold to foreigners and only after pre-construction approval by the canton.

Under present law, each canton annually pre-authorizes the number of sales that can be made to foreigners. This change effectively eliminates the sale-to-Swiss-citizens requirement. (However, the law requiring a holding period of five years before resale is still enforced.) The present law stipulates that the sale of a foreign-owned property to another foreigner is allowed if some portion of the annual allocation of foreign sales is unused at the time of the sale—and if the canton gives its approval.

Unless you have a Swiss residency permit, you cannot occupy your Swiss property for more than three months per calendar year. You can get around this by arriving at the beginning of the last quarter of one year and departing at the end of the first quarter of the following year. This allows for a six-month stay.

Financing can be obtained, using the property as security, on 60% to 65% of the purchase price. And many banks offer 100% financing with the deposit of additional collateral. It's usually possible to borrow back some of the equity at any time, using the arrangement as a limited line of credit.

Sample Swiss properties

Globe Plan S.A., *24 ave. Mon-Repos, CH-1005 Lausanne; tel. (41-21)22-35-12,* recently advertised the following properties:

• Half-chalets in Les Diablerets (a ski resort) with three or four rooms, garages, and spectacular views are on the market for SFr450,000.

• Residential apartments in Les Cristaux with two rooms are selling for SFr240,000; apartments with three rooms are available for SFr350,000.

• Half-chalets in Villars-sur-Ollon with three bedrooms, living rooms, kitchens, cellars, garages, and gardens are selling for SFr550,000 to SFr600,000.

REVAC S.A., *52 Montbrillant, CH-1202 Geneva; tel. (41-22)34-15-40,* recently advertised the following properties:

• One-bedroom chalets in the Four Valleys region of the Swiss Alps are available for SFr44,000 to SFr360,000.

• Two bedroom apartments in the smaller mountain resorts are selling for SFr69,000 to SFr213,000.

• In the less glamorous Jura region, two-bedroom residential chalets are available for SFr240,000 to SFr341,000.

• Two-bedroom chalets in Crans-Montana, a large resort in the Alps with downhill and cross-country skiing and seven lakes, are on the market for SFr295,000 to SFr750,000.

• Two-bedroom residences on the waterfront in Montreux are available for SFr350,000 to SFr1.5 million; one-bedroom residences are going for SFr305,000 to SFr795,000. (Mountain resorts, such as Villars and Gstaad, are only a half-hour away from Montreux by car.)

• A luxurious three-bedroom apartment on the waterfront between Geneva and Lausanne with a small private port and a magnificent view of the Alps is selling for SFr1.4 million.

Swiss real estate agents

• **A&G Associés S.A.,** *Philippe Allez et Zavier Givaudan, 4 Cours de Rive, 1204 Geneva.*

• **Alpe des Chaux S.I.,** *Bureau de Vente et de Renseignements, Hameau des Fracherets, 1882 Gryon.*

• **Candela-Immobiliern,** *P.O. Box 3343, 8049 Zürich.*

• **Emerald-Home Ltd.,** *Dorfstrasse, CH-8872 Weesen SG; tel. (41-58)43-17-78.*

• **Furer S.A.,** *Philippe Furer, administrateur-délegué, 38 ave. des Alpes, 1820 Montreux; tel. (41-21)63-52-21.*

• **Globe Plan S.A.,** *24 ave. Mon-Repos, CH-1005 Lausanne; tel. (41-21)22-35-12.* Globe Plan also can help clients obtain residency permits.

• **H. Sebold S.A.,** *6 Tour Grise, CH-1007 Lausanne; tel. (41-91)68-76-48.*

• **Hilary Scott,** *422 Upper Richmond Road W., London SW 14, England.*

• **Immobilien AG,** *Capitol, Bahnhofstr. 73, 8001 Zürich; tel. (41-1)211-6760.*

• **Immo-Treuhand Zürich,** *Jenni Company, Stockerstr. S4, 8001 Zürich; tel. (41-1)202-1817.*

• **Lincoln Property Company,** *European Headquarters, 70 Route de Florissant, Geneva.*

• **REVAC S.A.,** *52 Montbrillant, CH-1202 Geneva; tel. (41-22)34-15-40.*

• **Wellington Property Company Ltd.,** *K. Barton, director, 42-45 New Broad St., London EC2 M1QY, England.*

The aparthotel—a Swiss real estate bargain

A new real estate concept known as the aparthotel makes it easier for Americans to buy Swiss property. Buying an aparthotel has attractive tax advantages, and rental income is guaranteed. Swiss developers came up with the concept to overcome the barriers and expenses that prevent foreigners from buying real estate in Switzerland.

Aparthotels are similar to condominium hotels in the United States. Usually, they have dazzling mountain views and are located near tennis and golf facilities, natural hot springs, and ski lifts. Unlike most condos, they have nearly complete hotel facilities as well, including pools, saunas, restaurants, and maid service.

Staying in an aparthotel is both carefree and fun. And the financial advantages are substantial. You have to pay only 10% down. The balance is financed for as long as 45 years at low Swiss-franc interest rates. What's more, you pay interest only. The principal is paid off with a whole life insurance policy, an accumulation policy that matures with the mortgage.

It is relatively easy to rent out your condo when you are not there. Part of your contract may include a guarantee of rental income to offset the purchase price. Some owners spend as many as five months of the year in their Swiss properties, which still leaves the apartments available for maximum rental income during the peak season.

The tax benefits are also attractive. An exception to the rules that govern most rental properties allows you to consider any income from your aparthotel as *not* passive. Thus, losses can be deducted from your other income—just as was possible with real estate tax-shelter losses prior to the 1986 Tax Reform Act. You may be entitled to deduct mortgage interest, depreciation, property taxes, condo fees, maintenance costs, and even the costs of your transportation to Switzerland. As with all tax matters, you must pay careful attention to the details. But if you plan it carefully, your Swiss condo could virtually pay for itself.

Consider the numbers. The out-of-pocket cost of a typical $200,000 deluxe chalet-style condo, for example, may be about $26,000 net the first year (including the 10% down payment)—and about $6,000 each subsequent year.

But this condo could produce tax deductions of about $20,000 per year. If you get through the Internal Revenue Service (IRS) maze successfully, you'll end up the proud owner of a Swiss aparthotel almost for free—plus you'll be enjoying a free annual vacation in Switzerland!

Remember, however, that the provisions of the IRS laws dealing with these respective areas are much more complex than we're able to explain here. Consult your tax advisor.

For more information, write *Julia Guth,* **The Passport Club,** *824 E. Baltimore St., Baltimore, MD 21202.*

Renting in Switzerland

If you can't afford to buy property in Switzerland, you can always rent. Even if you are planning to buy, you may want to rent awhile anyway, before taking any permanent steps.

The most attractive rentals are in the mountains. It's easy to rent a mountain chalet, but the prices are high (skiers and hikers vie for these properties). Many rental agents deal in these areas, and nearly all speak English.

Two attractive villages that are slightly less expensive than the major resort areas are Saas Fee, in the next valley over from Zermatt, and Lenzerheide, along the road to St. Moritz. Both villages are sufficiently far from these popular resorts to be relatively inexpensive.

Chalets in the Alps rent for roughly SFr2,340 to SFr4,680 a month, depending on the season and the area.

Sample rental properties

A one-bedroom chalet in Montana with a balcony rents for SFr500 a week during low season and SFr940 during high season. The price includes the *taxe de séjour,* electricity, and heating.

A furnished apartment overlooking a peaceful garden in Geneva rents for SFr3,000 per month. It has a fireplace, a television, and a carport.

City rentals

It's not easy to find apartments for rent in Swiss cities, and rents vary widely, depending upon the region, location, amenities, and size. In urban districts, expect to pay SFr400 to SFr700 per month for a relatively new two-room apartment (unfurnished); SFr500 to SFr800 per month for a three-room apartment (unfurnished); and SFr600 to SFr1,000 per month for a four-room apartment (unfurnished). (These average rents are only estimates; it's difficult to give exact figures.)

Heat, hot water, and electricity add at least another SFr150 per month to the bill.

For help finding a rental

The following organizations and agencies should be able to help you with your search for a rental property:

• **Agence Plazer,** *3962 Crans-Montana, Switzerland; tel. (41-27)41-10-85.*

• *Arnaldo Corvasce,* **Bureau d'Affaires Touristiques,** *3961 Vercorin; tel. (41-27)55-82-82.*

• **Begg International,** *2121 Wisconsin Ave. N.W., Washington, DC 20007; (202)338-9065.* Gilbert Scharl, the agent in Switzerland, is helpful. His address is *52 Caudoz, 1009 Pully, Switzerland; tel. (41-21)28-82-81.*

• *Jean-Pierre Crettaz,* **Agence Jolival,** *3961 Chandolin, Switzerland; tel. (41-27)67-18-666.*

• **Nouvelle Agence,** *3962 Crans-Montana, Switzerland; tel. (41-27)41-40-64.*

The lay of the land

Choose your piece of Switzerland according to the sort of lifestyle you want. If you like to ski or hike, consider living in the Alps. If you're accustomed to big-city life, think about Zürich or Geneva. If you consider retirement a time to get away from the rat race, look into small towns or lakeside villages. Also consider what kind of culture would make you feel most at home. You can live in French, German, Italian, or Romansch Switzerland, depending upon your preference and knowledge of foreign languages. The Italian-speaking sections of Switzerland are the most open to foreigners and often the least expensive.

Zeroing in on Zürich

Zürich, a prosperous banking town, is a two-sided coin. The home of the Dadaists, it was also the site of youth riots in recent years (shockingly uncharacteristic of the Swiss).

Most of Zürich's population is staid and solid, but its German-speaking people have a jovial, witty side that becomes evident during the city's festivals. During **Sechselauten** (Zürich's spring festival, held toward the end of April), for example, Zürich's bankers don costumes and celebrate the end of winter by burning a huge straw dummy named the Boogg. And Zürich has produced writers as well as financiers. Joyce, Mann, Brecht, and Kleist all lived here at various times during their careers.

The **Bahnhofstrasse,** Zürich's main artery, is the cleanest street in the world. James Joyce once said, "Zürich is so clean that should you spill your soup on the Bahnhofstrasse, you could eat it up with a spoon." Some of the most powerful bankers in the world, known as the gnomes of Zürich, work here.

The Bahnhofstrasse is also known as Luxury Mile, because of its expensive, first-class shops. While it's fun to look at 18-carat gold shoehorns and watches, you're better off doing your shopping in

Zürich's department stores or along Marktplatz Oerlikon, a pedestrian district nearby. For daily shopping, try Migros, a chain of inexpensive food and department stores.

The **Altstadt** (old town), on the right bank of the Limmat River, is a maze of steep cobblestoned streets lined with cafés, sex shops, and nightclubs. A series of 17th- and 18th-century arcaded guild halls line the Limmatquai and surrounding streets. Inside, the halls are decorated with ornate friezes and ceilings. Most are now restaurants, so you can enjoy lunch as well as the surroundings.

Above it all is Zürich's massive cathedral, the **Grossmünster.** The Romanesque cathedral was a center of the Reformation. Here, Ulrich Zwingli preached against the sale of indulgences, common at that time in the Catholic church.

On the other side of the Limmat River, on Stadthausquai, is the **Fraumünster,** an austere Gothic cathedral enlivened with modern stained-glass windows by Chagall and Giacometti.

Zürich is also the home of Switzerland's finest museums, including the **Schweizerisches Landesmuseum** (Museum of Swiss History), *Museumstr. 2;* the **Kunsthaus** (Fine Arts Museum), *Heimplatz 1;* and the **Rietberg Museum,** *Gablestr. 15,* in a villa on Lake Zürich, which houses one of Europe's best collections of non-European art.

International Geneva

Geneva, a French-speaking city on shimmering Lake Geneva, is an international center and the home base of some 200 world organizations. This is the place in Europe to watch modern history as it unfolds.

The European headquarters of the United Nations is housed in the **Palais des Nations,** *14 ave. de la Paix.* Nearby are the World Health Organization, the International Red Cross, and the International Labor Office.

The tallest fountain in the world, the **Jet d'Eau,** spouts 476 feet in the center of Lake Geneva. It is striking, backed by the Swiss Alps.

Most of Geneva's monuments are in the **Vieille Ville** (old town). The most prominent is **St. Peter's Cathedral,** built between the 12th and 13th centuries. St. Peter's has been a Protestant church since 1536, when it became a center of the Reformation. You can see Calvin's seat in the north aisle. And the tomb of the Duc de Rohan, who headed the Reformation in France at the time of Louis XIII, is in the first chapel on the south side of the chancel.

372

The **Reformation Monument** stands against a 16th-century rampart of the old town. At the center of the 100-yard wall are statues of the four Presbyterian reformers: Calvin, Knox, Farel, and de Bèze. The monument was built in 1917 and includes texts that recall the origins of the reformed church.

Geneva's **Hôtel de Ville** (town hall), parts of which date back to the 15th century, has a courtyard with a cobblestoned ramp once used to carry litters to the upper floors. The Geneva Convention (which founded the Red Cross) was signed here Aug. 22, 1864.

Four good museums are located in Geneva. The **Voltaire Museum,** *25 rue des Délices,* in Les Délices, where Voltaire lived from 1755 to 1765, holds Voltaire's furniture, manuscripts, rare editions, and portraits. The **Musée d'Art et d'Histoire,** *2 rue Charles-Galland,* contains ancient art from Rome, Greece, and Egypt, as well as European paintings from the 15th through 19th centuries. The **Musée du Petit Palais,** *2 Terrace St. Victor,* features the works of impressionist artists, including Kisling, Van Dongen, Soutine, Chagall, Utrillo, and Suzanne Valadon. And the **Musée de l'Horlogerie** (Watch and Clock Museum), *15 Route de Malagnou,* traces the measurement of time from the Middle Ages to the present.

Mirroring the city is blue **Lake Geneva**—the deepest of the Alpine lakes (1,000 feet). It is 45 miles long and 7.5 miles wide at its widest point, and it covers 143,323 acres.

Chillon, a fortress perched on a rocky island at the opposite end of the lake from Geneva, inspired the poet Lord Byron to write the lyrical poem "The Prisoner of Chillon." François Bonivard was imprisoned in the castle dungeon for four years for trying to introduce the Reformation to Geneva. The Duke of Savoy, an ardent Catholic, had the prior chained to one of the pillars. If you visit the dungeon, take a close look at that pillar and the floor around it. The prisoner's footprints are traced in the rock here. Lord Byron carved his name on the third pillar in Bonivard's cell in 1816.

The best restaurants in Geneva tend to be French. But Geneva's own cooking can be delicious. Humble fare, it is generally served in informal places. Fish and cheese are the main ingredients.

Raclette—melted cheese scraped off a chunk of grilled Swiss cheese and served with boiled potatoes and gherkins—is a delicious local meal. You can try it in almost any brasserie in Geneva.

Fondue is another typically Genevan dish. Also a melted cheese, it is more refined—mixed with garlic, white wine, and kirsch. The best part of the fondue is the hardened brown cheese you scrape up at the end, known as *la religieuse* or *la dentelle*.

Capital Bern—the loveliest city

Switzerland's capital, **Bern,** with its turreted buildings, is one of the best-preserved medieval cities in Europe. It has more fountains per capita than any other city on the continent. The Alps surround the city, which is divided twice by the Aare River.

Established in 1191 by the Duke of Zahringen, Bern was originally a hunting ground. The duke and his cronies decided that the town should be named after the first animal caught on a particular hunt. The unfortunate beast was a bear (*Bär* in German), so the town was called *Bärn* (Bern is a corruption). A bear appears on the city's coat of arms, and for centuries mascot bears have been kept in the *Bärengraben,* or bear pits.

One of the most popular sights in Bern is the city's beach, where many sunbathe topless. These free-spirited sun worshipers caused a good deal of controversy when they first disrobed (probably because the beach is right beneath Parliament's windows).

Bern's attractions also include ancient cathedrals and fine museums. **St. Vincent Cathedral** (the *Münster*) is an impressive Gothic church with 16th-century statues depicting the Last Judgement. From the top of the 100-meter tower, you'll have a view of Bern and the Alps—but you'll have to climb 254 steps to get there.

The **Kunstmuseum** (Art Museum), *Hodlerstr. 12,* has the world's largest Paul Klee collection (Klee was a native of Bern). Works by Modigliani and Picasso are also displayed.

Gimmelwald—the most picturesque Swiss town

Gimmelwald (not to be confused with Grindelwald), a sleepy little town in the mountains near Interlaken, looks like something straight out of *Heidi.* You'll hear cowbells here and see farmers in lederhosen. Cars aren't allowed in Gimmelwald, making it delightfully quiet.

To get to Gimmelwald, take the Lauterbrunnen-Grutschalp funicular from Interlaken to Murten, where you'll find several good hotels. You have to hike the rest of the way from Murten.

Ski country

Glittering mountains crown Switzerland. The Rhine, Rhône, and Inn rivers originate in Swiss mountain glaciers, whose treacherous peaks challenge the world's finest skiers, hikers, and climbers. The ominous Matterhorn hovers above Zermatt. The Berner Oberland range guards Interlaken. Davos and St. Moritz sit snugly in Alpine valleys.

Scores of attractive resorts, spectacular settings for retirement homes, nestle in the mountains. **St. Moritz** is the most famous and elegant ski playground in the world. Gunther Sachs skis here—and once you've skied the five mountains at St. Moritz, you'll understand why. As you might expect, skiing here during peak season is expensive.

Most people don't realize that St. Moritz is also a spa. The town is divided into two sections, on two sides of sky-blue St. Moritz Lake. **St. Moritz-Dorf,** the ski resort, has the world's oldest ski school, dating back to 1927. The only vestige of the original village is the leaning campanile. **St. Moritz-Bad** is the spa quarter. Its curative mineral waters have been sought-after since the Bronze Age.

Zermatt's lifts reach as high as 11,500 feet, offering some of Europe's highest slopes and a whopping vertical drop of 6,300 feet. Zermatt's summer skiing is also Europe's best—as is its heli-skiing (if that interests you).

Lakeside idylls

The pearl of Swiss lakeside resorts is **Montreux,** on the shores of Lake Geneva. Blessed with an extremely mild climate, it has a six-mile lakeside promenade lined with palm trees and tropical flowers. The climate here is the mildest on the north side of the Alps, producing fig and almond trees, cypresses, magnolias, and bay trees.

Montreux is famous for its international music festivals, especially the jazz festival in July, the International Choral Recitals, which take place the week after Easter, and the Musical September concerts.

Lausanne, another resort on Lake Geneva, is a French-speaking city and a university center. Although its universities date back to the 16th century, its students keep the atmosphere young. Excavations in Lausanne have uncovered Neolithic skeletons and a section of Roman road where the Geneva-Lausanne highway now enters town.

The most picturesque section of Lausanne is around **place de la Palud,** in the old town. This square is bordered by the Renaissance facade of the town hall and centered around the 16th-century **Fountain of Justice.** Behind the fountain is an unusual covered staircase that leads to the town's 12th-century cathedral, one of the finest Gothic buildings in Switzerland. It shelters one of the last night watchmen in the world, whose duty is to call out the hour during the night. The south door of the cathedral, known as the Door of the Apostles, is covered with 13th-century sculptures. A 700-year-old rose window illustrates the elements, seasons, months, and signs of the zodiac.

Lausanne is also the home of the **Sherlock Holmes Museum,** which features editions of his books in dozens of languages, serious academic studies of the detective, and an uncannily lifelike reproduction of his study, complete with period microscope, violin, and opium paraphernalia.

A taste of Italy

Lugano's language is Italian, and its atmosphere Mediterranean. It was ceded to Switzerland by Milan in the early 16th century. Gardens bloom here year-round.

This lakeside town boasts a mini-Louvre. The **Villa Favorita,** *6976 Castagnola,* houses one of the finest private art collections in the world, collected by Baron Heinrich Thyssen-Bornemisza. Works from the 16th century through the end of the period of the French impressionists are included. Among the museum's many treasures are the painting of Henry VIII by Holbein and Monet's *Dejeuner sur l'Herbe.* (The collection has been deeded to the Prado in Madrid, so see it before it moves.)

Campione, located in the Swiss canton of Ticino but surrounded by Italy, is a good place for foreigners. No border controls are in effect, and no personal income or municipal tax is levied. Because Campione is such a popular region, it will take you years to get a residence permit. Furthermore, the demand for housing has made prices here skyrocket.

The best way to sample Switzerland

If you'd like to get a taste of Switzerland before actually moving there, consider arranging a three-week stay through a company called **Idyll Ltd.,** *P.O. Box 405, Media, PA 19063; (215)565-5242.*

Idyll's apartment-rental programs, called Untours, are great bargains and, because you stay with local Swiss hosts, give you a firsthand look at Swiss life. Programs to Switzerland cost $1,334 per person double occupancy, $1,206 per person four-person occupancy from May 31 through June 21; and $1,442 per person double occupancy, $1,314 per person four-person occupancy after June 21. These prices (which apply to the "Classic" program) include air fare to Zürich from New York or Boston, three-week apartment rentals, and one-month Swiss Holiday Cards, good for unlimited second-class travel on Switzerland's rail/bus/ship/tram network.

In addition, Untours include Idyll support services: pre-departure counseling, escort services, airport transfers, orientation sessions soon after your arrival in Switzerland, and two escorted sightseeing or cultural outings.

If you would rather arrange your own air fare, opt for Idyll's apartment-only rental program (called a "Custom" program). These programs are priced from $523 per person double occupancy, $402 per person four-person occupancy, including three-week apartment rentals and support services. You may add other features to these basic programs to tailor your stay to your exact preferences.

Although Idyll's host families are cordial and helpful, it's mutually understood that hosts are not expected to cart visitors around in cars, to arrange outings or sightseeing trips, or to tidy up apartments. Once settled in, you're on your own.

For more information

For more information on retirement in Switzerland and benefits for seniors, contact **Pro Senecute,** *Arnold-Boecklin-Str. 25, 4000 Basel 11,* or *Elsevier Sequoia, Box 851, 1001 Lausanne.*

For visa information, contact the **Embassy of Switzerland,** *2900 Cathedral Ave. N.W., Washington, DC 20008; (202)745-7937.* For general tourist information, call the embassy at *(202)745-7900.*

Chapter 18

Behind the Iron Curtain

"**I**ron Curtain." That just doesn't have an inviting sound. Yet some of the East bloc countries are lovely and inviting places for retirement. Yugoslavia offers miles of gorgeous coastline with hidden coves and quaint fishing villages. Romania's ancient spas are world-famous and renewing. Life in Czechoslovakia can be very cheap for an American retiree. Hungary's people have colorful traditions and love music. And Poland is filled with outdoor cafés and sidewalk artists, theater, film, and concerts.

Retirement on the other side of the Iron Curtain doesn't mean you have to defect. Nor do you have to be of East European descent, although most retirees to this area are. What you do have to do is apply for residency at the embassy of the country. Often acceptance involves getting an invitation from a friend or relative inside the country and proof that you can support yourself. Some countries are more inviting than others. Yugoslavia is quite open, while Poland is really only open to Americans of Polish descent. Hungary and Romania welcome immigrants, but aren't quite as used to the idea.

In most countries behind the proverbial curtain, it is much easier to retire if you were born there or if you have relatives still living there. However, this plus can turn into a minus in some cases. If you were born in an East bloc country, you may find that you are still considered a citizen of that country even if you are a naturalized U.S. citizen. This can be a problem if you ever want to leave. You may have to wait for long periods of time for exit papers.

A lesser problem you may face is the language. In this respect, too, Americans who hail from the area have an advantage. When we sought information at the various East European embassies, we found that few of the officials spoke good English, and obtaining necessary information was difficult. Hence the gaps in our knowledge. They were all extremely friendly, however. Persistence will get you what you need.

Retirement in Hungary

The Hungarian countryside is full of old palaces, medieval villages and towns, and elegant spas. The huge Lake Balaton is lined with resorts for swimming and sailing in summer and ice sailing in winter.

The settlers of Hungary came from the east, giving the country a colorful and slightly different atmosphere than the rest of Europe. The Magyar horsemen, as Attila the Hun and his tribesmen called themselves, came down into the wide Pannonian plain from Russia through a pass in the Carpathians. While he is a fearful memory in the rest of Europe, Attila is venerated in Hungary, where you can see statues of the warrior in public places. The Huns also settled in Finland, whose strange-sounding tongue is the only one related to the equally strange Hungarian.

The Huns left a legacy of great horses and dashing riders (*csikos*) that is still part of the Hungarian lifestyle, and a riding holiday is a superb way to see this country. The August Horse Show at Zichy Castle near Lake Balaton, with riders dressed in medieval costumes, is one of the best Hungarian horse shows.

Hungary is about the size of Indiana and home to about 10.5 million people.

Looking at Budapest

Budapest is a beautiful old city full of gypsy music. Hungarians are masters of the violin, and their love of music erupts in a number of music festivals throughout the year. Of special interest are the Gypsy Festival in February and the Summer Music Festival in August. A weekly musical event is the classical High Mass celebrated every Sunday morning in the 13th-century Matthias Church on **Castle Hill**, where kings Franz-Josef, Charles, and Matthias were crowned, as was Empress Maria Theresa.

The medieval palaces, villas, and inns on the narrow streets of Castle Hill house a number of fantastic old restaurants that serve some of Eastern Europe's best food. Not only is goulash a Hungarian specialty, but so are fish and wild game. Wine and beer cellars, coffee bars, and pastry shops are all part of the city's attraction. The best way to end a Budapest evening is with Danube caviar and cold Russian vodka, in the deep-red surroundings of an old-world cabaret. And sometime during the day you must have Hungary's two most famous wines—rich red Bulls Blood and sticky sweet Tokay.

Budapest is on the shores of the Danube and includes three islands and is crossed by eight bridges. The great river passes a string of medieval castles, churches, forts, and monuments on the Buda side. On the Pest side, it passes a huge neo-Gothic Parliament building, church domes and spires, Art Nouveau edifices, and modern hotels.

Once two separate cities, Buda and Pest were united in 1873.

Other Hungarian sights

Beyond Budapest is **Lake Balaton**, central Europe's largest lake. Along its shores are charming baroque towns and sunny vineyards. The lake is 50 miles long and as deep as 36 feet in some places. It is known for its sandy beaches, warm water (you can swim here from spring to late fall), resort hotels, and fine fishing. Sports of all kinds are popular on the lake, from swimming and sailing to horseback riding and ice skating. Sailing schools are located in Balatonfured, Siofolk, and Tihany. You can rent horses at riding schools in Tihany, Keszthely, Siofok, Nagyvazsony, Zamardi, and Szantod.

Lake Balaton served as a line of defense against the Turks for centuries. The remains of border castles can be seen in Tihany, Nagyvazsony, Szigliget, and Fonyod.

The most popular resorts are situated on the south shore of the lake, where the water is warmer and the beaches have a softer grade of sand. The north shore is relatively undiscovered and a good place to get away from the crowds. But the water is colder and the beaches aren't as nice.

Siofok, the largest town on the southern shore, is also the most crowded. If you would rather avoid the crowds, visit the small spa town of Balatonfured, on the northern shore of the lake. This hilly old town is covered with twisting streets. At the center of town is Gyogy Ter (Spa Square), where the waters of volcanic springs bubble under a pavilion. Also on the square is the Cardiac Hospital, where patients from all over the world come for treatment. Eleven medicinal springs reputedly good for the heart and the nerves can be found here.

You can bathe in a warm-water lake surrounded by rose-colored Egyptian lotus plants in Heviz, a town near Lake Balaton. Fed by thermal springs, the temperature of Heviz Lake varies from 82 degrees Fahrenheit to 100 degrees Fahrenheit. In cool weather, the warm lake steams, giving it a mysterious air. The waters of Lake Heviz are radioactive and said to be effective in curing locomotor, rheumatic, inflammatory, and articular diseases. The mud from the bottom of the lake also is therapeutic. It is dried and exported for mud packs. Cemeteries dating back to Roman times have been found along the lake.

The Great Plain, with its alien, Magyar atmosphere, is an area of small, low towns and villages almost lost amid the endless plain that stretches across the horizon. Debrecen, one of the largest and oldest towns in the Great Plain, has been inhabited since the Stone Age.

West of Debrecen is the Hortobagy, the most typical and romantic section of the plain.

Eger in the north and **Sopron** in the west are two of the loveliest baroque towns in Europe. Eger Castle was built after the devastating Tartar invasion. The cathedral was built in the 15th century. From 1596 to 1687, Eger was one of the most important Moslem outposts.

Hungary's heartland, where the Danube breaks through the Borzony and Visegrad mountains, has a chain of riverside spas, bare volcanic mountains, and limestone hills. Here, kings set up their residences and international forces met and fought. The region on the west bank is the most interesting. Be sure to visit three charming towns: Szentendre, Visegrad, and Esztergom.

Northern Hungary has low mountains crowned with castles. The state game reserve is home to herds of deer, wild boar, eagles, and falcons. Skiers play here in the winter. And grapevines flourish. Some villages are inhabited by people who still wear Hungarian national costume. Holloko is the most picturesque.

Western Hungary has more Roman remains than the rest of the country. Near the Austrian border, in the town of **Gyor,** a Roman fortress still watches over the hills. The Gyor cathedral's foundations go back to 11th century, and the Hedervary chapel contains a masterpiece of medieval art, the reliquary of King St. Ladislaw (1040-1095).

How to go about it

According to officials at the Hungarian Embassy, about 50 American families of Hungarian origin return to Hungary each year. Retirement there is quite common. To do so, first apply for admission to return through the Hungarian Embassy. If permission is granted, and it generally is, retirees can live there permanently. The process can take as long as four months. You must have guaranteed lodgings before permission is granted.

Roughly the same conditions apply to Americans who are not of Hungarian descent. But officials say only one or two such cases come across their desks every few years. If you do not have Hungarian relatives, you must apply for a permanent visa through the Hungarian Embassy. Again, you must have pre-arranged, guaranteed lodging before permission will be granted. And you must show your birth certificate and papers proving citizenship.

Immigration details

In addition to a passport, you must have a visa to enter Hungary. You can get an overnight tourist visa. If you arrive by air or car, you can obtain tourist visas at Ferihegy Airport or at the border; otherwise, you should apply to the Hungarian Consulate in your country or to an accredited travel agent at least 14 days before you wish to go to Hungary. To apply, you need two recent passport photos, a passport, a completed application form with copy, $15, and a self-addressed envelope stamped for certified mail with postage stamps—no meter imprints. The visa will be issued within 48 hours. Your passport must be valid for nine months after the date of entry. Visas are valid for six months for a stay of no more than 30 days.

Visas can be extended by applying to the **KEOKH (Aliens' Registration Office)** in Budapest at *Nepkoztarsasag Ut. 93,* or at county and district police headquarters. All visitors must register with the police. If you stay at a hotel, the hotel will do this for you. If you stay at a private home booked through a travel agency, the travel agent will see to the registration.

If you are a naturalized U.S. citizen of Hungarian origin, use caution. Unless the Hungarian government has accepted your application for renunciation of citizenship, it will consider you a Hungarian citizen. Hungarian officials usually will issue visitor visas in the U.S. passports of dual nationals. Occasionally, you will be asked to use Hungarian documentation to visit. If this happens, make sure the documentation will not prevent your departure.

A veterinary certificate is requested for pets.

If you plan to drive in Hungary, you will need an international drivers license.

For more information, contact the **Embassy of the Hungarian People's Republic, Consular Section,** *3910 Shoemaker St. N.W., Washington, DC 20008; (202)362-6769,* or the **Consulate General,** *8 E. 75th St., New York, NY 10021; (212)879-4126* or *(212)879-4127.*

Finding a home

Although foreigners cannot buy Hungarian real estate, they can lease property for 30 years—a long time if you are retirement age.

Hungary is one of the few East European countries with a flourishing private sector in real estate. The old town of Pest is full of 17th- and 18th-century townhouses that are being restored. The evidence of gentrification is exactly as you would expect. The old brass door fixtures are brightly polished, the wooden trim and doors stripped and restored, the stucco repainted in Williamsburg colors, and the wrought iron replaced. If you peek into the windows you see antique furniture, Oriental rugs, modern art, and entire walls full of books. Except that the books are in Magyar, you might be in Georgetown or Beacon Hill, Greenwich Village or Telegraph Hill.

Other Hungarians are saving their forints to restore weekend cottages around the Danube Bend, the castle- and crag-filled area where the river cuts its way through the mountains. From Friday afternoon to Sunday night, the roads are packed with cars, many bearing great slabs of plywood, evidence that do-it-yourself has come to Hungary. And Danube Bend home owners are protesting the pollution from a power plant across the river in Czechoslovakia that threatens their weekend retreats.

For years, Hungary's capitalistic neighbors from Austria led the Magyar property boom. The drive from Vienna to the picturesque medieval village of Sopron and the southern shore of Ferto Lake is shorter than to the more expensive Vienna Woods, where many Viennese have their weekend cottages.

One Hungarian real estate company that caters to foreign residents is **Pal Hessky of Immobilia,** *Szamuely Utca 38, H-1093 Budapest; (36-1)171255.*

In Hungary, newspapers do not advertise real estate. The only way to find out what is available is through the Vienna papers (which carry ads for Hungary) or a real estate agent.

Houses and apartments can be rented through the **General Banking and Trust Co.,** *Fzamuely 38, Budapest.* (The General Banking and Trust Co. also provides health insurance that is inexpensive compared to U.S. insurance.)

The cost of living

The cost of living in Hungary is low by American standards. You can rent an apartment for $200 to $800 per month. Dinner in an average restaurant costs between $8 and $10. And public transportation costs next to nothing.

Money matters

Exchange your dollars for forints at IBUSZ offices (the Hungarian National Tourist Office), banks, or hotels. Don't change too much at one time; Hungarian currency is non-convertible, so you cannot take it out of the country. Save your exchange receipts; customs may want to see them to make sure you haven't changed money on the black market. And don't depend on credit cards. Only the top hotels and IBUSZ shops accept them.

Language problem

Few Hungarians speak English. German, not English, is the most

384

common second language. So, if you plan to live there, we recommend you learn Hungarian, or at least German.

Don'ts

Don't drive even after only one drink. Hungary has a 0%-alcohol driving law.

Don't take pictures of people in uniform or of the buildings they occupy. It's against the law.

Traveling in Hungary

Most foreign travel to Hungary is handled by the offices of IBUSZ. It has many branches in Budapest, including desks in all major hotels. However, the overseas offices of IBUSZ don't actually arrange travel to Hungary. This can only be done by a travel agent accredited by the IBUSZ. These include major travel agents such as American Express and Maupintour. Agents can also make hotel reservations and other travel arrangements. Contact **IBUSZ,** *1 Park Plaza, Fort Lee, New Jersey, 07024; (201)592-8585.*

May to September is the best time to travel in Hungary, although June, July, and August are hot and crowded. The Budapest International Fair takes place in May and September. There are many music festivals, including: the Beethoven Memorial Concerts at Martonvasar, in southwest Budapest, in June and July; the Haydn Concerts at Fertod, in Western Hungary; and the Open-Air Opera and Drama Festival of Szeged, which runs from late July to late August. Budapest Musical Weeks are a traditional attraction in early autumn. Other special events include the Spring Festival Week in Budapest in March, the Film Festival in May and June, the Bartok Choral Festival in July, and the Chamber Music Festival.

Hotels

There can be a shortage of hotels in the summer in Budapest. Make a reservation ahead of time. If you arrive without reservations, the IBUSZ office at *Petofi Ter 3* or the tourist office at Ferihegy Airport will try to help you.

A few nice hotels are:

•**Thermal Hotel,** *Margitsziget, Budapest 1138; tel. (36-1)32-11-00* or *(36-1)11-10-00.* This luxury spa-hotel on Margaret Island in the middle of the Danube, has 206 rooms, a thermal swimming pool, tennis courts, riding trails, medieval ruins, and medicinal baths good for rheumatic ailments. Rooms are 7,000 forints per night;

•**Atrium-Hyatt,** *Roosevelt Ter 2, Budapest V; tel. (36-1)383-000;*

•**Budapest Hilton,** *Hess Andras Ter 1-3, Budapest I; tel. (36-1)885-3500;*

•**Duna-Intercontinental,** *Apaczai Csere Janos Utca 4, Budapest V; tel. (36-1)175-122;* and

•**Hotel Gellert,** *Szent Gellert ter 1,* has radioactive pools in mosaic-decorated Art Deco halls. Guests are supplied with thick bathrobes.

Hotel reservations can be made through any U.S. travel agency or at the following Hungarian travel agencies:

•**Malev Hungarian Airlines,** *630 Fifth Ave., Suite 900, New York, NY 10111; (212)757-6480;*

•**IBUSZ Hungarian Travel Bureau,** *1 Parker Plaza, 400 Kelby St., Suite 1104, Fort Lee, New Jersey 07024; (201)592-8585;* and

•**Hungarian Hotels Sales Office,** *6033 W. Century Blvd., Suite 670, Los Angeles, CA 90045; (213)649-5960.*

Hungarian spas

There are 447 curative and thermal springs registered in Hungary; 120 of them in Budapest. Thirty-two baths have been built over various springs in the city, and the Ministry of Health has given 10 of them the status of spas.

The cost of two or three weeks of therapeutic treatment for ailments ranging from rheumatism and gout to intestinal, respiratory, and gynecological complaints is available for a fraction of the cost of a visit to a Western spa. A stay at the Thermal Hotel, for instance, costs about 3,600 forints per night for a double.

Hungarian spas are not always as luxurious or pristine as those elsewhere in Europe, but they are wonderful nonetheless. The mineral waters that bubble up from beneath Budapest are genuine. This is where the ancient Romans "took the cure."

The Gellert and Thermal hotels (described above) are the best of the baths. But **Rudas,** *Dobrentei Ter 9, Budapest,* has baths dating back to the 16th-century occupation by the Turks. Hungary's intelligencia brainstorms here. Individual sunken marble baths are available to women.

One expat's Hungarian sojourn

Jane Butler, an American expat who teaches gymnastics in Hungary, describes Sopron, her adopted home.

The medieval town of **Sopron** is one of the few remaining places where you can see old Europe without modern distractions. Its historic buildings are well-preserved, horses and carriages still bring produce to market, and the squares and monuments are virtually free of crowds. Wide cobblestoned streets curve around ancient Roman walls. Each of the charming miniature medieval and Renaissance houses is different. Some have intricate stone carvings or niches that house figurines of saints. Some are colorfully painted. Others are so chipped away that you can see early Gothic interiors peeking through Renaissance exteriors. Great Gothic churches and onion-domed towers loom in the background.

The streets are peaceful. Old women in black kerchiefs sit in arcaded archways making white lace. Sometimes Hungarian folk music wafts through open windows.

The town holds other delights. At Fertorakos, about six miles from town, you can attend Franz Liszt concerts (he lived here) in a quarry. At the Esterhazy Palace in Fertod, about 16 miles away, you can listen to a Haydn symphony (Haydn was once composer-in-residence at the palace). Or you can follow the locals to the Fedett Uszoda for a swim, a medicinal bath, a sauna, and a massage.

Visit the churches on Gazda, Bécsi, Balfi, Bástya, and Pozsonyi utcas. Here and around Fötér, streets lead to the remains of an ancient Roman city; a 13th-century synagogue, *Uj utca 22*; an eerie Gothic graveyard; and a royal residence, *Fötér 8.*

Sopron's most visible landmark is Tuztorony, the Fire and Lookout Tower, built during the 16th and 17th centuries to protect the town from future destruction. Across from the tower is the **Patika Museum,** *Fötér 2,* which originally was an apothecary shop set up to battle epidemics.

Nearly everything in Sopron is a museum or an architectural landmark. To see the highlights, walk around Fötér and the streets and squares that lead to it, such as Uj, St. Gyuorgy, Templom, and Kolostor utcas and Orsolya tér.

The Fire and Lookout Tower is a good place to begin your tour. If you walk beneath the arch, you'll see to your left the big key to the city and to your right the remains of an ancient onion-domed Roman forum. Climb the 124 narrow winding stairs for a view of the old city. **Storno Ház,** *Fötér 8,* next door, is the late Renaissance-baroque palace where Liszt lived. **Fabricus Ház,** *Fötér 6,* contains ancient Roman statues and inscriptions.

In general, Sopron's museums are small and centrally located. You may find yourself the only visitor and be offered a personal tour. Usually, you must wear giant felt slippers so you don't mar the wooden parquet floors. Admission is nominal and often includes English-language guidebooks.

Just outside town is the Lövérek region, which borders the eastern foothills of Austria. In the Lövérek hills, you'll see vineyards and charming modern houses. You'll even catch a glimpse of Austria. Perhaps Sopron's biggest surprise is Taródi Var (the Hobby Castle), located in the Felso Lövérek region. The castle is not on the map, but if you follow Hársfa sor and Csalogány Köz, you'll find it. It looks like a medieval fortress. Ferocious stone animals carved into tablets flank the portals, a large chained wrecking ball hangs overhead, and chunks of the building have been lopped off. The castle even has an old Turkish bath that appears to have seen centuries of use—but hasn't. The entire complex was built in the 1950s by a man in his spare time. He's there today, still working on the place.

Medical care in Sopron

If you're thrown off a crazy horse in Sopron (because it thinks whoa sounds like the Hungarian word Jö, which means "run faster"— which is what happened to me), or if any other mishap or emergency puts you in the *kurház* (hospital), the state will pay the bill.

My experience with Hungarian bedside manner began the instant I was wheeled into the emergency room. The doctor fell head over heels in love with me. I think it had something to do with my tight riding breeches. The affair went on until I and his wife and children found out about each other.

If you need prescriptions (and even if you don't), visit **Gyógyszertár,** *Ujtelek utca 55.* This perfectly preserved apothecary shop looks exactly as it did 100 years ago. Although the remedies it dispenses have changed since then, the prices are still from another era. A bottle of multivitamins, for example costs about a dime.

Shopping in Sopron

Most of the shops are located on Lenin Körút. Walk all the way around this circle, or you'll miss some of the special little shops. Other stores are located on Uj utca and Kolostor utca in the heart of the old town.

Kézi Munka, *Lenin Krt. 36,* carries colorful hand-embroidered linens, doilies, and blouses at prices much better than at Intourist shops. **Antikuárium,** *St. György utca 14,* has Sopron's largest selection of Liszt, Bartok, and gypsy-music records, as well as old books. **Uveg Porcelan,** *Lenin Krt. 10,* sells handmade ceramics, metal objects, and fur-covered hunting canteens. **Labas Ház,** *Orsovla tér 5,* specializes in antique reproductions. The prices are cheap, cheap, cheap.

Kristaly, *Ogabona tér 1,* is simply *the* place to go for crystal.
Ikva Aruház, *Arpad utca,* off Lenin Körút, is Sopron's biggest
department store. It's the place to go for rugs, animal skins, furs, and
woolen items. **Herbaria,** *Lenin Krt. 87,* is the health-and-beauty
haven. Here you'll find Helena D youth cream, bath products, herb
teas, and granola.

Sopron hotels
Even top-class hotels in Sopron are inexpensive (and plain) by
Western standards.

•**Hotel Lövér,** *Varisi utca 4, Sopron; tel. (36-99)11-061,* is the
best in town. It has a beautiful lobby, an indoor pool, a sauna, a café,
and a nightclub.

•**Hotel Palatinus,** *Uj utca 23, Sopron; tel. (36-99)11-395,* is a
pleasant hotel in the heart of town. Rates are about $40 for a double
room; $26 for a single.

•**IBUSZ,** *Lenin Krt. 41, Sopron; tel. (36-99)13-281,* can place
you in private rooms with local families for about $10 per night.

Chowing down
Produce in Sopron is not always fresh, and menus are limited, but
the food is always inexpensive. Among Hungary's first-class restaurants (where full-course dinners with wine cost $10 to $15), Hotel
Lövér, address above, offers light entrées and game specialties. Hotel
Palatinus (address above), serves roast chicken, caviar, and goose
liver paté. It has the best selection of vegetables and salads. Prices are
lower than at Hotel Lövér.

To eat more cheaply, but still well, try **Bécsi Kapu,** *Bécsi utca 6,*
a cozy underground wine cellar. **Fenyves Etterem,** *Szabadsag Korut,*
is a low-priced and attractive place. Omelets, the best in town, cost 50
cents, as do bowls of soup large enough for two.

For more information
•**Embassy of the Hungarian Peoples' Republic,** *3910
Shoemaker St. N.W., Washington, DC 20008; (202)362-6730;* visa
section *(202)362-6769;*

•**Hungarian Consulate General,** *8 E. 75th St., New York, NY
10021; (212)879-4125;*

•**Hungarian Travel Bureau (IBUSZ),** *1 Parker Plaza, 400
Kelby St., Suite 1104, Fort Lee, NJ 07024; (201)592-8885* or
(212)582-7412.

•**U.S. Embassy,** *V. Szabadsag Ter 12, Budapest; tel. (36-1)329-*

375. Mailing address: **U.S. Embassy Budapest,** *APO New York 09213*.

Retirement in Yugoslavia

Yugoslavia is a beautiful country that has a coastline as lovely as Greece. It also has Byzantine treasures, Turkish minarets, and medieval fortresses. It lies between the East and the West. It has dramatic mountains, lovely beaches, tiny islands, and friendly people.

Retirement here offers beautiful beaches, sunny weather, inexpensive living, and fellow Westerners for company. Yugoslavia is flooded by tourists. While its population is 22 million, it hosts 25-million visitors a year.

Yugoslavia has a mountainous interior, the fabled Dalmatian coast along the Adriatic Sea, lovely lake Slovenia, and the flat plains of Vojvodina. Parts of Yugoslavia are still undeveloped, but its principal cities have well-dressed residents, impressive buildings, and well-stocked shops.

Yugoslavia is a nonaligned communist country that is considerably more open and Westernized than the other countries of Eastern Europe. Yugoslavs are free to travel and to exhibit Western tastes. They own cars, televisions, and household appliances.

There are six republics within Yugoslavia: Serbia, Croatia, Bosnia-Hercegovina, Slovenia, Montenegro, and Macedonia. Within the republics are four major Slavic nationalities. There are 220 lakes and 73,500 miles of rivers and streams. The coastline stretches 390 miles and three-quarters of the land is mountainous. Forests cover 36% of the land. Peruccia, which lies in a wilderness area between Bosnia and Montenegro, is Europe's last virgin forest. Animal life is abundant, including bear, deer, antelope, and all sorts of fish.

Weather in Yugoslavia is similar to that in Washington, DC (but less humid), cold in winter, hot in summer. Along the coast it is warmer. Temperatures range from 55 degrees Fahrenheit in winter to 100 degrees Fahrenheit in the summer.

Where to live?

One of the most beautiful retirement spots is **Lake Ohrid**, a 4-million-year-old lake in southwest Yugoslavia. It is home to fish that exist nowhere else in the world. Over 40 Byzantine churches and several fine beaches grace its shores. Yugotours brings senior citizens on tour here for very reasonable rates.

Yugoslavia's dramatic **Adriatic Coast** would make an attractive retirement home. Cliffs, islands, and coves break the shoreline. Coastal cities and towns are linked by a complex network of trains, buses, and ferries. Split and Dubrovnik are beautiful, historic towns. Korcula, Hvar, Losinj and Pag are secluded and lovely.

Built in A.D. 305, **Split** originally was the palace of a Roman emperor. Over the centuries, local residents moved into the palace's many rooms, embellishing them with Romanesque and Gothic touches. The rectangular walls of the old Roman town still exist. The palace halls are now streets and its rooms are houses.

Dubrovnik, a seventh-century coastal town, has lovely (but crowded) beaches and striking architecture. During the Dubrovnik Festival in July and August, it is difficult to get a room. This city was founded in the seventh century. South of Dubrovnik is the **Republic of Montenegro**, which has wonderful swimming areas. The 1,200-meter-deep Tara Canyon draws hikers and rafters.

Slovenia combines the natural beauty of Austria and the beaches of Italy. You can swim in the Adriatic and hike in the Julian Alps on the same day. Mountaineers climb Mt. Triglav, the country's highest peak. Ljubljana, a modern, industrial city, is a gateway to the mountains. Bled is another good base for exploring. During the winter there are splendid ski resorts: Zatrnik, Vogel, and Pokljuka.

Belgrade, the capital of Yugoslavia, makes a good home for culture lovers. Located at the confluence of the Sava and Danube rivers, it has been a settlement since the time of the Celts in the fourth century B.C. However, few monuments built before the 18th century have survived the region's many wars. The elegantly restored old quarter mixes nicely with the modern structures in Belgrade. Uphill from the River Sava is the Stari Grad (Old City). At the other end of Kneza Mihaila, the main street, is Kalemegdan, a fortress from which Romans, Serbs, and Turks controlled the confluence of the Sava and the Danube.

Zagreb, the center of Croatia and Yugoslavia's second-largest city, has a beautiful medieval old town as well as institutional apartment complexes. The Stari Grad has narrow cobblestoned streets leading past the cathedral and several other churches and museums. The neighborhood cafés are inviting.

A series of lakes and waterfalls can be enjoyed in the **Plitvice Lakes National Park**, where a network of paths lead through the thick forests.

How to go about it

American citizens can visit Yugoslavia for one year on a standard visa, as long as they leave every three months. If you wish to stay longer, your visa can be prolonged for as long as you need if you go to the police headquarters or the Secretary of the Interior of the province in which you decide to live. According to embassy officials, "This is not a problem."

For more information on immigration, contact the **Embassy of Yugoslavia,** *2410 California St. N.W., Washington, DC 20008; (202)462-6566;* or the **Consulate General,** *767 Third Ave., New York, NY 10022; (212)838-2300.*

Dual nationality

Yugoslavia does not recognize dual nationality. This means that all naturalized U.S. citizens of Yugoslav origin who have not renounced their Yugoslav citizenship are considered to be citizens of Yugoslavia. If taken into custody by Yugoslav authorities, they may be denied the opportunity to communicate with U.S. officials.

U.S. citizens of Yugoslav origin who wish to renounce their Yugoslav citizenship can get application forms from the Yugoslav Embassy in Washington, DC, or at Yugoslav consulates in New York, Cleveland, Pittsburgh, Chicago, or San Francisco.

Finding a home

Foreign purchase of property is illegal in Yugoslavia—with one exception: Americans. Under an old bilateral treaty, Americans are the only foreigners allowed to buy real estate in the country. However, Yugoslavia is very decentralized, and the powerful local communities tend not to be aware of the U.S. exception. As a result, buyers run into considerable red tape and delays.

If you do manage to convince local authorities that you can, indeed, buy (a difficult task), you will get a real bargain. Yugoslavia has world-scale tourist housing in sites that match the best of the French Riviera (along the Dalmatian, or west, coast, for example). One American spent two years seeking out a house on the island of Krk on the north part of the Croatian coast and then another seven months of back and forth while officials tried to determine his legal right to enforce the contract he had signed with the seller. But he has not regretted it since.

The U.S. consul-general in Zaghreb (for the coast) or the U.S. Embassy in Belgrade are the best sources to contact when you begin looking for properties. They can provide you with lists of lawyers. (In Yugoslavia, lawyers act as real estate agents.)

Rentals are also very inexpensive. To find an apartment or house, examine local newspapers. A two-bedroom apartment can be rented for $250 to $300 a month. A house in Belgrade can be rented for $400 to $500 a month.

Cost of living

The cost of living is low in Yugoslavia—you can easily live on $300 to $400 a month.

Your pension can be sent to a Yugoslavian bank, where you can keep it in U.S. or Yugoslavian money. Yugoslavian banks with branches in New York City include Yugobanka, Ljublyanska Banka, and Beobanka. The easiest to deal with is **LBS Bank,** *101 E. 52nd St., 30th Floor, New York, NY 10022; (212)980-8600,* an U.S.-registered bank controlled by Ljublyanska Banka. Each of Yugoslavia's provinces has its own bank and there are many smaller banks.

The Yugoslavian currency is the dinar. Travelers may import 1,400 dinars or export 1,500 dinars.

Health questions

Medical care is free for Yugoslavians, but Americans have to pay a small fee for medical insurance. To apply, go to the officials of the province where you wish to live.

For more information

•**Embassy of Yugoslavia,** *2410 California St. N.W., Washington, DC 20008; (202)462-6566;*

•**Yugoslav State Tourist Office,** *Suite 280, 630 Fifth Ave., New York, NY 10111; (212)757-2801;*

•**U.S. Embassy,** *Kneza Milosa 50, Belgrade; tel. (38-11)645-655;* mailing address: **U.S. Consulate General (BEG),** *APO New York 09213;* and

•**Yugoslav Airlines;** *(800)752-6528.*

Retirement in Romania

Romania's Carpathian mountains, the Black Sea, and the great Danube River form a natural fortress that protected Roman culture and allowed it to survive here long after the Roman empire retreated to Italy. The culture left by the Romans included their love of making good wine. Romania abounds with grape vineyards that have produced gold medal winners in international wine competitions. The Romans also left a lot of ruins, including a number of baths at the sites of many of Romania's famous mineral springs.

The beauty, culture, and the spas in Romania provide a secret, little-known retirement haven for the adventurous American. Adventurous is the key word, however. Romania is still closed to Westerners, and the standard of living is very low. Gasoline, which is purchased with coupons, is sometimes unavailable. And basic consumer goods are limited. During the winter, hotels rooms are often not heated.

What's it like there?

The lovely Carpathians guard the lifestyle of another age, where peasants still dress in medieval embroidered waistcoats and blouses, and wear soft moccasins secured to their legs by crisscrossed leather thongs. Here you'll find the best of the country's ornately carved wooden houses and old churches. Wood carving, in fact, is a Romanian specialty, along with the ancient folk arts of weaving and embroidery.

If Count Dracula is any indication, Romania extends a lifetime by centuries. Near the center of Transylvania, not far from Brasov, lies the castle of "Dracula" himself. The legendary vampire is based on an equally horrifying human being, Vlad the Impaler, who frightened off invading Turks by impaling hundreds of his own countrymen on tall stakes along the route of the enemy's march. It was a signal that he'd stop at nothing to fend them off.

While the legend of Dracula is frightening, his castle is charming. **Transylvania** has a fairytale prettiness with its many castles and rolling hills.

Brasov, an ancient city in Transylvania, preserves much of its medieval charm. This industrial city has famous old churches and is a good base for exploring the Carpathians and the countryside.

Nearby **Sibui** is an exquisite little medieval town. Not too far away, at the top of the mountain pass leading to Bucharest, is **Predeal**, the site of a posh ski resort.

Romania's other two provinces, **Walachia** and **Moldavia**, are just as charming, full of old castles, monasteries, and cheery villages.

Bucharest, Romania's 500-year-old capital, has broad, café-lined boulevards, restaurants, parks, lakes, monuments, dozens of museums, opera, ballet, and the Bucharest Philharmonic Orchestra. A major earthquake in 1977 killed more than 1,300 people and caused extensive damage to housing and industry. People, too, have caused havoc in Bucharest. The current regime, in the name of President Nicolae Ceausescu, is deliberately tearing down old buildings and monuments.

Constanta, the largest Romanian port, is part of the Romanian

Riviera. Located on the sunny Black Sea Coast, it contains vestiges of the Greeks, Romans, and Byzantines. It also has an elegant casino.

Facts and figures

Covering an area of 91,700 square miles, Romania is almost as big as the state of Oregon. Its borders Hungary, Yugoslavia, Bulgaria, and the Soviet Union.

Romania resembles a huge amphitheater. The lofty peaks of the Carpathians rise more than 8,240 feet around the Transylvanian plateau. The southern foothills slope gently toward the plains, which spread toward the Black Sea and the Danube. The Black Sea Coast stretches for 152 sandy miles.

The population of over 22 million speaks the Romanian language, a Romance language related to French and Italian. But you can get along without speaking Romanian.

How to retire there

It is easiest to retire in Romania if you are invited to live there by a Romanian citizen, or if you were born there. In order to get permission to immigrate, you must have arranged a place to live. Some U.S. citizens of Romanian origin do move back to the home of their forefathers. For more information, contact the **Romanian Embassy,** *(202)232-4747*.

Cautions

U.S. citizens of Romanian origin naturalized after Jan. 14, 1952, are still considered Romanian citizens by the Romanian government. It is important to discuss your legal status in Romania very carefully with a Romanian consular official when applying for a visa.

Attempts to bring in religious literature often leads to confiscation of the literature and denial of entry. Romanian officials say it is okay to bring in religious books for personal use but not to sell.

Romanians are prohibited by law from having foreigners, except for immediate relatives, spend the night in their homes. You are advised to respect this law.

Cost of living

The cost of living in Romania is dirt cheap. A kilo of potatoes, for example, costs 20 cents. Meat costs about $3 a kilo. Good seats at the opera cost less than $5, theater tickets can be as low as $2. You can rent an apartment there for about $30 to $33 a month. An average apartment can be purchased for approximately $6,500. To locate an apartment, contact **I.C.E. Terra,** *Bvdv Gheorghe Gheorghiu-Dej 16, Bucharest; tel. (40-0)15-30-63* or *(40-0)15-84-83.* Heating is unreliable; so is electricity.

Banking
Manufacturers Hanover Bank and Trust is an American bank with branches in Romania. It offers a convenient way to transfer pension funds to Romania.

Medical care
While medical care is free in Romania, non-citizens must purchase insurance. Contact the Ministry of Health (Ministerul Sanatatii) in Bucharest for information. Medical costs are cheap.

Romania's fountain of youth
Romania has a government-sponsored **National Institute of Geriatrics and Gerontology,** famous around the world for its wonder drug Gerovital H3, claimed to be effective in treating the problems of aging.

The Institute was founded in Bucharest in 1952 by cardiologist Dr. Ana Aslan. In what may be proof of the effectiveness of her discoveries, Dr. Aslan, now in her 80s, still directs the worked of the Institute and several other geriatric treatment centers around Romania.

Dr. Aslan's wonder drug Gerovital has been licensed by the Romanian government and is sold by prescription throughout the country. Among the afflictions it's claimed to help are memory loss, deafness, poor eyesight, skin diseases, ulcers, asthma, rheumatism, and Parkinson's disease.

The drug is administered by injection, pill, or liquid. The cold cream supposedly diminishes wrinkles, dryness, and age spots; the hair lotion is believed to stimulate hair growth, renew hair color, and reduce dandruff. Cosmetic treatment is one of the more popular programs at Dr. Aslan's spas.

Wonder drug or not, a visit to one of Dr. Aslan's health spas is likely to make you feel a lot better by virtue of the relaxing treatment you'll get in the midst of lovely surroundings. The regimen includes galvanic baths, Scottish showers, underwater massages, swimming, and saunas.

Each patient's regimen is tailored to his or her own medical needs, with an individual diet and exercise program. Most of Dr. Aslan's spa guests are over 40, but others are welcome. She recommends an early visit to delay the effects of old age.

Dr. Aslan's main treatment center is the luxurious **Flora Hotel,** *1 Polgrafiei Blvd., Bucharest.* You can arrange a visit if you call a day in advance. Or, book a two- or three-week stay through the Romanian tour agent, **Health Pleasure Tours, Inc.,** *(212)586-1986* , in New York, or **International Tours and Travel,** *(219)255-7272,* in Mishawaka, IN. Two weeks is the recommended minimum stay.

After your treatment you'll be given detailed instructions on how to continue your cure at home. The spa staff speaks English and a number of European languages. If Gerovital is part of your regimen, the Romanian government will allow you to export a two-years' supply (about $100). However, the U.S. government has not approved it for import into this country.

Other gerontology spas include **Savota Spa,** in the center of Transylvania on a salt-water lake surrounded by an ancient forest; the old **Roman Baile** and **Calimanesti-Caciulata Spas** in the Carpathians; and **Eforie Nord** on the Black Sea.

Rates at a spa stay are based on double occupancy and include full board. A stay at the Flora Hotel is $820 to $1,090 for two weeks in the low season; $1,435 to $1,554 for three weeks in the high season (June 15 to Sept. 15). Single supplements are $175 to $285. Stays at other spas begin as low as $545 for two weeks. Gerovital treatments are optional and require an additional supplement of $235 to $350.

Total packages with air fare from New York via TAROM Romanian Airlines are $1,652 to $2,198. Contact the **Romanian National Tourist Office,** *573 Third Ave., New York, NY 10016* for its brochure on spa packages.

Tourist information

Tritour offers three-day tours of Romania for $98 per person. Tours are arranged by the **National Tourist Office,** *573 Third Ave., New York, NY 10016, (212)697-6971.* Five-day tours are $150; seven-day tours are $210.

Tourist or transit visas are granted upon request at border crossings, without prior formalities or applications. To get one in advance, contact the **Romanian Consular Office,** *1607 23rd St. N.W., Washington, DC 20008.*

A minimum exchange of $10 per person per day of stay is required from travelers without pre-paid arrangements. This minimum exchange must be made at points of entry. Tourists entering Romania individually or in groups with pre-paid arrangements for the duration of their stay are exempt from mandatory exchange.

Gifts brought into the country should not exceed the value of

2,000 lei. Tourists may take out of the country goods purchased with the currency exchanged upon entry plus presents totaling 1000 lei. Works of art, and books of documentary, scientific, or artistic value can only be taken out with a "permitted for export" certificate issued by the shop that sold them.

Romanian Airlines, TAROM, provides direct connections to Romania from many world capitals. Pan Am and TAROM operate direct flights between New York and Bucharest.

For more information
•**Embassy of Romania,** *1607 23rd St. N.W., Washington, DC 20008; (202)232-4747;*

•**Romanian National Tourist Office,** *573 Third Ave., New York, NY 10016; (212)697-6971;* and

•**U.S. Embassy,** *Strada Tudor Arghezi 7-9, Bucharest; tel. (40-0)10-40-40;* mailing address: **U.S. Consulate General (BUCH),** *APO New York 09213.*

Retirement in Czechoslovakia

Czechoslovakia boasts one of the most beautiful cities in Europe—Prague. And if you are a snow-lover, this country has one of the most dazzling winters in the world. The snow-covered Tatras mountains look like crystal artworks laced in ice. For city-lovers and skiers, Czechoslovakia could make a fabulous retirement home.

Czechoslovakia is the sophisticate of Eastern Europe. Prague, filled with elegant palaces and spires, is one of the world's most romantic cities. It was made for walking and is particularly lovely just before dark, when its antique tint turns gold. It is prettiest in spring, when trees blossom and parks and palaces are filled with music.

Dubbed "the conservatory of Europe" in the 18th century, Prague still resounds with concerts and music recitals. The Prague Spring Music Festival is the most famous event in a national calendar filled with concerts. The National Theater produces opera, ballet, and drama. Prague has many theaters, all well-attended. The Czech Philharmonic Orchestra has a worldwide reputation. And the city has many other excellent musical organizations.

Prague residents take refuge in cozy medieval wine and beer cellars during the winter. In the summer, they relax in outdoor cafés. Its cuisine, like everything else in Czechoslovakia, is equally influenced by both the Slavs to the east and the Germans and Austrians to the west. The national drink is Pilsen, claimed by many to be the best beer in the world.

The countryside is just as wonderful, with castles, palaces, churches, and medieval towns. Bohemia is full of elegant spas, while Slovakia has some of the most spectacular scenery in Europe.

There are first-class skiing conditions in many parts of Czechoslovakia. The best resorts are Spindleruv Mlyn in the Krkonose (Giant Mountains) of northeast Bohemia and Strbske Pleso, Stary Smokovec, and Tatranska Lomnica in the High Tatras.

How to retire there

In order to retire in Czechoslovakia, you must first find a place to live there and then apply for permanent residence at the **Embassy of Czechoslovakia,** *3900 Linnean Ave. N.W., Washington, DC 20008; (202)363-6308.* Your Czechoslovakian address must be indicated on the application.

The easiest way to go about retiring in Czechoslovakia is to get the help of relatives who live there, if you are lucky enough to have any. If your relatives are willing to guarantee their dwelling for a certain period of time, this will do.

The local government, known as the National Committee, can also help with housing and medical insurance.

Real estate is not sold through private real estate agents. Law offices handle property. Two that might help are: **Advokatni Poradna CI,** *Narodnitr 32, Prague 1 11666;* and **Advokatni Poradna CI,** *Zahradnicka 6, Bratislava 81617.*

Prague has one bank where you can have an account in foreign currency: **Zivnostenska Banka,** *P.O. Box 412, Na Prikope 20, 113 80 Praha 1.* Most other banks require you to change your dollars into Tuzex bonds or Czech currency. Bonds allow you to shop at Tuzex stores, which sell the best quality goods. You probably will prefer the bonds, since they can be exchanged on the street for about six times the official rate. According to officials at the Czechoslovak Embassy, exchanging Tuzex bonds is not illegal as long as you received the bonds from one of the Czechoslovak banks. But it could be construed as illegal if the transactions are made for the purposes of speculation.

Cautionary note

Czechoslovak regulations forbid the import and export of materials that are "directed against the interests of the Czechoslovak Socialist Republic or other socialist countries." Citing these regulations, authorities have in the past confiscated printed and recorded materials critical of Czechoslovakia as well as religious publications and tapes.

If you carry religious items, expect to be searched thoroughly when entering or leaving Czechoslovakia. Proselytizing denominations, such as Jehovah's Witnesses and Mormons, are banned outright and their materials will be seized. Persons attempting to conceal such materials have been arrested and imprisoned upon entering or exiting the country.

Former Czechoslovak citizens should also be cautious. According to a bilateral treaty, a Czechoslovak citizen naturalized in the United States automatically loses his Czechoslovak citizenship upon becoming a U.S. citizen. However, this is not true for Czechoslovak nationals naturalized in the United States between Sept. 17, 1938, and May 7, 1957, a period not covered by treaty. Czechoslovak nationals naturalized during that period are considered dual nationals.

This is danger because dual nationals will be treated as Czechoslovak citizens, which limits the ability of U.S. officials to help if there are problems. In order to leave again, Czechoslovak citizens must be granted emigration passports, a time consuming process. And under Czechoslovak law, dual nationals who have served in non-Czechoslovak armed forces (including those of the United States) are subject to criminal penalties.

Czechoslovak citizens residing abroad must "normalize their relations" with the Czechoslovak government in order to return to Czechoslovakia. Czechoslovak embassies or consulates can provide details.

Cost of living

If you receive a U.S. pension, the cost of living in Czechoslovakia is very low. However, if you exchange your money at the unofficial rate, the cost of living is even cheaper—you would probably receive five times more Czechoslovak koruna for your dollars. This could mean the difference between renting a four-room apartment (under 600 koruna a month) and renting a charming mountain home or villa.

You can buy lunch at a Prague restaurant for about $2 per person. Prague hotels are about $60 per night. A bottle of Russian vodka is about $4. Crystal brandy snifters sell for about $3.50 apiece.

Health matters

Medical services are free for Czechoslovakians, but not Americans. Make sure your U.S. insurance covers you in Czechoslovakia.

Medical services are provided to resident foreigners in Prague by the Foreigners' Section of the Charles University Faculty Polyclinic, staffed by an English-speaking general practitioner, pediatrician, and dentist. A doctor is on call at all times. The Foreigners' Section refers patients to specialists for lab tests and hospitalization as necessary.

Local pharmacies stock locally prescribed medicines, but individuals can obtain most medicines in West Germany.

Costs for medical care and for medicines are lower than in the United States.

Since Czechoslovak equivalents of American medication are hard to identify and locate, bring a good supply of necessary medications or plan to order via mail. Many prescribed medications can also be obtained from the U.S. Army Hospital Pharmacy in Nürnberg, Germany.

U.S. Embassy personnel usually go to the U.S. Army Hospital, Nürnberg, Germany, for specialist care and all hospitalization.

Routine and emergency care in Prague are adequate, but the bureaucratic organization of medical care, the lack of choice of physicians, the shortage of hospital beds, and the language barrier can create significant problems.

For more information, contact the **Czechoslovakian Embassy,** *3900 Linnean Ave. N.W., Washington, DC 20008; (202)363-6315.*

Czechoslovakian spas

Spas in Czechoslovakia are world-renowned for the beauty of their surroundings. They are free with a physician's prescription. Most are located in lovely old manor houses and offer concerts, horseback riding, tennis, fishing, swimming, hunting, or skiing. Medical care is excellent. Packages range from $38 for a single or $31 for a double per person per day, low season, to $58 single or $48 double, high season. Czechoslovak Airlines (CSA) offers packages with air fare from New York for about $1,056 to $1,854. For information call *(800)223-2365.*

Marianski Lazne (Marienbad) in western Bohemia has been dubbed the most beautiful spa in central Europe. The success of the therapy must be related to the hikes through the lovely parks, gardens, and forests that surround the spa. Karlovy Vary, also in Bohemia and once known as Karlsbad, is the most famous Czech spa. Peter the Great, Beethoven, Goethe, Liszt, and Karl Marx are among those who have taken its waters. These two spas also have the best golf courses in the country. Contact **CEDOK (Czechoslovakian National Tourist Organization),** *10 E. 40th St., New York , NY 10016; (212)689-9729,* for information.

Tourist information

All visitors to Czechoslovakia must have a visa before arriving. Visas are available from any Czech diplomatic mission. For an application, write to CEDOK or the embassy. Enclose with your visa application a U.S. passport valid for at least another seven months; two passport photos; a self-addressed envelope stamped for certified mail (no machine stamps); and a money order for $16 made out to the Embassy of Czechoslovakia (no checks). You can get a visa on the spot if you go to the embassy in person.

The process takes two to three weeks. Your visa is not valid until you have exchanged about $15 per day into Czechoslovak koruna for the length of your stay. You must exchange the required amount at the border when you enter unless you have a voucher of prepaid services at hotels. For more visa information, telephone the visa section of the embassy, *(202)363-63-08*, Monday through Friday 10 a.m. to noon.

You must also account for each night spent in Czechoslovakia. Your visa should bear a stamp indicating where you stayed. If you stay in official accommodations, this will be done for you. If you make your own arrangements to stay in private homes, you must register with the local police. If you decide to prolong your stay, your visa can be extended for a modest payment.

A series of individual driving tours is available through CEDOK. You can purchase non-refundable gasoline coupons entitling you to an approximate 10% reduction from CEDOK and from the **Tuzex Information Center,** *Rytirska 19,* in Prague. You cannot buy diesel fuel without vouchers, which are available at border crossings, exchange offices of the Czechoslovak State Bank, or from foreign Tuzex offices.

Shopping

Most basic foods are regularly available in Prague. Fresh fruits and vegetables, however, are only available in season or when limited supplies are imported. Exceptions are some citrus fruits, carrots, cabbage, and potatoes, which are usually sold year round. Supplies of perishables are sporadic. The quality of both meat and vegetables varies greatly. Local dairy products are good. However, milk may spoil quickly because it is not refrigerated during distribution.

The Czechoslovak government store, Tuzex, maintains outlets in major cities and sells a limited variety of imported goods including food, liquor, cigarettes, and clothing. Local products are substantially cheaper through Tuzex than if purchased directly.

Driving

To drive in Czechoslovakia, you must have liability insurance. Third-party liability insurance must be bought from the Czechoslovak Insurance Co., which charges reasonable rates. It is valid throughout Europe.

A U.S. drivers license is valid in Czechoslovakia, but an international license is required for some neighboring countries and is recommended for all drivers. It is available from the **AAA,** *811 Gatehouse Road, Falls Church, VA 22047; (212)222-6000,* if you have a valid U.S. drivers license. A Czechoslovak license (which serves as an international license and is valid indefinitely) can be obtained through the embassy for a nominal fee with a valid foreign license. Without a valid license, a lengthy and expensive drivers training course and thorough exam are required.

Helpful addresses

•**Embassy of Czechoslovakia,** *3900 Linnean Ave. N.W., Washington, DC 20008; (202)363-6315;* visa section, *(202)363-6308* (mornings only).

•You can fly to Czechoslovakia via **Czechoslovak Airlines (CSA),** *545 Fifth Ave., New York, NY 10017; (212)682-5833* or *(800)223-2365.*

•For travel information, contact **CEDOK (Czechoslovak National Tourist Organization),** *10 E. 40th St., Suite 1902, New York, NY 10016; (212)689-9720.*

•The **U.S. Embassy,** *Trzeste 15, Prague; tel. (42-2)536-641/9.*

Retirement in Poland

Retirement in Poland can be difficult for Americans who are not of Polish origin. It's very difficult to get information on immigration procedures. Embassy officials are furtive when approached and there's little printed material available.

In order to retire in Poland, you must have a Polish relative send a letter of invitation and find you accommodations. Then you must get the agreement of the Polish passport office in Warsaw, which takes at least six months.

According to an embassy official, however, Americans are retiring to Poland. One reason, aside from the beauty of the country, is the incredibly low cost of living. One Polish-American told us that if you exchange your U.S. money for Polish money at the unofficial (black market) rate, you will get six times more for your money.

Theoretically, this could allow you to live like royalty. You could retire in a mountain chalet for $5000! Even if you don't trade your dollars on the black market you can live well. The mere fact that you can purchase services with dollars helps. For instance, if you decide to build a house you will find that building materials are scarce. With the appearance of dollars, the materials suddenly appear.

What is it like there?

The Poles are a musical, literate, and artistic people. Theater, film, concerts, books, and folk arts abound. The country resounds with Chopin festivals in the summer.

Most of Poland is a great, flat plain that has been easily overrun throughout history. Warsaw was devastated in World War II, but has been largely rebuilt. The city's pride and joy is the Old Town district, a new replica of the old city constructed from prints and family photos painstakingly collected by the city's architects after the war. An East-European Williamsburg, the Old Town is closed to traffic and plied by horse-and-buggy cabs.

Poland has thousands of churches. These churches and palaces run south from Warsaw's Castle Square. The city hints of Paris in the summer, when cafés move outdoors and sidewalk artists appear.

One of the most spectacular medieval cities in Eastern Europe is the old capital of Poland, **Cracow**, which managed to escape devastation during World War II. Its fine Romanesque and Gothic architecture was left virtually unharmed. A museum itself, Cracow is also the home of several great European museums as well as 11 colleges and universities.

The Czartoryski Palace houses the National Museum, which has collections of tapestries, pottery, weapons, and paintings by masters including Leonardo da Vinci and Rembrandt.

The state collections in Wawel Castle (once the royal seat and treasury) include Flemish and Polish tapestries, liturgical items, and precious metals.

The old city, in the heart of Cracow, has been restored. Pedestrians can climb medieval staircases and come face-to-face with masks or gargoyles. Buildings of the oldest universities are in this quarter. Jagiellonia University, founded in 1364 by King Casimir the Great, has 16,000 students. Copernicus is among its alumni.

The Main Market Square, one of Europe's largest and most interesting marketplaces, is the site of a national ritual every hour. A bugler sounds four short notes in memory of another trumpeter who once tried to warn his neighbors of a Tartar attack. His call was

404

interrupted by an arrow shot into his throat.

Northwest of Cracow is **Czestochowa**, a drab little town on the Warta River that comes alive on Assumption Day (Aug. 15) each year, when hundreds of thousands of pilgrims arrive to pay homage to a portrait of the *Black Madonna*, said to have been painted by St. Luke. The Madonna's dark cheeks are marred by two slashes that, according to legend, were made by an enraged Tartar who felt the painting getting heavier and heavier as he tried to steal it. The portrait is kept in a huge monastery called Jasna Gora (Hill of Light), founded in 1382 by Paulist monks. Swedish armies were halted here in 1655 and driven out of Poland.

The **Baltic Sea Coast** provides over 300 miles of spacious, sandy beaches, picturesque fishing towns, elegant spas, calm lagoons, lakes, steep cliffs, and dunes.

The spa of **Swinoujscie-Miedzyzdroje**, located on two islands, Uznam and Wolin, is very popular. Nearby Kamien Pomorski is also lovely. Kolobrzeg, Mielno, Ustka, and Leba are wonderful resort towns.

Gdansk, a large port city, is beautiful, with its historic quarter and Gothic and Renaissance buildings.

Northern Poland has a thousand lakes and picturesque wooded hills. The **Masurian Lake District** is the best-known section.

Red tape

You must have a visa to enter Poland. To apply, submit a visa application along with a passport that will be valid at least nine months after the date on your application; two passport photos; and a fee of $20 in most cases. It's a good idea to include a copy of a travel voucher or money exchange order from a travel agent. For an application, contact the **Consular Division,** *Polish Embassy, 2224 Wyoming Ave. N.W., Washington, DC 20008; (202)234-2501.* It takes two weeks to get a visa.

Tourists must exchange $15 a day into Polish currency while in Poland.

If you are a U.S. citizen of Polish origin or descent, use caution. If you were naturalized after Jan. 19, 1951, according to Polish law, you may not have lost your Polish citizenship. You can renounce it, however, before a Polish consul or at the Polish Embassy in Washington, DC. The renunciation could make your life a lot easier. Polish authorities have been refusing to issue visas to persons with dual nationality who have not renounced their Polish citizenship. Instead, such individuals are being required to obtain Polish consular passports in order to travel to Poland. Often, U.S. citizens of Polish heritage have traveled using Polish consular passports with no problems. However, if the visitor has problems in Poland, the U.S. Embassy may be unable to help.

Certification of citizenship status is especially important if you plan to live permanently in Poland. A U.S. citizen of Polish origin should not accept a repatriation visa. Under Polish law, acceptance of a repatriation visa means acceptance of Polish citizenship immediately upon arriving in Poland. A person who accepts a repatriation visa must get permission from Polish authorities in order to leave.

Shortages

Food supplies are short, and it is sometimes difficult to get good Polish fare. Meat and gasoline are not available without ration cards. Mushrooms, herring, and sour cream characterize the national cuisine. The national drink is vodka. Wyborowa is the best, and there are many flavored varieties.

Automobiles and apartments are especially difficult to buy, with long waiting periods required for both. If you use dollars, your wait probably will be shorter.

Transportation

Public transportation is cheap, but it's often crowded to the point of being unbearable. If you want to ride a bicycle, bring it from elsewhere. Steer clear of rental cars. Avis and Hertz rent cars in Poland for about twice the price you'd pay in the United States. (A sma.l Fiat goes for $277 a week, $39 each additional day.)

More for your money

Poland, whose own currency is so depreciated that its citizens are legally allowed to buy with dollars, is the center for a dollar-based subculture in Eastern Europe. In Hungary, the natives resent Polish traders who offer Western goods at prices the Hungarians cannot match.

One problem the ingenious Poles have had to solve involves change. Unlike bills, U.S. coins are not widely circulated in Eastern Europe. The Poles print up bits of paper with a face value of a nickel, a dime, or a quarter. These are circulated and accepted as change.

One frequent traveler to Poland reported that the dollar goes much farther than the Polish zloty. A woman offered to rent him a room for 5,000 Polish zlotys. At the official exchange rate, the cost was about $17 a night. But the czarny, or black-market exchange rate,

was more than triple the official rate. This brought the price down to
$5 a night.

Buying a Polish home

Thanks to the pioneering efforts of Polish-Americans, the Polish
real estate market has been open to other Americans for years. Officially, foreign citizens can buy Polish real estate only with permission
of the Ministries of Finance and Internal Affairs. They must pay a
price in Polish zlotys comparable to the free-market price of similar
properties, and they must bring in the dollars for the deal at the
official exchange rate.

Unlike Hungary, Poland has a free market in real estate. You'll
find newspaper advertisements and real estate agents working for
commissions, just as in the United States.

Poland allows its citizens to earn and hold U.S. dollars. The legal
controls on foreign real estate purchases are an attempt to prevent
two-tier real estate purchases, whereby only a fraction of the price of
the property is paid in legally imported zlotys. All the paperwork and
notarial registration take place as if this were the price. However, a
second dollar payment takes place under the table.

Unable to prevent the two-tier market from flourishing (even
when Poles sell to Poles), the government has created an arrangement
in which foreigners can buy Polish property in dollars for an intermediate rate between the official exchange rate and the black-market
rate.

For more information, contact **LOCUM,** *00828-Warsaw, Ul.
Marchaewskiego 13; tel. (48-22)200351, ext. 199, or (48-22)249134.*

Tourist information

Polorbis, the Polish national tourist organization, organizes
special tours, including riding vacations, gourmet-food trips, and
horse and caravan tours. The tours are equivalent to or cheaper than
tours to Western Europe. For information contact **Polaris,** *500 Fifth
Ave., New York, NY 10110, (212)391-0844.*

The least expensive, and perhaps the most convenient way of
visiting Poland is on a package tour with expenses prepaid. This
exempts you from having to exchange the minimum $15 a day, which
must be exchanged at the official rate. Even if you travel independ-
ently, however, you will find prices are very low.

Special events and festivals are held all year in Poland. In January, the International Jazz Jamboree is held in Warsaw. In February,
the Highland Carnival takes place in the Tatra Mountains. An Inter-

national Chamber Music Festival is held in Lancut in May. From May to October, Sunday Chopin recitals take place in Lazienki Park, Warsaw. Symphonic and chamber music concerts are heard from May to December in the Wawel Castle courtyard in Cracow. On June 23, throughout Poland, Midsummer is celebrated. Flower garlands attached to lit candles are thrown into the river, an echo of a pagan Slavic tradition. For more information, call the **Polish Tourist Office** in Chicago, *(312)236-9013.*

The most popular ski resorts are Zakopane in the Tatra Mountains and Krynicain the Beskidy Mountains. You can ski from November through April. Lower Silesia has resorts in Karpacz, Szklarska Poreba, Szczawno, Polanica, Kudowa, and Duszniki.

Poland is also great for hunting deer, elk, wild boar, lynx, wolf, fox, wood-grouse, blackcock, pheasant, and partridge. The best hunting grounds are the Bieszczady and Carpathian Mountains, Bialowieza Forest, Mazury, Augustown, and Koszlain.

An ancient tradition of riding and breeding horses survives in Poland. Riding holidays can be spent at the old manor houses and palaces in Czerniejewo, Dlusko, Ptaszkowo, Sierakow, Iwno, and Podkowa Lesna.

Hotels are plentiful but more expensive than those in other Eastern European countries. Top hotels are run by Polorbis. Independent hotels are less expensive, although it may be difficult to make reservations.

There are dozens of spas in Poland. The largest is Ciechocinek. The Polish Tourist Office will take care of arrangements.

Medical insurance is recommended.

LOT, the Polish airline, flies into 11 cities and towns. If you plan to fly within Poland, make reservations far in advance. Trains are the main method of travel. Seat reservations are mandatory on express trains and advisable on most trains.

The Polrail Pass is an excellent buy at about $40 to $72 for eight days.

Helpful addresses

•The **Embassy of Poland,** *2224 Wyoming Ave. N.W., Washington, DC 20008; (202)234-2501;*

•The **Polish National Tourist Office,** *(800)223-6037;*

•The **U.S. Embassy,** *Aleje Ujazdowskie 29/31, Warsaw 00-540; tel. (48-22)283041;*

•The **U.S. Consulate,** *Ulica Chopina 4, Poznan 61-708; tel. (48-61)585-86 or 585-87;* and

•The **U.S. Consulate** in Krakow, *Ulica Stolarska 9; tel. (48-12)2277-93.*

For the latest news

For the latest information on conditions affecting travelers in the above countries, call the **State Department,** *(202)647-4000,* or write to the **Citizens Emergency Center,** *Room 4811, Department of State, Washington, DC 20520.*

Currency Exchange Rates*

One U.S. dollar buys:

Austrian Schilling: 13.23
Barbados Dollar: 1.98
Bermuda Dollar: 1
British Pound: 0.5917
Canadian Dollar: 1.1855
Cayman Dollar: 0.80
Costa Rican Colon: 80
Czechoslovak Koruna: 9
Dominican Republic Peso: 6.28
Eastern Caribbean Dollar: 2.67
Ecuadorian Sucre: 503
French Franc: 6.3525
Greek Drachma: 160
Hungarian Forint: 50
Irish Punt: 0.6965
Israeli Shekel: 1.817
Italian Lira: 1367
Mexican Peso: 2425
Netherlands Antilles Florin: 1.80
Polish Zloty: 600
Portuguese Escudos: 153.65
Romanian Lei: 9
Spanish Peseta: 116.55
Swiss Franc: 1.6730
Yugoslavian Dinar: 10,000

* as of May 1, 1989

Recommended Reading

Algarve Magazine, Rua 25 Abril, 8400 Lagos, Algarve, Portugal; tel. (351-82)52850.

Costa Rica Report, Apartado 6283, 1000 San José, Costa Rica. $39 for 12 issues.

How to Retire to the Caribbean, by Sydney Hunt, Palm Tree Books, 5500 Little Falls Road, Arlington, Virginia 22207.

International Living, a monthly newsletter published by Agora Inc., 824 E. Baltimore St., Baltimore, MD 21202; (301)234-0515. $36 per year; $48 overseas airmail.

Island Properties Report, a monthly newsletter published by Gene Cowell, P.O. Box 88, Woodstock, Vermont 05091; (802)457-3734.

Living in France Today, by Philip Holland. Robert Hale Limited, London, England. 1985.

Living in Portugal, A Complete Guide, by Susan Thackeray. Robert Hale Limited, London, England. 1985.

Living in Spain in the 80s, by John Reay-Smith. Robert Hale Limited, London, England. 1985.

Lookout, Puebla Lucia, 29640 Ruengirala (Malaga), Spain; tel. (34-952)460950. A magazine about Spain written in English.

Moving To, Moving Publications Limited, 1939 Leslie St., Don Mills, Ontario M3B 2M3, Canada; tel. (416)441-1168. A quarterly magazine about Candian real estate.

People's Guide to Mexico, by Carl Franz. John Muir Publications, Santa Fe, New Mexico. 1982.

Property Ireland, Rockwood, Stocking Lane, Ballyboden, Dublin 16, Ireland. $25 per year surface mail; $35 per year airmail.

Retirement Paradises of the World, by Norman D. Ford. Harian Publications, Floral Park, New York. 1978.

The Retirement Letter, edited by Peter A. Dickinson, Phillips Publishing, In., 7811 Montrose Road, Potomac, Maryland 20854; (301)424-3700. $77 for 12 issues.

ing, In., 7811 Montrose Road, Potomac, Maryland 20854; (301)424-3700. $77 for 12 issues.

Travel and Retirement Edens Abroad, by Peter A. Dickinson. Phillips Publishing (address above).

Where to Retire on a Small Income, by Norman D. Ford. Harian , Floral Park, New York. 1979.

You and the Law in Spain, by David Searl, Lookout Publications SA, Puebla Lucia, 29640 Fuengirola (Malaga), Spain.

Acknowledgments

Many thanks to the scores of people who helped produce this book. The editorial staff at Agora Books was very helpful. Information was pulled liberally from past issues of *International Living,* edited by Bruce Totaro, and from Special Reports on Portugal, Great Britain, Costa Rica, France, Greece, Italy, Mexico, Spain, and Canada. Copy editors Kathleen Peddicord, Dianne McCann, and Anne Bonner combed the copy carefully for embarassing errors. Vivian Lewis, Editorial Director, kept me on the right track. Production staff—Denise Plowman and Becky Mangus—made sure the final book was attractive. Many hard-working interns (Anastasia Hudgins, Dave Robinson, Christoph Amberger, Deirdre Mullervy, Jennifer Delucca, Lynn Holden, and Nancy McElwain) checked facts and verified telephone numbers—a thankless task. Last, but not least, thanks to Bill Bonner, the publisher of this book. Without him, *The World's Top Retirement Havens* would not exist.

A special thank you is due also to Jane Parker, who spent hours poring over chapters on Portugal, Spain, and Costa Rica to make sure facts were up to date. Thanks also to Jack Hutchinson, who also spent hours of his personal time reading material and making corrections.

Writers who deserve my gratitude include Richard Aiken, Patrick Alexander, D.G. MacDonald Allen, Freya Basson, Alice Bingner, Victor Block, Jane Butler, Marilyn and Will Cantrell, Richard Carpenter, Kay Carroll, Gloria Cole, Douglas Casey, Norman Darden, Leo Dahlmanns, Audrey Davis, Peter A. Dickinson, Jane Dolinger, Lee Dudka, Trish Durbin, Susan C. Ellis, Alice C. Fleming, Annamarie Gregory, Michael House, John Howells, Stuart M. Hunter, Richard le Grelle, Lora Holmberg, Anastasia Hudgins, Stuart Hunter, Louisa Jones, Vivian Lewis, Lois Lucas, Annette Lyons, Mark Magowan, Francine Modderno, Patrice Mullin, Gene Murphy, Kathy Murphy, Chad Neighbor, Jane Parker, Kathleen Peddicord, Elizabeth W. Philip, Harry Portman, Charles Powell, Margaret Range, Charles Romine, Marjorie Rose, Michael Sedge, Lee Setomer, Jim Shaw, Gary A. Scott, Jo Ann Skousen, Sheila Signer, Bruce Totaro, Becky Tozier, Warren Trabant, Gene L. Tyler, Patti Watts, Jack G. Wilson.

I am also grateful to the many embassy officials and to the staffs at national tourist boards who took the time and effort to help me gather information. I know you are all busy and appreciate your help.

—Marian Cooper
Editor